D1756562

International Business
Finance

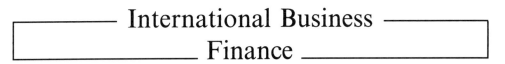

International Business Finance

A Concise Introduction

T. W. McRae

JOHN WILEY & SONS
Chichester • New York • Brisbane • Toronto • Singapore

Copyright © 1996 by T. W. McRae
Published © 1996 by John Wiley & Sons Ltd,
     Baffins Lane, Chichester,
     West Sussex PO19 1UD, England

     National 01243 779777
     International (+44) 1243 779777

Other Wiley Editorial Offices

John Wiley & Sons, Inc., 605 Third Avenue,
New York, NY 10158-0012, USA

Jacaranda Wiley Ltd, 33 Park Road, Milton,
Queensland 4064, Australia

John Wiley & Sons (Canada) Ltd, 22 Worcester Road,
Rexdale, Ontario M9W 1L1, Canada

John Wiley & Sons (Asia) Pte Ltd, 2 Clementi Loop #02-01,
Jin Xing Distripark, Singapore 0512

Library of Congress Cataloging-in-Publication Data
McRae, T. W. (Thomas W.), 1933–
 International business finance : an introduction / by T.W. McRae.
  p. cm.
 Includes bibliographical references and index.
  ISBN 0-471-96210-4 (cloth : alk. paper). — ISBN 0-471-96164-7
(pbk. : alk. paper)
  1. International finance. I. Title.
HG3881.M398 1996   95–44831
659.15′99—dc20   CIP

British Library Cataloguing in Publication Data

A catalogue record for this book is available from the British Library

ISBN 0-471-96210-4 (Cloth)
ISBN 0-471-96164-7 (pbk)

Typeset in 10/12pt Times by Keyword Publishing Services Ltd
Printed and bound in Great Britain by Bookcraft (Bath) Ltd
This book is printed on acid-free paper responsibly manufactured from sustainable forestation,
for which at least two trees are planted for each one used for paper production.

To Brian and Julie

Contents

exposure – transactions exposure – translation exposure – economic exposure – there is only one exposure position for one company – measuring exposure – PPP and foreign exchange strategy – monetary assets and liabilities – the IRPT and foreign exchange strategy – the international Fisher and foreign exchange strategy – is the forward rate an unbiased predictor? – hedging short-term cash flows – designing a foreign exchange information system – the frequency of reporting – can foreign exchange rates be forecast? – an empirical investigation – what next? – internal and external hedging techniques – hedging economic exposure – only one net exposure position for one company – what have we learned in this chapter? – further reading – tutorial questions – case studies

company – situations where holding companies are not tax efficient vehicles – the advantages to be derived from a holding company – setting up a "stepping stones" company – where should a holding company be set up? – the highly geared holding company – other tax advantages of holding companies – characteristics of tax regimes suited to setting up a holding company – setting up a management and finance centre – choosing a tax haven – using the facilities of a tax haven – anti tax-avoidance legislation – a case study in international tax planning – finding out about foreign tax – what have we learned in this chapter? – further reading – tutorial questions – exercise – case study

Preface

This book is targeted at those readers who have no knowledge of the world of international business finance but would like to grasp the fundamentals of the subject.

International trade is one of the fastest growing sectors of the world economy. In many countries the international trade sector is growing a good deal faster than the local trade sector. Today, in most of the countries of the world, the main outlet for expanding a business is to look abroad to foreign markets. The world is fast becoming a global village market in which anyone can sell to, or buy from, anyone else in the market.

In the past only the very large multinational companies had to worry about the complexities of international finance. This is no longer so. Medium and even quite small businesses are finding markets abroad and as they move abroad these businesses need to learn about the risks involved in handling foreign currency and how to hedge these risks, they need to learn about exotic payment systems such as forfaiting and counter-trading, they need to learn how to raise loans in a foreign currency, how to avoid or at least reduce the burden of foreign tax and how to circumvent the tough exchange control regulations imposed by some foreign governments.

These matters cannot be simply left to the "international treasurer", if a company can afford to employ such an exalted personage. Every manager operating in a foreign market needs to know about the fundamentals of international finance. The accountant who must decide on the payment system best suited to an export contract, the marketing manager who must decide on the volume of trade credit that can be safely offered to a foreign customer, the purchasing officer who needs to negotiate the currency in which a foreign purchase will be denominated, the engineer who must decide where to buy parts for a foreign contract, the tax officer who is scheming to minimize the global tax bill on her company, even the personnel manager who must design an attractive salary package for staff living abroad. All of these managers need to acquire a fair grasp of international finance since each of these problems has at least one facet that impinges on international finance.

International finance permeates into every pore of any business enterprise that is trading abroad.

This book is intended as an introduction to and not a full course on business finance. Every significant element of the subject of international business finance is covered but every stone is not turned to present a detailed description of every beastie beneath. We introduce the reader to the exotic world of options and swaps but we do not attempt to cover the menagerie of hedging products which have escaped from this particular stable in recent times. Many of these products seem to suffer from a very limited life-span although some others have transformed the financial world beyond recognition.

The book emphasizes a practical approach to solving the financial problems thrown up by international trading and does not dwell excessively on international economics or the formidable mathematics which underlie much of modern financial theory. However, we have tried to cite key references in the academic literature, where appropriate, and an extensive set of further readings, with thumb-nail descriptions, are appended to the end of each chapter.

The book has an international orientation since the problems faced by international treasury managers are much the same wherever the manager is working. Exchange control regulations are the major limiting factor since, where such controls apply, opportunities for applying sophisticated financial methods are much restricted compared to those enjoyed in countries operating free markets.

Many sets of questions, exercises and short case-studies are included in the text. In many instances solutions or notes towards solutions are provided. No solutions are provided for around one half of the problems set, to allow a tutor to use them as class exercises.

It is hoped that the book will prove helpful to students on financial management courses which include international business finance as a module but not as a full course. The book is also designed to assist managers who wish to expand their knowledge of the workings of the financial market in relation to international business dealings.

The book is based on the international finance elective run by the author on the MBA programme at the University of Bradford Management Centre, Yorkshire, England.

TWM
Ilkley, Yorkshire

List of Exhibits

Exercises and Cases

EXERCISES

CASE STUDIES

List of Abbreviations

ACT	Advanced corporation tax
CFC	Controlled foreign company
CIF	Cost, insurance freight
ECGD	Export credits guarantee department
EXIM	Export Import Bank (US trade bank)
FASB	Financial accounting standards board (US)
FOB	Free on board
FX	Foreign exchange
IMM	International money market (Chicago)
IRPT	Interest rate parity theory
IRR	Internal rate of return
LIFFE	London international futures exchange
MFC	Management and finance centre
NCM	Trade insurance agency
NRV	Net realizable value
PPP	Purchasing power parity theory
SSAP	UK accounting standard
TIEA	Tax information exchange agreement
WACC	Weighted average cost of capital

1
What Is So Different About International Financial Management?

INTRODUCTION

A wide range of textbooks are available on the subject of financial management and corporate finance so the reader might well ask the question "What is so different about international finance that a book needs to be written on the subject?". This is a good question that requires an answer.

International finance is concerned with all of those things that affect the finances of a company when the company crosses an international frontier. Once a company crosses its national boundary into another country many operating parameters may change. The distance of trading from home base may change by a substantial margin, the legal system will change, the currency of trading will change, the controls applied to currency conversion may change, the tax regime will change, the language used to conduct business affairs may well change and that rather nebulous but important concept, the culture, may be subject to substantial change.

Some of these changes are slight. The cultural differences between the UK and Canada are small. Some changes are large. The tax rules operating in the USA and the UK are very different. The French legal system is very different from the legal system operating in Japan. The financial philosophy applied in a Muslim country is very different from that adopted in a Christian country.

In this short chapter we will examine some of these differences and explain why they may impact on the operating procedures of a finance department working in a company that conducts a significant proportion of its business abroad.

DISTANCE

Up to the end of the 19th century the biggest problem faced by a company operating abroad was sheer distance. Reports and management instructions could take weeks if not months to be delivered from or to the local management in Argentina or India and the payment for goods exported to distant parts might take months to arrive. The performance of a foreign subsidiary might be measured on an annual or even biannual basis.

Most of these constraints have been removed with the introduction of wide-band telecommunication and satellite systems. So far as communication is concerned the world is now a global village. Instructions and payments can be sent around the world at close to the speed of light at any time of the day or night. Devices such as the telephone, the fax machine and the internet have contracted the size of the world to such an extent that an international company can be managed in much the same way as a company operating within a single country. Whether or not this close degree of control is a good thing is a matter of some controversy but what is undisputable is that distance is no longer a major barrier to effective management, financial or otherwise. Distance has been effectively abolished as a constraint on efficient financial management.

CURRENCY

At the present moment something of the order of 180 different currencies are used to facilitate the conduct of the world's trade. Exhibit 1.1 provides a listing of some of the more important of these currencies. The exhibit shows the country, the name of the currency issued and, where appropriate, the short form description of the currency.

Normally the currency of one country will be of little use to a trader in another country until it is converted into the local currency. French francs are of little use in the UK or the United States dollar in Japan. A given amount of the foreign currency must be exchanged for a given amount of the home currency before it can be used to purchase goods and services in the home country.

If a company wishes to buy goods or services from abroad or sell goods or services to a foreign buyer the company must decide whether to "denominate" the deal in the currency of the home or the foreign country. This decision can have a big impact on the eventual profit or loss on the foreign deal. We will return to this important topic in Chapter 4.

A financial officer whose company is trading abroad needs to know the "rates of exchange" currently offered by the currency dealers who trade one currency for another. The officer will need to find out the current "spot" rate of exchange ruling today and the "forward" rate of exchange ruling on some future date if a payment in foreign currency is due to be made or received on that date.

If the finance officer believes that the future rate of exchange might move against her company she can use various devices to "hedge" this foreign exchange risk. "Forward contracts", "futures contracts" and "option contracts" are examples of these hedging instruments. All such instruments fall into a class of financial products called "derivatives". Later in this book, in Chapters 2 and 5 we will explain how some of these hedging devices work.

The monitoring of the changing pattern of currency exchange rates and the mastery of currency hedging devices are two of the key skills that need to be learned by a financial officer if she wishes to control her company's exposure to foreign exchange risk.

RATES OF INTEREST

Many rates of interest operate at any one time within one country. The rate of interest charged by a lender of funds depends, among other things, on the credit rating of the borrower and the quality of the security offered by the borrower.

Exhibit 1.1   The Currencies of the World

Currency	Monetary unit	Short title
Afghanistan	Afghani	Af
Albania	Lek	Lk
Algeria	Algerian dinar	DA
Antigua	East Carib dollar	EC$
Argentina	Peso	Peso
Armenia	Rouble	Rb
Australia	Australian dollar	$A
Austria	Schilling	Sch
Bahamas	Bahamanian $	B$
Barbados	Barbadian dollar	BD$
Belgium	Belgian franc	B Franc
Bermuda	Bermuda dollar	$
Bhutan	Ngultrum	Ng
Botswana	Pula	P
Brazil	Cruzeiro	BRC
Cambodia	Riel	Riel
Cameroon	CFA Franc	Franc
Canada	Canadian dollar	C$
Cayman Islands	Cayman Is dollar	CI$
Chad	CFA Franc	Franc
Chile	Chilean peso	peso
China	Renminbi Yuan	yuan
Colombia	Colombian peso	peso
Costa Rica	Colon	C
Croatia	Dinar	Dinar
Cuba	Cuban peso	peso
Cyprus	Cypriot £	C£
Czech Republic	Koruna	Kcs
Denmark	Danish krone	Kroner
Ecuador	Sucre	sucre
Egypt	Egyptian £	£E
Ethiopia	Birr	EB
Finland	Markka	Mk
France	French franc	Franc
Gambia	Dalasi	D
Germany	Deutschmark	DM
Ghana	Cedi	Cedi
Gibraltar	£ Sterling	£
Greece	Drachma	DR
Haiti	Gourde	G
Honduras	Lampira	Lm
Hong Kong	Hong Kong $	HK$
Hungary	Forint	Frt
Iceland	Krona	Kr
India	Indian rupee	Rs
Indonesia	Rupiah	Rp
Iran	Rial	Rial
Iraq	Iraqi dinar	ID
Ireland	Punt	IR£
Israel	Shekel	Shk
Italy	Lira	Lire
Jamaica	Jamaican $	J$
Japan	Yen	Yen

(continued)

Exhibit 1.1   (*cont.*)

Currency	Monetary unit	Short title
Kenya	Kenyan shilling	Ksh
Korea: South	Won	Won
Kuwait	Kuwait dinar	KD
Laos	Kip	K
Lebanon	Lebanese £	L£
Lesotho	Loti	M
Libya	Libyan dinar	LD
Liechtenstein	Swiss franc	SF
Luxembourg	Luxembourg franc	LF
Madeira	Escudo	Esc
Malawi	Kwacha	K
Malaysia	Ringgit	M$
Mauritania	Ouguiya	UM
Mauritius	Rupee	Rs
Mexico	Peso	Ps
Mongolia	Tugrit	Tg
Morocco	Dirham	DH
Mozambique	Metical	MT
Myanmar (Burma)	Kyat	K
Namibia	Rand	R
Nepal	Rupee	Rs
Netherlands	Guilder	Gd
Neth Antilles	Guilder	Gd
New Zealand	NZ $	NZ$
Nicaragua	Cordoba	C$
Nigeria	Naira	N
Norway	Krone	Kr
Pakistan	Rupee	Rs
Panama	Balboa	B
Papua New Guinea	Kina	K
Paraguay	Guarani	Gs
Peru	New Sol	NS
Philippines	Peso	P
Poland	Zloty	Zl
Portugal	Escudo	Esc
Qatar	Riyal	R
Romania	Leu	Lei
Russia	Rouble	R
Salvador (El)	Colon	C
Serbia	Dinar	Dn
Singapore	Singapore $	S$
Slovenia	Tolar	Dinar
Somalia	Shilling	Sh
South Africa	Rand	R
Spain	Peseta	Ps
Sri Lanka	Rupee	Rs
Sudan	Dinar	£S
Swaziland	Lilangeni	E
Sweden	Krona	Kr
Switzerland	Swiss franc	SFr
Syria	Syrian £	S£
Taiwan	Taiwan $	T$

Exhibit 1.1   (*cont.*)

Currency	Monetary unit	Short title
Tanzania	Shilling	Sh
Thailand	Baht	Baht
Tonga	Pa'anga (T$)	T$
Trinidad	Dollar	TT$
Tunisia	Dinar	Dinar
Turkey	Lira	TL
Uganda	Shilling	Sh
Ukraine	Rouble	R
UAE	Dirham	Dr
UK	£ Sterling	£
USA	US dollar	US$
Uruguay	New peso	Ps
Vanuatu	Vatu	Vatu
Venezuela	Bolivar	Bs
Vietnam	Dong	Dg
Virgin Islands (US)	US$	US$
Western Samoa	Tala	WS$
Yemen (Rep)	Dinar	YD
Zaire	Zaire	Z
Zambia	Kwacha	K
Zimbabwe	Dollar	Z$

There are at least 180 currencies issued by the various countries of the world. Many of these currencies are accepted for trading in countries outwith the country that issues the currency. Multinational currencies such as the ECU issued by countries in the EU may become more common in the future. Currency values are changed and new currencies issued every year.

When a borrower or lender resides abroad an additional factor comes into play. Exhibit 3.2 illustrates the wide range of base interest rates operating on a specific date in the world's financial markets. The base interest rates charged to gilt edged borrowers on this date varied from a low of 1.7% per annum for a loan in Japanese yen to a high of 19% p.a. for a loan denominated in Greek drachma.

This huge difference between the cost of borrowing in yen and drachma did not result from a differential country credit rating on this date (although as we shall find in Chapter 7 such differences do exist) but from market expectations about future changes in exchange rates. The annual interest cost of a loan in drachma is 13.5% more expensive than an otherwise identical loan in pound sterling because the international money market believes that the drachma is going to fall in value against the pound sterling by around 13.5% over the next year. A loan in yen is 3.75% per annum cheaper than a loan in pound sterling because the market believes that the yen will cost around 3.75% more in terms of the pound sterling in a year's time.

If a financial officer is borrowing or lending in a foreign currency she must take these cost differences into account. Do these differences in interest costs reflect her own beliefs about future changes in exchange rates between the currencies? If they do not, the difference between the market's expectations and those of the financial officer might open up an opportunity to make a speculative profit on currency trading.

We will discuss the determinants of interest rate differentials on otherwise identical loans in different currencies in Chapter 3 and opportunities for making profits on currency speculation in Chapter 6.

THE TAX SYSTEM

The European Union (EU), WTO and other international trading forums are trying hard to standardize the tax systems and rates of tax applied in the different countries of the world. However, as the reader will find when he reads Chapter 10, very large differences still exist between the tax systems of the world. When a company begins to trade internationally it will soon find itself operating in an alien tax environment that is often quite different from that operating at home.

In order to minimize the global tax bill imposed on her company the financial officer needs to study the tax rules, the tax legislation and especially the tax rates and allowances applied to various forms of income and cost in each of the countries in which her company trades. This responsibility may require the finance officer to employ the services of an independent corporate tax adviser in her own country or in each of the countries in which her company trades.

Some countries, usually small islands outwith the control of a major power, charge almost no tax on the income of foreign companies who are registered within their legal jurisdiction but who do not trade there. These countries are called "tax havens" and provide foreign companies and rich individuals with much scope for reducing their global tax bill as well as providing the government of the tax haven with much needed annual revenue from licensing and registering the foreign companies who reside there. The tax authorities in other countries tend to be suspicious of companies who trade in "tax havens" but, despite this, most multinational companies do set up subsidiaries in tax havens. We will discuss the advantages and disadvantages of operating a subsidiary company in a tax haven in Chapter 10.

Whatever the foreign country with which her company trades the finance officer needs to study the global tax situation of the company with a view to minimizing the overall tax bill. International tax offers the assiduous finance officer much scope for reducing company tax and so increasing the net profit available for paying dividend to shareholders. Some types of expense are allowed against tax in one country but not in another, some types of revenues are subject to tax in one country but not in another, the rates of tax applied to corporate income vary a great deal from country to country.

Chapter 10 of this book is devoted to a discussion of these matters.

EXCHANGE CONTROLS

As recently as 1979 most of the governments of the world imposed tight controls on the movement of funds out of, and even into, their country. Such government restriction on the free flow of funds between countries is called "exchange control".

On October 23, 1979 the then British government under Margaret Thatcher abolished all UK exchange controls and since that date many other countries have followed suit. It is generally accepted that exchange controls tend to stifle trade between countries and so reduce overall world competition, which in turn makes the world trading system less efficient.

A great deal of research has been published in support of this view.

However, even in 1995 a good number of the governments of the world still impose rigid exchange controls on the movements of funds out of and even into their country. The raising of funds in these countries is strictly controlled especially if the fund-raiser is a foreign-based company. Most of the countries that still impose exchange controls are in that group of countries that have come to be known as "emerging economies". Some major trading nations such as Brazil and South Africa are currently in this group.

If a company is trading in a country that imposes tight exchange controls the financial officer needs to know what exchange controls exist and how these controls are applied. How, for example, will the rules on exchange control effect the repatriation of profits from subsidiaries registered in that country and what effect will the controls have on the repatriation and raising of funds in that country?

A veritable raft of devices have been devised to assist multinational companies in repatriating blocked funds and profits from countries with rigid exchange control regulations.

THE LEGAL SYSTEM

An action that is illegal in one country may be legal in another. Every company operating abroad is subject to the legal system of the country in which it operates, although the United States has attempted to impose its own tax and legal system on companies operating outside the USA.

A financial officer needs to be aware of any major differences in the law that might effect the legality of financial operations carried out in the foreign country.

For example, the legal philosophy that is applied in the United Kingdom and the USA is very different from the legal philosophy operating in continental Europe. Both of these systems are, in their turn, very different from the law as promulgated in Muslim countries where religious beliefs and statutes play an important role in legal matters.

Optimal financial strategies can be heavily influenced by legal constraints.

A company operating in a foreign country must employ the services of a lawyer in that country to ensure that the company does not unwittingly breach some important legal constraint in the foreign country that might be perfectly legal in the home country.

These matters are beyond the compass of this book but they are important and must be given proper consideration.

THE POLITICAL SYSTEM

Most of the developed industrialized countries of the world operate within a democratic political framework based on regular elections and allowing a reasonable degree of freedom in economic matters.

Under such a political and economic system governments do not interfere too much in business affairs. An importer in one country can do business with an exporter in another country without undue interference by government bureaucracy.

This freedom from interference is a recent development, even for developed industrialized nations. Many governments throughout the world still maintain a tight control over the international financial dealings of companies registered on their territory. In many countries of the world prior permission must be acquired from some monetary authority before imports are ordered from abroad or funds are transmitted outside the country.

If a country is governed by a dictatorship, such as in North Korea, interference in business affairs can be total and no foreign trading or foreign financial dealing is possible without long and detailed negotiations with the bureaucratic organization in the dictatorship that controls the import of goods and services and the export of funds from that country.

All of this can prove to be very tedious for a financial officer who is simply trying to finalize a trade deal.

In some countries trading is not feasible unless the foreign company is prepared to pay some kind of a bribe to the relevant official in the bureaucracy to obtain the necessary permissions.

Fortunately in the modern world something like 90%, by value, of the world's trade is carried on between democratic regimes and despotic, bureaucratic regimes are withering on the vine. However, the financial officer still needs to remember that the trading rules that apply between free-trading democratic countries may not apply when trading with organizations operating within alternative political systems.

CUSTOMS AND ETHICS

Customs, ethics and conventions differ from one country to another. Even within one country the customs can vary between regions. Behaviour that is considered ethical in one country may be considered unethical in another.

Business people in Western countries are particularly prone to assume that their own business practices are "normal" and that of other cultures "abnormal". In some countries, such as Japan and Saudi Arabia, committing what might seem to the Westerner to be a minor *faux pas* can cause grave offence to the host.

One well-known example is the charging of interest on loans. This is considered to be normal business practice within a Christian culture (although it was not always so!). The charging of interest on loans is not permitted in many Muslim, and particularly Arab, countries. Exhibit 1.2 illustrates the point.

Bribery is another example. What exactly is a bribe? The donation of a small gift to the other party after a business deal is struck is common practice in many cultures but any form of gift to the participants in a business deal is considered to be immoral within the business culture of the United States. The acceptance of any form of gift or benefit, however small, is severely punished even if the recipient is very rich.

Barry Zins of Meryl Lynch comments that: "Tax systems are cultural . . . harmonising the different systems would be well nigh impossible".[1]

There are many other examples. For our purpose the point to note is that an action that might be considered unexceptionable and even trivial in one culture may cause grave offence in another. The financial officer needs to educate herself in such matters by reading up on the culture of any country with which she is trading or by attending a course on the culture of any country with which her own company carries on business.

Exhibit 1.2   Credit Methods in Islamic Banking

An interesting example of the impact of culture on finance is the prohibition against the charging of interest on loans in many Muslim countries.

The Qur'ān explicitly prohibits the charging of interest on loans:

> "Those who devour usury will not stand except as stands one whom the Evil One by his touch has driven to madness. That is because they say 'Trade is like usury, but Allah has permitted trade and forbidden usury'".

Within a Muslim culture it is considered that a lender charging interest on a loan shares in the fruits of labour of the borrower without exerting effort himself. The matter is a bone of contention between Muslim scholars and Muslim economic theorists. The economists contend that while the charging of interest on consumption loans is wrong, the charging of interest on production loans ought to be acceptable.

Muslim banks have developed a series of alternatives to charging interest on loans. The basic approach in all cases is for the Islamic bank to participate in the risks attached to a venture and later to share in the profits arising from that venture.

Three methods of participation are in common use:

1. *Musharakah (participation)*. Under this system the bank enters into a profit-sharing agreement with the borrower of funds. The venture is agreed with a specific objective over a fixed time period. Profits or losses are shared in direct proportion to the initial contribution of capital. The *Shariah* allows such an arrangement and also allows the bank to ask for collateral from the customer to guarantee efficient management of the project.

This method of financing forces the bank to check out the feasibility of the project in some detail since it is a partner and not simply a financier of the project. In addition, once the bank is a partner it will not pressurize the customer as a Western Bank would if repayment is delayed for legitimate reasons.

2. *Modarabah*. This is similar to the Musharakah except for the fact that if the venture runs at a loss the bank bears the loss, the customer simply loses his capital, unless negligence on the part of the customer can be proved.

The customer is not allowed to guarantee the return of the amount contributed by the bank.

The Modarabah allows a form of "collective" investment, like an investment trust, whereby those who lack management skills or cannot afford to take big risks with limited capital can participate in large scale ventures.

3. *Murabahah (sale on credit)*. This process is similar to a "documentary letter of credit" (see Chapter 9). A customer requests the Islamic bank to purchase specific goods on his behalf and also promises to buy the goods back from the bank at an agreed price on a specified date. The price includes a profit for the bank, but since the buy-back is not guaranteed the bank takes a risk and this risk justifies a mark-up on the price paid by the bank for the goods.

The bank cannot accept an advance on purchase even though the goods are shipped in the name of the customer! The payment to the bank may be made in instalments.

The Islamic Development Bank promotes this method.

Financial techniques can vary between cultures. For example interest may not be charged on loans in many Muslim countries so various alternative forms of funding ventures have been devised by Islamic banks in the Near East, Malaysia and elsewhere.

Source: Abdeen and Shook, *The Saudi Financial System*. John Wiley, 1985.

WHAT HAVE WE LEARNED IN THIS CHAPTER?

1. When a company crosses an international frontier a number of important factors change. If a company wishes to operate successfully abroad the managers of that company need to learn how to operate in this new environment.

2. In the past distance was an important constraint on foreign operations. The recent dramatic improvements in telecommunications and speed of transportation has much reduced the importance of distance as a constraint on efficient operation abroad.

3. Foreign trading will bring a company into contact with foreign currencies. If foreign contracts are denominated in a foreign currency the finance officer must learn how to hedge foreign exchange risk. He or she must enter into the complex world of "derivatives".

4. The interest rates charged on long- and short-term loans denominated in a foreign currency will likely vary from the charge for similar loans in the home currency. The finance officer needs to understand why this is so and what to do about it.

5. The corporate tax systems of the various countries of the world vary a great deal one from another. The finance officer must learn how to use these differences to derive benefit from "tax arbitrage". The officer must learn how to use tax arbitrage to minimize the global tax bill of the company.

6. Currency can now flow freely between most of the advanced industrial countries of the world. This was not always so. Even today most developing and emerging economies and most of the countries that have recently escaped from the Soviet bloc impose tight exchange controls on the export of currency. The finance officer needs to learn about the intricacies of exchange control if he wishes to arrange trade deals with such countries.

7. The legal system of foreign countries can be quite different from that in the home country. A legal act in one country can be illegal in another. The finance officer needs to be aware of the important differences in corporate and tax law between the home country and those countries with which she trades.

8. Most advanced industrial countries work under a democratic system of government. The government must hold themselves accountable to the electorate every few years. Many countries, especially many developing countries, do not enjoy a democratic form of government. Trading with a country ruled by a dictatorship or a theocracy throws up many novel problems for the finance officer. The rules of trading can appear to be inflexible and irrational. The finance officer needs to adapt her style to such systems to conclude successful negotiations with a company or trading corporation resident in such a regime.

9. Customs and ethics vary a great deal between different countries. Religious or political conventions can be paramount in some countries and an act that is perfectly proper in one country can be considered unethical in another. Bribery and patronage are accepted in many countries of the world, although is seldom admitted in public. The finance officer needs to learn about such practices in advance of trading with a foreign country and decide how to re-act to such disparity in behaviour.

NOTES

1. Olivier, C. Tax man cracks down on treasurers. *Corporate Finance*, October 1994, 25.

TUTORIAL QUESTIONS

1. Approximately how many different currencies are used in world trade? What are the five most important currencies used in world trade? What is the name of the currency units used by Saudi Arabia, Guatemala, South Korea and Thailand?
2. If you receive a gift of 100 000 Korean Wan what will you have to do to turn this gift into currency you can use in the UK? If the rate of exchange is 2000 KW to the £ Sterling how many £ sterling will you get from the conversion?
3. What is meant by the term "denominate" in the sentence "Let us denominate the currency in which the deal will take place"? How is it that the currency in which a foreign trade deal is denominated can have a big impact on the eventual profit or loss from the deal?
4. Suppose the rate of exchange between the £ sterling and the German Deutschmark is 2.5 DM to the £ sterling. What is the value of one DM in terms of UK pence? If the rate of exchange between the French franc and the £ sterling is 8 francs to the £, what is the rate of exchange between the French franc and the DM? Assume efficient currency markets.
5. What is meant by the term "hedging" exchange rate risk? Your company have contracted to make a payment of two million Japanese yen in six months' time to pay for the importation of copying machines from a Japanese company. Is there any exchange risk incurred on this contract? If you believe that an exchange risk is incurred suggest two methods of hedging this exchange rate risk.
6. If the rate of interest on a one-year loan in Swiss francs cost 4% per annum and the rate of interest on an otherwise identical loan in Italian lire is 9% per annum what can we say about market expectations about the future exchange rate between the Swiss franc and the Italian lire over the next year? If you want a one-year loan and you must borrow in either Swiss francs or Italian lire which currency would you borrow in?
7. If a financial officer thinks that the difference between interest rates offered on six month loans in Swiss francs and Italian lire does not reflect her own expectations about the future exchange rates between these two currencies how can she make a profit out of this difference in expectations about the future?
8. How can different tax systems be used to reduce the global tax bill of a company?
9. What is a "tax haven"? Give two examples of the way in which a finance officer might use a tax haven to reduce the overall global tax bill of her company?
10. What exactly does "exchange control" control? Give two examples of the kinds of financial transactions that might be controlled by exchange control regulations. Why has the volume of exchange control regulations been reduced in recent years?
11. Your company, which is based in Sydney, Australia, has made a profit of 100 000 zylots in a foreign country. The exchange control authorities in this foreign country forbid you from repatriating these funds to your home country in the form of cash. Suggest how you could release these blocked funds so that the value can be used in Australia.
12. Why do most economists claim that exchange control regulations reduce the growth of the income of the world economy?
13. "Culture can effect international trade between countries". Suggest three aspects of international trade that might be influenced by cultural differences.
14. Suggest three ways in which the monetary authority of a country might interfere with the international financial affairs of a multinational company operating in that country?
15. Interest cannot be charged on loans in some Muslim countries. How do you think credit transactions can be effected under such conditions? Banks in Muslim countries make loans to their customers but how can they make a profit on these loans?
16. If you are trading with a foreign country that has adopted a communist form of government how will this effect the way you conduct the negotiations and fix a price for any deal made in that country?

17. How does the foundation of the legal systems of continental Europe differ from the foundations of the legal system of England and the United States?
18. "Modern methods of communication have abolished distance as a constraint on the efficient management of a company operating in several countries". Do you agree? How can the "internet" be used to improve the management of a multinational company?
19. Can you think of any custom or ethical practice that might effect the success or failure of a foreign project?

EXERCISE 1.1   TOOLGATE SOFTWARE

Assume that you are the finance director of a British company called Toolgate Software. The company writes computer programs that control the operation of machine tools in various manufacturing industries.

Up until three years ago the company only sold into the British and Commonwealth market but in the last three years Toolgate's sales force has tied up deals in Japan, Malaysia, Brazil and Argentina and is now seeking an even wider market for the company's highly specialized skills.

Some criticism feeds back to the managing director to the effect that the staff of Toolgate software "treat all foreigners as if they are British born". A number of deals have gone wrong because of the insensitivity of the salesforce and programmers to foreign attitudes and behaviour. The sales force have also made errors in the setting up of the financial aspects of foreign deals that have proved expensive to correct at a later date.

The MD decides to set up a two-day seminar to initiate the sales and other senior staff of Toolgate into the differences when a British company is setting up contracts with foreign buyers.

Assume that you are given the job of designing this two-day seminar.

Required: (a) Design a two-day lecture and discussion programme to familiarize the staff of Toolgate with the various differences that might arise when a foreign contract is being negotiated. (b) Which speakers would you invite from both inside and outside the company? Where could you find the outside speakers on such a programme? (c) Suggest the outlines of a case study that can be used in group discussions built around a contract with a large private company in Malaysia.

2
The Currency Markets

INTRODUCTION

The amount of money needed by the world community to finance international trade has increased tenfold over the last twenty years. In 1994 the various London FX markets handled no less than US$400 billion a day, a 80% increase on 1989. This huge increase in the demand for foreign currency has stimulated the growth of two types of market. The first type of market exchanges foreign currency for home currency in the present or in the future. These markets are called the "spot" (US$150bn) and "forward" (US$36bn) markets. The second type of currency markets to have expanded in recent years are the hedging or "derivatives" markets, these markets hedge the risk of a company incurring a loss because of a change in the value of the foreign currency against the home currency. The main derivatives markets are called the "futures" (US$3bn), the "options" (US$5bn) and the "swap" (US$106bn) markets.

More than one trillion US$ a day flow through the foreign exchange markets of the world, which makes these markets the largest markets in the world in any commodity.

This chapter will examine the nature of these markets and explain how they operate.

THE SPOT MARKET

If a finance officer wishes to buy foreign currency to pay a bill denominated in that currency or to sell foreign currency received from a foreign importer he must contact his bank or an independent currency dealer and ask for a "spot quote" in that currency. The currency dealer will quote a "buy" rate and a "sell" rate for that currency. The finance officer may contact several dealers to find the best quote on offer before making a decision. The finance officer can get a rough guide to the quote rates from a computer monitor linked to a quote system that lists the quotes offered by the various banks and dealers. Telerate offers such a system. After reviewing the rates quoted the finance officer will make a deal with one or other of the currency traders to buy a fixed amount of foreign currency at an agreed "buy" exchange rate or to sell a fixed amount of foreign currency at an agreed "sell" exchange rate. The actual switch of currency normally takes place two to three days after the deal is struck.

Table 1

	US$	£	DM
US$	**	0.633	1.551
£	1.579	**	2.449
DM	0.645	0.408	**

Smaller currency deals will normally be handled by the foreign exchange desks of the major banks. The specialized currency dealers trade large amounts of currency with the larger companies.

Spot rates on over 150 currencies are quoted on the major currency markets of the world at any one time. The currency prices quoted on free markets will always offer symmetric "cross rates" against one another. Let us study an example of symmetric cross rates.

If the rate of exchange between the pound sterling and the US$ is quoted at US$1.579 to the £, and the rate of exchange between the pound sterling and the German DM is quoted at DM2.449 to the £, then the following matrix of "cross-rates" must hold if the markets are free markets (Table 1).

If the £/US$ rate is 1.579 US$ to the £ and the £/DM rate is 2.449 DM to the £ then the US$/DM rate must be 1.551 DM to the US$ because $2.449/1.579 = 1.551$. If this rate did not hold then operators called "arbitrageurs" would soon spot the anomaly and buy or sell DM for US$ until the three rates came back into line. The figures are taken from the *Financial Times* of October 5, 1994.

Suppose, for example, that the £/US$ rate was 1.579 US$ to the £ and the £/DM rate was 2.6 DM to the £. A US arbitrageur would buy £100 000 for US$157 900 and sell the £100 000 for DM260 000. He can now sell the DM260 000 for $(260\,000 \times 0.645) =$ US$167 700. This is a money machine with no stop tap! In real life any cross-rate anomalies are soon competed away to bring the rates back into line.

An example of a foreign exchange deal offered on the spot market is shown in Exhibit 2.1. The data is taken from a screenful of information displayed by a rate quotation system such as "Telerate".

Direct and Indirect "Quote" Systems

In the UK market the exchange rates are quoted using the "indirect" method. In other words an enquirer is told the amount of foreign currency that can be bought with one pound sterling. Most other markets use the "direct" method of quotation. Under the direct quote method an enquirer is quoted the cost of one unit of the foreign currency in terms of so many units of the home currency.

For example, if the rate of exchange is quoted as US$1.6 to the £ sterling the rate is also $100p/1.6 = 62.5$ pence for one US$. If a UK dealer quoted the rate "directly" to a potential trader he would quote the rate as 62.5 pence to the US$. This does not happen in the UK. The rate is quoted "indirectly" as US$1.6 to the £ sterling. Indirect quotation can lead to a certain ambiguity. A newspaper might state, for example, that the US dollar "increased" in value from US$1.6 to the £ to US$1.5 to the £ over a given period!

Exhibit 2.1 Spot Rates of Currencies on a Telerate Screen

95-10-03   10.25 am

	Bank	City	Spot rate	Time
STG	Barclays	LON	1.5437–1.5448	10.17
	Swiss Bank	BAS	1.5444–1.5454	10.18
	B OF A	LA	1.5451–1.5462	10.21
DM	Christiania	OSL	2.4228–2.4239	10.18
	Lloyds	LON	2.4234–2.4246	10.19
	Citibank	NYC	2.4229–2.4241	10.21

A finance officer can find the current spot rates offered by various banks and dealers by bringing up the spot rate page on her computer screen. These rates change minute by minute. The screen shows the cost of buying and selling US$s and DM for pound sterling on October 3, 1995 at 10.25 am.

In the above Barclay's Bank are offering to buy US$ at US$1.5437 for a pound sterling or to sell US$ at 1.5448 to the pound sterling. Christiana bank in Oslo are offering to buy German DM at DM2.4228 for a pound sterling or to sell German DM at DM2.4239 for one pound sterling.

Spot rate contracts normally allow two days for delivery of the contract. If the finance officer buys DM100 000 for £41 274.56 on Monday October 3, 1995 the DM will be received on Wednesday October 5.

The difference between the selling and buying rate is called the "spread" on the spot quote. The spread on the Citibank quote on DM is (2.4241–2.4229) = 0.12 pf.

The figures appearing on the computer screen are only close approximations of the actual selling and buying rates quoted. These rates change quicker than the screen can change!

Exhibit 2.2 examines the problem of confusing direct and indirect quotes.

Spreads and Points

Returning to Exhibit 2.1 we see that "indirect" quotes are provided by several banks in several different countries. A buy rate and a sell rate is quoted on each currency. The difference between the buy rate and the sell rate is called the "spread". The width of the spread indicates the depth of the market or possibly the uncertainty of the dealer as to the future movement in the rate. A narrow spread indicates a deep market or a stable market, a wide spread indicates a shallow market, that is few deals per period, or a market with an uncertain future.

Rates quoted on screens, such as those shown in Exhibit 2.1, are often not contractual quotes but merely guides to the actual rates that will be quoted by a dealer via a telephone link to the trader.

Sometimes rates are quoted as "points" rather than absolute values. Points are taken from the last two digits in a quote. For example a quote of US$1.5864–1.5876 could be quoted as 64–76. The points system is used between experienced dealers to save time when providing a quote to another experienced dealer.

THE FORWARD MARKET

The forward market provides a facility for a finance officer to buy or sell a fixed amount of foreign currency at a fixed rate of exchange on some future date. A forward contract cannot be traded on a secondary market like a traded option or a future contract.

Exhibit 2.2 The Direct v the Indirect Method of Expressing Foreign Exchange Rates

UK dealers use the "indirect" method most foreign dealers use the "direct" method.

If we wish to express the value of any good or service we want to buy in terms of the national currency we always express the value as x units of the currency. For example:

> 1 apple = 40 pence
>
> 1 motor car = £16 000
>
> 1 railway ticket from Leeds to London return = £48.20.

When it comes to expressing the value of a foreign currency in terms of the pound sterling this usual procedure is reversed. For example, we express the value of US$, German DM or French francs, as:

> £1 = US$1.65 not 1 × US$ = 60.6 pence
>
> £1 = DM2.57 not 1 × DM = 28.9 pence
>
> £1 = FF8.5 not 1 × FF = 11.76 pence.

This is called the "indirect" method of expressing the value of foreign currencies.

This simple difference in the mode of expressing the value of foreign currency causes serious problems for newcomers to foreign exchange management. For example, it might be said that the US$ "rose in value over the month from US$1.65 to US$1.61." "The French franc collapsed from FF8.5 to FF11.3 to the £ over a three-year period."

The problem is simply that all other goods and services are expressed as so many units of the local currency for one unit of the good or service. The value of a foreign currency, using the indirect method, is expressed in the opposite direction.

For this reason it might be advisable for all newcomers to the foreign exchange markets to take any exchange rates quoted "indirectly" and re-express them "directly" as x units of the local currency (£ sterling in the case of British citizens).

For example:

> Not £1 = US$1.65   But US$ = 1/1.65 = 60.6 pence.
>
> Not £1 = DM2.97   But DM = 1/2.97 = 33.7 pence.
>
> Not £1 = FF10.5   But FF = 1/10.5 = 9.52 pence.

Newcomers to foreign exchange will find that this simple transformation will simplify their understanding of exchange rate movements.

It often happens that a finance officer knows that his company is due to receive a fixed amount of foreign currency on some date in the future or that his company will have to pay a fixed amount of foreign currency on some date in the future.

In such a situation there will be uncertainty as to the rate of exchange that will apply on the date when the foreign money is due to be received or paid out. Rates of exchange have been known to swing by as much as 25% over a few days or even over a few hours.[1]

If a finance officer in the UK does not want to live with this uncertainty he needs to find a way of ensuring that the sterling value of the foreign payment or foreign receipt is fixed in advance. One method of doing this is to set up a "forward contract" to buy or sell the foreign currency at a fixed price on a future date. The dates offered are usually 30 days, 60 days, 90 days, 180 days or 12 months forward although other dates can be negotiated by banks if the client so wishes.

Forward markets are run by the foreign exchange departments of all the major banks. If a financial officer wishes to buy forward DM500 000, which is due to be paid out in three months' time he will contact the foreign exchange desk of his bank and ask for a "forward quote" on DM three months forward. He may extend his search by contacting several foreign exchange dealers to find a "best quote". Eventually he will set up a forward contract with a foreign exchange dealer to buy forward DM500 000 at a fixed exchange rate on a specific date in three months' time.

When the bill for the DM500000 arrives from the German company in three months' time, on instruction from the client, the importer's bank will debit the UK importer's account with the sterling amount at the agreed rate of exchange and credit the foreign bank account of the exporter with the DM500000 as instructed by the client.

Movements in the forward rate are heavily influenced by movements in the current spot rate. The forward rate is not a market estimate of the future spot rate. Chapter 3 will demonstrate that the forward rate is, in fact, a rather poor predictor of the future spot rate.

Spot exchange rates are offered on most currencies against the US$. Forward rates are available on a more restrictive set of currencies. The larger forward markets are in US$, German DM, Japanese yen, the pound sterling, the Swiss franc and the French franc. Forward markets in some currencies open and close quite frequently depending on the financial and political state of the country issuing the currency.

Exhibit 2.3 sets out the spot and forward markets operating in early 1995.

An example of a forward rate contract is illustrated in Exhibit 2.4. Stenpak PLC wish to cover against the possibility of a sharp rise in the Canadian dollar against the £ sterling over a three-month period. Stenpak expect a rise greater than that predicted by the forward rate.

The Forward Premium or Discount

The difference between the spot rate quote on a foreign currency and a forward rate quote on that date is called the forward premium or forward discount on the currency.

For example if on a given date the spot rate of exchange between the US$ and the German DM is DM1.85 to the US$ and the six months forward rate on the same date is DM1.87 to the US$ then the US$ is becoming more expensive in terms of DM. The forward rate on the US$ is standing at a two cent "premium" to the spot rate. Conversely the DM is standing at a forward rate discount to the US$.

The premium or discount on a forward currency plays an important role in determining the difference in rates of interest on short-term loans denominated in the two currencies. We shall explain this relationship between the currency premium or discount and differences in the short-term rates of interest for the same period in more detail in Chapter 3 when we discuss the "interest rate parity theory".

The premium or discount on the forward rate on a currency can be converted to a rate of interest by using the following formula:

(Forward rate − spot rate)/(spot rate × 12/no of months forward).

For example in the case quoted above relating the US$ to the DM the differential rate will be:

$$(1.87 - 1.85)/1.85 \times 12/6 = 2.16\%$$

Exhibit 2.3 A Listing of Spot and Forward Markets

Currency	London spot market	London forward market	Local forward market
Algeria	NA	NA	NA
Argentina	S	NA	NA
Australia	A	A	A
Austria	A	A	A
Bahrain	A	A	A
Bangladesh	S	A	A
Belgium	A	A	A
Bermuda	A	NA	NA
Brazil	A	NA	LLM
Burma	A	NA	NA
Burundi	NA	NA	NA
Canada	A	A	A
Chile	A	NA	LLM
China	A	A	A
Colombia	S	NA	NA
Denmark	A	A	A
Egypt	NA	NA	NA
Finland	A	A	A
France	A	A	A
Germany	A	A	A
Ghana	A	NA	NA
Greece	A	NA	A
Hong Kong	A	A	A
India	A	NA	NA
Indonesia	S	NA	NA
Iran	NA	NA	LLM
Ireland	A	A	A
Italy	A	A	A
Japan	A	A	A
Kenya	A	NA	LLM
Kuwait	A	A	A
Korea: South	A	NA	LLM
Malawi	NA	NA	NA
Malaysia	A	A	A
Mexico	A	NA	NA
Morocco	A	NA	NA
Netherlands	A	A	A
New Zealand	A	A	A
Nigeria	A	NA	NA
Norway	A	A	A
Pakistan	A	NA	NA
Peru	NA	NA	NA
Philippines	S	NA	NA
Portugal	A	A	A
Qatar	A	A	A
Salvador (El)	S	NA	NA
Singapore	A	A	A
South Africa	A	A	A
Spain	A	A	A
Sri Lanka	A	NA	NA
Sweden	A	A	A
Switzerland	A	A	A

Exhibit 2.3 *(cont.)*

Currency	London spot market	London forward market	Local forward market
Taiwan	A	NA	LLM
Tanzania	A	BA	NA
Thailand	S	NA	NA
Trinidad	A	NA	NA
Tunisia	S	NA	LLM
Turkey	NA	NA	NA
Uganda	NA	NA	NA
UK	A	A	A
United Arab Emirates	A	A	A
Uruguay	S	NA	NA
USA	A	A	A
Zaire	NA	NA	NA
Zambia	A	NA	NA
Zimbabwe	NA	NA	NA

A = market available, NA = market not available, LLM = limited local market, S = sellers only.
There are over 180 currencies issued by the various countries of the world. All of these currencies have a local spot market but many do not have a local forward market. London and New York provide a spot and forward market in all the major currencies and some of the minor currencies. Countries encountering foreign exchange problems usually do not allow trading on a forward market especially on a foreign forward market.

In addition to the conventional forward contract there is an "option" forward contract that allows the buyer of the forward contract to buy or sell the currency between two dates rather on a specific date. This kind of option contract should not be confused with a "currency option contract", which we shall discuss later in the chapter.

Sometimes the forward rate is expressed in terms of the premium or discount on the spot rate rather than as an absolute rate of exchange. When a forward is expressed in this fashion it is called the forward "swap" rate of exchange between the currencies. Again this type of swap rate should not be confused with "currency swaps", which will be discussed later.

Exhibit 2.4 expresses the forward rate as a swap rate rather than as an absolute rate. The spot rate between the C$ and the £ sterling is quoted as 2.1219–2.1280 and the forward rate is quoted as 1/4 cpm and 3/4 c discount. This translates into a 2.1194–2.1355 forward rate as is shown in the Exhibit.

The relationship between the forward rate's premium or discount on the spot rate and the interest rate differentials on loans in the two currencies are so close that one can be calculated from the other. If the exchange rate difference or "agio" is out of line with the interest rate "agio" traders called "arbitrageurs" will bring them back into line.

The exchange rate agio is calculated by using the formula:

$$\text{forward rate} - \text{spot rate/spot rate}$$

The interest rate agio by using the formula:

$$\text{foreign rate of interest} - \text{home rate of interest/1} + \text{home rate of interest}$$

If the agios differ by more than about 0.20% it pays the arbitrageurs to borrow in one currency and cover the loan forward in the forward market. This forces the agios back into line.

Exhibit 2.4 An Example of a Forward Market Contract

Stenpak PLC buys reinforced cardboard boxes from Canada. A contract is signed on October 1, year 1 for C$220 000. The finance officer of Stenpak is worried about the future of the C$ to £ sterling exchange rate. She thinks that the C$ may rise in value by a significant amount over the next three months. The Canadian contract is due to be paid on December 31, year 1.

The current exchange rates between the C$ and the £ sterling are as follows:

Exchange rates quoted on October 1, Year 1.	Dealer will:		
	sell at	buy at	
Spot rate (dealer's sell and buy rates for C$)	2.1219	2.1280	for £ sterling
Forward rate: three month forward	1/4 c pm − 3/4 c discount		
Therefore the forward rates are: C$	2.1219 − 0.0025	2.1194 sell C$	
(Note: 1/4 c pm = 0.0025 cents) C$	2.1280 + 0.0075	2.1355 buy C$	

The exchange rate quoted on December 31, Year 1 is:

		Dealer will:		
		sell	buy	
Spot rate	C$	2.1013	2.1087	to the £ sterling

What do these quotes mean?

1. The dealer will sell C$s to Stenpak on the spot market on October 1, year 1 at the rate of C$2.1219 for one pound sterling. The dealer will buy C$s from Stenpak at the rate of C$2.1280 for one pound sterling.
2. The spread on the three month forward rate is C$2.1355 − 2.1194 = 0.0161:
3. The actual quotes on the forward rate for the three month forward contracts are:

   3 months   2.1194–2.1355, i.e.,   C$2.1194   The dealer will sell C$ at this rate
   C$2.1355   The dealer will buy C$ at this rate

4. If the finance officer was to buy the C$220 000 on October 1 she would pay:

   C$220 000/2.1219 = £103 680

5. But she will not need to pay the C$220 000 until December 31. Buying this amount forward six months means that when the C$220 000 is due to be paid on December 31 it will cost:

   C$220 000/2.1194 = £103 802

6. If the Canadian company fails to pay the C$220 000 on the due date on December 31, Stenpak must still honour the forward contract so the finance officer will need to buy the C$220 000 on the spot market at that date. This will cost Stenpak:

   C$220 000/2.1013 = £104 697

In this case the forward rates are quoted as either a premium or a discount on the spot rate. A premium must be deducted from the spot rate to find the actual forward rate. A discount must be added to the spot rate to find the actual forward rate.

THE CURRENCY FUTURES MARKET

By using the forward market a financial officer can fix the value of a future contract denominated in a foreign currency in terms of the local currency. This contract cannot be traded on a "forwards" market although it can be cancelled, at a cost, by setting up a forward contract in the opposite direction.

The currency "futures" market was set up to solve this problem. In a futures market the financial officer can buy a futures currency contract to buy or sell a fixed amount of currency for a fixed date of delivery and this futures contract can be traded on a "futures" market.

The currency futures market offers a "standardized contract" for the delivery of a package of currency at a fixed price for a future date. For example on the international money market (IMM) a sterling futures package of £62 500 is traded for March, June, September and December. The cost of hedging via the futures market is almost identical to the cost of hedging via the forward market.[2]

The main differences between a futures contract and a forward contract are as follows.

1. A futures contract is for a fixed value package, i.e., £62 500, Yen 12 500 000, DM125 000, etc. A forward contract can be arranged for any amount.
2. A futures contract is made between the buyer of the futures contract and a futures "clearing house", not with a bank as in the case of a forward contract.
3. A futures contract can be traded on a futures market. For example on the IMM market in Chicago. A forward contract cannot be traded.
4. The buyer of a futures contract can realize the profit or loss on the contract at any time, not simply at the end of the contract period.
5. In the case of a futures contract daily margins (% deposits between 1% and 5% of the contract value) must be maintained with the clearing house to reflect movements in the exchange rate. In effect the contract is rewritten each working day. Note that the margin can be covered by offering an interest bearing bond as security. No margin is required on a forward contract.
6. There is no buy–sell spread on the futures price as in the case of a forward contract. The broker charges a small commission of around 0.05% to 0.10% of the value of the contract.

The futures contract is based on a quarterly fixed date cycle of March, June, September and December.

All of this means that currency futures contracts are highly liquid. They can easily be reversed by selling the contract on the open market. Very few futures contracts are carried to maturity. Most are cancelled before maturity via a reverse contract.

Currency futures contracts are not popular hedging instruments in the UK but they are still popular in the USA on the IMM and in Singapore and Australia.

Futures are discussed further in Chapter 5 where an example of a futures contract is set out.

THE CURRENCY OPTIONS MARKET

If a finance officer fears that his company might suffer a loss by reason of an unexpected change in exchange rates then a fixed value hedging instrument such as a forward is the best hedge available. But suppose the finance officer expects a change in exchange rates but is not sure in which direction the rate will move? He thinks that a substantial gain or loss on exchange rate movement are both possible and the possibility of a gain or a loss are equally balanced? What should he do? What type of hedge is appropriate?

In such a situation the finance officer may well opt for a "currency option" as the favoured hedging instrument.

A currency option gives the buyer of the option the right but not the obligation to buy or sell a given amount of currency at a given price at a given time at the end of the option period or possibly during the lifespan of the option.[3]

For example let us suppose that a financial officer operating in the UK knows that his company are contracted to pay out DM625 000 in three months' time. The current spot rate is DM2.65 to the £ sterling. An election is due in the UK in two months' time and this might affect the exchange rate either way. What should he do?

He may decide to buy a currency option to cover the risk. He buys 10 × DM62 500 "call" option currency contracts for three months ahead at an exchange rate or "strike price" of DM2.5 to the £ sterling. This might cost the officer, say, £2000.

If the £/DM exchange rate remains above DM2.5 to the £ then the (European) option contract will never be exercised, it is "out-of-money". It is cheaper to buy the required amount of DM on the open market. However, if the DM/£ exchange rate rises to, say, DM2.45 to the £ then the officer has protected his company against any rise in the DM/£ exchange rate beyond DM2.5 to the £.

As the DM strengthens against the £ above DM2.5 to the £ sterling so the call option contract rises in value. The 10 call option contracts that cost £2000 might now be worth £6000 on the traded option market![4]

Two types of options can be bought. A "traded" option, which can be bought or sold on the options market and an "over-the-counter-option", which is arranged by a bank but which is not traded on a market. OTC options are usually of much larger value than traded options.

Options can also be of the "European" or "American" variety. A European option can only be exercised at the end of the option period. An American option can be sold during the option period. The sell–hold decision is a good deal more complicated for an American option since it is not so easy to evaluate the American option at a specific point in time.

We see that a currency option contract is both an insurance policy protecting a company against adverse changes in exchange rates and a gambling chip allowing a company to speculate on unexpected future changes in exchange rates. For this reason a currency option contract that is "out-of-the-money" (the spot rate is preferable to the strike price) still has a market value since it may move "into the money" before the option expires.

The huge rise in the volume of trading in currency options in recent years suggests that both financial officers and portfolio managers have found them to be excellent value for money despite the fact that they are a good deal more expensive per money unit covered than forward or futures contracts.

Currency option markets have been opened in Philadelphia, Chicago, London and Amsterdam.

The option contracts are standardized packages. The packet is standardized as to amount, expiry date and the spread of the strike prices offered. If the spot rate changes so the spread of the strike (exercise) prices offered change.

We will return to a further discussion of currency options in Chapter 5 when we describe the various devices available to a finance officer for hedging currency risk.

Exhibit 2.5 Currency Option Quotes on the Philadelphia Exchange

London Stock Exchange: £/US$ options
One contract = £31 250
Option costs are quoted as US cents per £
Spot exchange rate £1 = US$1.579

	Calls			Puts		
Strike price	Oct.	Nov.	Dec.	Oct.	Nov.	Dec.
1.500	7.68	7.65	7.78	****	0.03	0.24
1.525	5.24	5.34	5.71	****	0.13	0.59
1.550	2.83	3.27	3.87	0.04	0.55	1.23
1.575	0.94	1.71	2.45	0.59	1.42	2.22
1.600	0.13	0.72	1.41	2.28	2.87	3.61
1.625	****	0.22	0.74	4.57	4.86	5.41

Source: *Financial Times*, October 5, 1994.

The table shows the cost of taking out an option to buy (call) or sell (put) a fixed amount of currency on October 4, 1994 on the Philadelphia currency traded option market. Six strike prices are offered between US$1.50 and US$1.625. Future dates for completion of the contract are offered for the end of October, the end of November or the end of December 1994.

The standard contract is for an amount of £31 250, so one contract to buy US$ forward at US$1.525 for the end of December would cost 31 250 × 5.71 cents = US$1784.37.

Note that these options are traded options. Over the country (OTC) options are tailor made by banks to suit the needs of the client. OTC contracts are usually much larger than traded options, often trading millions of US$, and are not usually marketable.

Questions:
1. What is the cost of taking out an option to sell two contracts for the end of November at US$1.575 to the pound sterling?
2. What is the cost of taking out an option to buy around £100 000 at US$1.600 at the end of October 1994?

Exhibit 2.5 provides an example of the strike prices offered in a currency option market trading in £/US$ options.

The data is taken from quotes on the Philadelphia option exchange in the USA. The standard option contract is for a value of £31 250. The option premiums are quoted as US cents per £. The strike (exercise) prices offered vary from US$1.5 to the £ to US$1.625 to the £. Call and put options are being offered each month for three-month operiod ahead.

THE SWAP MARKET

The currency swap market is concerned with swapping streams of currency denominated in one currency for streams denominated in another currency. If a company owes money denominated in one currency but would prefer the obligation to be denominated in another currency it can approach an international bank to arrange a "swap".

The swap market is concerned with swapping two types of obligations. Fixed-rate-interest loans can be swapped for variable rate interest loans and vice versa, this section of the swap market is not our immediate concern. The other section of the swap market is concerned with swapping "tranches" of currency. Most, but not all, currency swaps are organized by the large international banks on behalf of customers.

Most currency swaps are short-term swaps but some are long-term lasting for several years. A section of the short-term swap market is now automated via a telecommunication channel and computer screen.

An example of a long-term swap is as follows.

An Australian company wishes to arrange a currency swap of FF10 000 000 into Australian dollars for a three-year period ahead. The company approaches an international bank and asks if such a swap can be arranged. The bank examines its own loan portfolio in the required swap currencies and if an additional "tranche" of one of these currencies will not unbalance its existing currency portfolio of the bank it arranges the swap for a fee of a fraction of 1% of the value of the swap.

Most swaps are made into or out of US$. In the above example the swap may consist of two parts. A French franc swap into US$ plus a second swap of US$ into Australian dollars.

Swapping "tranches" of currency obligations allows a multinational company to restructure its currency portfolio to suit its changing pattern of currency inflows and outflows.

If a currency officer believes that a future movement in exchange rates, which has not yet been anticipated by the market, will adversely effect his company he can use the swap market to get out of the given "dangerous" currency into a "safer" currency at relatively low cost.

The swap market allows a multinational company to balance its spread of liabilities in a given currency against its spread of assets in that currency and also to "match" its changing cash flows.

The swap market has been growing so fast in the 1990s that the US Congress among others has expressed concern that this relatively uncontrolled market might destabilize the world economy if a major player should go bankrupt.

The consequence of not hedging against substantial changes in the exchange rate are illustrated in Exhibit 2.6. This shows some of the losses incurred by some companies during the substantial peso devaluation of December 1994.

The mechanics of the currency swap market will be examined further in Chapter 5.

The Euromarkets

The swap and other currency markets can only operate because of the existence of the Euromarkets, which process vast sums of money each day. The Euromarkets trade financial debt products denominated in currencies other than the currency of the country in which they are sold.

Only the very largest MNCs trade on the Eurocurrency markets, which are mainly used by the international banks. However the Euronote and Eurobond markets provide useful financing facilities for larger companies that wish to raise finance internationally.

A brief introduction to the Euromarkets is appended to this chapter.

Exhibit 2.6   The Impact of the Mexican Peso Crash of December 1994

Between December 19, 1994 and December 27, 1994 the value of the Mexican peso fell from 3.5 peso to the US$ to 5.7 peso to the US$. A fall of 40% in value relative to the US$. The fall was not anticipated by many Mexican companies and foreign companies operating in Mexico. The fall in the value of the peso would not appear to have been adequately hedged by many companies.

Some of the consequences of this fall in the value of the Mexican peso are outlined below.

1. The shareholding in *Femsea Cervesa* owned by the Canadian Brewer *John Labatt's* fell by US$148 million. The holding was not hedged against a fall in the value of the peso.
2. Concrete-maker *Cemex*, which has 75% of its debt denominated in US$ and revenues denominated in peso was reviewed by Moody's credit grading service for possible downgrading.
3. *Mattel*, the US toymaker, stated it will lose around US$20 million on the devaluation.
4. *Grupe Gigante*, a large Mexican retailer, states it has suffered a foreign exchange loss of US$17 million in the fourth quarter of 1994.
5. *Grupa Tribasa* reports a foreign exchange loss of US$47 million in the fourth quarter of 1994.
6. *Nissan, GM, Ford* and *Chrysler* announce that they will raise the price of their cars in Mexico by 10%.
7. *Empresas ICA Sociedad Controlada* states that it expects a forex loss of around US$194 million in 1994.
8. *Volkswagen de Mexico* suspends production for one week in January 1995 because of a fall in demand caused by the devaluation of the peso.
9. *Internacional de Ceramica*, which pays for 40% of its materials in US$ and owes US$98 million in US dollar denominated debt, reported that a US$52 million forex loss was in prospect.

In December 1994 the Mexican peso fell in value by around 40% against the US$ and most other currencies. Many companies in Mexico and multinational companies trading with Mexico lost a good deal of money in this fall. The companies had not hedged their foreign exchange bets!

Source: Ball and Oliver, From test case to basket case. *Corporate Finance*, February 1995, 16–19.

WHAT HAVE WE LEARNED IN THIS CHAPTER?

1. The markets that trade and hedge currency are the largest and fastest growing markets in the world today.
2. The spot market trades one currency for another for delivery in three days' times. A dealer, usually working for a commercial bank, quotes a "buy" and "sell" rate for the currency. The difference between these quotes is called the "spread". The quote can be "direct" or "indirect". "Cross rates" between currencies must be consistent with one another.
3. The forward market buys and sells currency at a fixed rate for future delivery. Movements in the forward rate are heavily influenced by movements in the spot rate. Forward rates are quoted on fewer currencies than spot rates.
4. The difference between the spot rate and the forward rate is called the "premium" or "discount" on the spot rate. The forward rate can be expressed in terms of the premium or discount on the spot rate, this is called a "swap" rate.
5. The premium or discount on the spot rate can be converted into an interest rate differential between the two currencies involved. This is the basis of the "interest rate parity theory".
6. A "futures" currency contract allows a finance officer to buy a fixed amount of foreign currency at a fixed date for delivery on some future date. The cost is similar to a forward contract but provides greater liquidity since the standardized contract can be traded on a "futures" market.

7. A currency option gives the buyer of the option the right but not the obligation to buy or sell a given amount of currency at a given price at a given time at the end of the option period or possibly during the life-span of the option. An option is both an insurance policy and a gambling chip, it is thus more expensive per money unit covered than a forward or futures contract. A wide range of option products are offered on the currency markets of the world.

8. The currency swap market is concerned with swapping streams of currency or obligations denominated in one currency for streams denominated in another currency. The swap market allows a finance officer to move out of one risky currency into a safer currency. Swaps also allow money to be raised in a cheap market, so far as the swapper is concerned, and then swapped into a more desirable currency.

NOTES

1. When the UK opted out of the exchange rate mechanism on September 16 1992 the pound sterling fell by almost 25% in a few hours.
2. See Cox, J. et al. (1981) The relation between forward prices and futures prices. *JFE*, vol. 9, 321–45.
3. There are two kinds of options. A so-called "European" option and an "American" option. The European option can only be exercised at the end of the option period. The American option can be exercised within the option period. Most currency options are American options.
4. Garman, M. and Kohlhagan, S. have devised a model for valuing currency options (see (1983) Foreign currency options values. *Journal of International Money and Finance*, December, 231–7.

FURTHER READING

Brown, B. (1986) *The Forward Market in Foreign Exchange*, Croom Helm.
Coggan, P. (1986) *The Money Machine: How the City Works*, Penguin Books.
European Bond Commission (1991) *The European Options and Futures Markets: An Overview and Analysis for Money Managers and Traders*, Chicago, USA, Probus.
Gregory, I. and Moore, P. (1986) Foreign exchange dealing. *Corporate Finance*, October, pp. 33–46.
Heller, L. (1986) *Euro-commercial Paper*. Euromoney Publications.
Honeygold, D. (1989) *International Financial Markets*, Woodhead-Faulkner.
Hull, J. and White, A. (1987) Hedging the risks from writing foreign currency options. *Journal of International Money and Finance*, June, pp. 131–52.
Price, J. and Henderson, S. K. (1992) *Currency and Interest Rate Swaps*, Butterworth.
Sweeney, R. J. and Edward, J. (1990) Trading strategies in forward exchange markets, *Advances in Financial Planning and Forecasting*, vol. 4, pp. 55–80.

TUTORIAL QUESTIONS

1. Given the following exchange and interest rates answer the following questions:

US$ for £ sterling.

Date	1.11.95
Spot rate	1.92
Forward rate	1.85 one year forward

Rate of interest on one year bonds. UK£ = 15%   US$ = 10%

Questions:
(a) Does the forward rate on the US$ stand at a discount or a premium to the £ sterling? What is the value of this discount or premium?
(b) Would it pay a speculator to buy a US$ bond with sterling, take out a forward contract to cover the exchange risk on this bond, and when the US$ bond matures in one year's time convert the proceeds back into £ sterling?

2. What is a cross rate? Why are cross rates always symmetrical in a free market? If the rate of exchange between the pound sterling and the Canadian dollar on a specific date is one pound sterling equals C$1.95 and the rate of exchange between the £ and the French franc on the same date is one pound sterling equals 8.5 French francs, what is the rate of exchange on that date between the Canadian dollar and the French franc? How can you be so sure that this is the exchange rate on that date? What makes it so?

3. If a currency exchange market regularly shows a wide spread between the offer and bid exchange rate on a currency what does this fact tell us about the market? If an experienced currency dealer quotes sterling against French francs to another experienced dealer as 34–71 what does this mean?

4. What is the "agio" in foreign currency dealing? How can an arbitrageur use this "agio"?. What is the value of the minimum "agio" that must be exceeded to induce an arbitrageur to enter the market?

5. What is a futures currency contract? What factors are standardized in a futures contract? Why take out a futures currency contract if a forward contract for the same amount is available and is simpler to arrange? What margin must be provided on a futures contract?

6. Explain in your own words the meaning of the term "currency swap". What is being swapped? Who usually arranges the swap? Provide three examples where a currency swap might prove useful to a company that is trading internationally. Who guarantees that a currency swap will be reversed at the end of the contract period?

7. What is a currency "call" option? How does it work? If a currency option can remove exchange rate risk from a buyer of an option who takes on this risk in the currency option market? What is the maximum loss possible if you buy a currency "call" option? What is the maximum loss possible if you "write" a currency "call" option?

8.
Table 2   Cost of Call Option

DM per £	Strike price	Sept.	Oct.
	280	12.4	13.1
(today's	285	8.3	9.4
price 293 pf)	290	3.4	4.1
	295	2.0	2.8
	300	0.7	1.1

You buy a £25 000 call option for end October at DM2.95 to the £ and another for end September at DM2.80 to the £. What is the cost in DM and £s of these call options? If the spot rate on the 30 September was DM2.85 per pound and the spot rate on October 31 was DM2.73 per £ sterling would you exercise the options?

9. In Exhibit 2.5 what is the cost of taking out a currency call option to buy $31 250 in two months' time at US$1.60 to the £ sterling? To sell £62 500 in three months time at US$1.50?

10. Explain the conditions under which a forward contract, a futures contract or an option contract is the best contract to enter into to handle exchange rate risk?

11. Explain the procedure if a finance officer wishes to take out a forward contract to sell ten million Italian lire forward now that is due on a contract to be paid to your company in six

months' time. What will happen if the Italian importer fails to pay the amount due to you in six months' time?

12. An option contract is said to be "in-the-money"? What does this mean? How is it that a currency "call" (buy) option contract still has some value even when the current spot exchange rate is well below the exercise price?

13. Do you think that the US government has cause to be worried about the possibility that the swap market might destabilize the financial markets of the world? How could this happen?

14. Some countries, such as South Africa, have two spot markets for their currency, a commercial market and a financial market. The external value of the currency differs in these two markets. What possible advantage can be gained by the South African economy from having two spot markets? What advantage can be gained from the rand having two different values at the same time?

15. On February 15 1996 a British company, Cartel PLC, wins an export order to export US$2 million worth of glass fibre cable to an United States importer. The credit terms on the contract are for the US$2 million to be paid to Cartel PLC in six months' time.

The exchange rates quoted to CARTEL by its bank on February 15, 1996 are as follows:

Spot rate on 15.2.96:   1.5623–1.5711 (US$ per £)

6 months forward   1/8th cent premium (0.125)
                          − 3/8th cent discount (0.375)

Spot rate: 15.8.96   1.5344

Required: (a) Calculate the six months forward rate in terms of the US$. (b) What is the cost of buying one US$ six months forward in terms of pound sterling? (c) what will Cartel do on August 15, 1996? (d) How much money will Cartel receive on August 15, 1996 in terms of £ sterling? (e) What was the cost of the forward cover to Cartel?

EXERCISE 2.1   APPLEGATE PLC

Applegate PLC exports carbon dyes to the United States. A large contract has just been signed on May 1, year 1 for US$540 000. The finance officer of Applegate is worried about the future of the US$ to £ sterling exchange rate. She thinks that the US$ may fall in value by a significant amount over the next six months. The US contract is due to be paid on October 31, year 1.

Given the facts about the spot and forward exchange rates set out below write down:

1. The cost of buying and selling the US$ on the spot market on May 1, year 1.
2. The spread on the 3 month and 6 month forward rate in terms of the US$.
3. The actual forward rate for three month and six month forward contracts in US$.
4. If the $540 000 could be sold on March 1, year 1 how much would be received in £ sterling?
5. If the finance officer sells the US$s six months forward how much will she receive in terms of £ sterling on October 31, year 1?
6. Suppose the US company fails to pay up on October 31, year 1. What is the situation regarding the forward contract?

Exchange rates quoted on May 1, year 1.

        Spot rate (dealer's buy and sell rate) US$ 1.4711–1.4789 to the £ sterling
        Forward rate: three months forward   1/4 c pm–3/4 c discount
        Forward rate: six months forward   3/4 c pm–1 1/2 c discount

Note: 1/4 c pm = 0.0025

Exchange rate quoted on October 31, year 1:

        Spot rate   US$ 1.4500–1.4597   to the £ sterling

EXERCISE 2.2 IRPT PROBLEM

Assume that on June 15 1996 the following exchange rates between the French Franc and the £ sterling are printed in the financial press:

Spot rate: 14 June 96	£1 = FF8
Forward rate (3 months)	£1 = FF7.9
Forward rate (one year)	£1 = FF7.7

1. Is the franc standing at a premium or a discount to the £ sterling on the forward market?
2. What would you expect the interest rates to be on short-term 12 and 3 month loans in French francs if the UK rates of three month loans (on an annualized basis) and one year loans are respectively:

$$\text{3 months' loan in sterling} = 12\%$$

$$\text{One year loan in sterling} = 14\%$$

Assume free movement of loan funds between Paris and London.

EXERCISE 2.3 CURRENCY OPTION PROBLEM

London Stock Exchange: £/DM options
One contract = £20 000
Option costs are quoted as pfennig per £
Current spot exchange rate £1 = DM2.56

Table 3

	Calls			Puts		
Strike price	Oct.	Nov.	Dec.	Oct.	Nov.	Dec.
2.500	11.52	11.58	11.67	****	0.05	0.36
2.525	7.86	8.01	8.57	****	0.20	0.89
2.550	4.25	4.91	5.81	0.06	0.83	1.85
2.575	1.41	2.57	3.68	0.89	2.13	3.33
2.600	0.20	1.08	2.12	3.42	4.31	5.42
2.625	****	0.33	1.11	6.86	7.29	8.12

Table 3 shows the cost of taking out an option to buy (call) or sell (put) a fixed amount of DM on October 10, 1996 on the London currency traded option market.

Questions:
1. What is the value of a standard contract?
2. What is the cost of taking out an option to sell two contracts for the end of December at DM2.6 to the pound sterling?
3. What is the cost of taking out an option to buy £80 000 at DM2.5 at the end of October 1996?
4. What is the cost of taking out both a call and put option for one contract at DM2.550 for the end of November?

If the DM to pound sterling exchange rate at the end of October, November and December is:

October: DM2.54   November: DM2.51   December: DM2.48

What profit or loss would have been made on these option contracts?

ANSWERS TO EXERCISE 2.1 APPLEGATE PLC

1. The dealer will sell US$1.4711 to Applegate on the spot market on May 1, year 1 for one pound sterling. The dealer will buy US$ from Applegate at the rate of US$1.4789 per £.
2. The spread on the three month forward rate is 0.0075 cents less 0.0025 cents = 0.0050 cents. The spread on the six month forward rate is 0.015 cents less 0.0075 cents = 0.0075 cents.
3. The actual quotes on the forward rate for three month and six month forward contracts are:

3 months	$1.4711 - 0.0025 =$	1.4686	The dealer will sell US$ at this rate
	$1.4789 + 0.0075 =$	1.4864	The dealer will buy US$ at this rate
6 month	$1.4711 - 0.0075 =$	1.4636	The dealer will sell US$ at this rate
	$1.4789 + 0.015 =$	1.4939	The dealer will buy US$ at this rate

4. If the finance officer could sell the $540 000 on May 1 she would receive:

$$US\$540\,000/1.4789 = \qquad £365\,136$$

5. But she will not receive the $540 000 until October 31. Selling this amount forward six months means that when the $540 000 is received on October 31, she will receive:

$$US\$540\,000/1.4939 = \qquad £361\,470$$

6. If the US company fails to pay the US$540 000 on the due date on October 31 Applegate must still honour the forward contract so the finance officer will need to buy the US$540 000 on the spot market at that date. This will cost Applegate:

$$US\$540\,000/1.4500 = \qquad £372\,414$$

Notes:
1. The forward rates are quoted as either a premium or a discount on the spot rate.
2. A premium must be deducted from the spot rate to find the actual forward rate.
3. A discount must be added to the spot rate to find the actual forward rate.

APPENDIX 2.1 THE EUROMARKETS

Introduction

The markets that provide much of the funding for the various financial products described in Chapter 2 are called the "Euromarkets". This collection of markets represents a comparatively recent development in the world of finance. Prior to 1970 the Euromarkets contributed a comparatively small fraction of world finance, which was, at that time, centred on the United States.

The name "Euromarket" is something of a misnomer since these markets include most financial debt products that are denominated in a currency other than the currency of the country in which they are sold. Euromarket products are traded in New York and Tokyo and Hong Kong as well as in London or Frankfurt or Paris. The name "Offshore" markets or "External" markets would provide a more accurate description of the geographical location of these markets.

The Euromarkets developed as a consequence of certain communist states being unwilling to invest in the USA and the USA itself wishing to discourage foreign institutions from raising funds in the USA. This aim was effected via such legal devices as the interest rate equalization tax of 1963 and the notorious regulations Q and M in 1966, which limited the level of interest that could be paid on term deposits in the USA and the reserve requirements of US banks. The oil price rise of the 1970s also pumped large amounts of funds into the Euromarkets from Middle Eastern states.

Whatever the causes of the growth of these markets the Euromarkets now provide a substantial fraction of the funding of multinational institutions and also account for a substantial fraction of the non-equity based securities held in the portfolios of investment institutions throughout the world.

The huge expansion of the swap market described in Chapters 2 and 5 would not have been possible without the parallel development of the Euromarkets.

The dominant currency in the Euromarkets is the US$ but the DM, £ sterling, Japanese yen and French franc are also popular currencies in this market. The ECU, the European unit of account, is popular among supranational institutions and a few MNCs such as IBM, Toyota and Ford.

The Size of the Euromarkets

The amount of money raised and invested through the Euromarkets is huge. The total amount currently on issue may exceed US$ 10 000 000 000 000. Ten trillion US dollars.

Some Definitions

A Euromarket is any financial market that exists outside of the country that issues the currency in which the particular financial product is denominated. For example, a French company issuing Eurofranc bonds in Germany will probably use the facilities of the Euromarket to make the issue.

A Eurocurrency is any freely convertible currency deposited in a financial institution outside the country issuing the currency. For example, £10 million pound sterling deposited by a UK company in a Swiss bank account.

Eurobonds are bonds issued in a country other than the country that issues the currency in which the bond is denominated. Since they are not traded in a specific domestic market the conditions attached to the bonds are not directly regulated by any government although issuers may be constrained by issue regulations in their own domestic market. Most Eurobonds are bearer bonds although they may be registered by some stock exchange authority. There is often no with-holding tax imposed on Eurobonds since there is no domestic tax authority to collect the tax. These attributes may provide opportunities for maximizing tax efficient investment.

Eurobonds differ from "foreign bonds", which are issued by MNCs. Foreign bonds are denominated in the currency of the country in which they are issued.

The Eurocurrency Market

The Eurocurrency market is the largest market operating within the Euromarkets. The Eurocurrency market is a wholesale money market that allows short-term fixed-interest loans to be bought and sold at competitive prices. Most loans so issued have a maturity of less than a year.

Only very large institutions such as international banks, government institutions and major MNCs use this market. The minimum value loan offered has a value equivalent of one million US$.

The market is popular because of (1) the lack of regulation, especially regarding the reserve requirements of the banks issuing the loans. (2) the loans having a lower cost and providing a higher revenue than in domestic markets and (3) the absence of a with-holding tax on interest repatriated abroad.

In addition to the short-term fixed-interest loans the Eurocurrency market also offers Eurocredit bank loans for longer periods of time from one to ten years. These loans are normally floating rate loans at x% above some base rate such as LIBOR or PIBOR, which are used as the base rate.

The Euronote Market

This market issues short-term debt instruments denominated in foreign currencies.

The main instruments are Eurocommercial paper, Euro medium term notes (EMTNs) and note issuance facilities (NIFs). These instruments provide the buyer with liquidity via a secondary market and a superior rate of interest compared to the domestic market.

The Eurobond Market

Eurobonds are issued by large multinational institutions and underwritten by international banks. Although in bearer form they are usually registered with a stock exchange to prevent fraud. The bonds are issued for a fixed period of time at a fixed or floating rate of interest. The floating rate is fixed at a base rate plus some percentage, say LIBOR plus 1.7%. A minimum rate of interest may be guaranteed.

Most short-term Eurobonds are used to fund the "swap" market, longer term bonds provide a suitable form of investment for financial institutions such as pension funds and investment trusts. Around 65% of the Eurobonds currently on issue were issued to support the swap market.

Types of Eurobonds

There are three main types of Eurobonds offered on the Eurobond markets. Fixed rate bonds, floating rate notes and some more exotic instruments.

Fixed rate bonds are priced at between US$1000 and US$10 000 and offer maturities of 3, 5, 7 and 10 years. The bonds normally do not offer collateral security in the event of borrower default but are otherwise subject to strict legal conditions. Normally the bond is repaid at the end of the lending period, in other words most fixed-interest bonds are "bullet" bonds. However variations on this theme exist. Dual currency bonds offer interest and repayment denominated in another currency. Warrant bonds have a warrant attached to the bond that allows the owner to buy another bond at a fixed price when the first is repaid or to convert the bond into a fixed number of equity shares. Instalment bonds are also on offer that repay the bond in instalments.

Floating rate notes (FRNs) are bonds which offer a rate of interest related to some base rate such as LIBOR plus a fixed percentage, for example six month LIBOR plus 2%. The rate is revised on a regular basis, for example six month LIBOR is revised every six months. Several other types of FRNs are offered for example "capped and collared" FRNs which place an upper and lower limit on the rate of interest to be paid during the life of the bond. "Convertible FRNs" have also been offered, which allow the owner to convert into a fixed-rate bond under certain circumstances.

The Secondary Market

The International Securities Market Association (ISMA) supervises the Eurobond markets. It publishes a regular bulletin on the prices offered and the number of transactions in the Eurobond market.

Eurobonds are traded on many stock exchanges as an over-the-counter (OTC) market. Bond dealers, who are registered with ISMA, make a market in specific types of bonds offering bid and offer prices.

The custody of Eurobonds and the clearing of Eurobond deals is organized by two dealing systems called EUROCLEAR and CEDEL. Buy and sell transactions are effected via SWIFT and the EUCLID and CEDCOM systems.

The issue cost of a Eurobond generally varies between 1.5% and 2.5% of the value of the bond.

The Special Advantages Provided by the Euromarkets

The Euromarkets are unregulated and do not normally impose a with-holding tax on interest payments.

Funds raised on the Euromarkets are normally cheaper as to both issue costs and interest rate compared to funds raised on domestic markets. Returns obtained by investors in the Euromarkets normally provide a higher rate of return than from comparable investments in the domestic markets, possibly by reason of tax advantage.

The fact that most Eurobonds are issued in bearer form offers the potential for secrecy to the holder, which might again offer certain tax advantages.

It is claimed by some commentators that funds, particularly of large amount, can be raised more quickly from the Euromarkets than from the domestic markets.

The secondary markets for Eurobonds organized via EUROCLEAR and CEDEL provide an efficient method of buying and selling bonds before the maturity date of the bond.

3
Theories of International Finance

INTRODUCTION

Economists have studied the operation of the international financial markets for over a century. Their research has produced a number of interesting theories as to how these markets work. Some of these theories have been tested so many times that there can be no reasonable doubt as to their veracity, other theories are more controversial.

In this chapter we will briefly examine some of the more important theories that are relevant to a financial officer when he is devising a blueprint for managing his exposure to foreign exchange risk.

THE PURCHASING POWER PARITY THEORY

The purchasing power parity theory is one of the oldest theories to be promulgated in international economics.[1]

The theory claims that the future exchange rate between two currencies is related to the difference between the future inflation rates expected in each of the countries using these currencies. If the future inflation rate in the two countries can be forecast then a financial officer should be able to estimate the future exchange rate between the currencies with a fair degree of accuracy.

Let us take an example (Table 4).

Table 4

| Country | Index of expected inflation End of: | |
	1996	1997
UK £	100	103
Australian dollar	100	110

The PPP theory claims that the anticipated change in the £/A$ exchange rate will be given by the equation:

$$c = (0.10 - 0.03)/(1 + 0.03) = 0.068$$

The PPP theory suggests that if the inflation rates turn out to be as forecast the £ sterling will appreciate by about 6.8% against the Australian dollar over the next year.

The PPP theory assumes a free flow of funds between the £ sterling market and the Australian dollar market over the year. If exchange controls are imposed on the movement of currencies between the two markets then the adjustment of the exchange rate can be delayed but not eliminated.

THE INTEREST RATE PARITY THEORY

In Chapter 2 we explained that on any given date the difference between the "spot" exchange rate between two currencies and the forward rate is called the "forward premium" or "forward discount" on the currency.

The interest rate parity theory (IRPT) claims that this premium or discount is related to the difference between the interest rates charged on short-term loans denominated in the two currencies over the given time period.[2]

The interest rate differential should approximate to the forward rate premium or discount for the given period. If this is not so the markets cannot be in equilibrium.

An example of the working of the IRPT is provided in Exhibit 3.1.

The Exhibit provides an example of the working of the IRPT between the £ sterling and three other currencies, the US$, the Italian lire and the French franc.

At the beginning of the period the spot rate on the US$ is standing at US$1.84 to the £ sterling. The forward rate one year forward is US$1.78 to the £ sterling. Thus the US$ stands at a premium of 6 cents to the £ sterling over the period of one year.

The IRPT claims that this difference of 6 cents will be reflected in the difference between short-term interest rates in the USA and the UK on one-year loans.

Thus there is a relationship between the spot rate (s), the forward rate (f), the short-term interest rate in the home currency (s%) and the short-term interest rate in the foreign currency (f%).

An equation has been devised which relates all of these factors:

$$(1 + s\%)/(1 + f\%) = s/f.$$

For example if the short-term loan rate in the UK is 10% per annum and in the foreign country, the USA, it is 6.41% per annum and if the spot rate is currently US$1.84 dollar to the £ then the forward exchange rate, f, between the currencies must be:

$$(1 + 0.10)/(1 + 0.0641) = 1.84/f$$

$$f = 1.84 \times ((1.0641)/(1.10)) = US\$1.78 \text{ to the pound.}$$

The IRPT assumes a free flow of short-term funds between the currency markets in the UK and the USA.

If the short-term interest rates should get out of line with the forward premium or discount on the currency then "arbitrageurs" will soon step in to make a profit by

Exhibit 3.1 An Example of the Working of the Interest Rate Parity Theory

Suppose the spot rate and the forward rate on three currencies were as follows on April 1 1994

Currency	Spot rate	One year forward	Premium discount	Value
Pound sterling	1	1	Nil	Nil
US dollar	1.84	1.78	Premium	6 cents
Italian lire	2000	2300	Discount	300 lire
French franc	10	10.5	Discount	50 cents

The number of pounds sterling that can be bought with 1000 units of the foreign currency is thus:

Currency	(a) Spot at 1.4.94	(b) Forward 3.1.95	(c)	(d) Rate of interest %
1000 pound sterling	£1,000.00	£1,000.00		10.00
1000 US$ buys	£543.48	£561.80		6.41
1000 Italian lire buys	£0.50	£0.43		?
1000 French francs buys:	£100.00	£95.24		?

The equation required to calculate the short-term rate of interest in the US$ market, the Italian lire market and the French franc market given the 10% rate in the UK market is:

$$(1 + s\%)/(1 + f\%) = s/f$$

where: $s\%$ = the short-term rate of interest in the home market

$f\%$ = the short-term rate of interest in the foreign market

s = the spot rate of exchange

f = the forward rate of exchange

therefore:

$$f = s \times (1 + f\%)/(1 + s\%) = 1.78$$
$$s = f \times (1 + s\%)/(1 + f\%) = 1.84$$
$$f\% = (f \times (1 + s\%)/s) - 1 = 6.41\%$$
$$s\% = (s \times (1 + f\%)/f) - 1 = 10.00\%$$

If the US$/£ spot rate is US$1.84 to the £ sterling, the one year forward rate is US$1.78 to the pound and the annual short-term interest rate on pound sterling loans is 10% per annum then, if the IRPT is working, the short-term rate of interest on US$ loans will be 6.41% per annum.

Readers can work out the rate of interest on Italian lire loans and French franc loans for themselves.

The interest rate parity theory relates the premium or discount on the spot rate to the difference between the short-term loan rates in the two currencies over the relevant period.

eliminating the difference. Arbitrageurs would take out loans in the "cheap" currency and lock in the profit on the deal by covering the loan repayment value forward on the forward market.

Note that the true rate at which the premium is compounded is not simply the rough approximation of $10\% - 6.63\% = 3.37\%$. The true rate is a slightly lower rate at 3.16%, that is $(1.10)/(1.0663) - 1 = 3.16\%$.

THE INTERNATIONAL FISHER THEORY

The PPP theory claims that future exchange rates are influenced by differences in inflation rates between two currencies. A higher inflation rate in Argentina compared to the USA will, over time, reduce the value of the Argentinian peso relative to the US dollar.

If the bond market expects Argentinian inflation to be higher in the future than US inflation this expectation will have an impact on the relative cost of long-term fixed-interest bonds in the two countries. If it is expected that the inflation rate in Argentina will, in the future, be higher than in the USA then Argentinian companies will have to pay a rate of interest above that paid on US$ bonds if they wish to float fixed interest bonds denominated in pesos on the US market.

Roughly speaking if the inflation rate in the USA is expected to average 4% over the next five years and the inflation rate in Argentina is expected to average 20% per annum over the same period then the Argentinian peso bond will have to pay around $(20\% - 4\%) = 16\%$ more per annum to investors to persuade international investors to invest in peso bonds.

The difference is not exactly 16% it is actually:

$$(1.20)/(1.04) - 1 = 15.384\%.$$

This brings us to the International Fisher Theory. The International Fisher Theory claims that the difference between interest rates on fixed-interest long-term loans or bonds in different currencies will reflect "expected" differences in inflation rates in the various countries over the period and so will be rated to allow for future "expected" gains or losses in exchange rates.[3]

If international markets were perfect markets and the International Fisher Theory worked then the real cost of fixed interest loans in the various currencies of the world would always be the same[4] in terms of the home currency! Unfortunately international markets are not perfect markets and many such markets are not even efficient markets so finance officers must take care when selecting the currency in which to raise their foreign currency loans. We will return to this important topic in Chapter 7.

We have highlighted the word "expected" to emphasize the fact that unexpected jumps in the inflation rate will not be allowed for by the interest rate differential on fixed-interest loans in different currencies. It has been shown that although interest rate differentials may be unbiased predictors of future changes in exchange rates they are rather poor predictors of such changes. We will expand on the difference between unbiased prediction and poor prediction in the next section of this chapter.

Exhibit 3.2 illustrates the base rate cost of a set of otherwise identical fixed-interest loans offered to the finance officer of a UK company in various currencies in 1993. The highest cost, at 19% per annum, is the cost of a loan denominated in Greek drachma. The cheapest cost, at 1.75% per annum, is the cost of an otherwise similar loan denominated in Japanese yen.

If the international Fisher effect is to be believed the difference between the interest cost of loans in the various currencies reflects market expectations about future changes in exchange rates over the period of the loan.

The table in Exhibit 3.2 also shows the difference between the fixed-interest cost of a loan in pound sterling and the cost of otherwise identical loans in other currencies

Exhibit 3.2 The Base Rate of Interest in 14 Countries on December 7, 1993

	Base rate of interest (%)	Cost (%) difference from sterling
Greek drachma	19.00	13.5
Portuguese escudos	13.40	7.9
Spanish pesetas	9.50	4
Danish krone	8.75	3.25
Italian lire	8.00	2.5
Swedish krone	7.00	1.5
French francs	6.50	1
German DM	5.75	0.25
Belgian francs	5.50	0
UK £	5.50	0
Dutch guilders	5.25	−0.25
Swiss francs	4.25	−1.25
USA$	3.00	−2.5
Japanese yen	1.75	−3.25

Exchange controls were abolished in the UK on October 19, 1979. From that date UK companies have been able to raise loans in any foreign currency they choose so long as the Central Bank in the foreign country approves the removal of funds for investment in another country. The nominal cost of funds varies a great deal between countries. The difference between the highest and lowest base rates in the above table is 17.25%!

The difference in cost represents the markets best estimates of the likely future rate of inflation in the two countries. In other words the market believes that over the next year the difference in the rate of inflation between Greece and Japan is likely to be 17.25%!

These represent the base or prime rates. Large, very safe companies will be able to raise loans at a few percentage points above the base rate. Smaller and riskier companies will have to pay a much higher premium to the lender to cover the greater risk involved.

over one year. The Swiss franc loan costs 1.25% per annum less than a sterling loan, a loan in Italian lire costs 2.5% more per annum than the cost of a sterling loan.

Thus the market appears to believe that the Swiss franc will rise in value by about 1.25% per annum, actually $(1.055/1.0425) - 1 = 1.20\%$, against the pound sterling over the period of the loan and that the Italian lire will fall by about 2.5% per annum, actually 2.37%, against the pound sterling over the period of the loan.

Again a free flow of funds must be allowed between the two currency markets for this theory to hold.

The equation required to calculate any of the four factors involved in the international Fisher for one year given the other three factors is:

$$h\% - f\% = (s_{t+1} - s_t)/s_t$$

where $h\%$ is the interest cost per annum in the home currency, $f\%$ the interest cost per annum in the foreign currency, s_{t+1} the rate of exchange at the end of the loan period and s_t the rate of exchange at the beginning of the loan period.

For example, a one-year loan in Greek drachma costs 19% per annum. A one-year, otherwise identical, loan in pound sterling costs 5.5% per annum. The current rate of exchange between the Greek drachma and the £ sterling is Dr373 to the pound sterling.

What does the market expect the drachma to pound sterling exchange rate to be in one year's time?

$$(1 + 0.19)/(1 + 0.055) \times 373 = 421 \text{ Dr to the £.}$$

In one year's time the market expects the rate of exchange between the drachma and the £ sterling to be Dr421 to the pound sterling.

Nominal Versus Real Interest Rates

The international Fisher assumes that the real interest rate differential remains constant in the two countries involved. It could be that a sudden shortage of funds in one country raises the real interest rate to encourage saving in that country or to attract funds to that country. In this case the nominal interest rate differential is made up of two factors, expectations about future relative inflation in the two countries and a greater demand for funds in one country compared to the other. The interest rate differential may not, in such a case, provide an accurate measure of future exchange rates.

Political uncertainty can also effect the differential.

IS THE FORWARD RATE AN UNBIASED PREDICTOR OF THE FUTURE SPOT RATE?

In the previous discussion we explained that market values frequently imply estimates for the likely value of future exchange rates. How accurate are these predictions? Do these predictions consistently undervalue or overvalue a currency over time or, on average, are the predictions unbiased? An example of the bias problem is set out in Exhibit 3.3.

The first column in Exhibit 3.3 shows the three-month forward rate on the Spanish peseta to £ sterling exchange rate over a twelve-month period. The second column lists the actual future spot rate on these dates.

The third column lists the differences between the forward rate and the actual spot on each date.

If we add these differences up over the year we find that the total of the differences sum to zero. Note that in only one case, December, did the forward rate predict the actual spot rate accurately but, on average, over the twelve-month period the forward rate did not consistently underestimate or overestimate the actual future spot rate.

In such a case we can say that the forward rate is an "unbiased predictor" of the future spot rate. Research has shown that for many exchange rates that operate in free markets the one-, three- and six-month forward rate is an unbiased predictor of the future spot rate. There is some doubt about the one year forward rate.[5]

In the second example shown in Exhibit 3.3 the forward rate on the German DM is compared to the actual spot rate on these dates. In this case the three-month forward rate appears to consistently overvalue the DM over this period. The forward rate is a "biased" predictor of the future spot rate.

The biased nature of the forward prediction of spot is currently a matter of some controversy among economists.

Exhibit 3.3 Illustration of the Unbiased Nature of the Forward Rate as a Predictor of the Spot Rate

	Peseta per £			DM per £		
Date	Forward rate 3 month	Future spot rate on this date	Difference	Forward rate 3 month	Future spot rate on this date	Difference
Jan.	180	175	5	2.50	2.47	0.03
Feb.	177	171	6	2.53	2.49	0.04
Mar.	178	174	4	2.56	2.53	0.03
Apr.	181	184	−3	2.61	2.57	0.04
May	179	188	−9	2.57	2.53	0.04
June	176	183	−7	2.64	2.63	0.01
July	174	181	−7	2.61	2.63	−0.02
Aug.	171	177	−6	2.58	2.57	0.01
Sep.	174	168	6	2.56	2.51	0.05
Oct.	173	167	6	2.51	2.49	0.02
Nov.	178	173	5	2.48	2.44	0.04
Dec.	180	180	0	2.46	2.41	0.05
Total difference			0			0.34

In the case of the peseta the forward rate only gives an accurate prediction of the future spot rate in one month, December. However, when the differences between the forward rate and the future spot rate in each month are added up they sum to zero. The forward rate is a poor but unbiased predictor of the future spot rate.

In the case of the German DM the forward rate is also a poor predictor of the future spot rate but in this case it is also a biased predictor. In 11 of the 12 months the forward rate has underestimated the strength of the DM against sterling.

Research suggests that the one month, three month and six month forward rates tend to be unbiased predictors of the future spot rate.

If the forward rate is an unbiased predictor of the future spot then it would be foolish for a finance officer to cover on the forward market on a regular basis. Forward cover costs money and on average, in the long run, it will give no better cover than not taking out forward cover!

This recommendation will not apply to large "one off" exposure risks.

The Risk Premium and the Forward Rate

Some currencies are riskier to hold than others so it has been argued that the forward rate will include a currency risk premium that might upset the unbiased nature of the exchange rate prediction.

Research on this topic has found that the risk premium effect seems to be small compared to other factors. The probable reason for this is that currency risk can be removed or at least much reduced by holding a diversified portfolio of currencies.

These are technical matters that are of more interest to the professional economist than to the financial officer. All the financial officer needs to remember is that the forward rate has been found to be a poor but reasonably unbiased predictor of the future spot rate.

We shall return to the practical implications of this fact later.

THE EFFICIENT MARKETS THEORY

The efficient markets theory is probably the most important theory to be promulgated in modern finance.[6]

The theory claims that if a financial market is efficient then all past information is already discounted into the value of the financial products being traded on that market. Even more importantly, it is claimed that in an efficient market new information made available to the market is very quickly discounted into the value of all financial products traded on that market.

If the theory is correct then past movements in such things as a share price can provide the investor with no useful information about the future movements in the value of the share. Only new, currently unknown, information can effect movements in the future value of the share.

The efficient markets theory suggests that a market may enjoy various degrees of efficiency. The precise definition of an efficient market and the various degrees of efficiency that can apply in that market will not be pursued here.

If currency markets are efficient then all of the information that may effect currency prices is very quickly incorporated into exchange rates and so the pattern of movement in past exchange rates can provide no useful information about future exchange rates.

If currency markets, like the spot and forward market, are efficient then currency prices are "fair" prices. Currency prices represent the markets best estimate of the true value of the currency at a given point in time with all relevant information taken into account. All publicly available information will be incorporated into the currency price very quickly, within minutes of the information becoming available.

But are currency markets efficient? The answer is not certain. The markets trading in the major currencies such as the US$, the DM, the £ sterling and the Japanese yen are probably pretty efficient but the markets in minor currencies are probably subject to substantial inefficiency. Thus the value offered on exchange rates in minor currencies may not be a "fair" price. Such markets might be rigged.[7]

THE LIMITATIONS OF GOVERNMENT CONTROL

Almost all the theories set out above assume free markets. That is they assume that exchange controls and fixed exchange rates are not being imposed on the free movement of funds between countries.

Exchange controls do not cancel these theories but they do result in unpredictable effects. For example, currency exchange rates cannot be forecast with any degree of accuracy if the market is a free market but once exchange controls are imposed on the movement of funds or once a currency is fitted into a "currency snake" limiting the free movement of the exchange rate, then profits from forecasting become at least a theoretical possibility.

The currency speculator is competing against an opponent, the government, who does not mind losing money, it is not their own money! It is rumoured that George Soros's money fund made close to a billion dollars from speculating on the fall of the British pound on September 16, 1992.

However, as each year goes by international financial markets are processing information more efficiently and becoming more free from government control. They are thus moving towards the efficient market ideal.

WHAT HAVE WE LEARNED IN THIS CHAPTER?

1. Economists have suggested several theories to explain how the international financial markets work.
2. The purchasing power parity theory claims that the future exchange rate between two currencies is related to the difference between the future inflation rates expected in each of the countries using these currencies. It follows that if the inflation rates can be predicted with a fair degree of accuracy the future exchange rates can also be predicted.
3. The interest rate parity theory (IRPT) claims that the forward premium or discount on the spot exchange rate on a currency is related to the difference between the interest rates charged on short-term loans denominated in the two currencies over the given time period. In an efficient market if the premium or discount gets out of line with the interest rate differential operators called "arbitrageurs" bring them back into line.
4. The International Fisher Theory claims that the difference between interest rates on "fixed interest" long term loans or bonds in different currencies will reflect the market's expectations about differences in inflation rates in the various countries over the period and so will be rated to allow for future "expected" gains or losses in exchange rates. Since arbitrageurs do not operate in the international loans market and since international loans markets are not very efficient the theory does not appear to work well at the level of the firm.
5. The forward rate is a poor predictor of the future spot rate of exchange between currencies. However, there is some evidence that the forward rate is an "unbiased" estimator of the future spot rate although this is disputed by some recent research.
6. The efficient markets theory claims that if a financial market is efficient then all past information is already discounted into the value of the financial products being traded on that market. Even more importantly, it is claimed that in an efficient market new information made available to the traders in the market is very quickly discounted into the value of all financial products traded on that market. Efficient currency markets give the buyers and sellers of currency a "fair" price. The currency markets trading major currencies appear to be efficient as long as governments do not interfere with the market.
7. Governments like to interfere with the free operation of currency markets, particularly before elections! Exchange controls and "currency snakes" make currency markets less efficient and so open up the theoretical possibility that profits can be made from speculating on changes in exchange rates.

NOTES

1. See Officer, L. H. The PPP theory of exchange rates: a review article. *IMF Staff Papers*, March 1976, 1–60 for an extensive review of the literature up to 1975.
2. See Aliber, R. Z. The interest rate parity theorem: a reinterpretation. *Journal of Political Economy*, December 1973, 1451–9.
3. See Gailliot, H. J. PPP as an explanation of long-term changes in exchange rates. *Journal of Money Credit and Banking*, August 1970, 348–57.
4. Assuming equal risk.
5. See Cornell, B. Spot rates, forward rates and market efficiency. *JFE*, January 1977, 55–63 and Hansen, L. and Hodrick, R. Forward rates as optimal predictions of future spot rates. *Journal of Political Economy*, October 1980, 829–53.
6. See Fama, E. F. Efficient capital markets: a review of theory and empirical work. *Journal of Finance*, May 1970, 383–417 for an extensive survey of the key literature, most of which was published prior to 1969.
7. See Giddy, I. and Dufey, G. The random behaviour of flexible exchange rates. *Journal of International Business Studies*, Spring 1975, 1–32 for a useful discussion of this question.

FURTHER READING

Abuaf, N. and Jorion, P. (1980) PPP in the long run, *Journal of Finance*, March 1990, 157–74.
Bilson, J. (1983) The evaluation and use of exchange rate forecasting services in R. Herring (ed.). *Management of Foreign Exchange Risk*, Cambridge University Press, pp. 149–179.
Copeland, L. S. (1994) *Exchange Rates and International Finance*, Addison-Wesley.
  A lucid presentation of many of the economic theories relevant to international financial management. The emphasis is on exchange rate determination but much else is covered.
Fama, E. (1984) Forward and spot exchange rates. *Journal of Monetary Economics*, vol. 14, 319–38.
Huang, R. (1987) Expectations of exchange rates and differential inflation rates: further evidence on PPP in efficient markets. *Journal of Finance*, March, 69–79.
Kindleberger, R. and Lindert, S. (latest edition) *International Economics*.
  A standard university text on the subject. Many of the theories of international finance are covered in some detail.
Levich, R. (1979) Are forward exchange rates unbiased predictors of future spot rates? *Columbia Journal of World Business*, Winter, 49–61.
Manzur, M. (1990) An international comparison of prices and exchange rates: a new test of PPP. *Journal of International Money and Finance*, March, 75–91.
Mishkin, F. (1984) Are real interest rates equal across continents? *Journal of Finance*, December, 1345–57.
Solnick, B. H. (1982) *International Investments*, Addison-Wesley.
  The book is aimed at an audience working in the field of international investment rather than in international financial management but much of the theory described is relevant to both disciplines.
Wolff, C. (1987) Forward foreign exchange rates, expected spot rates, and premia: a signal extraction approach. *Journal of Finance*, June, 395–406.

TUTORIAL QUESTIONS

1. What do you understand by the term "Interest Rate Parity Theory"? What is the mechanism that makes this theory work? Why can the IRPT seldom be applied beyond one year? Why is it that the IRPT does not apply to every currency?
2. What do you understand by the International Fisher Theory? Let us suppose that you are the international treasurer of a multinational company (MNC). You believe in the International Fisher theory. Your company needs to borrow approximately £50 million for five years to develop factories in Italy and Spain. You wish to borrow all the money in one currency. The amount can be borrowed in £ sterling, Spanish pesetas or Italian lire. Suppose the current rates of interest on fixed interest five-year loans borrowed in these three currencies

are:

£ sterling 12% per annum, Spanish peseta 10%, Italian lire 15%.

Ignore tax and legal costs.

What currency of loan would you recommend to your Board? How would your belief, or otherwise, in the International Fisher theory effect your decision?

3. What do you understand by the Purchasing Power Parity Theory? If a UK multinational holds SP160million net working capital in Spain and a 5% devaluation of the Spanish peseta (SP) against the £ sterling is expected in the next few months what advice would you give to the board of your UK company regarding the SP160 million net working capital denominated in Spanish pesetas?

Working capital held in Spain:

Inventory SP100, Debtors SP70, Cash SP40, Creditors SP50.

4. Provide a numerical example over a six-month period showing the forward rate on the Swedish krone against the £ sterling to be an unbiased predictor of the future spot rate of the krone against the £ sterling. If the forward rate really is an unbiased predictor of the future spot rate what implications will this have for covering foreign currency deals forward?

5. What is the "International Efficient Markets Theory?". What is meant by the word "efficient" in this context? What is efficient? If the spot market on the £–US$ is "efficient" what does this tell us about those who chart the past movements of the exchange rate in order to find patterns which can be extrapolated to forecast the future £–US$ exchange rate? Explain your reasoning in your answer to this question.

6. In 1980 a UK travel firm raised $US120 million of loans denominated in the US$ to buy passenger aircraft from firms in the USA. The exchange rate at the time was US$2.45 to the £. In 1983, when the loans were due to be repaid, the rate of exchange stood at US$1.41 to the £. The travel firm could not repay the loans and went bankrupt despite the fact that it was making a substantial operational profit at the time. Why could the travel firm not repay the loans? Do you think this case has any bearing on the truth or otherwise of the International Fisher Theory?

7. Why is it that the truth or otherwise of the Interest Rate Parity Theory has been tested many times and yet the truth of the international Fisher theory has been tested so seldom, especially at the level of the firm?

8. The Spanish peseta is expected to devalue or revalue by how much against the German DM and £ sterling over the next year given the predictions in Table 5 regarding inflation?

Table 5

Country	Predicted index of inflation	
	Beginning of year 1	End of year 1
UK	100	110
Spain	100	130
Germany	100	95

Assume that the PPP theory is working in all cases. What stops the PPP theory from working?

9. Assume that the cost of a one-year loan in Canada on 1.1.96 is 10% per annum and in the United States the cost of an otherwise identical loan is 4% p.a. Also assume that the

spot rate on the C$ to the US$ on 1.1.96 is C$1.32 to the US$. Calculate the one-year forward rate on the C$/US$ currency market assuming that the IRPT is working.

10. Assume that a three-year bond in Australian dollars costs 8% per annum and an otherwise identical bond denominated in German DM costs 5% per annum. Calculate the markets expectations with regard to the annual average change in the A$ to DM exchange rate over the next three years assuming that the International Fisher Theory is working between these two currencies.

11. Give two reasons why the International Fisher Theory may not work in practice.

12. If it is true that the forward rate is a poor predictor of the future spot rate why do currency managers bother to take out forward contracts on currencies?

13. Some currencies are riskier to hold than others. This fact would suggest that a "risk premium" should make these risky currencies more expensive to hold than safer currencies. In practice, empirical research has shown this assumption to be incorrect. Why do you think the assumption is incorrect?

14. "If currency markets are efficient currency exchange rates are 'fair' prices". Explain why this is so.

15. What is a "currency snake"? Why do groups of countries, such as the EU, decide to place their currencies within such a snake? Why is it that profits on currency speculation can probably be made when a currency is placed within a currency snake but not otherwise?

EXERCISES

1. Assume that international financial markets are efficient and currencies can flow freely between different countries.

Calculate the future exchange rates expected by the markets if the predicted inflation rates are as follows:

(a) For the next year the inflation rate in the UK is expected to be 3% and in Canada 5%. The current exchange rate between the £ and the Canadian dollar is C$1.9 to the £.

(b) From the beginning of year 1 to the end of year 4 the inflation rate in the UK is expected to be 4% and in South Africa 7% per annum. The current exchange rate is 6 rand to the pound sterling.

(c) The current exchange rate between the US$ and the Japanese yen is 130 yen to the US$. The exchange rate in five years' time is predicted to be 100 yen to the US$. If the annual inflation rate in the USA is expected to be 4% over the five-year period what is the expected inflation rate in Japan over the same period?

2. Use the interest rate parity theory to make the following calculations:

(a) The current rate of exchange between the £ and the US$ is US$1.5 to the £. The US$ stands at a premium of 5 cents to the £ on the six-months forward market. If the rate of interest on six-month loans in the UK is currently 10% per annum calculate the rate of interest on six-month loans in the US$.

(b) The rate of interest on three-month loans in New Zealand is 12% on an annual basis. The rate of interest on three-month loans in Australia is 9% on an annual basis. The current rate of exchange between the NZ$ and the A$ is NZ$1.23 to the A$. Calculate the three-month forward premium of the A$ on the NZ$.

(c) The current rate of exchange between the Italian lire and the UK£ is 2469 lire to the £. The one-year forward rate is 2528 lire to the £. The rate of interest on one-year loans in the UK is currently 9% per annum. What is the rate of interest on one-year loans in lire if the IRPT is working?

3. If the international Fisher effect works calculate the following:

   (a) The rate of interest on a fixed interest five-year French franc loan is 7% per annum. The rate of interest on an identical fixed interest five-year loan in German DM is 5% per annum. The international bond market expects the French franc to depreciate in value against the DM by what % each year over the five-year period? If the current exchange rate is FF 3.41 to the DM, what do the markets expect the exchange rate between the FF and DM to be in five years' time?

   (b) The country of Lilliputia has an exchange rate with the UK£ but no bond market. The rate of interest on fixed interest three-year bonds in the UK is 8% per annum. The current exchange rate between the UK£ and the Lilliputian "gullivar" is G$12 to the £. A currency forecaster predicts that in three years' time the rate of exchange will be G$15 to the £. If a British company wishes to raise a fixed interest G$200 000 loan in Lilliputia what rate of interest should be attached to the loan if the cost is to be competitive to raising the money in the UK?

   (c) A British company raises a fixed interest 10-year loan at 6% in DM. The company could have raised the same amount of money in Swiss francs at 4% per annum for the same period. On the date the loan was raised the rates of exchange were as follows:

   One pound sterling = 2.5 DM = 2 Swiss francs.
   Ten years later the rates of exchange are:
   One pound sterling = 2.2DM = 1.8 Swiss francs.
   At the end of the ten years the British company reconsiders the decision to raise the loan in DM rather than Swiss francs. Did it make the right decision?

4. The rates of exchange in Table 6 show the three-month forward rate and the actual spot rate of exchange on these future dates between the UK£ and the Spanish peseta over two six-month periods. Is the three-month forward rate an unbiased predictor of the future spot rate? In which of the two six-month periods is the forward rate the more accurate predictor of the spot rate?

Table 6

Month	1	2	3	4	5	6
Forward rate	202	203	204	202	203	205
Future spot rate	200	201	205	202	204	203
Forward rate	202	203	204	202	203	205
Future spot rate	195	210	211	196	196	211

5. Assume that the currency market trading the UK£ and the US$ are efficient markets. Making this assumption what is the UK£ to US$ exchange rate likely to be in period 6 given the rates of exchange in periods 1 to 5 in Table 7?

Table 7

Period	1	2	3	4	5	6
Rate US$ per £	1.5	1.52	1.53	1.55	1.56	?

On Devising a Foreign Exchange Exposure Strategy

INTRODUCTION

The previous chapters have introduced introductory material that a financial officer will find useful in planning a strategy for handling foreign exchange risk.

In order to devise an FEM strategy the financial officer must (1) identify those values that are exposed to the risk of loss if exchange rates should change by a significant margin; (2) decide whether he or she believes that foreign exchange rates can be forecast; and (3) devise a strategy for hedging the identified foreign exchange risk by choosing from among the many hedging devices available those particular devices best suited to the needs of the company.

This chapter will discuss steps (1) and (2) whereas Chapter 5 is devoted to describing and discussing the various hedging techniques and devices available for handling step (3).

FOREIGN EXCHANGE EXPOSURE RISK

If any cash inflow, cash outflow, asset or liability is denominated in a foreign currency then it is potentially exposed to exchange rate risk. A significant change in the exchange rate between two currencies might be of benefit to the company so exposed or it might damage its interests. Financial officers are mainly concerned with those forms of exposure that might damage the interests of their company.

Let us investigate an example of foreign exchange exposure.

A debt of A$3 000 000 is owed to a British company by a company in Australia. The debt is due to be paid in three months' time. If the rate of exchange is currently $A2.1 to the £ and in three months' time the rate of exchange is $A2.3 to the £ then the British company might lose £124 223 if it ignores the exposure risk. The loss occurs because $A3 million/2.1 = £1 428 571 and $A3 million/2.3 = £1 304 348. If we subtract these values from one another the difference is the value of the loss, which turns out to be £124 223. A substantial loss by any standard.

Let us look at another example. A British company buys three passenger aircraft from a US aircraft manufacturing company for US$60 000 000. The company raises a loan of US$60 000 000 in the USA at an interest charge of 8% per annum to pay for the aircraft. The loan is to be repaid at the end of five years. The loan is a "bullet" loan, which means that only interest is paid during the five-year period, the capital is to be repaid in one lump sum at the end of the five-year period.

When the loan is taken out in 1995 the rate of exchange is $US1.55 to the pound sterling. When the loan is repaid in the year 2000 the rate of exchange is US$1.40 to the pound sterling.

When the loan was taken out it was worth US$60 million/1.55 = £38 709 677 in terms of pound sterling. When the loan is repaid the amount due to be repaid is US$60 million/1.40 = £42 857 142 in terms of pound sterling. The value of the loan in local currency, that is in terms of pound sterling, has increased by £42 857 142 − £38 709 677 = £4 147 465. We shall discover in Chapter 7[1] that a lower interest rate in the USA compared to the rate in the UK may compensate, at least to some extent, for this increase in the terminal value of the loan in terms of sterling, but this is not invariably the case. The point of the example is to illustrate the fact that the UK company is exposed to a substantial amount of exchange rate risk over the five-year period.

Let us take a final example. A French company buys one million 686 computer chips from a company in the USA at US$200 a chip. The contract will run over five years. When the deal is struck the French franc to the US$ exchange rate is FF5.3 to the US$. The French franc weakens against the US$ over the five-year period as shown in Table 8.

Table 8

Year	0	1	2	3	4	5
US$	5.3	5.4	5.6	5.6	5.8	6.0

The computer chips have increased in cost by 13.2% in terms of the local currency, French francs, over the five-year period of the contract yet they have remained unchanged in cost in terms of US$. An increase in cost of this magnitude might well make the contract uncompetitive for the French company by year five of the contract. The French company needs to work out some way of hedging this exchange rate risk on the contract.

In all three cases the weakening of one currency against another has exposed the home company to the risk of a substantial loss in terms of the home currency.

Foreign exchange management strategy attempts to identify such potential exposure to exchange rate risk and then either eliminate the risk or control the magnitude of the risk.

TYPES OF FOREIGN EXCHANGE EXPOSURE

Financial analysts have identified three primary types of foreign exchange exposure. These are called:

- Transaction exposure.
- Translation exposure.
- Economic exposure.

Let us now examine each type of exposure in turn.

Transaction Exposure

Companies that export goods and services to, or import goods and services from, abroad must receive or pay for these goods and services. Many of these receipts and payments will be denominated in a foreign currency.

Since exchange rates can and do fluctuate in value minute by minute, all of these payments and receipts that are denominated in a foreign currency are subject to exposure to exchange rate risk.

This form of foreign exchange exposure is called "transaction exposure".

Translation Exposure

If a company operates abroad it may well own warehouses abroad or run subsidiaries abroad that hold assets such as land and buildings, inventory, debts, or manufacturing equipment. The value of these assets are likely to be denominated in the currency of the foreign country. If the company owns a subsidiary abroad the subsidiary may be financed by loans raised in the foreign country, if so these loans will also be denominated in the foreign currency. In addition the subsidiary is almost certain to owe money to trade creditors and banks in the foreign country.

The rules of accounting in many countries require that when a company, which is registered in that country prepares its annual accounts it must "consolidate" the profit and loss accounts and the assets and liabilities of its foreign subsidiaries into a set of group accounts to arrive at a "consolidated" balance sheet and profit and loss account for the group.

It would be meaningless to add together the values of all the assets, liabilities, revenues and expenditures of the foreign subsidiary accounts as denominated in their local currencies. The values of the assets, liabilities, revenues and costs from each of the foreign subsidiary accounts must be "translated" into a set of consistent values denominated in a single currency, normally the "home" currency.

Exhibit 4.1 shows the balance sheets of a British company with subsidiaries in Canada and Australia. The Canadian accounts are expressed in Canadian dollars, the Australian accounts in Australian dollars.

Since the accounts of both subsidiaries are denominated in a foreign currency it follows that all of the assets and liabilities of these foreign subsidiaries are potentially subject to foreign exchange exposure. This form of exposure is called "translation exposure".

Later in this chapter we shall argue that only "monetary" assets and liabilities are really exposed to exchange rate risk. Note that Exhibit 4.1 calculates the net monetary exposure position of both subsidiaries, one in C$ the other in A$. Both subsidiaries owe more than they are owed in their local currency.

Exhibit 4.1 Example of Balance Sheets of Parent Company and Two Foreign Subsidiaries

	UK £m			Canada C$m			Australia A$m
Buildings		132			266		95
Equipment		95			153		101
Fixed assets		227			419		196
Current assets							
Inventory	67			111		234	
Debtors	58			92		107	
Cash	14	139		27	230	15	356
Current liabilities							
Creditors	47			83		97	
Tax due	33	80	59	51	134	96	12	109	247
Total net assets	£m	286		C$m	515	A$m	443
Finance							
Equity plus reserves		100			200		150
Long-term debt		186			315		293
Total financing		286			515		443

NET MONETARY ASSET POSITION

	£m			C$m			A$m	
Debtors	58			92			107	
Cash	14	72		27	119		15	122
Creditors	47			83			97	
Tax due	33			51			12	
Long-term debt	186	266		315	449		293	402
Net monetary asset position	£m	−194		C$m	−330		A$m	−280

As the subsidiaries are owned by a British parent the assets and liabilities of the foreign subsidiaries are exposed to exchange rate risk.

If the PPP theory is correct the non-monetary assets will float up in value with local inflation. Therefore, only the monetary assets and liabilities such as debtors and long-term debt are exposed to exchange rate risk.

The lower half of the table shows the net monetary position of all three companies. Both the Canadian subsidiary and the Australian subsidiary are in a negative net monetary asset position. The companies owe more monetary liabilities than they own monetary assets.

If the Canadian dollar or the Australian dollar falls in value the parent company will gain since the real value of the foreign debt will fall in terms of £ sterling.

This assumes that the international Fisher theory does not work!

Economic Exposure

The FX risks involved in transaction exposure and translation exposure have been known to financial officers for many years and methods have been evolved for minimizing these risks. The FX risks arising from "economic exposure" have been identified much more recently.

Economic exposure is concerned with guarding the long-term cash flows of a company from the dangers inherent in substantial but gradual changes in exchange rates. Economic exposure can best be understood by studying two examples.

A British company has built its success on importing hi-fi equipment from Korea and selling the equipment in Europe. When the company started out on this policy the Korean wan stood at 1300 wan to the £. As the years passed the company continued to import from Korea but gradually the wan strengthened in value against the £ sterling until it reached 1000 wan to the £. The profits of the British company were gradually being eroded as the cost of imports in terms of sterling rose in value and the British company was unable to pass all of this increase in import cost on to its customers. This was despite the fact that the import cost of the hi-fi equipment had actually halved in value in terms of wan!

In 1972 a Dutch company found a successful market for its lorries in South Africa. The market was a very profitable market up to 1985 when the South African rand began to fall sharply against the Dutch florin. By 1990 the rand had halved in value against the florin. The Dutch company were unable to raise their prices in South Africa sufficiently to keep their profit margins constant. Profitability per unit sold fell year by year until in 1992 the Dutch company was forced to pull out of South Africa completely.

In both of the above cases the company had failed to monitor its long-term economic exposure. "Economic exposure" is concerned with protecting the long-term cash flows of a company in terms of the home currency from damage caused by gradual changes in exchange rates over a long period of time.

There Is Only One Exposure Position for One Company

Although there are three types of exposure to consider the financial officer must always remember that one company or group of companies has only one exposure position at any one point in time.

The net value of each type of exposure can be offset against any of the others to arrive at a net exposure position in each currency. For example, the possible loss on a large cash inflow in Canadian dollars can be offset against a debt of approximately equivalent value in Canadian dollars owed to a Canadian company in Canada.

We will return to this point later in the chapter. It is an important point that is often overlooked.

MEASURING EXPOSURE

Exhibit 4.2 provides a logic diagram designed to assist a financial officer to measure the foreign exchange exposure of her company at a given point in time.

Exhibit 4.2 A Logic Diagram to Assist in Deciding on the Degree of Foreign Exchange Exposure Facing a Company

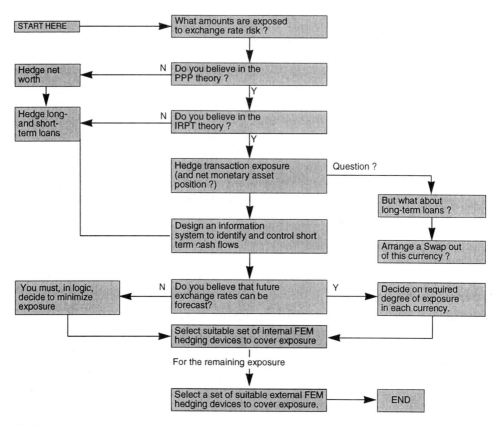

The flow chart suggests a method of identifying the amount of foreign exchange exposure faced by a company at a given point in time.

The PPP theory and the IRPT theory eliminate non-monetary assets and short-term loans from the equation.

Once the net amount of exposure has been calculated the treasurer must decide whether or not she believes she can forecast future exchange rates. If she decides she cannot then the objective must be to reduce exposure to a minimum. If she believes she can forecast future exchange rates then the way is open to take positions and speculate in currency futures.

The amount of the net FX exposure position of a company can vary depending on the attitude of the financial officer to the veracity or otherwise of the various economic theories set out in Chapter 3.

The first step in measuring the exposure position of a company at a specific point in time is to collect certain information.

First, the financial officer must prepare a cash flow statement for the designated future period, say six months forward, setting out all of the cash inflows and outflows of the company in each foreign currency. These cash flows may be contractual or may simply be expected cash flows that are not yet certain. The second step is to prepare a listing of all of the assets and liabilities of the group of companies which are denominated in currencies other than the home currency.

The financial officer is now in a position to measure the net foreign exchange exposure of the group in each currency for the next accounting period.

PPP and Foreign Exchange Strategy

Let us first consider the impact of the purchasing power parity theory on foreign exchange exposure.

The PPP theory claims that only those assets and liabilities whose terminal values are fixed in terms of money are subject to exchange rate risk. The value of non-monetary assets like inventory, equipment, vehicles and buildings will, in time, float up with local inflation. Such assets are, to a substantial extent, self-hedged against inflation.

Since the PPP theory claims that in the long run future exchange rates are tied to inflation differentials between countries it follows that non-monetary assets are self-hedged against changes in exchange rates if they are self-hedged against inflation!

Thus, as shown in Exhibit 4.2, as far as assets and liabilities denominated in foreign currencies are concerned in the long term the financial officer need only worry about hedging monetary assets and liabilities against exchange rate risk.

Monetary Assets and Liabilities

What then is a "monetary" asset or a "monetary" liability?

A monetary asset is an asset whose value is fixed at the outset as a given number of money units. Suppose a US citizen owes a debt of US$50 000 to a German citizen who uses German DM for trading in Germany. The debtor owes 50 000 money units, called US$s, to the German citizen. If the value of the US$ should rise or fall compared to the German DM over the period of the loan then, since the loan is denominated as a fixed number of US$, one party to the deal will benefit and the other party will lose. If the US$ falls against the DM over the loan period then, when the capital portion of the debt is repaid in US$, the German citizen will receive fewer DM than he granted as a loan. The interest rate on the loan may, or may not, compensate for this fall in the value of the loan in terms of DM.

We conclude that money assets and liabilities denominated in a foreign currency are subject to exchange-rate risk. Non-monetary assets are not subject to exchange-rate risk in the long term since the value of such assets are determined by the normal forces of supply and demand for the asset. As long as assets can be internationally traded then local inflation will drive up the value of the non-monetary asset to the "world" price. If goods or services can be bought more cheaply in a foreign market and if trading between the markets is possible then arbitrageurs will soon buy the products and services in the cheap market and sell them at a profit in the dearer market.[2]

Note that the value of an equity (ordinary) share depends on the value of future profits and dividends made by the company issuing the share, thus equity shares are non-monetary assets. The value of an equity share depends on the balancing of demand and supply on the local stock exchange.

Debt is the most common form of monetary asset or liability, either trade debt and long-term company debt or government debt such as a fixed interest government stock.

Since monetary items are subject to exchange rate risk a financial officer needs to calculate the net monetary asset position of each subsidiary in the group on a regular basis.

Exhibit 4.1 illustrates the net monetary asset or liability position of three companies, one parent and two subsidiaries. In all three cases the company is in a net monetary liability position, this means that the company owes more than it is owed in its local currency.

The Canadian company owes C$330 million net and the Australian company A$280 million net. If the C$ or the A$ should rise in value against the £ sterling then the sterling value of these debts will rise. If the C$ or the A$ falls in value against the £ sterling then the sterling value of these debts will fall.

A rise in the sterling value of the foreign debts may or may not be a problem. It all depends on the overall cash flow position of the Group in each of these currencies.

The important thing so far as FX exposure is concerned is to ensure that the current net monetary position of each of the subsidiaries is calculated on a regular basis and that the hedging of this position is considered.

The IRPT and Foreign Exchange Strategy

In Chapter 3 we discovered that in a free market the differences in short-term interest rates (up to about one year ahead) on currencies are related to the forward premium or discount on the exchange rates between the currencies.

In other words short-term loans have a built-in hedge against future "expected" changes in exchange rates. The finance officer need not construct an additional hedge to cover this risk. The only risk that needs to be covered is the risk of "unexpected" changes in exchange rates that would impact on differential short-term interest rates. Such a change in rates could impose a capital loss (or offer a gain) on the company when the time comes to convert the fixed-interest loan denominated in the foreign currency back into the home currency. However, the absolute value of such a loss is likely to be small in most cases. If the potential loss is considered to be significant it can be covered relatively cheaply on the currency option market by buying options that are "out-of-the-money".[3]

We conclude that, under normal circumstances, any FX exposure on a short-term foreign currency loan is self-hedged. If the uncovered risk is considered to be substantial it can be hedged relatively cheaply on the derivatives market or elsewhere.

The International Fisher and Foreign Exchange Strategy

As shown in Exhibit 4.2 we have now eliminated non-monetary assets and short-term foreign loans from the exposure picture. What items are left? Following the logic of Exhibit 4.2 we are left with long-term loans and transaction cash flows.

If the IRPT provides automatic exposure cover for short-term loans surely the international Fisher does the same for long-term loans? Are long-term loans not simply a linked series of short-term loans?

The international Fisher can be interpreted as meaning that the difference between the cost of otherwise identical loans in different currencies represents the markets' best guess as to the future change in exchange rates between the currencies over the period of the loan.

The additional interest paid on a loan taken out in a foreign currency will be eliminated in terms of the home currency by a fall in the capital value of the foreign currency relative to the home currency over the period of the loan, and vice versa. The only thing the financial officer needs to worry about is any "unexpected" change in exchange rates. Unexpected, that is, by the currency market.

We shall return to this point later.

Is the Forward Rate an Unbiased Predictor?

It is claimed that even if the interest rate differential between loans offered in different currencies is not a good predictor of the future exchange rate between the currencies it is an "unbiased" predictor of the change. If this claim is valid it might provide the finance officer with a debt-raising strategy.

If interest-rate differentials are an unbiased predictor of future exchange rates, then as long as the financial officer is able to select a "portfolio" of foreign loans from a range of currencies then any poor guessing by the market as to the future rates of exchange on individual currencies can be eliminated by "diversifying" the total debt of the company over a sufficient number of currencies.

Many economists support the proposition that interest rate differentials are an unbiased predictor of future FX rates. If this is so, then, as long as a finance officer diversifies her company portfolio of debt over a sufficient number of currencies the debt becomes, in effect, self-hedging. The long-term exposure risks attached to foreign debts in individual currencies can be ignored.

Unfortunately, for the finance officer, the matter is not as simple as this and we will return to the problem later in the chapter. A possible solution is to arrange a currency swap to cover the FX risk. Chapter 7, which is devoted to a study of foreign borrowing, discusses the problem in more detail.

It is worth noting that the PPP theory and the IRPT theory are both subject to the attention of arbitrageurs who profit by identifying profitable arbitrage opportunities in the market. This is not so in the case of the international Fisher theory. No arbitrage mechanism exists to make this theory work.

We conclude that the implications of the international Fisher for foreign currency debt raising strategy are uncertain.

Hedging Short-term Cash Flows

Although it has been argued by some economists that all assets and liabilities denominated in a foreign currency are self-hedging to a degree, everyone seems to accept that short-term cash flows are subject to exchange risk.

The exposure of short-term foreign cash flows to changes in exchange rates is called "transaction" exposure.

As shown in Exhibit 4.2 the finance officer must set up an information system and a hedging system to cover this particular type of FX risk.

DESIGNING A FOREIGN EXCHANGE INFORMATION SYSTEM

As we noted above an FX information system needs to (a) collate information on budgeted cash flows in each foreign currency and (b) list all assets and liabilities denominated in a foreign currency.

The frequency of reporting will depend on the extent of foreign trading and the stability of the currencies being monitored.

Exhibit 4.3 sets out a suggested list of the types of statements that need to be prepared on a regular basis if the finance officer wishes to monitor and control the currency exposure of her company.

McRae and Walker (1980), after studying several currency information systems, suggested that the following principles should be employed in setting up an effective FX information system.

1. *Information should be anticipatory.* In other words the system should concentrate on future not past events.
2. *The frequency of the reporting period is important.* The finance officer must tailor the frequency of reporting to the specific needs of the company and the stability of the currencies used by the company. A standard reporting period for every subsidiary is not likely to work efficiently.
3. *The information should be sent directly to the officer controlling foreign financial operations.* Some companies send all currency information first to the chief accountant or controller who redirects it to the relevant foreign exchange department. This approach slows the control system down and makes it inflexible. The reaction period to new information is slowed down. The managers who need the information must be clearly identified and the information sent directly and speedily to those individuals.
4. *The benefits of the FX information system must be carefully explained to all users of the system.* There is evidence that many managers do not fully understand the impact of foreign currency on profit.[4] If the importance of efficient currency management is explained to staff this should improve the accuracy and speed with which the information is processed through the system.
5. *The same type of information system should not be applied to all foreign operations.* It is wise to tailor the system to the specific needs and size of each individual foreign operation. This will improve the relevance of the information processed and ensure better co-operation from the foreign operators.

The Frequency of Reporting

As noted above the frequency of reporting is important. Annual information should be confined to financial statement projections, future credit operations and investment plans.

Quarterly reports on currency flows need to be prepared in much more detail. Balance sheet and income projections should be analysed by currency and country of operation. These reports are particularly useful for efficient corporate tax planning.

Cash flow budget projections should be prepared daily, weekly or monthly depending on the volume of transactions involved. The budgets should be prepared by each foreign

Exhibit 4.3 A Set of Foreign Exchange Exposure Statements

Type of statement	Frequency

The following statements should be prepared by each subsidiary

Projected cash flow

in each currency	For 6 months ahead
inter-group cash	For 6 months ahead
cash to and from third parties	For 6 months ahead

Actual and projected hedging cover

Forward contracts	Monthly
FDRs	Monthly
Future contracts	Monthly
Currency options	Monthly

OTCs
Traded options

Balance sheets

Actual figures	Every three months
Budgeted figures	For 3, 6 and 12 months ahead
Identifying net monetary position	For 3, 6 and 12 months ahead

By currency

Income statements

Actual figures	Every three months
Budgeted figures	For 3, 6 and 12 months ahead

By currency

Capital projects

Actual currency liabilities	Monthly
Budgeted currency liabilities	As decisions are taken
Budgeted currency inflows	Over life of project

Exposure position

Gross exposure in each currency	Monthly for 6 months ahead
Net of hedging exposure in each currency	Monthly for 6 months ahead
Foreign exchange gain or loss projection	Monthly for 6 months ahead
Long-term economic exposure analysis	Annually

Currency rates

Spot rates	Daily
Currency forecasts	For 1, 3, 6, 12 months ahead
Long-term currency forecasts	For 1, 3, 5 and 10 years ahead (if available)

If a finance officer wishes to identify and control the foreign exchange exposure of her company she will need to arrange the regular preparation of a set of statements such as those listed above.

Each company will need to design a foreign exchange information system suited to the specific needs of that company. In most cases transaction exposure is the more important form of exposure but some companies are more exposed to shifts in the value of assets and liabilities and foreign projects caused by unexpected movements in exchange rates.

These statements will now be consolidated into a group based total exposure position by the head office treasury department. Each group of companies has only one exposure position in each currency.

operational unit who will set out future budgeted costs and revenues in each currency. These reports should differentiate between:

Inter-company and extra-company cash flows.
Capital and trade flows.
Contractual and non-contractual flows.

Any existing hedging arrangements must also be listed together with a note of any limitations imposed by foreign countries on taking out forward cover.

Once the information system is in place the finance officer is now in a position to collate this data and then calculate the net exposure position in each currency for each future period.

Exhibit 4.4 sets out an example of a consolidated currency exposure statement prepared by a medium-sized British company. The volume of exposure is related to the expected movement in the exchange rate in each currency over the next year. The statement shows, for each currency, the volume of exposure, the expected % change in the exchange rate forecast by the company, the value of this change, the current spot rate of exchange, the forward rate one year forward and the forecast exchange rate for one year forward made by a professional forecaster.

Exhibit 4.4   A Consolidated Currency Exposure Statement

ELEK CORPORATION PLC
FOREIGN EXCHANGE PROJECTIONS

TIME HORIZON: One year   PREPARED BY William Murray
DATE: 15/03/95   FORECASTER Jane Beckit

A	B	C	D	E	F	G
	Estimated	Forward		Spot		Forecast
	volume	rate %	Expected	Rate	Forward	exchange
	of	change	gain or	of	rate	rates
Currency	exposure	re £ sterling	loss	exchange	one year	(one year)
unit	000s	%	000s	unit	unit	unit
US$	534	1.05	5.61	1.5785	1.562	1.55
DM	1275	1.57	20.02	2.4495	2.411	2.35
FF	8744	0.98	85.94	8.3637	8.2815	8.4
C$	439	4.85	21.31	2.2129	2.1055	2.1
A$	777	−0.96	−7.46	2.1361	2.1566	2.2
Malaysian RM	619	1.31	8.10	4.0481	3.9951	3.9
Japan yen	56 732	4.58	2600	157.53	150.31	145

The company treasurer in the parent company collects the monthly cash flow statements from all the subsidiaries and consolidates them into a group exposure statement.

This statement will identify the total gross exposure position in each currency.

The treasurer will now have to decide whether to minimize the exposure position by using the various hedging techniques described in Chapter 5 or to take up a position in each currency.

CAN FOREIGN EXCHANGE RATES BE FORECAST?

In Chapter 3 we examined a theory called the efficient markets theory. This theory claims that an efficient financial market can very quickly encapsulate all new information impacting on the value of financial instruments traded by that market. The change in value can occur very quickly, within minutes, to alter the market value of the financial instrument to its new correct value. This means, among other things, that an efficient market provides a "fair" price on products traded on the market and that past information on prices cannot assist in estimating future prices.

If all existing information is already encapsulated into the value of a currency then the future value of that currency cannot be forecast. Only new, currently unknown, information can alter the value of the currency.

We repeat that if currency exchange markets are truly efficient then no profit can be made from exchange rate forecasting.

This statement is only true if the exchange is dealing in currencies that are freely traded. If exchange controls, "currency snakes" or other intervention mechanisms are in operation the markets are not free markets, therefore, they are not efficient markets. Profits can be made from currency forecasting when currency values are being controlled or manipulated by governments. The currency speculator is gambling against an opponent, the government, who does not mind losing money.

If currency is not being traded in a free market then it may be possible to make money out of speculating on the future value of a currency.

How does all of this effect the finance officer charged with reducing risk on transaction exposure?

If the finance officer believes that she cannot forecast exchange rates she must, in all logic, set out to "minimize" the net foreign exchange exposure position of her company in all currencies. The objective will be to reduce foreign exchange exposure to a minimum and so to reduce the risk of loss (and lose the possibility of gain!) on currency revaluation to a minimum.

If, on the other hand, the finance officer believes that she, or some forecasting agency, can forecast exchange rates (that is can beat the forward market's guess as to future exchange rates) then she can restructure her net position in each currency so as to maximize the speculative profit her company can make from this prediction. In other words she can speculate in currency futures.

Can foreign exchange rates be forecast? If the market is a free efficient market the answer is almost certainly no! A few studies have claimed that one or other of the forecasting agencies have consistently beaten the market over some years[5] but most studies have reached the opposite conclusion.

If, however, the market is not a free market because the government is interfering in the free operation of the market then it is likely that profits can be made from forecasting exchange rates. The currency speculator is not making a symmetrical bet. The exchange rate can usually go up as far as it likes but the government's monetary authority will prevent the rate from falling below a fixed minimum value. The speculative loss on the downside is contained.

We conclude that research on currency forecasting suggests that in a free market profits cannot be made out of forecasting exchange rates so a financial officer must aim to minimize exposure. In a controlled market profits can be made, at least theoretically, from currency forecasting so a finance officer might decide to go long or short in various currencies if she believes that this policy will earn significant profits for her company.

An Empirical Investigation

The author interviewed the international treasury officers of 12 UK multinational companies. Ten of these officers believed that exchange rates can be forecast, even in a free market, but only two admitted to speculating in currencies!

Many multinational companies, particularly British companies forbid their finance officers from speculating in currency futures. The boards of US multinationals appear to be more sympathetic to currency speculation.[6]

WHAT NEXT?

Let us suppose that the finance officer has listed all foreign assets, liabilities and cash flows. She has eliminated all self-hedging assets and liabilities from her calculations. She has designed a currency information system that allows her to collate all relevant information about currency on a regular basis. She has decided whether or not she believes that future exchange rates can be forecast, which means that she has decided whether or not to minimize the exposure position in each currency. The final step is to calculate the desired net exposure position in each currency and then decide on which of the many hedging techniques available to the company should be used to cover the remaining exchange risk.

Internal and External Hedging Techniques

Andy Prindl of Morgan Guaranty suggested that currency risk hedging techniques can be divided into two basic classes of techniques. These are techniques internal to the firm and techniques based on financial products produced externally to the firm.[7]

Examples of internal techniques are netting inter-company debts, matching inflows and outflows in the same currency and changing the currency of invoicing.

Some examples of external techniques are forward cover, currency futures, currency options and the factoring of debts denominated in a foreign currency.

Internal techniques for covering foreign exchange exposure tend to be cheaper to implement than external techniques so a wise finance officer will first exhaust the internal techniques available and only use external techniques for hedging the balance of exposure that cannot be covered internally.

Chapter 5 is devoted to a discussion of the many internal and external techniques that can be used to hedge FX exposure risk.

HEDGING ECONOMIC EXPOSURE

Economic exposure is concerned with exchange losses arising out of long-term trends in the exchange rates between currencies.

Only the top level board of a company are in a position to permit the hedging of long-term FX exposure. If a company is buying from a country with a strengthening exchange rate or selling into a country with a declining exchange rate this situation can only be altered by diversifying purchases towards countries with a more benevolent trend in the exchange rate and diversifying sales in a similar manner.

These are top level decisions. The duty of the finance officer is to identify these trends in exchange rates and inform the board accordingly. It is up to the board to ensure that the prediction is reasonable and then find suitable alternative markets.

ONLY ONE NET EXPOSURE POSITION FOR ONE COMPANY

We repeat what was emphasized earlier in the chapter. Each company has a single exposure position in each currency. Different types of exposure, transaction, translation or economic exposure can be offset against one another to arrive at a net exposure position.

This netting process is a powerful hedging technique yet it is seldom attempted.

WHAT HAVE WE LEARNED IN THIS CHAPTER?

1. The key factor in devising a foreign exchange exposure strategy is to identify those items that are exposed to foreign exchange risk.
2. A company is at risk to three types of exposure. Transaction exposure, translation exposure and economic exposure.
3. If the finance officer believes in the PPP then non-monetary assets are not exposed to exchange risk in the long term. Thus only monetary assets and monetary liabilities need to be hedged.
4. Short-term loans in foreign currencies are self-hedged against "expected" changes in exchange rates via the interest rate differential that is directly related to the forward premium or discount on the exchange rate. Only "unexpected" changes in the exchange rate are uncovered.
5. Long-term loans are more problematic. The international Fisher suggests that interest rate differentials will cancel out currency losses due to future exchange rate changes but empirical study disputes this conclusion. There is some evidence that interest rate differentials provide an "unbiased" estimate of future exchange rate changes but even this finding is disputed by some recent research.
6. The PPP and the IRPT are supported by arbitrage mechanisms operating in the market. The international Fisher theory is not.
7. Once the decision is taken on the volume of exposure to which the company is subject an information system must be designed to collect the required currency information on a regular basis. This information needs to be centralized to have maximum impact.
8. If a finance officer does not believe that foreign exchange rates can be forecast she must, in all logic, attempt to minimize exposure. If she believes that rates can be forecast then long and short positions can be set up in each currency. The ability

to forecast exchange rates is closely linked to the efficiency of the market that trades the currency.

9. It is unlikely that a company can eliminate all of the exposure to which it is subjected. A residue of exposure will remain. This exposure needs to be hedged by one means or another if exposure is to minimized.

10. Devices for hedging exposure can be segregated into two groups. Internal hedging devices organized by the company itself and external hedging devices offered by the external market.

11. Internal hedging devices are, on the whole, cheaper to operate than external devices so these should be exhausted before turning to the external markets.

12. Chapter 5 will describe various devices that are designed to hedge exchange rate risk. The finance officer must know enough about hedging techniques to be able to choose the hedging device that is best suited to a given exposure situation.

NOTES

1. There are many ways of hedging this risk. Some of these ways are explained in Chapters 5 and 7.
2. An interesting example of the operation of this theory is the recent dramatic increase in the production of computer software in India for the US and European markets. The wages of programmers are much lower in India than in the West so computer departments in Europe and the USA subcontract the writing of their computer software to Indian firms.
3. See the discussion of options in Chapter 5.
4. From questionnaires sent to the author.
5. Several recent studies have found that forward predictions of future spot rates are biased but none has found that a profit can be made consistently from any forecasting model. See Copeland, L. S. (1990), Chapter 11.
6. See for example Rogriguez, R. M. and Carter, E. E. *International Financial Management*. Prentice-Hall, 1990.
7. See Prindl, A. R. *Foreign Exchange Risk*. John Wiley, 1976, Chapters 7 and 8.

FURTHER READING

Batten, J. et al (1993) Foreign exchange risk management practices and products used by Australian firms. *Journal of International Business Studies*, Autumn, 557–73.

Belk, P. and Glaum, M. (1990) The management of foreign exchange risk in UK multinationals: an empirical investigation. *Accounting and Business Research*, vol. 21, no. 81, 3–13.

DeRosa, D. (1991) *Managing Foreign Exchange Risk*. Chicago, USA, Probus.

Eiteman, D., Stonehill, A. and Moffett, M. H. (1995) *Multinational Business Finance*, Addison-Wesley.
    Parts 3 and 4 of this book present a detailed plan for designing a foreign exchange management strategy.

Froot, K. et al (1993) Risk management: co-ordinating corporate investment and financing policies. *Journal of Finance*, vol. 48, no. 5, December, 1629–58.

Jacque, L. (1981) Management of foreign exchange risk: a review article. *Journal of International Business Studies*, Spring, 81–101.

Levi, M. and Sercu, P. (1991) Erroneous and valid reasons for hedging foreign exchange rate exposure. *Journal of Multinational Financial Management*, vol. 1, no. 2, 25–37.

McRae, T. and Walker, D. (1980) *Foreign Exchange Management*, Prentice-Hall.
    A practical introduction to handling foreign exchange including a discussion of the logic of devising an overall strategy.

Moffett, M. and Karlsen, J. (1994) Managing foreign exchange rate economic exposure. *Journal of International Financial Management and Accounting*, vol. 5, no. 2, 157–75.

Prindl, A. R. (1978) *Foreign Exchange Risk*, John Wiley.
  A dated but primal book that sparked the debate on setting an overall foreign exchange management strategy in a multinational company. Written by one of the world experts on this subject. Still relevant.
Ruesch, O. (1992) Protecting your profits with foreign exchange procedures. *Journal of European Business*, May, 34–6.
Wunnicke, D. et al (1992) *Corporate Financial Risk Management*. New York, John Wiley.

TUTORIAL QUESTIONS

1. Explain the meaning of the word "exposure" in the context of foreign exchange management. What exactly is "exposed" and exposed to what?

2. Explain the difference between translation exposure and transaction exposure. Which of these two types of exposure do you think is the more important to a company that trades internationally? Give your reasons.

3. It is claimed by some experts that only the value of the "monetary" assets and liabilities of a foreign subsidiary are at risk to future unexpected changes in exchange rates. What is a monetary asset or a monetary liability? Why is the value of a non-monetary asset owned by a foreign subsidiary not at risk to unexpected changes in exchange rates? Why are ordinary (equity) shares not considered to be monetary assets?

4. "Economic exposure" is a relatively recent concept first suggested by Andy Prindl in 1975. What is meant by the term "economic exposure" in the context of foreign exchange management? Suppose a British company is buying key parts for its copying machines, which are assembled in the UK, from Japan and selling most of its manufactured products in Eastern Europe. Discuss this situation in the context of economic exposure. Why might a finance officer need to warn her Board about this situation? What, if anything, can be done about it?

5. Why is the price elasticity of demand for the products of a company so relevant when adjusting to changing patterns of economic exposure?

6. A well-known free market economist from Chicago University once said at an international conference on Foreign Exchange Management: "It does not matter where you buy your goods or where you sell them. Your average long run profit will be the same. Foreign exchange exposure is a short run problem." Whatever does the speaker mean by this statement? Do you agree?

7. Explain the difference between a "risk minimizing" and a "profit maximizing" FEM strategy. What are the three essential conditions that must be satisfied before a profit maximizing strategy can be adopted by a company that trades internationally?

8. It has been claimed that the attitude of management to currency speculation is different in the UK and the USA. Some researchers have stated that this difference of attitude can be traced to differences in the incentive systems applied to motivate finance officers in the UK and the USA. Can you think what these incentive systems might be that can have this differential effect?

9. What are the necessary market conditions that must be present before profits can be made, except by chance, from exchange rate forecasting? How do these conditions arise?

10. The following assets and liabilities are held by MADRAX (Malay) a subsidiary of a British company operating in Malaysia. If the Malaysian ringitt is expected to fall by 5% in value against the £ sterling over the next six months which of these assets and liabilities, if any, are exposed to exchange rate risk?

Loan to MADRAX (Malay) from MADRAX (UK)	R25 million
Inventory of glass manufactured in the UK	R35 million
Shares in other Malaysian companies	R20 million
Debt owing to MADRAX (Malay) by MADRAX (UK)	R10 million
Trade creditors of MADRAX (MALAY)	R15 million
Shares in MADRAX (Malay) owned by MADRAX (UK)	R60 million
Bank loan owed by MADRAX (Malay)	R32

What is the net amount exposed to exchange rate risk?

11. "The only thing the international treasurer needs to worry about so far as short-term foreign currency loans are concerned is 'unexpected' changes in exchange rates." Explain this opinion. Why is so much emphasis placed on the adjective "unexpected".

12. What principles should be employed in designing an information system to control currency management?

13. A finance officer wishes to set up an information system to monitor foreign exchange exposure. What information should the officer collect on a regular basis to achieve this objective?

14. Suggest what annual, quarterly and monthly information about currencies should be prepared by companies operating within a Group.

15. Describe the difference between an internal and an external exchange risk-hedging technique? Give two examples of each.

16. "Every company has only one net foreign exchange exposure position at any one time." Do you agree with this controversial statement? What does it mean? Do you consider that the concept is a useful one?

17. If the forward rate is an unbiased predictor of the future spot rate should a finance officer use the forward market to hedge currency exposure?

18. The international Fisher is simply a long-term version of the IRPT. Do you agree?

CASE STUDY: DUNDAX

History of Company

Dundax PLC was established fourteen years ago. The company manufactures and sells chemical blending equipment. It is a "niche" market that has not been entered by the larger manufacturers because of the specialized nature of the product.

In 1992 the foreign sales of the company contributed only 20% of sales. Then Dundax bought out one of its few rivals, an Italian company situated in Genoa, and the European sales "took off". In 1995 sales in continental Europe made up 39% of total sales.

In 1989 Dundax moved into the US market via an agency and in 1990 set up its own US subsidiary. By 1995 US sales contributed 20% of total sales.

Dundax, by 1995, was fast becoming an international company.

The New Financial Director

For the first 17 years of life the financial director of Dundax was James Wood C.A., a Scottish accountant. He had run the finance department in an efficient and conservative way and was highly respected by the main board members. In January 1994 Mr Wood reached the age of 65 and retired.

After much discussion at board level Mr Wood was replaced by Mr Stephen B. Hadley B.Sc. (Eng), M.B.A. Mr Hadley is 33 years of age. Mr Hadley has worked in the finance division of Specialized Weapon Systems, a US company located in California, at Boston

Wire and for six months as a financial adviser with the Steinberg merchant bank before accepting his appointment with Dundax PLC.

Mr Hadley decided to look at four key areas of the Dundax financial set-up in his first month with the company. These were (1) the financial reporting system; (2) the costing system; (3) the organization of foreign exchange; and (4) the use of computers by the finance division. His initial review of the overall financial set-up has persuaded him that these four areas are in need of substantial overhaul.

The Foreign Exchange Set-up

Hadley seeks the assistance of Mr Alan Bloomberg, the company accountant, in preparing the set of documents set out in Tables 9, 10, 11 and 12.

Dundax control three companies resident in the UK, Italy and the USA and they deal in six currencies. However four of the currencies the £, US$, Lire and DM account for over 90% in value of all transactions.

Hadley finds out that despite the relatively low volume of foreign sales at the time Dundax suffered substantial losses through unexpected changes in currency values between 1989 and 1991 and that experience had persuaded Mr Wood to follow a very conservative foreign exchange policy from that date.

Hadley finds a note from Mr Wood to the board dated February 15, 1989 which states:

"After extensive discussions with Mr Simpson from our bankers Southwest Bank plc I am of the opinion that only by hedging the entire net worth of our foreign subsidiaries can we avoid the substantial foreign exchange losses of recent years. This is an expensive policy but it removes all risk of foreign exchange loss on holding assets denominated in foreign currency. I will also continue to take out forward contracts on all substantial sales contracts once they are signed and will also cover forward on all large payments in foreign currency. These measures should prevent the recurrence of our recent unfortunate losses on currency fluctuation. Our experience of forecasting in recent years proves beyond all reasonable doubt that forecasting foreign exchange rates is quite impossible."

Hadley notes that Mr Harold Simpson, an outside director of Dundax, is also a local director of Southwest bank. Hadley is of the opinion that the foreign exchange rate forecasters called Kurfor have a very good track record in foreign exchange forecasting up to two years ahead.

Mr Hadley decides that the foreign exchange strategy of Dundax is much too conservative. It needs a shake-up.

He studies the data on foreign exchange set out in the attached Appendix and decides that Dundax needs a new foreign exchange strategy.

He decides that he must work out the foreign exchange exposure position of Dundax and then select an economical method or methods of hedging exposure risk.

Hadley also needs to consider his relation to the Board of Dundax. Are there any facets of his foreign exchange strategy that he should put to the Board before he implements them?

Required: (a) Criticize the existing foreign exchange strategy devised by Mr Wood. (b) Identify the various forms of foreign exchange exposure to which Dundax is subject (c) Suggest ways of hedging these FE exposure risks (d) Suggest the types of questions Mr Hadley should put to the Board of Dundax before he implements his FE management strategy.

Appendix: Dundax PLC

Table 9 Balance Sheets as at December 15 1995

Assets	£ DD (UK) m		Lr DD (Italy) b		$ DD (USA) m
Buildings at cost (net of dep)		80		60	75
Equipment (net)		64		150	10
Inventory (at cost)		25		45	120
Debots and cash		20		37	80
		189		292	285
Less: short-term debts					
Loans 15%, 22%, 10%	20		35		50
Creditors	15	35	30	65	46	96
Net assets		154		227	189
Finance:					
Equity + reserves		94		107	119
Long-term debt		60 (10%)		120 (13%)	70 (6%)
		154		227	189

NOTES
1. All the equity shares in the Italian and US subsidiaries are held by Dundax UK.
2. The loan finance has all been raised locally in the local currency. Mr Wood always insisted on this financing policy. When the lire loan was raised in 1991 the exchange rate was £1 = 2000 lire it is now £1 = 2400 lire. When the US$ loan was raised in 1990 the exchange rate was £1 = $1.82 it is now £1 = $1.71.
3. The buildings and equipment of the Italian company were bought in 1991 and those of the US company in 1990. Neither have been revalued since.

Table 10 Estimated Quarterly Cash Flows Over the Next Year

DD(UK) PLC	Qrt 1	Qrt 2	Qrt 3	Qrt 4
		million		
$ sterling	70	97	85	62
Lire billion	−23	−14	−54	−5
US$	26	−31	−28	22
DM	−21	−56	−5	−63
DD(ITALY)				
$ sterling	−23	−38	4	−75
Lire billion	97	85	79	51
US$	21	−76	43	18
DM	−31	−5	−49	−19
DD(USA)				
£ sterling	−27	−12	28	−18
Lire billion	−14	−10	−11	−6
US$	58	64	22	33
DM	−5	−3	−4	−6

Table 11 Net Position in Each Currency

	Qrt 1	Qrt 2	Qrt 3	Qrt 4	Total
$ sterling £m	20	47	117	−31	153
Lire 000m	60	61	14	40	175
US$m	105	−43	37	73	172
DMm	−57	−64	−58	−88	−267

Table 12 Forecasts by Kurfor as to Future Value of the Currencies

Foreign Currency Units per £

	Spot	3 months	6 months	Year	3 years
USA: US$	1.71	1.69	1.67	1.63	1.5
Germany: DM	2.9	2.84	2.81	2.7	2.4
Italy: lire	2400	2450	2520	2640	2900

% of Sales Denominated in US$

	1992 %	1993 %	1994 %	1995 %
UK	80	65	42	33
USA	3	10	22	20
Germany	5	8	6	4
Italy	10	13	17	25
East European	2	4	7	10
South America	0	0	6	8
	100	100	100	100

% of Purchases Denominated in US$

	1992 %	1993 %	1994 %	1995 %
UK	81	66	51	40
USA	5	12	18	20
Germany	4	10	18	27
Italy	10	12	13	13
	100	100	100	100

CASE STUDY: ROLLS ROYCE

Rolls Royce is one of the most distinguished names in the pantheon of British Industry. The company no longer makes Rolls Royce cars but has diversified its production into a wide range of engineering products.

Rolls Royce now operates through two groups, one concentrating on aerospace products, the other on industrial power products.

The industrial power products division manufactures equipment for power generation and transmission, marine propulsion, equipment for the oil and gas industry and materials handling equipment.

The aerospace division manufactures engines for aircraft and associated products.

Rolls Royce treasury division handles a range of currencies in selling and buying a wide range of products to many customers worldwide. However the US$ to £ sterling exchange rate is the major currency variable at risk to exchange rate fluctuation. Rolls Royce deals in over 30 currencies but the US$ is "80% of the problem".

For defence business Rolls Royce prices in pound sterling but the aerospace division mostly prices in US$s.

The two main competitors to Rolls Royce aerospace division namely General Electric (US) and Pratt and Whitney are US-based firms who naturally price in the US$.

The industrial power division handles a much wider range of currencies than aerospace. Typical FX exposure extends to four years in this division with contract size varying all the way from £100 000 to £50 million.

Rolls Royce usually quotes in US$ or £ sterling but will quote in another foreign currency if this offers a competitive advantage. Typical US$ exposure on aerospace contracts extends out to 10 years or even longer. Aerospace contracts are valued at between US$150 million to US$450 million, a few contracts are as large as US$1.5 billion:

"A typical contract lasts five and a half years...six months tender to contract risk and then five years between the contract being awarded and the goods delivered and paid for."

The foreign exchange strategy has been stated to be that Rolls Royce will "not have an overall loss when we look at the portfolio of currencies under management". The treasury have stated that their exposure philosophy is to be risk averse. "We are a manufacturing industry not a financial institution" (p. 47).

In 1993 Rolls Royce made pre-tax profits of only £76 million on sales of £3.5 billion. More than 70% of sales were made outside the UK market. The net US$ exposure of Rolls Royce is estimated to be equal to 25% of group sales in any one year. It has been estimated that "for every cent that the exchange rate moves it can either add or subtract £6.5 million to our bottom line...a 10% to 12% adverse movement in the exchange rate would have wiped out our profit last year" (p. 47).

The treasury at Rolls Royce consider that, so far as US competitors are concerned, a neutral rate of exchange between the US$ and the £ sterling in 1994 would be around US$1.6 to the £.

The treasury state that:

"Ensuring that the risks are recognised as part of the bidding process is absolutely essential. The identification of the creation of the exposure is the key to solving all the exposure problems."

Required: Write a memo to the Board of Rolls Royce suggesting a suitable foreign exchange strategy for covering the exposure to exchange rate risk faced by Rolls Royce in both the Aerospace and the Industrial Power Group. Note that the aerospace division handles very large contracts mainly denominated in US$ and the industrial power division handles a much larger number of smaller contracts denominated in a wide range of currencies.

Source M. Ball, Coping with the swings and roundabouts *Corporate Finance* July 1994, 47–8.

CASE STUDY: RINOGLASS

History of Company

Rinoglass PLC was established 20 years ago. The company manufactures and sells toughened glass, which is resistant to bullets.

The company has expanded recently with the growth of terrorism and the attacks on political and other leading figures throughout the world.

As recently as 1991 all of the company sales were to police and government departments in the UK. In 1992 the company found a good market for their products in South Africa and later they started exporting to the United States and Germany. An enquiry from Russia in 1993 led to exports to that country and later a market was found in the Philippines. Foreign sales of the company has expanded to 73% of turnover by 1995.

In 1992 the South African sales had become so substantial that Rinoglass set up a subsidiary company in Port Elizabeth in the Eastern Cape to manufacture Rinoglass for the African market.

Rinoglass, by 1995, was fast becoming an international company.

The New Financial Director

In 1994 the financial staff of Rinoglass had little knowledge of international marketing or international finance. The Chairman and major shareholder in Rinoglass, John Adams, decided that some new blood was needed and so he appointed a new Marketing and Financial Director.

The new Financial Director, Keir Maxton, MBA, ACA decides to make a thorough appraisal of the foreign exchange position of the company.

The Foreign Exchange Set-up

Mr Maxton orders a set of schedules to be prepared setting out the following details about the foreign currency position. These schedules are set out in Tables 15–19 attached to the end of this case.

The schedules show (a) The revenues and costs of Rinoglass over the last five years expressed in terms of the pound sterling. The exchange rate used for translation is the average exchange rate ruling during the year; (b) The balance sheet of the South African subsidiary as at July 1, 1995, the company year end. The balance sheet is expressed in rand; (c) the expected net cash flow in each currency over the next six months. Inter-company payments have been eliminated from this statement; and (d) Exchange rate forecasts in the five main trading currencies for six months forward, one year forward and three years forward. Mr Maxton has a high opinion of the forecaster making these forecasts.

The current foreign exchange strategy of Rinoglass is very simple. All export contracts are denominated in the currency of the importing country. The marketing department has found that this policy greatly improves their chance of winning foreign contracts. All export contracts are covered forward as long as a forward market exists in that currency. The exports to Russia are covered by an expensive credit insurance contract with Trade Indemnity, but this insurance does not hedge changes in exchange rates. Mr Maxton is very worried about this contract.

Maxton knows the importance of keeping the Board of Rinoglass informed about his foreign exchange management strategy. Particularly regarding any facets of his foreign exchange strategy that might expose the company to substantial risk.

Required: (a) Criticize the existing foreign exchange strategy currently applied by Rinoglass. (b) What additional information would Mr Maxton need to collect before completing his appraisal of Rinoglass' exposure position? (c) Identify the various forms of foreign exchange exposure to which Rinoglass is subject. (d) Suggest ways of hedging the foreign exchange exposure risks that you have identified. (e) Suggest the types of questions Mr Maxton should put to the Board of Rinoglass before he finalizes his FE exposure strategy.

Appendix: Rinoglass PLC

Facts About Rinoglass

1. The sales and costs of Rinoglass in each currency as expressed in £ sterling over the last five years to the year end of July 1, are shown in Tables 15 and 16.

Table 15 % of Sales Valued in Pound Sterling

	Year				
	1991 %	1992 %	1993 %	1994 %	1995 %
£ sterling	100	92	70	52	28
South African rand	0	8	17	24	24
US$	0	0	10	12	15
German DM	0	0	3	8	13
Russian roubles	0	0	0	4	12
Philippine peso	0	0	0	0	8
	100	100	100	100	100

Table 16 % of Costs Valued in £ Sterling

£ sterling	100	73	52	37	27
South Africa rand	0	9	12	13	14
US$	0	11	20	22	24
German DM	0	7	16	21	22
Russian rouble	0	0	0	5	7
Philippine peso	0	0	0	2	6
	100	100	100	100	100

The % is calculated by translating at the spot rate of exchange at the year end.

2. Rinoglass set up a subsidiary company in South Africa called Rinoglass (RSA) in 1992. The balance sheet of this company as at July 1, 1995 is shown in Table 17 (in Rand).

Table 17

Assets	Rand m	Finance	Rand m
Buildings and land	30	Equity and reserves	54
Machinery	21	Long-term debt 16% (2002)	23
Inventory	27	Creditors	12
Debtors	9		
Cash	2		
	89		89

3. The expected net cash flows in each currency over the next six months are estimated as shown in Table 18.

Table 18

	July	Aug.	Sept.	Oct.	Nov.	Dec.	Total
Rand (m)	15	12	18	12	24	29	110
US$ (m)	−3.6	−1.6	2	−4.8	−3.5	−5.1	−16.6
German DM (m)	−2	−12	6	−43	−4	−15	−70
Russian roubles (m)	2300	2600	3100	3300	3700	4000	19 000
Philippine peso (m)	70	80	−50	120	210	320	750

4. Currency forecasts for six months, one and three years ahead from a forecaster whom the finance officer of Rinoglass believes to be reliable are as shown in Table 19.

Table 19

	Spot rate	Six months forward	One year forward	3 years forward
Rand	5.5	5.8	6.1	7.3
US$	1.5	1.45	1.4	1.3
German DM	2.33	2.3	2.2	2.1
Russian rouble	2000	2400	3000	4000
Philippine peso	40.1	40.8	42	45

DUNDAX PLC: NOTES TOWARDS A SOLUTION

Mr Wood's Approach to Redesigning a Foreign Exchange Management Strategy

The first thing Mr Woods must do is identify the three types of exposure called transaction exposure, translation exposure and economic exposure.

Criticism of the Existing Foreign Exchange Strategy

The current strategy is much too conservative and therefore expensive. When only a small fraction of sales and assets, etc., were expressed in terms of a foreign currency then the cost of hedging all foreign currency items may have been acceptable. Now it is much too expensive, a more discriminating approach is needed.

Mr Woods believes that forecasting is a worthwhile activity and in controlled currencies this is supported by empirical research. The ability to make money out of forecasting within a free floating exchange rate regime is much more questionable.

Mr Woods believes that the accuracy of past Kurfor forecasts has made forecasting worthwhile so he will use the Kurfor forecasts. If Mr Woods believes in the Purchasing Power Parity (PPP) Theory, and surely he must, then non-monetary assets become self-hedging. This allows Mr Woods to concentrate his attention on the net monetary asset position of the Italian and US subsidiaries.

He must, however, be careful to check out the likely future value of the foreign loans in terms of sterling. Are the interest and capital repayments fully covered in foreign currency or should a sinking fund be set up to repay them?

Finally, he must consider the economic exposure of the company. What is the likely future value of the foreign currency receipts and payments in terms of the home currency? Is it possible that inputs may grow more expensive (in terms of £ sterling) and outputs (sales) of less value (in terms of £ sterling). If so what can be done about it?

Transaction Exposure

A monthly cash budget must be set up in each currency. The monthly net position in each currency noted and internal hedging tactics devised to control foreign exchange risk (netting, matching, leading and lagging etc). Any remaining unwanted balances can be offset by using external hedging devices such as forward exchange contracts, futures or options.

If, however, the monthly exposures are small relative to the wealth of the company then external hedging can be ignored if the forward rate is an unbiased predictor of the future spot rate. A series of small future exchange rate losses would be cancelled by a series of small gains in the long run.

Since Mr Wood believes that forecasting is a worthwhile activity he may even decide to deliberately unbalance the "natural" exposure position of the company in order to speculate in currency. He will need to consult with the Board of Directors on this decision.

Translation Exposure

This refers to the balance sheet position of the subsidiaries. The non-monetary assets such as inventory and equipment are self-hedging through different internal rates of inflation therefore Mr Wood will concentrate on examining the net monetary asset position of the Italian and US companies.

It could be that a large debt is building up abroad because of a rise in the £ sterling value of the foreign loans, which, we recall, are denominated in foreign currency values. Table 20 sets out the net monetary position of each subsidiary.

Both subsidiaries enjoy a substantial net monetary liability position therefore Dundax gains if these currencies devalue against the £ sterling. However, if either currency revalues (rises in value) against the £ Dundax could be in trouble if it does not have access to sufficient amounts of the foreign currency to (a) pay the interest and (b) repay the loan.

Table 11 suggests that a large surplus of US dollars is being generated annually so an insufficiency of US$ is not a problem. A sinking fund in US$ should be set up if a rise in the US$ relative to the £ might cause financial problems in the future.

On transaction cash flows the lire is just in balance overall. From past experience a substantial revaluation of the lire against the £ is most unlikely. Mr Wood would consult Kurfor but the situation seems well covered.

The buildings and equipment in Italy were bought some four years ago. If they are still valued at their cost price in 1991 they may well be substantially undervalued in the Italian subsidiary accounts in terms of lire. Therefore, they should not be consolidated at the closing rate of exchange. If the closing rate is to be used these Italian assets should be revalued. The US asset values may be more acceptable because the assets were acquired in 1990 and there has been no substantial change in the US$ to £ exchange rate over the period.

Economic Exposure

As shown in the appendices the long-term cash flow pattern of the group is changing. Sales are building up in Italy, Eastern Europe and South America. Past history suggests that these countries do not have strong currencies against the pound sterling. On the other hand Dundax is buying a higher proportion of its purchases from the USA and Germany. These currencies are historically strong against the pound sterling. A common EU currency may solve this problem in the long run of 10 years or more but not in the near term.

The company is caught in a "currency nutcracker" and Mr Wood must warn the Board about this and suggest switching purchases to less hard currency countries and selling more aggressively into these hard currency countries.

Appendix: Dundax PLC: Notes Towards a Solution

Table 20 Calculation of the Net Monetary Position of Each Sudsidiary

		Lire Italy		US$ USA
Debtors and cash		37		80
Less: Loans	−35		−50	
Creditors	−30		−46	
Long-term debt	−120	−185	−70	−166
Net monetary liability				
Position		−148		−86

Techniques for Hedging Foreign Exchange Risk

INTRODUCTION

Once the finance officer has completed the procedures outlined in Chapter 4, he will have identified the exposure of his company to changes in exchange rates in several currencies.

Various financial products have been devised for hedging this foreign exchange risk. All of these products are not suited to, or available to, all companies. A finance officer needs to select from among those products those best suited to the structure and pattern of cash flow of his company.

Foreign exchange hedging techniques can be usefully segregated into two categories—those that are internal to the company and those that are external of the company. External hedging techniques are provided by external markets such as the forward, futures, options and swap markets. External techniques of hedging foreign exchange risk tend to be more expensive than internal techniques. The cost of running the world's currency hedging markets is around 3% of the value of the currency hedged.

Exhibit 5.1 provides a listing of the more popular devices that are used for hedging foreign exchange risk.

The remainder of this chapter is devoted to a description and discussion of these various techniques and products.

CONSTRAINTS ON SELECTING A HEDGING TECHNIQUE

Exhibit 5.1 demonstrates the wide range of hedging techniques that are available to a finance officer for hedging foreign exchange risk. All of these techniques are not available to every company trading abroad, much depends on the structure of the company, the currencies traded and the pattern of cash flows.

The size and structural complexity of a company are important factors in selecting a suitable hedging technique. The larger the company and the more countries and currencies in which it trades, the wider is the range of hedging techniques that are likely to be available to that company. For example the values of "parallel" currencies tend

Exhibit 5.1 Some of the More Popular Devices Used to Hedge Foreign Exchange Risk

Internal hedging techniques
Netting inter-company debts
Matching cross frontier currency flows
Leading and lagging inter-company debts
Adjusting the contract price based on expectations as to future currency movements.
Changing the currency in which the invoice is denominated.

Hedging devices that use external markets
A forward currency contract
Arrange a short-term loan in the foreign currency
Discount a bill of exchange denominated in the foreign currency
Factor the foreign currency debts
Buy a currency option for a future date
Arrange a currency swap
Arrange an exchange risk guarantee
Mix a currency cocktail.

A wide range of devices are available to the company treasurer to cover against exposure to foreign exchange risk.

These devices can be classified into two categories: internal techniques of hedging and external techniques of hedging. On the whole the internal techniques provide cover at a lower cost than external techniques.

to move together and this allows a company trading in many currencies to offset one currency against the other. Some internal hedging techniques are only available to a company of a certain size.

When selecting a suitable hedging technique the following strategic factors also need to be considered.

Overall Business Strategy

The Board of a company considering how to hedge its currency exposure will have promulgated a set of business policies covering such things as currency speculation, risk taking, autonomy of subsidiaries and relationships with foreign governments. Some hedging devices can impinge on one or other of these matters. The finance officer must ensure that the hedging techniques chosen do not breach any basic business policy guideline set down by the Board of the company.

Psychological Factors

Some hedging tactics, for example, those involving tax havens, require managers of foreign subsidiaries to give up a good deal of their autonomy to the "management and finance subsidiary" set up in the foreign tax haven. For example the marketing department may resent invoicing a tax haven company, switching the currency in which contracts are denominated or altering the timing of payments to suit some hedging tactic such as being told to slow down or speed up payments to avoid possible FX losses or to make speculative gains.

The board and the finance officer will need to weigh up and balance the financial benefits derived from tight control of foreign currency management against the psychological cost of reducing the autonomy of managers in other parts of the organization.

Incremental Costs and Benefits

Finally the finance officer needs to calculate the precise incremental cost of each hedging technique and weigh these costs against the benefits derived from reducing the potential foreign exchange losses.

It is relatively easy to calculate the precise cost of forward cover or the cost of buying an option but it is difficult to measure the precise "incremental" cost of most of the internal hedging techniques currently in use.[1] This might cast some doubt on the frequent assertion by treasury managers that internal hedging techniques are cheaper than external hedging techniques.[2]

Measuring the exact cost of any hedging technique is not easy. For example, the full cost of switching the currency of invoicing may take a long time to manifest itself in lost orders and the cost of hedging via a factor is very difficult to disentangle from the costs of the other facilities provided by a factor.

A finance officer ought to make a point of estimating the incremental costs and benefits associated with each of the hedging techniques available to him otherwise, in time, an inefficient mix of hedging techniques are likely to be adopted.

We will now briefly describe some of the more popular hedging techniques used by treasury managers for hedging exposure to foreign exchange risk.

INTERNAL HEDGING TECHNIQUES

Netting End of Period Balances in the Same or Parallel Currencies

This is not strictly a hedging technique but a way of minimizing the cost of hedging: end of period inter-company debts in the same or a parallel currency are set off against one another at the end of each accounting period. Only the net balance owing requires to be hedged.

"Parallel currencies" are currencies that tend to move in tandem with one another. These currencies can be used as substitutes for one another in a hedging situation. For many years the value of the German DM and the Swiss franc ran parallel to one another in terms of the US$. Parallel currencies should not be confused with currencies that are tied to one another like the Bahamanian dollar and the US$.

Netting may be bi-lateral or multilateral. An example of multilateral netting is where debts of subsidiary A in currency A are offset against debts of subsidiary B in currency B that are, in fact, owed to subsidiary C in currency C within the same group, where A and C are parallel currencies.

The mechanics of netting are simple. Each subsidiary sends a fax, e-mail or telex of company debts in each currency to the head office at the end of each period. Head office decides on the best netting arrangement and instructs the subsidiary accordingly. The subsidiary instructs their bank of these arrangements.

The method can speed up inter-company settlement of debts and reduce the cost of currency transfers by around 0.5% to 2% of the value of the gross cash flows. The technique provides improved control of group liquidity and may even assist with tax planning. Netting can also allow the parent company to operate a leading and lagging of inter-company payments, a technique that we will be describing later in this chapter.

There can be problems in implementing the technique despite its apparent simplicity. The exchange control regulations of some foreign countries may prohibit the netting of debts (Kenya, Brazil) or the monetary authority in the country may require special permission to be sought before the technique can be employed.

The technique may set off some disagreement between the management at head office and the management of the subsidiary being instructed. For example, there may be disagreement on the currency of the final net payment or even on the date when the final net payment is to be repatriated.

Matching Payments in the Same or a Parallel Currency

The central treasury at head office matches individual payments and receipts in the same or a parallel currency as regards amount and timing.

The head office treasury collects the cash flow budgets of each subsidiary, usually via a cable or internet link, and collates them into a single group cash budget for each individual currency. The projected dates of individual currency transactions are now shifted around to minimize excess exposure in any particular currency at any one time. The subsidiaries are then instructed as to the precise date of payment or receipt.

The technique of matching is performed with the aid of a computer program designed to identify and match payments and receipts in the same or a parallel currency.

Matching allows the future cash exposure position in each currency to be continuously monitored by the finance officer. The technique reduces the amounts that need to be hedged in any one currency at any one time. The technique can even be applied to third party payments and receipts if the third party agrees to participate. The technique is best suited to larger companies but it can be used by small companies who only export and import from the UK if they can afford the cost of the information system and can persuade their foreign agents or associates to participate in the scheme.

Certain difficulties limit the use of the technique. The centralization of currency control is an essential condition. This can be expensive to effect. A tight control of the timing of cash flows within the group needs to be imposed to make the system work successfully. Subsidiaries may resent this degree of discipline since they may perceive no direct benefit to themselves in the arrangement. Persuading third parties to go along with the arrangement might present even bigger problems for the same reason. Opening a foreign currency bank account can run into exchange control problems in some emerging economies and such accounts can prove expensive to run.

Leading and Lagging

If a finance officer believes he can beat the market at forecasting changes in exchange rates he may wish to speed up or slow down certain payments or receipts from or into a foreign currency. This hedging technique is called "leading and lagging".

Leading and lagging adjusts the timing of payments or receipts to alter the future exposure position of a company in a particular currency. Leading and lagging is a form of currency speculation.

The mechanics of leading and lagging are similar to those used in matching except that the degree of switching transactions in time are more radical. The exposure position is being optimized to maximize speculative profits whereas "matching" is normally used to minimize the exposure position of a group.

The benefits of leading and lagging are derived from the possible profits that may arise out of currency speculation if the speculator's exchange rate forecasts are correct. Leading and lagging is therefore an important tool of any finance officer who adopts a "profit maximizing" rather than "risk minimizing" strategy.

Leading and lagging can also offer the finance officer an efficient method of providing inter-company loans. A speeded up payment is the equivalent of a short-term loan.

A centralized currency control system is essential to operating the technique. A tight control over the cash flows of subsidiaries is required and, as with netting and matching, leading and lagging might well run into strong objections from the managers of subsidiary companies. The future liquidity position of the subsidiary will be effected and an interest credit may have to be imputed to a subsidiary company that loses short-term funding to another company in the group by reason of leading and lagging.

The technique can be applied to debts due to third parties but this is a risky tactic. Local minority interests in foreign subsidiaries, if they find out, may complain that their profits are being reduced to benefit a company in another country.

But by far the greatest risk a company faces in applying leading and lagging to international payments is the possible objection by a foreign government. Many foreign governments forbid the technique outright either by their own nationals or by foreign companies resident in the country. This applies particularly to governments in Africa and South America. Leading and lagging has acquired a certain notoriety in these continents and many foreign governments have become somewhat paranoid about the use of the technique. Some governments in emerging countries require foreign companies to assign a "fixed payment time" to all debts to allow the monetary authority in that country to audit the timing of foreign payments.

Leading and lagging may also have implications for overall tax planning by shifting costs and profits about in time. For example, if the company tax rate is due to change in a foreign country the speeding up of payments between subsidiaries may assist in reducing the global tax bill of the group if the subsidiary is assessed on a cash basis.

Adjusting the Contract Price to the Forward Rate

In Chapter 2 we noted that with most major currencies a quote is provided by currency dealers for both a spot rate and a forward rate. The forward rate quote may be up to one year ahead.

Description: If a contract is being quoted in the home currency rather than in the importer's foreign currency the price in the home currency can be based on the forward rate of exchange rather than on the spot rate.

This builds into the contract price the expected rise or fall in the exchange rate between the date the contract is signed and the payment date. If the payment date is six months ahead the contract can be priced in home currency based on the six-month forward exchange rate on that currency.

This technique can only be used with non-standard contracts priced in the home currency. The price of mass produced goods cannot be altered continuously in this way.

The marketing department may object to the use of this hedging technique because it impinges on their control of pricing policy. It is also possible that the monetary authority of a foreign country may become suspicious of continual changes in price, although this is unlikely if the contract is for non-standard goods or services.

Changing the Currency in Which Contracts are Invoiced

A company trading abroad may decide to switch the currency in which contracts are invoiced if this change is thought likely to improve the profitability of the company as measured in the home currency.

In the early 1980s many British companies stopped invoicing in pound sterling and switched to invoicing in foreign currency as the pound fell in value against most major foreign currencies. South African companies adopted the same strategy, by invoicing in US$ and £ sterling, following the collapse of the rand on the world's currency markets in 1985.

Description: The mechanics of the technique are simple. The exporter informs the customer that in future invoices will be denominated in some alternative currency. Possibly the importer's own currency or the exporter's currency or some third country currency such as the US$. Some excuse for this change in policy needs to be thought up by the finance officer or the marketing manager. For example it can be argued that by invoicing in the importer's own local currency the importer will be able to estimate his cash budgets more accurately in the future.

It has been claimed by some authorities that a switch in currency may allow the exporter to maximize profits without the importer being aware of the change in price. On the other hand the importer may not be that naive and may take offence!

Many importers are happy to be invoiced in their own currency because it provides a known fixed cost for imports and so the costs associated with hedging the import price denominated in a foreign currency can be avoided.

Sometimes the reverse strategy is employed when an exporter deliberately invoices the importer in a weak currency to make exports more price competitive. The success of this strategy depends on the price elasticity of the product to the importer. Will he buy more of the product if the price falls? Will he even perceive the fall in price?

The technique needs to be applied with caution. Frequent changes in the currency of invoicing is not feasible, it would annoy the customer. The monetary authority in the importing country might forbid the practice. The marketing department, as we noted above, might object to altering the currency of invoicing since the currency of invoicing might be a key factor in selling the product in that particular country.

EXTERNAL HEDGING TECHNIQUES

Many types of financial products have been devised to provide cover against unexpected changes in exchange rates. Several of the markets that produce, buy and sell these products were described in Chapter 2.

Some currency markets, such as the forward market, are of ancient lineage. The forward market dates back to the Austro-Hungarian Empire in the 1870s, other markets are of a more recent vintage. The currency market that trades "traded" options dates from 1982 and the currency "swap" market dates from around 1986. Many finance officers are still learning how to use the products offered by these more recently formed markets.

In 1970 the Bretton Woods agreement of 1944 fell apart. This agreement had set the relative value of most of major trading currencies against the US$.[3] From that date the currency values of the world were no longer linked to either the price of an ounce of gold or to the value of one US$. Financial officers were thus forced from this date to seek out ways of protecting their company from the substantial costs that could be inflicted on the profits of the company by unexpected swings in exchange rates.

All the devices we are about to describe are traded on free markets. In theory everyone has access to these markets and to the hedging products traded on these markets, but whether or not a particular market is open to a finance officer may depend on the size of the currency deal he is contemplating. The forward market and the "traded" options market can handle relatively small amounts of cover. The swap market deals in much larger amounts of money, one million US$ is a minimum size deal.

Several of the hedging devices we are about to describe have already been discussed in Chapter 2.

The Forward Market

Description: The forward market offers a contract to buy or sell a fixed amount of currency at a fixed price on a specific date in the future. The dealer will offer the financial officer a buy price and a sell price for the required currency, this is called the buy–sell spread. The currency dealer does not know whether the enquirer is buying or selling currency when the enquirer asks for a forward quote. The buy–sell spread provides the dealer with a profit on the deal.

A forward contract is usually contracted with the foreign exchange department of a commercial bank via telephone or possibly via an automated dealing system using a computer terminal and screen.[4] Large multinational companies have direct lines into the dealing rooms of the banks.

The forward contract may be set for completion on a fixed date in the future or it may be a "forward option" contract, which can be implemented between two dates. The latter type of contract is the more expensive because it offers a greater degree of flexibility to the buyer of the contract.

A forward contract can eliminate foreign exchange exposure on a business deal. Once the forward contract is set up the exporter or importer knows exactly how much home currency he will receive or have to pay on the foreign contract on the future date. The cost of the cover is fixed and will not change before the forward contract matures. If the financial officer selects a "forward option"[5] contract, which can be implemented between two dates, he is then in a position to choose the most suitable settlement date to pay out or receive the foreign currency. This facility can prove useful if the date of the future payment or receipt is not certain.

The forward market suffers from a few constraints. Forward contracts are not available in all currencies, although synthetic forward contracts can now be created by using options, sometimes in parallel currencies. Some forward markets are very shallow and tend to dry up if the currency market becomes turbulent. This happened to the forward market in the Australian dollar some years ago.

Some financial officers consider forward contracts to be an expensive form of hedge. This belief is probably due to a misunderstanding. The cost of a forward contract is found in the buy–sell spread not in the difference between the spot and the forward rate. The latter difference represents a loss or gain on the forward value of the currency which has already occurred, it is not a current cost of the forward contract. However, the buy–sell spread does vary a great deal between currencies. The more efficient and the deeper a market is the narrower is the buy–sell spread. The buy–sell spread also widens with uncertainty, for example, as the period before settlement is extended forward so the buy–sell spread grows wider.

As the future spot rate can differ from the prior forward rate offered for that date a finance officer can make a profit or a loss on a forward contract. The tax treatment of the profits and losses made on derivative contracts is complex. The treatment by the tax authorities is not entirely symmetrical in all countries. We discuss the problem further in Chapter 10.

Some foreign governments forbid the setting up of forward currency markets in their country and even forbid companies registered in their country from using forward markets in other countries! The law regarding the use of forward markets by foreign subsidiaries is often uncertain and the financial officer of a foreign subsidiary needs to beware lest he annoys the foreign monetary authority by hedging their currency on his own forward market.

We have already noted in Chapter 4 that if the forward rate is an unbiased predictor of the future spot rate then there is little point in a finance officer using the forward market as a hedging device if a company is involved in a continuous series of relatively small foreign currency transactions. In the long run he would lose as much as he would gain by hedging all transactions and this series of forward contracts would cost money. If, however, a single currency transaction of significant value is found to be in the currency budget then this particular transaction should be covered forward.

Exhibit 2.4 provided an example of a forward contract.

Short-term Borrowing

Description: One simple method of covering exchange risk forward is to take out a loan in the foreign currency. For example, if a fixed amount of foreign currency is expected in six months' time a finance officer can take out a six months' loan in that currency now and repay this loan in six months' time out of the proceeds of the foreign contract.

Suppose, for example, that a Canadian company sells an electrical transformer to a French company for FF2 million, the bill is due to be paid in French francs in nine months' time. The deal exposes the Canadian company to an exchange rate risk of FF2 million over the next nine months. One method of hedging this risk would be for the Canadian company to ask its Canadian bank to arrange a FF2 million loan for a period of nine months, to convert the FF2 million immediately into Canadian dollars, and then repay the French franc loan out of the proceeds of the contract in nine months' time. The Canadian dollars provided by the loan can be used by the Canadian company as additional liquidity over the nine-month period or the money can be invested in the Canadian money market for the same period.

This complex procedure has eliminated exchange risk on the FF2 million contract over the nine-month period.

This procedure for covering exchange rate risk is complex but in certain circumstances it is the most appropriate method to use. The exposure risk is eliminated. The cost of cover is known. The loan will provide useful liquid resources to the Canadian company at low cost since excellent security is being provided to the lender of the French francs as long as the French company enjoys a good credit rating with ADEF, the French rating agency.

If the foreign exchange exposure is in the form of a payment rather than a receipt the company can buy French francs now and lend them over the nine-month period to a French borrower.

The forward market and the short-term loans market are so closely interlinked that they are both run on the same computer network.

Hedging foreign exchange risk by taking out short-term loans in the foreign currency raises a few problems. The method is more expensive than forward cover because of the legal costs involved. Loans in the required foreign currency may not be available, or more likely, the foreign government will not allow loans to be taken out in its currency for this purpose. These limitations are only likely to apply to currencies issued by countries with underdeveloped financial markets.

The tax effect of any profit or loss arising out of exchange rate changes over the period of the loan may be complex and unpredictable. Much will depend on the rules agreed between the tax authorities in the two countries involved in the loan.

The Garston Electrics case study set out at the end of this chapter illustrates how to use foreign currency loans to hedge FX risk.

Using a Bill of Exchange Denominated in a Foreign Currency

For many hundreds of years the bill of exchange has been a staple method of paying for and financing exports.

Description: The foreign importer gives the exporter a promise in writing to pay a fixed amount of foreign currency to the exporter on some future date.

Bills of exchange can be negotiable instruments. This means that the exporter can immediately discount the accepted bill of exchange with a bank or acceptance house who pay the exporter a fraction, say 96%, of the face value of the bill. The rate at which the bill is discounted depends on the level of the inter-bank rate at that time. The new owner of the bill signs the back of the bill and can then sell the bill on to another company or institution. The bill of exchange has become a kind of money.

A bill of exchange can provide cover for foreign exchange risk if the discounter takes over the risk of a change in the exchange rate between the date when the bill is discounted and the date when the bill is honoured (paid) by the foreign importer at maturity.

The bill may be accepted by a discount house or a commercial bank at home or abroad. The rate at which the foreign bill is discounted is adjusted to take into account the forward premium or discount on the exchange rate for the date the bill is due to be paid. Discounting the bill provides the exporter with early liquidity.

Insurance guarantees can be taken out at a modest cost to guarantee the security of the bill. This procedure will increase the negotiability of the bill.

This form of hedge is only available on export receivables and it may be prohibited by the exchange control authority in some countries. It is also claimed by some authorities to be an expensive form of cover although in some currencies it may be the only form of cover available if no forward market exists in that currency.

We will examine bills of exchange in more detail later in this book when we come to discuss methods of paying for exports and imports in Chapter 9.

Factoring Foreign Debts

Once an exporter has concluded a contract with a foreign importer and dispatched the goods to the importer the exporter may have to wait for some considerable period of time before the bill is paid. This delay in receiving the cash from credit sales may extend to several months. In addition to the cost of financing this delay in payment there is additional work involved in checking the credit rating of the buyer, invoicing the buyer and keeping account of the buyer's credit record.

Description: A "factor" is an organization that takes over a debt from an exporter and pays the exporter a fraction of the debt in cash. A factor may also make a check on the creditworthiness of the importer, invoice the importer, collect payment from the importer including chasing the importer up on late payment and keeping the credit account of the importer up to date.

In recent years the international factoring of debts has grown rapidly in most of the industrialized countries of the world.

In addition to the other services mentioned above the factor may also take over the foreign exchange risk attaching to the debt if the debt is expressed in a foreign currency.

When the factor takes over the debt from the exporter he pays the exporter a fraction of the face value of the debt, say 80% of the face value. Later, when the debt is paid, the factor makes a second payment to the exporter of the balance due less the factor's charge for his services.

In effect the receivables are assigned as collateral security to the factor allowing the factor to finance the deal. The factor may be a specialist international factor or a department of a commercial bank.

As an international factor is likely to hold many debts in many different currencies at any one time he may be able to "net off" debts in the same or parallel currencies and so cover the exchange risk internally. This form of internal self-hedging is likely to be less costly than hedging the foreign exchange risk externally.

Factoring has proved to be a useful facility for medium-sized businesses who have little knowledge of trading internationally. The factor takes over the credit risk, the exposure risk and also finances the foreign deal.

The only disadvantage of factoring is the cost. The cost of international factoring can be high although it is difficult to disentangle the precise costs of each of the several services involved in factoring a company's debtor's ledger.

An exporter needs to take care that factoring a debt does not void existing insurance cover on the export contract.

Currency Futures

A currency futures contract is a contract to buy or sell a fixed amount of foreign currency at a fixed price on a given future date. Futures contracts are standardized tradeable contracts. Normally a finance officer will buy several standard futures contracts at one time to cover a given exposure risk.

Futures contracts are only available in a small number of currencies. However, all of the major currencies of the world are covered. The most commonly traded contracts trade the US$ against the DM, the Swiss franc, the yen, the £ sterling and the ECU. Note that most of these currencies are European currencies.

In recent years currency futures contracts appear to have fallen somewhat in popularity as a hedging device compared to forwards and currency options. Currency futures can no longer be bought in London. Currency future contracts can be bought and sold in Chicago on the IMM market and in Sydney, Australia and Singapore.

Let us suppose that on March 10, 1996 a French company knows that it will be required to pay US$10 000 000 on September 30, 1996 to a US company for computer chips. The French company decides to cover itself against exchange exposure on this deal so it buys US$/FF futures with French francs. The current rate of exchange on March 10 is FF5.2987 to the US$. The cost of US$/FF September futures on March 10 is FF5.1 to the US$. Assume that a standard sized US$/FF future costs FF250 000. The French company must buy 210 September French Franc future contracts to cover the risk, the value of these contracts approximates to US$10 000 000 because the contracts will cost (210 × FF250 000)/5.1 = US$10 294 118. On September 30, the French company can sell the future contracts, collect the US$ at the agreed exchange rate and pay for the contract on chips in US$.

If the exchange rate falls below FF5.1 to the US$, say to FF5.3 to the US$, then the value of the futures contract will rise accordingly. However, the futures market is not an exact mirror of the spot market. The terminal value of a futures contract value might not exactly match the required number of US$ required, but it should be close.

The cost of a futures contract will approximate to the cost of a forward contract on the same amount since arbitrageurs will eliminate any cost discrepancy between the two hedging devices.

Currency Options

We discussed the currency option market in Chapter 2. In recent years, since 1985, currency options have become a popular method of hedging FX risk if the direction of the future movement in the exchange rate is uncertain.

Description: There are two kinds of currency options, "traded options" which are bought and sold through traded option markets like the PHLX exchange in Philadelphia, and "over-the-counter" (OTC) options, which are set up by the large commercial banks.

Traded options are standardized contracts and can be traded at any time on the traded options market. OTC options are individually designed and are normally of much larger value compared to traded options. OTC options are designed by banks to the specific needs of their customers and are not normally traded before the maturity date.

A currency option of either type can be used to hedge against the risk of loss resulting from unexpected swings in the exchange rate between currencies. If the swing would have resulted in a loss the owner of the option is protected against this loss. If the swing in the exchange rate would have provided a gain, the owner of the option will still benefit from this gain. An option is both an insurance policy and a gambling chip!

If an option offers the buyer the right to "buy" a fixed amount of currency the option is called a "call" option. If the option offers the buyer the right to sell a fixed amount of currency in the future it is called a "put" option. Traded options are guaranteed by the market on which they are bought or sold.

As we noted in Chapter 2 an option gives the buyer a right to buy or sell a fixed amount of currency at a fixed price on a future date or between two dates. However, an option places no "obligation" on the buyer of the "call" or "put" option to exercise these rights.[6] If the buyer does not wish to execute the option he has bought he simply tears up the option contract. His maximum loss is the cost of the option plus the interest lost on the amount invested in the option. This cost is usually no more than a few percent of the value of the currency hedged with the option.

Currency options provide the buyer with an insurance policy against large "unexpected" swings in exchange rates over a fixed period of time, thus most currency options are never exercised.

In recent years traded options have replaced futures contracts as the favourite "standardized" hedging product in fluctuating currency markets.[7] Options have even impinged on the demand for forward contracts, although most large currency deals are still covered by forward contract and the forward market has expanded in recent years.

Exhibits 2.5 and 5.2 provide illustrations of quotes for traded currency option contracts. Exhibit 5.2 illustrates a "call" option bought by a finance officer working for a UK company. The officer wishes to cover for exposure on DM190 000 to be paid in three months' time to a German company. The officer secures the right to buy the required amount of currency at a fixed price on any date between July 1 and September 30, 1995.

Exhibit 5.2 An Example of a Currency Option Contract

The Omera company, resident in Germany, signs up to buy a transformer from Hamstead PLC, a UK company, on July 1 1995. The contract stipulates that Omera will pay an amount of £600 000 to the UK company on September 30 1995. Omera decides to buy a set of traded options to cover the exchange risk on this contract. The current rate of exchange is DM2.5 to the £ sterling. Thus if Omera buys the £ sterling currency now it will cost Omera £600 000 × 2.5 = DM1 500 000. Omera expects the £ sterling to strengthen against the DM over the next few months so it buys an American traded currency "call" option at DM2.5 to the £ for September 30 at a cost of 2 pfennigs per £. An American option gives Omera the right to buy the currency at this price at any point between the first July and September 30 1995.[8]

Omera buys thirty standard contracts at £20 000 a contract (30 × £20 000 = £600 000). This costs 600 000 × DM0.02 = DM12 000 (£4800).

If the option is exercised the cost of buying the £ sterling in terms of DM will be fixed at £600 000 × 2.5 = DM1 500 000. However this option might never be exercised. If the £ is cheaper than DM2.5 to the £ sterling between July and September Omera might decide to buy the currency on the open market and scrap the option or sell it in the option market if it still has value.

If the option is exercised because the DM/£ exchange rate moves to, say, DM2.7 to the £ then the cost to Omera will be fixed at DM1 500 000 (£600 000) plus the cost of the option DM12 000 (£4800) plus interest on this amount for the three month period. A total of DM1 512 000 (£604 800) plus lost interest of say DM300 (£110).

If Omera had not taken out an option contract the cost of the contract in terms of sterling on September 30 would have been £600 000 × 2.7 = DM1 620 000 assuming an exchange rate of DM2.7 to the £.

In the above example, Omera has benefited by taking out the option contract. In this case a forward contract or a futures contract would have provided alternative forms of cover.

He may never exercise the option if the DM stays above DM2.40 to the £ (that is below 41.67 pence for one DM).

The main advantages provided to a buyer by hedging via an option are that the cost of the hedge is fixed and the option need never be implemented. However, as we noted above, an option is a "gambling chip" in addition to being an insurance policy. If the exchange rate moves favourably the owner of the option can make a substantial profit as the spot rate moves away from the strike price and the option moves "into the money". The option is a highly levered gambling chip. On the downside, as we noted above, the loss is limited to the cost of the option plus the interest lost on the investment in the option.

A currency option will always be more expensive than an equivalent forward or futures contract designed to cover FX risk on the same value of currency. However, when the possibility of making a speculative profit on exchange rate changes is taken into account currency options provide a relatively cheap form of cover while leaving open the possibility of making a speculative profit.

On the downside currency option markets are only available in a few major currencies such as US$, DM, Swiss franc, £ sterling, Japanese yen, Canadian dollar, Australian dollar, French franc and recently the European ECU.

Valuing a Currency Option

As a currency option can change in value minute by minute on the option market the problem arises of pricing the fundamental value an option at a specific point in time.

Options can be executed on a fixed date or between two dates. If a currency option is to be executed on a fixed date it is called a European option, if it can be executed between two dates it is called an American option. A European option can be valued using a valuation model developed by Garman and Kohlhagen.[9] This model is a variation on the well known Black–Scholes option valuation model.

The G–K model requires the following information. The spot rate, the difference between the short-term interest rates in the two currencies, an estimate of the variance in the exchange rate over the period of the option and the duration of the option.

From the G–K model it is possible to calculate a number of useful measures, namely:

1. The delta: that is the sensitivity of the option premium to a change in the spot rate.
2. The gamma: that is the rate of change in the delta with respect to a given rate of change in the spot rate.
3. The theta: that is the diminishing value of a call option with respect to time, or more precisely with respect to the amount of time before the call option expires.
4. The vega: that is the sensitivity of the value of the option premium with regard to changes in the volatility of the exchange rate.

Option dealers can use these measures as an assist in evaluating an option. The dealer can decide whether to buy, sell or hold an option when these factors take on specified values.

Note that once a "call" option has been evaluated it is a relatively trivial matter to calculate the value of the equivalent "put" option.

Writing Options

Thus far our discussion of options has concerned itself with buying "call" and "put" options, but if an option is bought someone must be selling it! Option dealers do not talk about "selling" options but about "writing" options.

Writing, i.e., selling, an option is a very risky business unless the writer knows what he or she is doing. An option that has been written cannot be torn up like an option that is bought. A written option must be executed if the buyer of the option decides that he wants the contract executed.

Writing options is a job for professionals in the option market and need not concern us but for the fact that by mixing "bought" options and "written" options it is possible to manufacture various highly sophisticated hedging products.

A detailed description of the design and use of the many sophisticated hedging products that have, in the last few years, been manufactured by merchant banks and others is well beyond the scope of this book. Some suggested readings on this complex subject will be listed at the end of the chapter.

We will limit our discussion to describing two option products. These two products should give the reader a flavour of the wide range of option products now on offer to a finance officer for hedging FX risk. One product is called a "straddle" and the other a "butterfly spread".

The Straddle

Suppose two options of equal value are bought at the same time. One option is a "call" the other a "put". Both options have the same strike price and the same termination date. This option based product is called a "straddle".

Such a product covers the owner of the straddle against any move in the exchange rate in either direction while still offering the potential for a profit on the deal. The larger the move in the exchange rate the greater the profit on the "straddle". A small movement in the exchange rate will result in a small loss if the change in the exchange rate is not sufficient to cover the cost of buying the straddle. Let us work through an example.

Let us suppose that an American sets up a straddle on the US$ to £ sterling with the strike price on a US$ option at US$1.65 to the £ sterling and the joint cost of both options, the call and the put, at 0.05 cents. The straddle makes a profit if the rate rises to $1.65 + 0.05 = US\$1.70$ or falls to $1.65 - 0.05 = US\$1.60$; otherwise the straddle makes a loss.

If the options are taken out for the same terminal date but at a different strike price the product is called a "strangle". An analysis of this situation will demonstrate that if the rate of exchange remains between the two strike prices then the owner of the twin option loses the total cost of the option. Even if the strike price is above the higher or below the lower exchange rate a profit is not guaranteed. A profit is not made until the cost of setting up the option is recovered.

A "strangle" is a good deal cheaper to set up than a "straddle" because a strike price within the "strangle" is likely to be "out of the money" when it is bought and option strike prices that are out-of-the-money are cheap.

The writing, as against the buying, of straddles and strangles is a very risky business. In theory the loss is unlimited while the gain is strictly limited.

The Butterfly Spread

Two calls are written (sold) at the same strike price. Both calls must be "in the money". On the same date one call is bought which is "well out of the money" and one call is bought which is "in the money". We need to remember that the designer of the butterfly spread receives the premiums on the calls he sells but pays the premiums on the calls he buys.

   If the reader works out the possible outcomes of this situation she will find that the money that can be lost by using a butterfly spread is limited while the potential for profit is considerable.

Other Option Products

A veritable menagerie of option-based products have poured onto the financial markets in recent years as shown in Exhibit 5.3. Some of these products are solutions looking for problems but others have proved their worth to finance officers.

Exhibit 5.3   Some Exotic Derivatives

Simple derivative products have been on offer for hedging exchange rate and other forms of risk for many years. Since 1990 a new range of derivatives have come on stream. In some cases these derivatives are not tradeable and cannot be valued easily. However, in other cases they can provide a very economical hedge for certain kinds of risk.

   A few of the more useful products among the 1000 or so on offer are described below.

   1. A "vanilla " option: a simple uncomplicated option product.
   2. An option on an option: the buyer obtains the right to take out an option at a fixed price if the need should arise. Much cheaper than the plain vanilla above.
   3. A "look-back" option: the owner of the option can buy or sell the underlying asset at the highest or lowest value ruling during the life of the option. A very expensive option to buy!
   4. A "Quanto" option or swap: the amount of currency paid in the local currency increases or diminishes depending on the value of the underlying asset or liability as valued in the foreign currency. For example, in a quanto £ to US$ floating interest rate swap a corporation receives variable interest in sterling and pays variable interest in US$ but both payments are denominated in sterling.
   5. A "path-dependent" option: this is a variety of option whereby the strike price depends on the path the value of the underlying asset takes over the life of the option. For example in the case of a "floating-strike" option the option pays out the difference between the average value of the underlying asset over its life and the spot price when the option is exercised. It is difficult to evaluate the price to pay for such an option.
   6. "Knock-in" and "knock out" option: these path dependent options have a "trigger" value attached. In the case of the "knock-out" option the option expires without value if at any time before the maturity date the underlying asset sells at or below the trigger price. In the case of the "knock-in" option the option expires without value unless, before maturity, the value of the underlying asset reaches the trigger price. Options with triggers attached should, in theory, be cheaper than plain vanilla options offering the same cover but they can be risky if large unexpected changes in rates occur.
   7. "Contingent premium" option: the premium need only be paid if the option expires "in-the-money". This is a useful hedge for covering against improbable events. It is a form of catastrophe insurance.
   8. "Step down premium" option: no initial premium is paid but as the option moves towards being "in-the-money" so a part of the premium is paid. The closer the option gets to being useful the higher the fraction of the premium that must be paid.
   9. A "swaption": provides the owner with the right to undertake a swap under certain conditions.
   10. A "shared" option: the option is bought by several buyers only one of whom will need to exercise it.

The above list only includes a small fraction of the hundreds of option products now offered to treasury managers. Some of these are very useful but many are not tradeable since they are customized to the needs of a specific company. Often they are difficult to evaluate.

For example, an option can be bought on "taking out an option"! This product provides a financial officer with a cheap way of covering against changes in the foreign exchange cost of trade deals which might never take place.

A normal option gives the buyer the right to buy or sell the currency at the strike price. An "average rate option" gives the buyer the right to the difference in value between the strike price and the arithmetic average of the spot exchange rates on each day during the life of the option contract. A useful alternative to taking out daily options to cover each day's foreign cash flow!

A "look-back option" gives the buyer the right to buy or sell the foreign currency at the lowest or highest rate of exchange ruling during the life of the option. Such a right is of great value to the buyer so a look back option costs about double the cost of a conventional option.

A "shared option" allows the "call" option to be taken up by any of the parties who contribute towards buying the option. For example, four British companies might tender for a contract in Canada. Only one company, the winner of the contract, will need to cover the currency risk in Canadian dollars. So all four might take out a "shared" option and the company that wins the contract will exercise the option at one quarter the cost of buying the option by itself.

If the finance officer decides to write option contracts or buy into the menagerie of esoteric hedging products now on offer he may be placing his company into a risky position as is demonstrated in Exhibit 5.4.

Few financial officers are familiar with the full range of option products now on offer but there can be little doubt that these products offer much potential for hedging a wide range of foreign exchange risk situations.

Options v Forwards v Futures

If a finance officer wishes to cover exchange rate risk on a fixed amount of foreign currency he will find that a forward contract or a futures contract will always be cheaper than an equivalent option contract. Why then should a finance officer ever buy a currency option to cover exchange rate risk?

If a finance officer is confident that exchange rates will move in one direction only, either up or down, then he should either not hedge the risk or use a forward or a futures contract to cover the risk. As between forwards and futures the futures contract will provide the superior liquidity, if liquidity is important.

If the finance officer is not sure in which direction the exchange rate will move he may well decide to cover the FX risk via a currency option contract. In this way he will cover against the cost of a negative movement in the exchange rate but will still be able to benefit from any favourable movement.

The greater the uncertainty the greater the advantage of a currency option as a hedging device over forwards and futures. A currency option is a particularly appropriate hedging device to use if a substantial movement in the exchange rate is expected but the finance officer cannot predict the direction of the change. Such a situation can arise, for example, just before a general election.

When exchange rates are stable a forward or a futures contract are likely to prove to be the more appropriate hedging devices simply because they are simpler and cheaper than options.

Exhibit 5.4 Derivatives Can Be a Risky Business

Currency derivatives are normally used to insure against substantial unexpected changes in exchange rates. On the other side of the equation companies can "write", that is sell, options and swaps and buy a range of customatized exotic hedging instruments designed by the merchant banks. Trading and evaluating such derivatives, even if possible, can prove to be a profitable but also a very risky enterprise.

In 1994 Edwin Artz, the Chairman of Proctor and Gamble, warned his shareholders that the company would take a US$160 million pre-tax speculative loss in the first quarter on its treasury management operations. The loss was incurred on "leveraged" swaps. A type of interest rate swap.

In 1991 Allied-Lyons PLC lost £150 million on writing uncovered currency options.

In 1994 the German Company Metallgesellschaft uncovered no less than US$ one billion of losses on uncovered speculative oil futures.

The Japanese company, Kashima Oil, is said to have lost no less than US$1.5 billion on currency trading losses in 1994. While the British Merchant Bank, Baring's, lost around one billion US$ on trading on Japanese Stock Exchange index futures in February 1995 and was wiped out.

We repeat that these losses arise out of writing uncovered options or buying esoteric financial instruments that are not properly understood by the buyer or swapping into the wrong interest rate or the wrong currency at the wrong time. Buying simple currency options is a safe hedge.

Most of these losses could have been much reduced, but not eliminated, by setting up tight trading rules capping the cumulative amounts of currency at risk and balancing the books on a continuous basis. Specific rules can be set up between the treasury department of a company and its banks and dealers to limit the net value at risk at any one time.

A study by the accountants KPMG found that a majority of the larger MNCs interviewed by them permitted their treasury departments to be selective in setting up cover. This implies that currency speculation is permitted. (See Chapter 4.)

There is some evidence that the majority of senior directors do not have a good understanding of derivatives. A study by the "Group of Thirty", a Washington think tank, found in 1993 that only 28% of senior directors in the USA claimed to have a good understanding of derivatives while 65% relied on the competence of more junior staff.

A further study by a UK based consultancy called Record Treasury Management in 1993 found that 7% of UK treasurers could make deals up to £50 million without Board approval, 18% deals above £10 million without Board approval while 50% needed to obtain Board approval for derivative deals above one million pounds. 14% needed Board approval for all derivative deals.

But do directors understand the intricacies of the derivatives market? The same study found that among the 90 firms surveyed 36% of the Directors thought the explanations of the deals presented to them were "inadequate" and 18% thought the presentations to be "poor".

Simple currency options are safe and well understood but some of the more exotic hedging instruments recently introduced onto the markets are creating problems for the companies who use them.

The above listing of losses is only the tip of the iceberg. Huge amounts of money have been lost (and made?) over the last 10 years on derivative based deals. Most of the losses were due to foolish speculation.

How much does a finance officer need to know about derivatives? In the USA the case of *Brane* v *Roth* in 1993 found that a company director had a duty to understand hedging techniques and were liable if such techniques were not used to protect company assets for the benefit of the shareholders. The case has no legal force outside Indiana, USA, but it may be a harbinger of things to come.

The Currency Swap

Description: A currency swap occurs when a company swaps a liability denominated in one currency for a liability of another company denominated in another currency for a period of time at an agreed exchange rate. A swap is useful for hedging the FX risk associated with future payments of interest and capital on a foreign loan. A currency swap is not a swap of the loan itself but a swap of currencies, so neither party incurs any liability for the loan obligations of the other party.

In 1990 49% of the treasurers polled by *Euromoney* hedged through currency swaps with 42% of their total exposure covered in this way.[10]

Most swaps are organized by international banks who have found from experience that mediating swaps is a lucrative business.

In the case of most swaps mediated by banks one side of the swap is denominated in US$. The bank may swap a given amount of US$s as the intermediary currency between two other currencies. For example, a pound sterling for DM swap may be separated into two independent swaps, a DM for US$ libor swap plus a US$ libor for £ sterling swap.

The bank acts as an intermediary in this swap arrangement. The bank is happy to arrange both swaps so long as it does not unbalance its own currency portfolio. Naturally the bank charges a fee for the services provided, this fee usually amounts to a fraction of 1% of the value of the swap to both parties.

Some banks use the Monte Carlo simulation technique to keep their currency exposure position in balance.[11]

Advantages of Swaps

A currency swap can provide many benefits to the parties to the swap.

For example, swaps can be used to reduce the cost of debt by arbitraging the debt raising ability of a company into that financial market where their debt raising ability is strongest (and cheapest). Swaps can be used to remove FX exposure on loans denominated in a "hard" foreign currency. Swaps can be used to gain access to currencies that are otherwise "off-limits" to the company and possibly to by-pass exchange control and "blocked" currency regulations. Last, but by no means least, swaps can be used to manufacture long-term "synthetic" forward currency contracts for as far forward as five to 10 years when no such contracts are offered on the conventional forward markets.

The entire financial structure of a company can be altered, off balance sheet, by using swaps but a detailed discussion of this complex topic is well outside the compass of this book.

The benefits provided to multinational companies by the currency swap market are so considerable that the swap market has shown the fastest growth of all currency markets in recent years. In 1990 the value of all the swaps traded on all the swap markets of the world summed to about US$1 000 000 000 000, by 1994 this value had grown to an astonishing US$4 000 000 000 000!

The precise figures are not known but the volume is such that several research reports have been commissioned by governments and international institutions in recent years to test the safety of the swap system.

A joint study of the markets was undertaken by the US Federal Reserve, the Federal Deposit Insurance Corporation and the Comptroller of the US currency. This committee reported to the US Congress in February 1993. The report gave derivatives a "cautious thumbs up". Despite the fact that many of these markets are unregulated the report considered that the failure of a large swap dealer is "unlikely". The one major problem is thought to lie within derivatives that span several markets. If one market should go down the crisis could spill over into other markets via the derivatives.

A 1992 report on the same problem by the Basle Committee of bankers was less sanguine. This report concluded that bankers need to improve their risk control procedures on derivatives.

A report published by the General Accounting Office of the US Congress in May 1994 warned that the unregulated derivatives markets must be brought under the surveillance of a US regulator if a future meltdown of the world's financial system is to be averted.

An Example

Since currency swaps have many uses they also have many variants. One possible scenario is as follows.

An Australian company, Ozsoft, wishes to acquire a £100 million sterling loan for five years to buy a British company. The Australian company finds that it will cost 10% p.a. to raise this money on the UK market. However, the company Treasurer knows that she can raise the Australian dollar equivalent of £100 million, A$200 million at the current rate of exchange, at 7% on the Sydney market where Ozsoft is known, compared to 10% on the UK market where it is not known. The difference of 3% in interest cost is much greater than future expected exchange rate differences would justify.

Ozsoft approaches the swap department of the AA International bank (AAI) and asks if a swap of approximately A$200 million can be arranged from Australian dollars into £ sterling over a five-year period. The AAI bank contacts its swap bank to find if there is a company wishing to swap a roughly equivalent amount of pound sterling into Australian dollars over the same period.

The AAI bank finds a UK leisure company, Aquamast PLC, which wishes to develop an ambitious leisure centre opposite the barrier reef in NE Australia. The cost of this project will be around A$200 million. Aquamast had intended to raise the money in Australia but the AAI bank points out that it can raise the money more cheaply in its own currency, the pound sterling, than in Australia where it is an unknown quantity, and then swap the £100 million out of pounds into Australian dollars.

The AAI bank now acts as a broker and arranges the matching swap. A £100 million sterling bond at 8% is issued by Aquamast in the UK and a A$200 million bond at 7% is issued by Ozsoft in Sydney. The bank charges a fee of 0.20% on the value of the swap to each customer for arranging the swap.

Aquamast pays the £100 million to the AAI bank who passes the money to Ozsoft. Ozsoft pays its A$200 million to the AAI bank who passes the money to Aquamast.

For each of the next five years each company will make an interest payment to the AAI bank who will pass the money to the counter-party. For example, Aquamast, who is now earning Australian dollars from its Reef project, will pay A$14 million to the AAI bank who will pass the money to Ozsoft to allow it to make its interest payments on its bond denominated in A$. Ozsoft will pay £8 million to the AAI bank who will pass this money to Aquamast to pay its interest charges on the pound sterling bonds.

At the end of five years Aquamast will pay A$200 million to the AAI bank who will pass the money to Ozsoft to repay its Australian bondholders. Ozsoft will do likewise with the £100 million sterling to allow Aquamast to repay its UK bondholders. Both companies have raised money more cheaply via the swaps route.

Since this is simply a swap of currency and not of the actual loans the cost of default by either party is not so high as if loans were being swapped. If one party should default the risk involved is the risk attached to unexpected changes in the exchange rates over the five-year period of the swap.

Where interest payments are swapped a fixed interest rate swapper is rather more at risk than the variable rate swapper since the swap is subject to both exchange rate risk and the risk of an unexpected change in market interest rates over the period of the swap.

Recently some swappers have asked for collateral to insure against the counter-party failing to honour its swap obligations. Other swappers will only deal with a counter-party who enjoys a triple A credit rating grade from a major credit rating agency.

Most swaps are arranged by commercial banks. Sometimes the bank acts as a broker as in the above example, introducing the parties to one another and guaranteeing the deal against default by either party. Sometimes the bank acts as dealer taking the swap into its own swap portfolio until a suitable counter-party can be found.

International banks have found swapping to be a lucrative activity since the risk attached to a swap between well known customers is quite low.

Problems with Swaps

Various technical problems are associated with swaps. It is difficult for market makers, such as banks, in the swap market to hedge both currency and interest rate movements at the same time while keeping a balanced net position in each foreign currency in each forward period.

The spreads are much wider in the swap market than in the other markets that hedge exchange rate risk. This makes swapping a relatively expensive operation for the customers of the bank.

The currencies available in the primary swap market are rather limited. The principal currencies offered are the Yen, DM, US$, Swiss franc, £ and ECU, although swaps linked via the US$ to other currencies might be arranged.

Exchange Rate Guarantees

The governments of some countries provide exchange rate guarantees for a small fee (say 0.3% to 0.7% of the value of the export contract) to encourage their local companies to increase their export effort.

Description: The conventional approach to providing an exchange rate guarantee is to compensate local companies who lose money on export contracts because of a substantial unexpected change in exchange rates between the time a contract is signed and the date the payment is received.

The change in the exchange rate over the period of the contract must exceed some given threshold, say 3%, before the compensation allowance is triggered. If the exchange rate moves in favour of the exporter then the government claims any excess profit over the 3% threshold.

With so many other hedging devices now available to hedge FX risk exchange rate guarantees have fallen out of fashion. Today they are mainly used by governments in developing countries to encourage export promotion or by governments in advanced industrial countries to encourage their own companies to trade with countries which offer no forward market, or other hedging devices, to cover FX risk.

If an exchange rate guarantee is entered into by an exporter then any exchange rate fluctuation outside the 3% band can be ignored by the exporter. Usually, but not invariably, the exporter must include all foreign currency exports into the guarantee and not simply those exports denominated in risky currencies.

Currency Cocktails

Description: If the value of a debt is denominated in a currency cocktail the unit of currency used to value the debt is expressed as a mixture of several currencies.

The advantage of such a valuation procedure is that the value of a debt denominated in a "cocktail" currency is likely to vary rather less in terms of the home currency of the debtor than a debt denominated in any single currency within the cocktail (except for the home currency). The variance on the value of the debt in terms of home currency is reduced but the cost is lower.

Debts expressed in terms of ECUs, the European Currency unit (ECU), are expressed in terms of a currency cocktail.

Currency cocktails are difficult to set up since the rules regarding the valuation and weighting of the currencies in the cocktail need to be strictly laid down and agreed by all the parties concerned. Currency cocktail denominated debts have not been very popular except with international organizations and companies resident in countries that are unfashionable for one reason or another.[12]

However, the ECU may provide a useful hedging technique for finance officers during the transitional period before the European Union adopts a single currency. For this reason the popularity of ECU bonds tends to mimic the popularity of a single European currency. When a single currency was thought likely in 1991 and 1992 the sale of ECU bonds boomed, the debacle of September 1992 almost finished them off but by 1994 their popularity was returning once more.[13]

AUTOMATING CURRENCY DEALING

Up until recently most currency deals, whether spot contracts or derivative contracts, were agreed via a telephone link between a trader and a currency dealer. The dealer might be working in the foreign exchange department of a bank or be a specialized currency dealer or broker.

A substantial proportion of currency dealing is now automated via cable and computer screen. Automated dealing systems using Reuter's Citywatch, Telerate or Cognotec are becoming increasingly popular. Cognotec now offers automated deals on swaps, money market deposits and forward dated or time options. These systems provide rate histories, graphs and calculation suites for potential traders. Exhibit 5.5 illustrates a screen offering a swap deal using Barclay's TAG autodealing system via Cognotec.

Even if a finance officer is bargaining with a dealer over the phone, access to a computer screen provides an advantage. If she has access to the current rates and costs

Exhibit 5.5   Screening of an Automated Swap Deal

Barclay's Bank Automated Dealing (TAG)
Swap Transaction

DATE	120794			
Near swap component				
Co buys	DEM			12345.67
Co sells	GBP			4769.06
Period		Value date	160794	
Far swap component				
Co buys	FBP			4760.6
Co sells	DEM			12345.67
Period	3M	Value date	81094	
Request (Y/N)		Y	Near rate	2.5887
			Swap pips	0.0046
			Far rate	2.5933
Deal (Y/N)		Y		
			DEAL COMPLETED	
Deal number		Near	31765	Far 31766
	Press Q to quit		Press C to continue	

Questions to be asked of an automated dealing system:

1. How many currencies can one deal in?
2. How large and small can the transactions be?
3. Does the system update in real time?
4. How long do I have to make a decision? (25 to 60 seconds).
5. Can standing orders be inserted into the system?
6. What type of markets are covered? (Spot, forward, options, swaps, futures?)
7. Is a history of past transactions available?
8. What kind of security systems are installed? (Audit trail? Dealer limits? ID? Passwords?)
9. Does the system interface with other systems or an automated advice system?

Swap and other deals can now be completed by using an automated dealing system sited in the office of the company treasurer. The computer is linked via a communication system like Cognotec, Tag or Trader to a dealer. The deal shown swaps DM for £ sterling.
Before a treasurer decides on the trading system to use she needs to ask some key questions about the system.

of financial products quoted on the computer screen while she is bargaining with two currency dealers over the phone she is in a strong position to obtain the best deal possible.

The future of the currency markets lies with automation.

WHAT HAVE WE LEARNED IN THIS CHAPTER?

1. Various financial products have been devised for hedging foreign exchange risk. All of these products are not suited to, or available to, all companies. A finance officer needs to select from among those products those best suited to the structure and pattern of cash flow of his company.

2. Foreign exchange hedging techniques can be usefully segregated into two categories, namely those techniques that are internal to the company and those techniques that are external of the company.

3. The techniques chosen will be constrained by the size and complexity of the company plus such additional factors as the overall business strategy, business ethics, certain psychological factors and, of course, cost.

4. The internal hedging techniques available to a finance officer include such devices as netting, matching, leading and lagging, adjusting the contract price to the forward rate and changing the currency of contract.

5. The external markets available for hedging exchange rate risk include the forward market, the short-term loans market, bills of exchange, factoring foreign debts, the currency futures market, the currency options market, currency swaps, exchange rate guarantees and currency cocktails.

6. The derivatives markets in futures and options can be very risky markets to enter if the finance officer is not fully conversant with the operation of these markets.

7. A growing proportion of currency deals are being channelled through automated dealing systems. These systems give the finance officer easy access to an extensive data bank of information on movements and projections in the currency markets.

NOTES

1. The author is not aware of any study that has attempted to calculate the costs associated with each type of internal hedging technique.

2. The claim that internal techniques are cheaper than external is based on discussions by the author with the treasury managers of 12 large UK multinational companies.

3. Or linked to the price of gold. One troy ounce of gold was valued at US$35 in 1935. The value of other currencies were linked to the US$ in 1944.

4. For example, via Reuters, Telerate or Cognotec.

5. Not to be confused with an option on a forward contract. See ahead.

6. This statement is only true for the buyer of the option. On the other side of the deal is a person or institution who "writes" the option. The writer must implement the option if asked to do so by the buyer of the option, so writing an option is a very risky investment unless the writer already has that amount of currency in his portfolio.

7. Although it should be noted that Chang and Shankar (1986) found that currency futures outperformed currency options (used as synthetic futures) as a hedging instrument in investment portfolios.

8. Unlike a European currency traded option that can only be exercised on the closing date, that is September 30, 1995.

9. Garman, M. and Kohlhagen, S. Foreign currency option values. *Journal of International Money and Finance*, December 1993, 231–7.

10. *Euromoney*, May 1990, 120.

11. See First pick your target. *Euromoney*, July 1994, 94. Comment by Kenneth Lay, World Bank.

12. For example, South Africa before 1994 and Taiwan.

13. See *The Economist*, April 24, 1993, 111.

FURTHER READING

Andersen, T. (1993) *Currency and Interest Rate Hedging*. New York Institute of Finance.

Beidleman, C. (1985) *Financial Swaps*. Dow-Jones Irwin.

Black, F. and Scholes, M. (1973) The pricing of options and corporate liabilities. *Journal of Political Economy*, May, 637–59.
    The primal article on valuing options.

Brown, B. (1986) *The Forward Market in Foreign Exchange*. Croom Helm.

Euromoney (1992) *Dictionary of Derivatives*. June.

European Bond Commission (1991) *The European Options and Futures Markets: An Overview and Analysis for Money Managers and Traders*. Chicago, USA, Probus.

Garman, M. and Kohlhagen, S. (1983) Foreign currency option values. *Journal of International Money and Finance*, December, 231–7.

Giddy, I. (1983) The foreign exchange option as a hedging tool. *Midland Corporate Finance Journal*, Fall, 32–42.

Johnson, R. and Giaccotto, C. (1995) *Options and Futures: Concepts Strategies and Applications*. New York, West Publishing.

A thorough but not too mathematical introduction to the option and future markets that includes the foreign exchange markets. Includes an instructor's guide.

Koziol, J. D. (1990) *Hedging Principles: Practices and Strategies*. New York, John Wiley.

A practical introduction to these techniques with many examples.

Morgan Guaranty Trust Company (1991) Swaps: volatility at controlled risk. *World Financial Markets*, April, 1–22.

Price, J. and Henderson, S. K. (1992) *Currency and Interest Rate Swaps*. Butterworth.

Ross, D. (1990) *International Treasury Management*. Woodhead-Faulkner.

A detailed description with examples of most of the hedging techniques introduced in this chapter. A readable book unlike many on this topic.

Tucker, A. (1990) *Financial Futures, Options and Swaps*. West Publishing Company.

An excellent textbook for those who wish to learn "how to do it". Includes many practical examples and has an accompanying instructor's guide.

TUTORIAL QUESTIONS

1. What is a "parallel" currency? If two currencies are parallel currencies how can this fact be used to hedge exchange rate risk in either currency?

2. "The hedging techniques adopted by a company trading internationally can have an unforeseen psychological impact on the managers operating in other parts of the organization" Explain this comment. What psychological factors can be effected by currency hedging techniques?

3. Describe three benefits that may be derived from using a centralized "netting" technique to reduce FX risk.

4. Explain the difference between the hedging techniques called "netting" and "matching". These techniques are often confused with one another.

5. Why must a strong discipline be applied to the management of cash flow if a company with many foreign subsidiaries uses the "matching" technique to hedge exchange risk?

6. Provide an example where the lagging of a payment in pesos to a foreign subsidiary in Argentina might gain a speculative profit for a company. Provide a set of figures illustrating the gain in terms of the home currency.

7. How can the forward market be used in the pricing of foreign contracts? Can this pricing technique really be described as a "hedging" technique?

8. Describe the circumstances under which a change in the currency of invoicing foreign sales might induce higher profits for the exporter?

9. Why did the exchange value of most of the world's currencies, which had been stable up to 1970, become so unstable after 1970?

10. What is the buy–sell spread on a forward contract? If this spread widens what does this tell us about the market on which the forward contract is quoted? Why does the buy–sell spread widen as the length of the forward contract increases?

11. How does a foreign currency dealer make a profit on a forward contract? How does a futures dealer make a profit on a futures contract?

12. If a company is exposed to a large number of small-scale foreign currency deals should the finance officer use the forward market to hedge the exposure risk involved on these deals? What has the forward rate's ability to predict the future spot rate got to do with your answer to this question?

13. An Italian exporter sells furniture to Australia worth 200 million lire. The contract is due to be paid in Australian dollars in six months' time. Describe the steps that need to be taken by the Italian company if the Italian company wishes to cover the exchange risk incurred by this contract by taking out a loan in Australian dollars to cover the exchange risk on the deal. Why might such a hedging tactic not be (a) possible (b) wise?

14. How does the discounter of a bill of exchange expressed in a foreign currency allow for foreign exchange risk?

15. What services can an international factor provide to an exporter? Why can a factor hedge foreign exchange risk more cheaply than the average exporter?

16. Why is it that the use of currency futures as a hedging device has declined somewhat in popularity in recent years?

17. A traded currency option is what is called a "standardized contract". What attributes of the currency option contract are standardized? Why does this process of standardisation improve the efficient working of the currency options market?

18. Compare a "traded" option with an "over-the-counter" option. What are the advantages enjoyed by either option over the other?

19. "A traded currency option is an insurance premium plus a gambling chip." Explain and illustrate this definition of a traded currency option.

20. An Australian company has issued a 10-year bond in the USA for US$50m at 8% per annum in 1993. The Australian company finds after five years that its access to US$s is rather limited and it would like to swap this US$ liability for Australian dollars of about the same amount at current rates of exchange. Describe the steps the Australian company will need to take to achieve this objective.

21. How can a British company use a currency swap to create a "synthetic" forward contract covering for a liability of DM25 million which is due in three years' time? Assume that the current exchange rate between the £ and the DM is DM2.5 to the pound sterling?

22. Currency swaps are "off-balance sheet". What does this mean? Why are governments so opposed to "off-balance" sheet financial transactions?

23. Why should an exporter enter into an exchange rate guarantee contract with a government agency rather than covering forward in the forward market in the usual way?

24. A company wishes to issue a Eurodollar bond denominated in a "currency cocktail" of £ sterling, German DM and French francs. Describe how the currencies would have to be evaluated and weighted within the bond to achieve this end.

THE BARING'S AFFAIR

In late February 1995 rumours swept through the City of London that Baring's Bank, one of the oldest and most distinguished banks in the City of London, was in serious financial trouble. The trouble, it was claimed, stemmed from derivative operations in Singapore.

The rumours, for once, turned out to be true. Within three weeks of these reports, Baring's Bank, with a capitalization of around £500 million, was wiped out, or to be more accurate was sold to the Dutch financial group ING for a single pound sterling.

The precise details of what happened may never be known. Subsequent reports claim that the head of Baring's Singapore future's business, a young man called Nick Leeson, lost the bank some $1.4 billion (£860 million) on futures trading.

Mr Leeson was trading in derivative instruments called "Nikkei 225 futures". The value of these futures depends upon the average value of shares quoted on the Tokyo stock exchange. The Osaka Stock exchange publishes data on the trading position of dealers and it seems that between the beginning of January 1995 and late February Mr Leeson built up a position in "buy" contracts (gambling on the Nikkei to rise) which rose from 3000 contracts in mid-January to an astonishing 20 000 contracts in late February. This represented around 10% of the entire market in Nikkei 225 futures.

The Nikkei index stood at around 16 000 in mid-January and it seems that it would have to have risen to around 18 000 for the future trades to have made a profit.

On the day before the final crash Baring's is rumoured to have built up a market position worth US$27 billion!

The Kobe earthquake on January 17, 1995 may have precipitated the collapse, but the astonishing lack of control of futures trading in Singapore by Baring's management in London was at the root of the disaster.

A memo written as far back as 1992 by James Bax, head of Baring's securities in Singapore, to his head office in London ran as follows: "My concern", writes Mr Bax, "is that we are . . . setting up a structure which will subsequently prove disastrous." Prophetic words indeed. An internal audit of the Singapore futures operation carried out by Baring's own audit team in August 1994 pointed to the dangers that might arise from allowing Mr Leeson to control both the trading and settlement operations. A combination of activities which were actually banned by SIMEX, the Singapore international money market, at the time.

Baring's Bank was wiped out as an independent entity but the damage extended much further. SIMEX, the Singapore international money market, was growing very fast, by 53% in turnover in 1994 alone. The reputation of SIMEX for efficiency and probity was damaged by the Baring's fiasco. The City of London itself came out of the affair badly. What was the Bank of England doing in allowing Baring's to transfer £569 million of funds from London to Singapore in January 1995? Under EU rules a bank is not allowed to transfer more than 25% of its equity capital into a single investment without the approval of the Bank of England. Baring's total equity capital did not exceed £325 million in January 1995.

Baring's management claim that they thought that Nick Leeson was trading on behalf of a third party, but if this was the case why the need for the £569 million for margin calls? Banks are not allowed to pay collateral on futures contracts on their client's behalf.

The Baring's fiasco is a monument to poor management control. In June 1995 the Bank for International Settlements published a paper which the Bank of England circulated to firms in the City of London. The paper concludes that:

> "As a matter of general policy, compensation policies, particularly in the risk management, control and senior management function, should be structured in such a way that is sufficiently independent of the performance of trading activities, thereby avoiding the potential incentives for excessive risk-taking that can occur if, for example, salaries are tied too closely to the profitability of derivatives".

In other words a derivatives' trader should never again be placed in a position whereby he or she can gamble with a billion dollars of other people's money to make two million dollars for him, or herself.

CASE STUDY: GARSTON ELECTRICS PLC

Garston Electrics PLC is a British company based in Leeds, Northern England. On June 30, 1996 Garston sign a contract to sell some heavy electrical equipment to Santo Barco S.A., a Spanish company based in Barcelona, Spain. The contract is denominated in Spanish pesetas. The contract is valued at SP170 000 000.

The payment for the contract is due to be sent to the UK by Santo Barco on September 30, 1996.

On June 30, 1996 the financial director of Garston, Mr Emyln Thomas, is considering the currency risk involved in this deal. Currently the pound sterling is floating against the peseta and the pound/peseta exchange rate had fluctuated widely in recent years. Mr Thomas is worried that the peseta might fall in value by a substantial margin against the pound sterling over the next three months. He thinks that political problems in Spain may cause the peseta to fall by as much as 10% in value against the £ over this short period of time! The currency market, however, is only expecting a 2% fall in value.

Mr Thomas considers three approaches to handling the problem of the possible loss in value in terms of the pound sterling of the Santo Barco contract:

1. Sell the SP170 million forward three months using a forward contract. He can then use the proceeds of the Santo Barco contract to pay out the SP170 million in three months' time.
2. Borrow SP170 million in Spanish pesetas for three months at 18% per annum and convert this money immediately into pound sterling. Repay the loan out of proceeds of the Santo Barco contract in three months time.
3. Do nothing about the FX risk attached to this contract. Simply convert the SP170 million at the spot rate ruling on September 30, 1996. This is sometimes called self-hedging the risk.

Some relevant facts about the contract:

1. The interest rates ruling on three-months loans in pound sterling and pesetas on June 30, 1996 are:

UK pound sterling   10%,   Spanish pesetas   18%.

2. The spot and forward rates on the pound/peseta exchange rate on June 30, 1996 are:

Spot rate:	172 Ps to the £ sterling
Forward rate (three months)	176 Ps to the £ sterling

Required:

1. Given the information available to Mr Thomas on June 30, 1996 calculate which of the three options is likely to provide the highest income in £ sterling as at September 30, 1996.
2. If we now assume that the actual spot rate on September 30, is 180 pesetas to the pound sterling calculate, in retrospect, which option Mr Thomas should have chosen to maximize income in terms of the pound sterling.
3. What other important factors not given in the question would Mr Thomas need to know before he can make a final decision on how to handle the FX risk attached to the Santo Barco contract?

CASE STUDY: ZENINK PLC

Zenink PLC, a subsidiary of the Zenarc corporation is a British company that exports high purity ink-jet dyes around the world.

Zenink has contracted to sell two large orders to Canada and South Africa. Zenink won both contracts because they were willing to denominate the deals in terms of the foreign currency, namely Canadian $s and South African rand. The contracts are worth C$10 million and Rand 50 million respectively. The ink will be delivered over the next year and both contracts are due to be paid in one year's time on June 30, 1995.

The deal was pushed through by the marketing department but the treasurer of Zenink is rather worried about these two contracts because the profit margin is low and he suspects that both the Canadian dollar and the South African rand may fall in value against the pound sterling over the next year. A currency forecaster whom the treasurer believes to be reliable is forecasting that the C$ will fall by 5% against the £ over the next year and the rand by 10%. Forward rates are available on both currencies and the spot and one-year forward rates along with other relevant data are shown below.

The treasurer decides to work out the cost of three options for hedging this currency risk: (a) Take out a one-year forward contract in both currencies; (b) raise a loan in C$ and rand equal in value to both contracts in the Eurodollar market. The loan will be repayable in one year's time out of the proceeds of the contracts; (c) do nothing and accept the risk of a fall in the value of both currencies.

Required: calculate the cost of these three options given the following information (ignore tax):

Spot rate on July 1, 94	C$2.00 per £
Spot rate on July 1, 94	rand5 per £
Forward rate: one year forward	C$2.04 per £
Forward rate: one year forward	rand5.25 per £

Current interest rate on one-year loans in the currencies.

Canadian $	11%
South African rand	14%
UK £	9%

Required: Which option would you choose? Explain your reasoning.

If the actual spot exchange rates on June 30, 95 were as shown below which, in retrospect, was the better option?

Canadian $	C$2.02 per £
South African rand	rand6 per £

GARSTON ELECTRICS PLC: NOTES TOWARDS A SOLUTION

Part 1

Which of the three suggested options provides the highest income for Garston in terms of pound sterling?

1. Alternative 1: Take out a forward contract

Garston enters into a forward contract to deliver Ps170 million on 30.9.96 at 176. On 30.9.96 Garston receives Ps170 million from Spain and sells these pesetas for 170m/176 = £965 909.

2. Alternative 2: Do nothing

Garston receives Ps170 million on 30.9.96 and expects to convert these pesetas at a spot rate of 191 pesetas to the pound. Thus Mr Thomas expects to receive 170m/191 = £890 050.

Why 191 Ps to the £? 172 Ps cost 100 pence on 30.6.96. Therefore, one peseta costs 100/172 = 0.581 pence. If the peseta falls in value against the £ by 10% then one peseta will cost 0.581 × 90/100 = 0.523 pence. Therefore, 100 pence (£1) will cost 100/0.523 = 191 pesetas. QED

3. Alternative 3: Take out a loan in pesetas

Garston borrows Ps170 million in pesetas for three months in the UK or Spain.

The Ps170 million are immediately converted into pound sterling on 30.9.96 at the rate of 172 pesetas to the £.

This brings in Ps170 million/172 = £988 372.

If this amount is invested in the UK market for three months it can earn interest at 10% per annum.

$$£988\,372 \times 10\% \times 3/12 = £24\,709$$

However, we must deduct the cost of the loan in pesetas:

$$Ps170\,000\,000 \times 18\% \times 3/12 = Ps7\,650\,000$$

If these pesetas are bought on 30.9.96 at the expected spot rate on that date they will cost:

$$Ps7\,650\,000/191 = £40\,052$$

The net income from alternative 3 is thus:

$$£988\,372 + 24\,709 - 40\,052 = £973\,029$$

The loan alternative brings in the highest income under these set of assumptions.

However, many other permutations are possible. For example, Mr Thomas need only cover for the loan net of interest payable in pesetas. Also the interest due to be paid on the peseta loan could be covered forward (although this is unlikely if Mr Thomas believes that the peseta is going to fall in value against the pound sterling over the next three months). We have ignored tax in these solutions.

Part 2

If the actual exchange rate on 30.9.96 is 180 pesetas to the £ what would be the result under each of the three options?

1. Alternative 1: Enter into a forward contract.

Result: Unchanged at 170m/176 = £965 909.

2. Alternative 2: Do nothing

Result: Ps170m/180 = £944 444.

3. Take out a loan of Ps170 million.

Result: The immediate conversion of the Ps170 million and the interest earned in the UK remain the same.

However, buying Ps7 650 000 for the interest payment is now more expensive:

$$\text{The cost of the interest in £ sterling is } Ps7\,650\,000/180 = £42\,500$$

Thus the income from the loan option is:

$$£988\,372 + 24\,709 - 42\,500 = £970\,581$$

Conclusion: The loan option still brings in the highest income so, even in retrospect, Mr Thomas would have chosen the loan option to hedge the FX risk.

Note: that the interest rate parity theory (IRPT) is not working exactly in this case. The market expects the peseta to fall from 172 to 176 over the three-month period, an annualized fall of 9.3%. The annualized differential interest rate between the £ and the peseta is only 8% (18% - 10%).

6
Risk and Foreign Investment

INTRODUCTION

The problems involved in direct foreign investment are legion and cannot be adequately covered in a book of this size. In this chapter we will be concerned with only one aspect of direct foreign investment namely the nature and degree of risk attached to direct foreign investment and how such risks can be hedged.

Foreign investment is said to be "direct" when a company invests to take control of a venture abroad. For example, a company might buy land, buildings, equipment and inventory to set up a company abroad.

If a company invests in foreign shares or other financial assets that do not provide control of a foreign venture the investment is said to be "indirect" or "portfolio" investment. Most foreign indirect investment, that is portfolio investment, is conducted by the managers of "collective" investment schemes such as insurance companies, investment trusts and unit trusts.

From an analytical point of view direct investment abroad is little different from direct investment at home. In order to assess the worth of the investment the financial officer needs to identify and set out the cash flows from the foreign investment, calculate the cost of the funds to be invested in the foreign investment, make an estimate of the riskiness of the foreign investment and then decide whether the returns from the foreign investment justify the risks involved.

The usual progression that leads to a company investing abroad is as follows. In the beginning the company exports to a foreign country, then, finding a rising demand for its products abroad, it sets up an agency in the foreign country or it issues a licensing agreement to a foreign company to sell its goods in that country. Later it may enter into a joint venture with a local company in the foreign country and finally, if demand is still not satisfied, the parent company may decide to set up a subsidiary company abroad.

Some form of investment will be required to set up any of these foreign entities but this chapter is concerned with that form of foreign investment which results in an operating subsidiary being set up in a foreign country.

WHY DOES A COMPANY INVEST ABROAD?

There are a myriad of reasons why a company decides to invest abroad. It may be seeking new customers, it may find that there is a higher profit margin abroad, it may wish to benefit from economies of scale by increasing total output, it may wish to access new sources of material or new technology abroad, it may face high tariff barriers if it does not invest directly in a foreign country rather than export to that country and so on.

However, the most common reason for making a direct investment abroad is the need to diversify the sales outlets of the company into foreign markets. The company decides to reduce its dependence on the vagaries of a single home market.

The wide variation in the return to be expected on investments in the different countries of the world is illustrated in Exhibits 6.1 and 6.2. Exhibit 6.1 shows the average real return on portfolio investment in various advanced industrialized countries for the period 1983 to 1992. Exhibit 6.2 demonstrates the return and the degree of risk attached to that return from a wider range of countries. Note the wide variation in the ordinal ranking of the returns when comparing the simple return and the risk-adjusted return on these portfolios for the period 1989 to 1993.

The simple investment return must always be adjusted for risk to truly assess the worth of the investment.

Exhibit 6.1 Real Return on Portfolio Investment in 10 Countries, 1983–92, in Terms of US$

	Equities %	Bonds %	Cash %
France	20	13	9
Holland	17	9	7
UK	14	8	7
Germany	14	8	6
Switzerland	13	6	5
Japan	12	11	9
USA	12	8	4
Australia	11	7	5
Italy	10	13	10
Canada	5	9	6

Source: UBS Philips and Drew.

The table shows the real return on a portfolio of investments invested in equity shares, bonds and cash instruments over the 10-year period from January 1983 to December 1992.

The real return is the gross monetary return adjusted for United States inflation over the period. The returns are expressed in terms of US$ so changes in exchange rates over the period affect the returns shown.

The French equity portfolio performed best. Bonds performed well in France and Italy while the Italian cash instrument portfolio performed best over the period because of high real interest rates.

Exhibit 6.2 Annual Return and Associated Risk in Various Markets, 1989–93

Country	Return %	Risk (SD)	Return/risk
	Sorted by return %		
Venezuela	63	71.6	0.88
Argentina	62	116.8	0.53
Mexico	61	29.7	2.05
Latin America (IFC)	50	35.3	1.42
Thailand	40	32.7	1.22
Emerging markets (IFC)	33	20.3	1.63
Malaysia	30	23.5	1.28
Philippines	30	40.2	0.75
Asia (IFC)	29	22.5	1.29
Brazil	23	89.8	0.26
USA	13	12.7	1.02
UK	11	20.3	0.54
Indonesia	7	35.8	0.20
Japan	−5	29.4	****
	Sorted by risk adjusted return		
Mexico	61	29.7	2.05
Emerging markets (IFC)	33	20.3	1.63
Latin America (IFC)	50	35.3	1.42
Asia (IFC)	29	22.5	1.29
Malaysia	30	23.5	1.28
Thailand	40	32.7	1.22
USA	13	12.7	1.02
Venezuela	63	71.6	0.88
Philippines	30	40.2	0.75
Argentina	62	116.8	0.53
UK	11	20.3	0.54
Brazil	23	89.8	0.26
Indonesia	7	35.8	0.20
Japan	−5	29.4	****

Source: *The Economist*, January 22, 1994, 80.

The table shows the annual return on a portfolio of shares in various stock markets of the world over a period from 1989 to 1993. The table also shows the risk, measured as the standard deviation of the return, over this period.

The first table is ranked in order of % return. Return being measured as dividend plus capital gain or loss over the period. The second table show these returns adjusted for risk.

Note that the relation between risk and return is not linear over the period but, in most cases, a high return is associated with a high risk. The emerging markets provided a higher return than the UK but had the same associated risk.

WHAT ARE THE KEY VARIABLES IN THE DIRECT FOREIGN INVESTMENT MODEL?

The following questions need to be asked before a company decides to make a direct investment in a foreign country:

1. What increase in "incremental" demand for the products of the company will result from the foreign investment?
2. At what price, in terms of foreign currency, can the goods or services be sold in the foreign market? What is the price elasticity of demand for the product in the foreign market?
3. What are the fixed cost and variable costs of production in the foreign market at various levels of output?
4. What is the full cost of the investment? How much of this cost can be recovered if the project fails? What proportion of the cost of the investment can be bought in the foreign country and how much needs to be imported? Imported from where? What grants and tax concessions can be negotiated with the government in the foreign country?
5. What are the working capital requirements for the foreign project? Will these requirements be very different from the requirement in the home country? For example, must higher levels of inventory be maintained to service production because of increased distance from suppliers?
6. What is the expected future rate of inflation in the foreign country? How disruptive would a high rate of inflation be to production and sales abroad? How will the predicted rate of inflation impact on the exchange rate between the home and the foreign currency?
7. What is the cost of funds in the foreign country? What proportion of these funds can be raised locally and what proportion must be imported from abroad? How has the cost of funds moved in recent years in the foreign country?
8. Is this investment project likely to be a permanent project or a capital venture with a fixed life? If the lifetime is short what is the likely terminal value of the project?
9. What are the exchange control regulations in this country? What are the rules regarding repatriation of profits from this country? Are these rules applied rigorously?
10. How stable is the exchange rate between the foreign and home currency? Are devices such as forward markets, options and swaps available in the foreign country or elsewhere to hedge exchange rate risk?
11. How stable is the government of the country in which the investment is to be made? What is the political risk index attached to this country by political risk assessors?
12. What tax rates and regulations are imposed on the profits made by companies in the foreign country? Are any subsidies available to encourage foreign investment? What is the with-holding tax rate on dividends?

    The above set of questions presents a formidable list of things that need to be found out before a foreign direct investment can be properly assessed, yet it represents only a fraction of the facts that need to be garnered by an investment team before a decision can be taken to make a foreign investment.

    Most of the remainder of this chapter is devoted to examining one particular question, namely "is direct investment in a foreign country riskier than direct investment in the home country?"

IS FOREIGN INVESTMENT RISKIER THAN HOME INVESTMENT?

The traditional view of foreign direct investment is that this type of investment is riskier than investment in the home country. The main differential factor is knowledge, a company knows more about local conditions than conditions in a foreign country. In Chapter 1 we listed the many factors that differentiate foreign operations from operations at home, factors such as currency, level of interest rates, rates of tax, the law, exchange controls, culture and customs.

In recent years the traditional view that foreign investment is riskier than home investment has been questioned. It is now claimed that foreign direct investment actually "reduces" the risk attached to the overall cash flows of a multinational company. How can this be?

The incremental risk added to the earnings of a company undertaking a direct foreign investment can be measured in much the same way as one can measure the risk added to the current earnings of the company by introducing a new product or project onto the market.

A new product can diversify the existing product portfolio of a company in such a way that it reduces the variance on the income from the product portfolio. The new product can help to stabilize the earnings of a company and so reduce the "beta" or risk attached to the earnings figure.[1]

Much of the research that found that foreign trading and investment actually reduces the risk attached to the earnings of a company worldwide was conducted and published in the 1970s.

Rugman (1975), after adjusting for several factors, found that the share price of US companies with a higher than average percentage of foreign sales was less volatile than companies with a lower percentage of foreign sales.[2]

Agmon and Lessard (1977) found that the shares of multinational companies with a high fraction of foreign sales enjoyed lower betas than companies with a low fraction of their sales being sold abroad.[3] For example, firms with 1% to 7% of foreign sales had betas averaging 1.04. Firms with 42% to 62% of foreign sales had betas averaging 0.88. As one would expect companies with a high fraction of foreign sales tend to invest more abroad.

The basic cause of this apparent anomaly is the lack of correlation between the growth rates of the different countries of the world. Whereas local sales are falling during a recession in one country the sales in some other country are booming. It is true that the growth rates of the economies of the advanced industrial countries are auto-correlated (correlated through time) but the rise and fall in economic activity do not coincide in time. If the US economy is booming in 1994 the boom may not reach Europe until 12 to 18 months later.

Madura (1995) provides the correlation matrix shown in Table 21 for stock market movements in four major industrialized countries for the years 1972 to 1992.[4]

These are low correlations and demonstrate that when one economy is booming or in slump another major economy may be enjoying or suffering from quite different economic conditions.

When this low correlation between the growth pattern of different countries is plugged into the model of foreign investment the result reduces the variance on the income stream of the multinational company whose income is diversified over many countries.

Table 21

	Canada	Japan	USA	UK
Canada	1.00			
Japan	0.42	1.00		
USA	0.57	0.42	1.00	
UK	0.51	0.45	0.55	1.00

This reduction in the earnings variance reduces the "beta" on the quoted shares of the company, which, in turn, reduces the cost of funds to the company.

A contrary view, however, was expressed by Jacquillat and Solnick (1978). They found that the betas of home companies did not differ much from MNCs of the same size. Mainstream opinion seems to favour Agmon and Lessard[5] and later studies which support their position.

AN ILLUSTRATION OF THE BENEFITS OF FOREIGN INVESTMENT

Let us suppose that a UK company called ARC PLC with a market capitalization of £80 million is considering investing a further £20 million either in a new product for the UK market or into starting up a new French subsidiary. Funds are not available for financing both ventures. Only one of the two ventures can be undertaken.

The risk–income profile of each of these investment opportunities is set out below.

Some Key Facts About the Two Projects

The portfolio of projects run by the existing business has managed to achieve a net of tax return on capital of 25% per annum in recent years. The variability of this return, as measured by the standard deviation, is 0.07.

The risk–return profiles of the two new projects are shown in Table 22.

The return expected on the new UK project is estimated to have a correlation of around 0.9 with the return on the existing UK projects. The return expected on the French project is estimated to have a correlation of only 0.3 with the average returns on the UK projects.

Table 22

	Return (% per annum)	Standard deviation
New product launch in UK	30	0.15
Investment in French subsidiary	30	0.18

Discussion

The estimated returns on both projects are estimated to exceed the average net of tax returns on existing projects by a substantial margin, 30% p.a. against 25% p.a., however, the specific risks attached to these new projects might cancel out this apparent advantage.

What impact will each project have on the risk–return profile of the company as a whole?

Solution

The overall expected after tax return of the existing UK projects plus either of the new projects is:

$$(0.80 \times 0.25) + (0.20 \times 0.30) = 26\%.$$

If risk is ignored then taking on either project would appear to increase the overall returns of the company. However, the returns cannot be viewed as equal once risk is included in the equation. The standard deviation on the income from the UK project is 15% against a projected standard deviation on the French project income of around 18%.

From these figures it might be assumed that the UK project is to be preferred since it provides the same return as the French project and is less risky. This approach, which is the traditional approach with regard to foreign investment, ignores the projected correlation through time between the rates of growth in the UK and France.

When this correlation factor is inserted into the investment equation the result is as follows:

$$\text{Variance on UK project} = (V_e{}^{\wedge 2} \times S_e{}^{\wedge 2}) + (V_n{}^{\wedge 2} \times S_n{}^{\wedge 2}) + (2 \times V_e \times V_n \times S_e \times S_n \times C_{uk}).$$

Where:

Variance = the risk attached to the total income of the company after including the new venture.

V_e = the % of current UK investment in the total company

S_e = the standard deviation on the income from current UK investment

V_n = the % of total investment made up of new investment

S_n = the standard deviation on the income of the new UK investment

C_{uk} = the correlation between the year on year return on the new UK investment and the existing UK investment

The total risk attached to the return on existing investments plus the new UK investment is thus:

$$R = ((0.80)^{\wedge 2} \times (0.07)^{\wedge 2}) + ((0.20)^{\wedge 2} \times (0.15)^{\wedge 2})$$

$$+ (2 \times (0.80) \times (0.20) \times (0.07) \times (0.15) \times (0.90))$$

Variance on total return = 0.00706

If we apply the same equation to the French project the result turns out to be:

$$R = ((0.80)^{\wedge 2} \times (0.07)^{\wedge 2} + (0.20)^{\wedge 2} \times (0.18)^{\wedge 2})$$
$$+ (2 \times (0.80) \times (0.20) \times (0.07) \times (0.18) \times (0.30))$$
$$R = 0.006080$$

The overall variability of income generated by the existing UK investment plus the French project is around 20% lower than the variability of the income of the existing UK investment plus the new UK project since:

$$(1 - (0.005642/0.00706)) = 1 - 80\% = 20\%$$

We conclude that the risk–return profile of both projects suggests that if the company can only choose one project it should choose the French project. The French project provides the same return as the UK project but reduces the overall risk attached to the income of the multinational company.

The key to the success of the French project lies in the assumed lower correlation of only 0.3 between the annual rate of growth in the UK and France in each year over the period of the project. This low correlation has a substantial impact on the overall risk attached to the income of ARC when the project is plugged into the total investment portfolio of the company.

WHAT COST OF CAPITAL SHOULD BE USED AS THE HURDLE RATE IN THE FOREIGN INVESTMENT DECISION?

When an investment project is contemplated the cost of funds is an important determinant of the investment decision. Will the risk-adjusted returns from the project cover the cost of funds invested in the project?

The cost of funds is conventionally measured as the weighted average of the cost of capital (WACC) to the company. Funds can be raised from profits, a new issue of shares, long- and short-term debt and other sources. Under normal conditions the WACC will be applied to all projects undertaken by the company, a cost of funds will not be calculated for each individual project.

This is the conventional view but it may not be appropriate to companies that invest internationally. Shapiro (1993), for example, argues that if the foreign financial market is isolated from the world's major markets or if the foreign investment is of a different risk class to the conventional type undertaken by the company then the cost of funds applied to the foreign project should be adjusted to reflect these differences. Other academics have argued that the appropriate cost of funds is the cost of funds to a similar company in the given foreign market (Stonehill and Stitzel, 1989). It has even been argued that the cost of funds in the home country is the appropriate hurdle rate to use on all investment projects wherever in the world they be undertaken!

Since there appears to be no agreement among academics as to the appropriate hurdle rate to use in assessing foreign projects it may be of interest to review the hurdle rates actually used by multinationals.

Baker (1988) sent a questionnaire to 435 MNCs asking about their investment procedures. He received 125 usable returns.

Table 23

	US firms	European firms
WACC (Company wide)	42	26
Long-term debt (Company-wide rate)	6	20
Long-term debt (Local rate)	6	17
Long- and short-term debt (Company wide)	8	14
Long- and short-term debt (Local)	6	18
Other rates	35	29
Total	103	124

The results were as follows. Eighty-three per cent made some use of IRR in assessing foreign projects and 66% made some use of the NPV approach. These firms were then asked what discount rate they used in foreign projects. The answers were as shown in Table 23.

We conclude that a wide range of methods seem to be used by MNCs when calculating the cost of funds to apply to foreign projects; in practice there is little unanimity on the best approach. Company-wide WACC seems to be the more popular method especially among US multinationals.

There is one exception to this rule. If a foreign project has access to "cheap" funds that are unique to the project, funds, for example, from a development bank in the foreign country, then most analysts agree that this cheap source of funds should be used as the appropriate cost of funds for the project.

Diversified multinationals may prefer to use the CAPM[6] approach to measuring the required cost of funds. An appropriate "beta" can be found from among quoted companies in the foreign market whose output and structure are similar to the foreign subsidiary.

Baker also asked the same group of multinationals how they adjusted the return on the foreign project for risk. The answers provided were as shown in Table 24.

Most of the companies in the survey used more than one method to adjust for risk thus the above figures sum to more than 100%.

Table 24

	US firms %	European firms %
Shorten the payback period	34	55
Increase the discount rate	38	45
Decrease future cash flows	19	36
Increase accounting ROR	16	18
Other methods	57	24

A wide range of alternative methods of adjusting for risk were mentioned. Some examples of these methods were increasing the size of the dividend distribution from risky projects, using sensitivity analysis to identify the key risk variables that needed to be hedged, using Monte Carlo simulation to find the shape of the risk distribution on the project return and using a Delphi approach to the same end by getting managers to estimate a three point probability distribution on key variables.

Once again no single best method predominated. This has been the finding in other studies on risk assessment methods in investment.

HEDGING THE RISKS INVOLVED IN FOREIGN INVESTMENT

Whatever the method used for measuring the risk attached to foreign investment and adjusting the return for this risk all analysts agree that an attempt should be made to eliminate or at least minimize the risks attached to a specific foreign project if this is feasible.

Diversification of the investment portfolio is not the only approach to hedging the risks involved in foreign investment. Many devices are available for hedging the risks attaching to specific foreign ventures.

The more common risks encountered in foreign ventures are:

> Country and political risk
> Technological risk
> Exchange rate and inflation risk
> Cost and pricing risk
> Credit risk

Some of these risks will be related to one another. For example, political risk can obviously influence exchange rate, cost and credit risk.

Some of the methods available for hedging these risks are discussed below.

Political Risk: Engaging Government Support

Most governments are keen to support the export of goods and services by local companies and some, but by no means all, foreign governments are keen to encourage inward investment.

Many governments throughout the world have set up institutions such as the ECGD in the UK and Hermes in Germany to assist exporters by providing insurance cover for risks which may not be adequately covered by the private sector. Risks such as the risk of expropriation of assets by a foreign government, the temporary freezing of the funds of a subsidiary company by the foreign exchange control authority, severe limitations being placed on the repatriation of profits to the home country or artificial exchange rates or high with-holding taxes being imposed on repatriated funds. Government intervention of this sort is much less common today than it was in the past but state sponsored insurance against such risks is still offered in many countries.

The government of the USA sponsors the EXport IMport bank, the UK the Export Credits Guarantee Department (ECGD), Japan has MITI and JEXIM, France has

COFACE and Germany has HERMES. The activities of these government sponsored organisations have been much reduced since the mid-1980s but they are still active in certain sectors of the export market.

Any company investing abroad should take full advantage of these subsidized forms of insurance that provide cover at a reasonable cost against the many kinds of political and country risks that lurk in politically unstable countries abroad.

Before a foreign investment is set up in a politically unstable country it may be that the investing company can use these government sponsored organizations to absorb a substantial fraction of the investment risk at relatively low cost to themselves.

We will discuss these matters further in Chapter 9.

Political Risk: Local Participation

Political risk, as we noted in the previous paragraph, usually expresses itself in the form of government intervention in the investment process.

One popular method of discouraging government intervention is to invite local companies and local citizens to join in the foreign venture via equity participation. This is the classic hedge against government interference in a foreign investment project. If the partner in the foreign venture is the government itself this makes negative intervention by the government even less likely.

Another way of hedging the political risk attached to a foreign project is to raise funds for the project in the local capital market. This hedging technique is particularly apposite if the funds are raised in the form of debt since debt finance provides a hedge against both unexpected local inflation and appropriation or other form of intervention by government. However, many governments in developing economies will only allow a foreign company to invest locally if a substantial proportion of the funds invested in the venture are brought in from abroad. There are also rules against "thin capitalization" of foreign ventures being used to repatriate funds out of the country.[7]

A company investing in an underdeveloped economy can improve its local image somewhat if it makes the maximum use of local labour and other local resources. The foreign subsidiary may be able to maximise "local content" by using the services of local industries operating in such sectors as construction and transport. Local labour should be trained to take over as many jobs as possible in the project rather than importing trained foreign workers.

The basic objective must be to show the government of the foreign country that the management board of the investing company has the interests of the foreign country at heart and is not simply a "carpet-bagger" out to extract as much money as possible from the foreign country in the fastest possible time.

By adopting such a policy a multinational company can provide itself with a strong hedge against government intervention in the investment process.

Exchange Rate Risk: Hedging Foreign Currency Flows

Every foreign investment project is exposed to the risk of unexpected changes in exchange rates. Substantial changes in exchange rates are likely to be associated with high relative inflation in either the foreign or the home country.

Chapter 5 discussed the many devices that are available to a finance officer for hedging exchange rate risk. We shall not repeat our discussion of these devices here. The reader will recall that the devices available external to the firm are forwards, foreign loans, futures, options and swaps. All of these devices are not available for hedging the cash flows of every foreign venture, particularly when the investment is in an emerging or underdeveloped country, but some form of hedging device is almost certainly available, at least in the short term.

In recent years hedging devices called "synthetic derivatives" have been devised by operatives who work in the option markets of leading financial centres. Synthetic derivatives mimic hedging devices that are desired but not currently available on the currency markets of the world. "Synthetics" can sometimes be manufactured to hedge currency flows in currencies that lack adequate hedging markets of their own.

We conclude that currency flows, even from developing countries, can usually be hedged by conventional means but if not then "synthetics" may be available to solve the problem.

Technological and Cost Risk: Hedging Via the Law

One company often employs another specialist company to conduct a survey of a foreign investment project, say the construction of a dam or the extraction of gold from a difficult site in inhospitable terrain. Under these circumstances, if the conclusions of the survey are found to be very inaccurate, the investing company can sue the survey company for damages in the courts.

Companies such as Bechtel, the giant US survey company, carry heavy insurance to cover themselves against this type of risk. The cost of the insurance is added to the survey fee. The conclusions of survey companies are usually somewhat conservative for this reason.

Such cost guarantees provide a useful method of covering exposure to certain types of foreign investment risk, particularly technological risks, which may be difficult to cover in any other way. For example, the survey company might estimate a project cost of US$300 million based on a given extraction process. If the process is found not to work under the given conditions the company making the foreign investment who has employed the services of the survey company can sue for the additional cost.

A similar situation occurs when a company subcontracts a part of the work on a foreign project using a fixed price contract. This is particularly appropriate if the part of the contract that is subcontracted encompasses a process in which the investing company is not experienced. If the subcontractor fails to perform as contracted, or the cost of the part subcontracted rises well above what is expected, either the investing company can sue or the subcontractor must pay the additional cost himself.

Pricing Risk: Hedging the Future Price of the Product

In most investment projects the return on the project is very sensitive to a variation in the price of the product produced by the project. For example the price of gold is almost invariably the "key variable" in gold extraction projects. Unfortunately it is exceedingly difficult to hedge the "long-term" future price of a product in a free market.

Long-term fixed price contracts for any product are hard to come by. The best that can be achieved is a "ratchet" price contract which allows the price to vary by only a fixed percentage from period to period (following the trend of the free market price).

For short periods of time commodity "futures" and "option" contracts are available to fix the future price at which the raw material is sold or bought, but such devices seldom extend beyond one or two years at most.

Many attempts have been made in the past to fix or hedge the future price of raw material products for long periods ahead. This has been attempted with products as diverse as sugar, oil and gold, but all such attempts have failed unless the producer was a monopolist or monopsonist. The US government managed to fix the price of gold at US$35 an ounce from 1935 up to the late 1960s.

Price fixing in a free market is not really feasible since alternative sources are found or substitute products are developed if the free market price of the product rises above its historical trend line.

We conclude that, in a free market, the fixing or hedging of the long-term price of a product or service is not feasible. Price fixing or hedging the price in the short term of one or two years ahead is feasible via derivatives.

Hedging the Credit Risk

The risk of non-payment by the buyer for goods or services received from the seller is always possible if the goods are sold on credit. The credit risk is increased if the credit is given to a buyer living abroad since it is more difficult for an exporter to take legal proceedings against a debtor living within a foreign legal jurisdiction.

For this reason, as we noted above, many governments run export support agencies to provide credit insurance to cover the risk of default by a foreign buyer. In the case of the UK the ECGD no longer provides credit guarantees on short-term credit, this aspect of credit insurance, previously offered by the ECGD, has been privatized and taken over by a Dutch company called NCM. However, the risks attached to medium- and long-term credit sales by a UK company, particularly credit offered to foreign buyers of large contracts, are still covered by the ECGD. A similar situation exists in most major industrial countries.

When an export contract is agreed with a buyer resident in a developed country insuring the deal is not a major problem. Private credit rating agencies and credit insurance companies are on hand to assist the exporter in hedging the credit risk involved. Insurance cover for credit sales to underdeveloped and emerging economies is harder to come by. Private credit agencies in the home country may not be prepared to provide credit insurance on such risky contracts "at a reasonable cost".

If a government sponsored credit agency cannot or will not cover these risky credit sales the exporter will need to insist on pre-payment or for the importer to provide a documentary letter of credit or to enter into a "forfaiting" agreement or suchlike. Both of these legal forms are guaranteed by a bank who guarantee that payment will be received on the due date or at least before the goods are delivered to the buyer. The various payment systems such as "letters of credit" and "forfaiting" are described in some detail in Chapter 9. In both cases international banks will normally be expected to provide the ultimate credit guarantee on payment.

This completes our discussion of the methods available for hedging foreign investment risk. Later in this chapter we will apply some of these methods to an actual case study.

ASSESSING COUNTRY RISK

We have already discussed some of the risks attached to investing in a foreign country. All foreign countries do not suffer from the same degree of what has come to be known as "country risk". This means that the projected risk-adjusted return on a foreign investment project will be effected to some degree by the risk attached to specific country where the project takes place.

Exhibit 6.2 illustrates the rate of return that would have been received on a portfolio of equity shares invested in the stock markets of a range of countries over the period January 1, 1989 to December 31, 1993.

The return, not adjusted for risk, varies from 63% per annum in the case of Venezuela to a loss of 5% per annum in the case of Japan. The return is measured as the dividend received in each year plus or minus any change in the market value of the particular share in that year.

Clearly, there is a wide variation in the return achieved from a portfolio of shares invested in each of these countries over this period.

The worth of an investment cannot, however, be measured by this annual return alone, the risk attached to the return must also be taken into consideration. An adjustment for risk, measured as the standard deviation on the return, is provided in Exhibit 6.2. In most cases a high relative return is correlated to a higher relative risk, but the relation is not absolute. Investment in the emerging market portfolio provides a risk equal to that in the UK portfolio but the average return is much higher for emerging markets, at 33% per annum, compared to only 11% p.a. from the UK portfolio.

These figures apply to the shorter period of 1989 to 1993. Earlier or later periods or a longer run of figures might provide a very different result.

These figures are provided simply to emphasize the point that the return and the associated risk vary between markets and that a high return from a country need not necessarily be cancelled by the associated risk.

We conclude that a finance officer who is considering investing in a foreign country needs to take into account the "country risk" involved in this investment. Just how risky is this country compared to others for the purpose of investment?

How is "Country Risk" Measured?

Several agencies provide regular measures of country risk. Some of these agencies are listed in Appendix 6.1 at the end of this chapter.

The *Euromoney* index of country risk, which is published regularly in that magazine, selects a number of criteria and then weights them to arrive at an average figure which provides a single index of country risk.

Exhibit 6.3 provides a sample of countries taken from the *Euromoney* 1993 "country risk" index.

The *Euromoney* index uses two "analytical indicators", namely economic performance

Exhibit 6.3 A Sample from the *Euromoney* Political Risk Index

Country	Total risk	Economic performance	Political risk	Credit rating	Access to capital markets	Access to short-term finance
Maximum score	100	25	25	10	5	5
USA	96.74	25.00	21.74	10.00	5.00	5.00
Netherlands	96.38	22.10	24.28	10.00	5.00	5.00
Switzerland	95.73	21.14	25.00	10.00	5.00	5.00
France	95.55	21.28	24.28	10.00	5.00	5.00
Germany	95.21	20.57	24.64	10.00	5.00	5.00
Singapore	94.39	24.19	22.26	9.23	5.00	3.75
UK	94.20	22.64	21.56	10.00	5.00	5.00
Japan	93.80	20.66	23.14	10.00	5.00	5.00
Malaysia	80.43	22.67	21.15	6.15	3.50	2.75
South Africa	60.25	12.63	15.28	0.00	4.50	2.25
India	55.39	12.61	14.68	2.13	2.50	1.25
Pakistan	47.34	12.33	11.05	0.00	2.00	1.00
Brazil	47.19	11.32	10.85	0.19	1.50	2.00
Zaire	23.44	2.43	1.78	0.00	0.50	0.25
Ukraine	22.73	6.16	5.07	0.00	1.00	0.50
Korea, North	19.02	2.09	5.43	0.00	0.00	1.50
Afghanistan	14.87	0.00	3.62	0.00	1.00	0.25
Cuba	10.52	5.81	3.21	0.00	0.00	1.50

Source: *Euromoney*, March 1994, 178–80.

The total "country risk" is calculated from a weighted index of various risk factors such as economic performance, political risk, debt default risk, credit ratings derived from credit agencies and access to various forms of international finance.

The table only provides a sample of the factors considered and the countries analysed.

and political risk, two measures of the national debt position of the country, a credit rating index based on the average of Moodie's and Standard and Poor's credit indices, and four measures of the degree to which the country has adequate access to sources of international finance. Each of these measures is given a weight varying from 25 to 5 and the results are averaged to arrive at a composite "country risk index", that can vary between 100 and 0.

In the case of the index for 1993 shown in Exhibit 6.3 the USA scored the highest ranking and so, at 96.74, was awarded the lowest risk. Cuba scored the lowest ranking (highest risk), being awarded an index score of only 10.52.

However, Cuba was not awarded the lowest ranking on all counts. Cuba was awarded a higher score on "access to short term finance" than 13 other countries on the list and a better score on "discount on forfaiting" than seven other countries.

The organization called Political Risk Services "provides a systematic process whereby country risk analysis can be calculated into probabilities for specific outcomes".[8]

This index is based on the "Prince" model designed by W. Coplin and M. O'Leary. The model identifies the key "players" influencing the outcome of events such as political parties, trade unions, individual leaders, military groups and so on. The model assesses the impact of changes in these entities on such things as stable government, investment restrictions, exchange controls and export credit risk.

The model asks three questions about the player's attitude to an outcome. For example, with regard to a possible restriction on remittance of dividend from the country the model would ask (1) "Does the player support or oppose the outcome?" (2) "How much power does the player have with regard to this decision?" (3) "How important is this decision to the given player?"

The model now weights the players according to their importance and strength of feeling and translates these factors into a probability measure which can be attached to the outcome occurring.

The inputs to the model are supplied by a team of international experts in politics, economists, etc.

PRS, via ICRG, also publishes a monthly "Country risk guide", which includes a ranking of 130 countries. The ranking is based on 13 political factors, six economic factors and five financial factors. The composite ranking is calculated from a weighted average, 50% political, 25% financial, 25% economic.

The Economic Intelligence Unit (EIU) publishes regular reports on 82 countries worldwide. The EIU runs a network of analysts who are resident in each country and these analysts feed important political, economic or social changes into the centre in London. The quarterly reports on individual countries are based on global assumptions regarding the growth of world trade, commodity prices, exchange rates, interest rates etc. The reports evaluate such things as economic and political stability, level of corruption, amount of bureaucracy and investment potential.

The Institute of International Finance (IIF) evaluates the country risk of non-OECD countries for commercial banks. These regular reports provide data on the financial flows, the debt servicing ability and the creditworthiness of the countries surveyed. The institute evaluates each country from the point of view of a financial institution. Current sources of finance to each country are listed.

S.J. Rundt Associates publish regular reports on export credit risk, exchange rate forecasts and country risk indices for a wide range of countries. Reports are published weekly, monthly, four monthly and annually.

The reports cover such things as changes in exchange control regulations, exporter's recent experiences in various countries, availability of export insurance, likely changes in exchange rates and other related matters.

The risk indices provided by SJR can be "customized" to meet the specific needs of the client. For example, clients who deal mainly with government departments can assign a higher weight to political stability or bureaucracy.

Multinational Strategies (MNS) provide risk measures on individual projects. They also advise companies how to create their own country risk assessment measures. They claim that "Countries don't have risk, projects do". MNS is willing to tackle the difficult job of assessing the degree of risk attached to non-standard projects with unusual attributes.

All of the above institutes provide impartial objective advice on foreign projects that are not biased by the specific subjective attitudes of the company making the investment.

Nagy (1990) describes how to build a country risk index.[9]

Case Study: The Kandywood Project

Let us now carry out a risk assessment on a foreign venture being considered by a company called Highland Woodproducts PLC, a UK company that operates in the "special woods" industry and sells its products mainly to Europe and Japan.

Highland Woodproducts PLC, a UK company with extensive investments in forest products in Scotland and Canada, have been searching for a source of "special" woods for some time. These woods are needed to complete a full portfolio of the different types of woods supplied by the company to European and Japanese markets.

"Special woods" are only available in a few countries in South East Asia and South America and are currently in short supply.

In 1988 a forestry expert discovered a wooded valley in an island in Central Indonesia that contained many of the trees that provide special woods. The trees were standing in substantial groups suitable for felling. Unfortunately the extraction area is found to be extremely inaccessible and the cost of building sufficient roads etc into the area to extract the wood is considered to be prohibitive. The rivers are considered as a possible outlet but they suffer from many cataracts and so are not suited to floating the logs downstream. The local name of the valley translates as "Kandywood" so the project is entitled the "Kandywood" project.

Highland's initial interest in the Kandywood project is abandoned in 1990 after receiving a cost estimate from Kando, a Korean construction firm, on the likely cost of constructing roads out from the site to the coast.

In 1992 Alex Dury, the MD of Highland, reads a report in *Time* magazine about the introduction of reinforced helium airships, which, it is claimed, can be used to transport raw materials out from inaccessible regions of the world.

Dury asks his engineering department to look into the possibility of using airships to extract wood products from the Kandywood site in Indonesia. The subsequent report reaches a positive conclusion. However, the report only examines the technical feasibility of the project. The financial viability of the project is not considered.

Dury's next step is to ask the Finance Director of Highland to rough out a cash flow statement on the project in consultation with the marketing, production and engineering departments.

The Finance Director, William Hallam, chooses Richard Hardaker MBA, ACA, a qualified accountant who has recently returned from taking an MBA at a leading UK business school, to undertake the difficult job of estimating the cash flows from the project.

Hardaker flies to the USA where he interviews the company called "Transair", which is building and leasing the airships. He finds that the directors of Transair are keen to participate in the project since it would seem to open up a huge potential market for the airships if the Kandywood extraction process is successful. Transair offer to lease the airships at half the normal price for the term of the Kandywood contract.

Hardaker now flies to Jakarta in Indonesia where he hires a helicopter to visit the remote Kandywood valley. He finds a long green heavily forested valley with many flat sites, which seem suited to being converted into airship ports. The valley is surrounded by high rocky hills which would make road access difficult and expensive.

Hardaker next visits the Projects section of the Ministry of Economic Development in Indonesia. The department is enthusiastic about the project because it would bring work into an area that has been, up till now, very underdeveloped. The Minister suggests a project tax regime under which Highlands would pay an annual royalty to the Indonesian government of 20% of the market value of the wood extracted from Kandywood plus a corporate tax rate at 20% of the annual operating net cash flow. No withholding taxes will be imposed on dividends, interest or "know-how" charges. A tax holiday on the annual corporate tax charge is offered for six years from initial start-up. This latter concession is made to encourage rapid development of the project.

Hardaker now flies on to Vancouver, Canada, where he interviews the timber extraction consultants "Timbercon". Timbercon agree to advise on the technical side of felling, cutting and extracting wood from the remote site. A topic on which they are considered to be the world's most experienced firm.

Hardaker returns to the UK and spends a month preparing his report for the Finance Director of Highland. His final cash flow estimates and a sensitivity analysis matrix on the yield on the project are set out in Exhibits 6.4(a) and (b).

Some additional notes prepared by Hardaker are appended as Exhibit 6.4(c)

Hardaker identifies three main problems which need to be solved:

1. The key risks attached to this project need to be identified. Methods of "hedging" these risks must be worked out, if they can be hedged.
2. The impact on the return of any changes in the value of the main project variables need to be assessed. Changes to variables such as price, budgeted output of wood, exchange rates, costs, etc.
3. The best method of financing the project needs to be worked out. How much funding is needed? When is it needed? From which lender and in which currency?

Hardaker hands over the project report to the Finance Director, Mr Hallam, who immediately sets up a small team of experts from the production, marketing and finance staff to review Hardaker's report. The review team is required to make recommendations as to the financial viability of the Kandywood project, to identify any key problems that Mr Hardaker may have overlooked and to consider how to finance the project.

Required: Assume you are a member of this review team. Identify the key risks involved in the project. Suggest how these risks might be hedged. How should the project be financed? In what currency? In your opinion is the project a viable project for Highland Woodproducts?

A suggested solution to these questions is appended to this chapter.

WHAT HAVE WE LEARNED IN THIS CHAPTER?

1. Foreign investment can take the form of "direct" investment or "portfolio" investment. Most foreign investment by MNCs takes the form of "direct" investment.
2. A company invests abroad for many reasons but the main reasons are to find new markets for its products and to diversify its markets.
3. Investing abroad introduces several new variables to the investment model. Variables such as exchange rates, exchange controls, differential interest rates and novel tax

Exhibit 6.4(a) Estimated Cash Flows from the Kandywood Project (£'000)

Item	1995	1996	1997	1998	1999	2000	2001	2002	2003	2004	2005	2006	2007	2008	2009	2010	Totals £'000
Output (000 blocks)	0	0	0	0	0	4	14	22	30	24	18	14	10	8	6	4	154
Price per block: US$	400	400	400	400	400	400	400	400	400	400	400	400	400	400	400	400	
Exchange rate: $ per £	1.8	1.8	1.8	1.8	1.8	1.8	1.8	1.8	1.8	1.8	1.8	1.8	1.8	1.8	1.8	1.8	
Sales: gross cash flow	0	0	0	0	0	889	3111	4889	6667	5333	4000	3111	2222	1778	1333	889	34222
Costs: capital																	
Exploration (£)	180	260	310	220													970
Prelim cutting (R)	70	120	140	80													410
Construction (Y)			100	850	1000	520	40										2510
Airship (US$)			50	60	20	180	110	120									540
Other equipment (Y)		200	120	140	80	90											630
Airship port (R)	70	230	240			30											570
Total capital cost	320	810	960	1350	1100	820	150	120	0	0	0	0	0	0	0	0	5630
Costs: operating																	
Wages (30% £, 70% RUP)							22	76	119	162	130	97	76	54	43	32	811
Maintenance (30% £, 70% R)							9	30	48	65	52	39	30	22	17	13	325
Fuel (US$)							6	23	36	49	39	29	23	16	13	10	244
Insurance (£)							4	15	24	32	26	19	15	11	9	6	161
Other (R)							2	8	12	16	13	10	8	5	4	3	81
Total operating costs	0	0	0	0	0	0	43	152	239	324	260	194	152	108	86	64	1622
Total cost	320	810	960	1350	1100	820	193	272	239	324	260	194	152	108	86	64	7252
Net cash flow	−320	−810	−960	−1350	−1100	69	2918	4617	6428	5009	3740	2917	2070	1670	1247	825	26970
Royalty (20% of sales value)						14	584	923	1286	1002	748	583	414	334	249	165	6302
Company tax (20% of NCF-royalty)									1028	801	598	467	331	267	200	132	3825
Total government tax	0	0	0	0	0	14	584	923	2314	1803	1346	1050	745	601	449	297	10127
Company net cash flow	−320	−810	−960	−1350	−1100	55	2334	3694	4114	3206	2394	1867	1325	1069	798	528	16843

Exhibit 6.4(b) Sensitivity Matrix Showing Yield on the Investment on Kandywood Products Under Various Assumptions

Variable	% Change in the variable								
	− 50	− 20	− 10	− 5	0	+ 5	+ 10	+ 20	+ 50
					Yield %				
Output	12.1	22.6	25.4	26.8	28	29.2	30.4	32.6	44
Price per block	12.1	22.6	25.4	26.8	28	29.2	30.4	32.6	44

	% Change in the variable								
	+ 50	+ 20	+ 10	+ 5	0	− 5	− 10	− 20	− 50
					Yield %				
Exchange rate	19	24	26	27	28	29	31	34	38
Capital cost	19	24	26	27	28	29	31	34	38
Operating cost	27.6	27.9	28	28	28	28.1	28.1	28.2	28.5
Royalty %	25.2	26.9	27.5	27.8	28	28.3	28.6	29.1	30.6
Company tax %	26.5	27.5	27.8	27.9	28	28.2	28.3	28.6	29.4

The table shows the impact on the yield from the project if a given variable is changed by a given percentage.

The "best estimate" of the yield is 28% per annum. Each variable is changed by percentages varying between − 50% and + 50%.

Only one variable is changed at a time, the other variables remain unchanged. This may not be a realistic assumption. Often a change in one variable will trigger a change in another variable. For example, if the US$ falls against all other currencies, including the £ sterling, this may trigger a rise in the US$ price of special woods.

With reference to exchange rates it is assumed that only the US$ to £ sterling exchange rate is important, thus other exchange rates will not affect the yield significantly.

Exhibit 6.4(c) Some Additional Notes on the Kandywood Project

1. An estimate of the future price of woodblocks.

(a) Probability of this average price	(b) Unit price per block (US$)	(c) (a) × (b) US$
0.1	275	27.5
0.1	325	32.5
0.2	375	75.0
0.3	425	127.5
0.2	475	95.0
0.1	525	52.5

Expected average price of blocks in US$ = 410.0

The price chosen for insertion into the model is US$400 per block.

The figures are based on the Timbercon best estimates.

The price per block for special woods has varied between US$240 and US$500 over the last 10 years. The trend is towards increasing price, especially in the Japanese market.

2. Cost of funds

The worldwide cost of funds to Highlands Woodproducts is estimated to be 12% net of tax, 15% gross of tax.

3. The CAPM return

The CAPM model of stock exchange pricing suggests that the shareholders of Highland Woodproducts are expecting an average return on all projects of around 25% per annum given the risk attached to this share.

Signed: *Richard Hardaker*

systems. Foreign investment is a good deal more complicated than investment at home.

4. Prior to the 1970s it was assumed that foreign investment must a good deal more risky than home investment and a "risk premium" must be added to the required return from foreign investment to compensate for this risk. In recent years academic research has found that foreign investment may actually reduce the risk attached to the cash flow of an MNC by diversifying the cash flow over many disparate economies.

5. The cost of funds that should be charged against a foreign investment project is a subject of much controversy. A company-wide WACC seems to be the most commonly used method of costing funds but in special circumstances this rate is not appropriate.

6. Foreign investments are subject to a wide range of specific risks. Risks such as country or political risk, exchange rate and inflation risk, credit risk, technological risk plus the conventional cost and pricing risks. Over the years finance officers and others have devised methods of hedging most of these specific risks.

7. Country risk, which includes political risk, is so important that several agencies devote their time exclusively to measuring this risk on a regular basis. Their findings are available to international investors, at a price.

8. In order to assess the worth of a foreign investment the investment team of a company must: (a) set out the estimated cash flows; (b) identify the risk factors involved; (c) carry out a sensitivity analysis on the project to identify the key risk factors; (d) work out ways of hedging these risks if this is possible; (e) study the correlation between the return on this project and the companies portfolio of projects; and (f) decide whether the adjusted return on the project justifies the net risk involved in undertaking the project.

NOTES

1. The total risk attached to the return from a company share can be segregated into "specific" risk and "market risk". The "beta" of a company share measures the market risk. The beta claims to measure the difference between the variation in company return relative to the variation in market return over a given period. The viability of the "beta" measure of the risk attached to the return on a share is currently a subject of intense controversy among academic economists.

2. See Rugman, A. R. Foreign operations and the stability of US corporate earnings risk reduction in international operations. *Journal of Finance*, May 1975, 233–6.

3. Agmon, T. and Lessard, D. Investor recognition of corporate international diversification. *Journal of Finance*, September 1977, 1049–56.

4. See Madura, J. *International Financial Management*, West Publishing Co., 1995, p. 490.

5. See Jacquillat, B. and Solnick, B. Multinations are poor tools for diversification. *Journal of Portfolio Management*, Winter 1978, 8–12.

6. Capital asset pricing model.

7. "Thin capitalization" means that a high fraction, say 75%, of the venture is funded by debt. This is a popular tax stratagem for reducing tax on dividends. See Chapter 10 for further discussion of this point.

8. See The risk analysts analysed. *Euromoney*, September 1993, 369.

9. Nagy, P. A. *Country Risk: How to Assess, Quantify and Monitor It*. Euromoney Publications, 1990.

FURTHER READING

Agmon, T. and Lessard, D. (1977) Investor recognition of corporate international diversification. *Journal of Finance*, September, 1049–58.

Baker, J. C. (1988) The cost of capital of multi-national companies. *Management Finance*, Autumn, pp. 12–15.

Eiteman, D., Stonehill, A. and Moffett, M. (1995) *Multinational Business Finance*, Part 6. Addison-Wesley. Part 6 of this book provides a wide-ranging discussion of the problems associated with foreign investment and the possible solutions to these problems.

Errunza, V. and Senbet, L. (1981) The effects of international operations on the market value of the firm: theory and evidence. *Journal of Finance*, May, 401–17.

Eun, C. and Resnick, B. (1984) Estimating the correlation structure of international share prices. *Journal of Finance*, December, 1311–24.

Fosberg, R. and Madura, J. (1991) Risk reduction benefits from international diversification: a re-assessment. *Journal of Multinational Financial Management*, no. 1. 35–42.

Jacquillat, B. and Solnick, B. (1978) MNC's are poor tools for diversification. *Journal of Portfolio Management*, Winter, 8–12.

Lee, S. H. (1993) Relative importance of political instability and economic variables on perceived country creditworthiness. *Journal of International Business Studies*, fourth quarter, 801–12.

Rogers, J. (ed.) (1988) *Risk Assessments: Issues, Concepts and Applications*. Global Risk Assessment Inc.

Rugman, A. (1975) Foreign operations and the stability of US corporate earnings: risk reduction by international diversification. *Journal of Finance*, March, 233–4.

Rummel, R. J. and Heenan, D. A. (1978) How MNC's analyse political risk. *Harvard Business Review*, January–February, 67–76.

Sethi, S. P. and Luthur, K. (1986) Political risk analysis and direct foreign investment. *Californian Management Revue*, Winter, 57–68.

Shao, L. and Shao, A. (1993) Capital budgeting practices employed by European affiliates of US transnational companies. *Journal of Multinational Financial Management*, vol. 3, no. 1/2, 95–109.

Solnick, B. H. (1992) *International Investments*. New York, Addison-Wesley. A rigorous treatment of the subject which emphasizes portfolio investment but is also relevant to direct investment abroad.

Stonehill, A. and Stitzel, T. (1969) Financial structure and multi-national corporations. *California Management Review*, Fall, pp. 91–96.

TUTORIAL QUESTIONS

1. Explain the difference between direct and portfolio investment. What is the objective of each of these types of investment?

2. A company is operating very successfully in its home market. Suggest three reasons why a company in this enviable position may decide to make a direct investment abroad.

3. List five key factors that need to be checked out before a company can make the decision to undertake a foreign investment. These facts would not need to be checked out if the investment was an investment at home.

4. What specific facts will need to be found out about tax and exchange controls?

5. What was the traditional view regarding the risk attached to foreign investment.

6. Why has this view changed? Why is foreign investment now regarded as the method of reducing overall investment risk rather than increasing it?

7. What does the "beta" of a share quoted on an efficient stock exchange actually measure?

8. "The growth rates of industrialized countries are 'auto-correlated' but this does not affect the thesis that diversification of income between different countries reduces the overall risk attached to the total earnings of the multinational company". Explain why this is so.

9. What was the correlation between stock market movements in UK and Japan between 1972 and 1992? Was the correlation of the share indices between UK and Canada greater or less than the correlation between UK and the USA over this period?

10. Provide an example of the income, variance and correlation analysis between two projects. One a home project and one a foreign project.

11. Discuss methods that might be employed to reduce the risks attached to foreign investment by enlisting the support of the local government of the country involved.
12. Foreign governments have been known to interfere with the operation, particularly the financial operation, of foreign subsidiaries located in their country. Suggest four forms of interference that might be employed by foreign governments. How can a company cover itself against this kind of potential government interference in the running of the company?
13. Name four government-sponsored organizations in four different countries which insure unusual risks encountered by exporters from their country. Why does the private sector not insure these risks?
14. What is a "synthetic" derivative? Why is it necessary to devise and use such an exotic device to hedge FX risk on currency flows arising from foreign investments?
15. How can the law be used to hedge risk on a foreign project?
16. Why is it almost impossible to fix the long-term price of a raw material sold in a free market?
17. If an exporter who is making credit sales to a buyer in a developing country cannot find credit insurance in the private sector in his own country what alternatives are available to him?

CASE STUDY: MEGATON PLC

Let us assume that you are the financial director of Megaton PLC a UK quoted company with a market capitalization of £400 million. Your company are considering the possibility of investing £100 million into introducing a new product into the UK market. However, it is suggested by the marketing director that a better option might be to invest the £100 million into a new subsidiary company in the United States because the US market is likely to be an expanding market over the next 10 years.

The risk–income profile of each project is assessed and set out below.

Required: Given the risk–income profile of each project as set out below calculate which option seems to be the better option for Megaton. The better option being the option giving the same return with lower risk to the company. As funds are not available to undertake both projects only one of the projects can be undertaken.

Key Factors on the Risk–Income Profile of Each Project

1. The after tax return on the capital invested in the existing UK business has been 25% per annum on average in recent years.
2. The variability of this return has been 0.07 (standard deviation) in recent years.
3. The risk-income profile of the two suggested options is as shown in Table 25.

Table 25

	Return (%)	Standard deviation
UK new product launch	30	0.12
New subsidiary in USA	30	0.15

Correlation of project returns with UK business:
(a) The correlation of the return on the UK project with average after tax returns of the UK business = 0.8.
(b) The correlation of the return on the US project with average after tax returns of the UK business = 0.3.

CASE STUDY: IZWETAN

Conolo PLC have developed a considerable expertise in underwater oil exploration from their 15 years' experience working in the North Sea. They own four undersea oilwells in the North Sea.

In 1986 Conolo applied to the government of Indonesia for permission to prospect for oil off the coast of Indonesia. In March 1987 a substantial underwater oil field, called the Izwetan field, is discovered and Conolo employ the large US engineering company called Bextel to estimate the cost of developing this oil field.

The financial director of Conolo is asked to provide an investment evaluation of the project to the board of Conolo. The board will meet on October 10, 1996 to decide whether or not to go ahead with the Izwetan project.

One key problem is the future price of oil. This is very difficult to predict but most forecasts are optimistic. Another key consideration is the royalty rate to be applied to the value of the oil extracted. The financial director provides a memo to the board suggesting that, on a world scale, this rate is rather high, he suggests that pressure should be put on the government of Indonesia to reduce it.

The investment evaluation sheet is provided as Exhibit 6.5(a) and a sensitivity analysis sheet on the yield on the project is provided as Exhibit 6.5(b).

Required: Study Exhibits 6.5(a) and (b). Do you consider the Izwetan project to be viable? What are the key risk factors in this investment model? Can you think of ways of hedging the various risks attached to this project? How important are the assumptions about the exchange rates ruling over the period? How important is the level of the royalty rate which is applied to the oil revenues?

1. Would you advise Conolo to put money into this project if you were the financial director of Conolo?
2. Let us suppose that you did go ahead with this project. How would you finance the project? In what currency? When is the finance needed?

Exhibit 6.5(a) The Variables in the Izwetan Evaluation Model

US$ per £ sterling	US$1.49
Annual expected fall in the £ sterling in terms of US$	−5% p.a.
Yen per £ sterling	150 yen
Annual expected fall in the £ sterling in terms of Yen	−5% p.a.
Indonesian rupee per £ sterling 1996	2000
Annual expected rise in the £ sterling in terms of the Indonesian rupee	+5% p.a.
Decrease in volume of oil from budget	×1
Oil price per barrel in US$ 1996	US$16 p.b.
Expected annual increase in oil price	+5% p.a.
Royalty % charged on oil extracted by government of Indonesia	20%
Corporation tax rate in Indonesia	30% of cash flow
Increase in operating cost from budget	×1
Increase in capital cost from budget	×1

The 23% "best estimate" yield in Exhibit 6.5(b) is based on the above assumptions. The other yields are obtained by varying the above figures by the given percentage and leaving all the other figures unchanged.

Exhibit 6.5(b) Sensitivity Analysis of the Yield on the Izwetan Project

					% Change				
Variable % change Foreign currency falls in value	− 50	− 20	− 10	− 5	Best estimate of % yield	+ 5	+ 10	+ 20	+ 50
US$/sterling	6	14	18	20	23	25	27	34	48
Yen/sterling	22	22	22	23	23	23	23	24	24
Rupee/sterling	23	23	23	23	23	23	23	23	23
Price of oil	− 4	13	17	20	23	25	27	32	44
Output of oil	− 4	13	17	20	23	25	27	32	44
Variable % change	− 50	− 20	− 10	− 5	Best estimate of % yield	+ 5	+ 10	+ 20	+ 50
Capital cost	48	34	27	25	23	20	18	15	8
Operating cost	26	24	23	23	23	23	22	21	20
Royalty rate	27	24	23	23	23	23	22	21	19
Company tax rate	25	24	23	23	23	23	23	22	20

The figures in the body of the table give the yield on the project if a single variable is changed by the given percentage and the other variables remain constant.

CASE STUDY: MEGATON PLC: NOTES TOWARDS A SOLUTION

The key point is to calculate whether the lower risk (standard deviation) on the local project is compensated for by the reduced risk arising from the international diversification into the US market. This trade-off depends on the correlation between the economies of the UK and US. The growth rate in these economies is known to have a relatively low correlation in any one year, although the growth rates are highly auto-correlated over many years.

1. The overall expected after tax return of the UK company on existing projects (80% of total) plus either new project (20% of total) is:

$$(0.80 \times 0.25) + (0.20 \times 0.30) = 26\%$$

2. However, the risk (SD) on each project and the expected correlation between the new project returns and the existing UK business return are not the same.
   The co-variance on the UK project is calculated to be:

$$\underset{A}{} \quad \underset{B}{} \quad \underset{A}{} \quad \underset{B}{} \quad \underset{C}{}$$

$$(0.80)^2 \times (0.07)^2 + (0.20)^2 \times (0.12)^2 + 2(0.80) \times (0.20) \times (0.07) \times (0.12) \times (0.8) = 0.005862$$

A = SD of return on existing UK business.
B = SD of return on UK project.
C = Correlation of return on new UK project with return on existing business in the UK.

The co-variance on the suggested US project is calculated to be:

$$\underset{(0.80)^2 \times (0.07)^2}{A} + \underset{(0.20)^2 \times (0.15)^2}{B} + 2\underset{(0.80)}{A} \times \underset{(0.20)}{B} \times (0.07) \times (0.15) \times \underset{(0.3)}{C} = 0.005044$$

Decision: Choose the US subsidiary project. The firm's overall variability of income is reduced by about 14% if the US option is chosen, yet the average return on both options remains the same at 26%.

Calculation of the 14% reduction in risk:

$$1 - (0.005044/0.005862) = 1 - 0.86 = 14\%.$$

CASE STUDY: THE KANDYWOOD PROJECT: NOTES TOWARDS A SOLUTION

A series of steps towards solving this problem might be:

1. Use the technique of sensitivity analysis to identify the key variables impacting on the yield on the project.
2. Assess the risk attaching to each of these variables.
3. Work out ways of hedging these risks.
4. The currency used in financing the project might also be a key variable so the method of financing the project and hedging the possible exchange rate risk on any foreign currency loans should also be considered in the light of the other aspects of the project.
5. Having identified the key variables, assessed the risk attached to these variables and worked out suitable methods of hedging these risks the project can now be evaluated. Does the likely return on the project justify the risks involved? This final evaluation will always be highly subjective depending as it does on the risk–return profile adopted by the management of Highlands Wood Products.

Sensitivity Analysis

Sensitivity Analysis can be used to find out if the following variables have a significant impact on the yield.

Output, price per block, exchange rate, capital cost, operating cost, royalty rate, company tax rate.

It is obvious, for example, that operating costs must vary by a substantial percentage to make a significant impact on the yield.

The local tax regime might have a significant impact on the yield. For example, is the project yield particularly vulnerable to a change in the low company tax rate and/or the tax holiday?

The sensitivity analysis matrix can be used to answer such questions.

Hedging Tactics to Reduce Risk on Specific Variables. Output

There seems to be very little risk of the volume of wood not meeting expectations. The wood is visible and has been thoroughly checked out by experts. There is a small probability of some disease harming the trees in the future but experts consider this probability to be so low that it can be ignored.

The felling and cutting of the trees uses low technology and Timbercon say the conditions in Indonesia present no problem whatsoever on this score. The conditions for felling have been described as "ideal".

The transport risk is much more substantial. Movement of wood by airship is a novel technology and problems during the monsoon season are possible although the builders of the airships, Transairship Corporation (TAS), say this is not likely to be a problem.

Possible Hedge for Airship Transportation?

HWP can try to subcontract the shipment of the wood to TAS itself. If TAS will sign a contract to ship the wood out, this will show that TAS believes in the technical feasibility of the project. HWP will insist on a penal clause being inserted into the contract making TAS pay a substantial fine if the project proves technically not feasible or if there are substantial delays on the budgeted rate of shipment. Highlands will also insist on a bank guarantee on this value, up to an amount equal to the maximum fine. These terms, if accepted by TAS will, of course, increase the cost of the contract to HWP but will also provide a substantial hedge against the major transportation risk involved. HWP will need to rework the sums after incorporating these new costs but can also reduce the total risk attached to the project.

Hedging the Price Per Block

HWP have an estimate from Timbercon, the world's leading expert on wood pricing, that the expected value of the average price per block over the relevant period will be $410.

HWP have used an average unit value per block of $400 in their calculations so this difference would appear to provide a small hedge on price.

HWP may be able to sign a "rolling" forward or futures contract on price for short periods ahead with potential buyers if the wood is scarce but normally the profit margin is the only viable hedge against long-term changes in commodity prices.

Hedging the Exchange Rate

As the selling price of wood is denominated in US$ the simplest solution is to raise the required finance in US$. This tactic provides sufficient dollars to repay the interest on the loans. However, since the UK £ is expected to decline over the next few years against both the US$ and the Japanese yen the company might consider raising the loans in sterling and investing in fixed interest US$ or Yen bonds which can be called down to pay the interest in UK £ when needed. HWP would then be effectively gambling on a devaluation of the UK £ against the US$ and/or Yen.

A change in the £ sterling to Indonesian rupee exchange rate is unlikely to present a problem to the company. We have already noted the negligible impact of changes in operating costs on yield.

Hedging the Capital Costs

The risk attached to the airships has already been discussed. The cost of building the airport at both ends of the transport corridor will be subcontracted.

The felling and cutting equipment uses low technology presenting a low technological and cost risk.

The remaining risks attached to the capital costs would appear to be low. These risks are acceptable to HWP.

Hedging the Government Charges

It is essential for HWP to lock in the benefits of the favourable tax regime applied to the project. A change of government or even of ministers in Indonesia might cause the terms to be changed once the company is clearly committed to the deal. HWP should employ the services of a "country risk" consultant to assess this risk.

The Projects Department of the Export Credits Guarantee Department (ECGD) in the UK is designed to provide insurance against such changes in government policy. The capital projects section of the ECGD will provide insurance cover against such changes for a fee of a small percentage of the value of the contract. If the foreign tax regime is changed, despite the initial guarantee that it will not be, the ECGD will pay HWP about 90% of the value of the loss caused by the enforced change in a legally binding deal.

It might also be wise to involve the World Bank or some such international institution in the deal to dissuade the foreign government from changing the initial contract. HWP might also offer the government of Indonesia some part of the equity so that it can participate in the profits from the project.

Adjusting the Numbers for Risk

The project cost of funds for HWP is calculated to be 15% gross of tax and 12% net of tax. It is advisable to use these rates and not to increase them to allow for risk. Risk should be allowed for by applying a probability factor to the individual cash flows. Several computer packages on the market make this process a relatively painless one. An "add on" package to Lotus 1-2-3 allows an analyst to apply probabilities to the cash flows in a spreadsheet. However, recent research on investment techniques suggests that in practice few companies handle risk in this way. They simply use sensitivity analysis to measure the effect of changes in the key variables on yield and leave the allowance for risk to the subjective judgement of the investment evaluation team.

APPENDIX 6.1: SOME ORGANIZATIONS THAT MEASURE COUNTRY RISK AND OTHER KEY INTERNATIONAL VARIABLES ON A REGULAR BASIS

Dun and Bradstreet Ltd
Economic Analysis Department
Holmers Farm Way
High Wycombe
Bucks. UK

Economist Intelligence Unit
15 Regent Street
London SW1Y 4LR
UK

Institute of International Finance
2000 Pennsylvania Avenue
NW Suite 8500
Washington DC 20006
USA

Multi-national Strategies
67 Irvine Place
(North) 8th Floor
New York, NY 10003
USA

Political Risk Services
International Country Risk Guide
222 Teall Avenue, Suite 200
PO Box 6482
Syracuse, NY 13217-6482
USA

S.J. Rundt Associates
130 East 63rd Street
New York, NY 10021
USA

7
Raising Loans Denominated in a Foreign Currency

INTRODUCTION: BORROWING ACROSS FRONTIERS

Can a company reduce its cost of funding by borrowing abroad? The answer to this question is not certain. If the International Fisher Theory is correct then the answer is "probably not, if the international market for funds is a free and efficient market". The problem is that the funds flowing between many of the countries of the world are restricted in some way.

For up to a quarter of a century after the ending of the Second World War the above question was of purely academic interest. Severe restrictions were imposed by most governments on the free flow of funds out of their country. Funds were in short supply and governments believed that the existing funds available in a country should be conserved for local use.

From around 1970 this attitude began to change and countries such as Switzerland and Germany and then the United States began to free up their capital markets. This change in attitude has allowed companies to access funds denominated in currencies other than their own.

On October 23, 1979 the British government, rather dramatically and certainly unexpectedly, abolished all exchange controls on the pound sterling. The 10 000 banking staff responsible for implementing the UK exchange control regulations were shifted to other work.

Prior to 1979 the exchange control regulations applied to currency movements out of the United Kingdom were amongst the toughest in the world. Oddly enough their abolition made no appreciable difference to the value of the pound sterling.[1]

This abolition of exchange controls by the UK government prompted many other governments to follow suit so that today most governments in advanced industrial countries impose very light exchange controls on the flow of funds out of or into their countries.

This new freedom allows company treasurers to borrow from a wide range of foreign capital markets. Companies are no longer restricted to borrowing in their local currency.

Surplus funds can now be invested in that economy that is prepared to pay the highest real rate of interest for the funds. Funds can be borrowed from that financial market offering the "cheapest" source of funds, wherever that source may be.

By 1996 exchange controls have been abolished in most of the financial markets operating in advanced industrial countries, however, exchange controls have not been abolished in many less developed countries. Tight exchange controls are still applied by governments in many developing countries. Severe restrictions are applied to both the transfer of local funds out of the country and the use of funds in the country.

Most countries impose a "withholding" tax on dividend and interest payments repatriated out of the country to foreign shareholders and lenders.

Fortunately for the efficiency of the world investment programme over 90% of the funds that flow across international frontiers are flowing between advanced industrial countries. Thus a high proportion of the total of international funds crossing international frontiers are flowing between free capital markets.

THE COST OF FOREIGN BORROWING

Exhibit 3.2 illustrates the base rate for borrowing funds in 14 currencies on a specific date in December 1993. Note the wide variation in cost between the cheapest and the most expensive funds on offer. A difference of no less than 17.25% per annum!

If a naive British borrower were given this list and asked to choose a currency in which to borrow, and he could borrow in any one of these currencies, he would almost certainly decide to borrow in Japanese yen. The borrower, being naive, knows nothing about the relation between the level of interest rates and expectations about future changes in exchange rates.

The question the naive borrower fails to ask is, "Will the Japanese yen still prove to be the cheapest currency to borrow in "terms of the home currency" at the end of the five-year period?". No one knows the answer to this question, least of all the borrower. The difficulty lies in predicting the future movement in the sterling/yen exchange rate over the period of the loan.

This fact will not come as news to a reader who recalls the explanation and discussion of the International Fisher Theory in Chapter 3.

The cost of foreign borrowing is influenced by several other factors in addition to FX risk. First, there is the risk of a change in the real interest rate due to a change in the market's perception of the degree of political risk in that country. Secondly, in the case of a swap, there is the risk of default by the counter party to the swap. These factors are relevant but an unexpected change in the future exchange rate is the major risk attached to a loan denominated in a foreign currency. This brings us back to the International Fisher Theory.

If a finance officer decides to raise funds in a foreign currency he will need to take a position on whether or not he believes in the International Fisher Theory, so let us review this theory once more.

International Borrowing and the International Fisher Theory

Levich (1979) writes that:

> "for markets to clear, investors demand a higher nominal return on assets denominated in a depreciating unit of account . . . other things being equal exchange rate changes tend to equalise the rates of return across assets that are similar in all other respects except currency of denomination".[2]

The International Fisher Theory claims that differences in the cost of funds borrowed in different currencies represents the market's best guess concerning the future changes in the exchange rates between the currencies over the period of the loan. If, on a particular date, the cost of a five-year loan denominated in £ sterling is 12% per annum and the cost of an otherwise identical loan denominated in US$ is 7% per annum the market is guessing that over the period of the loan the pound sterling will depreciate in value on average "each year" by around $(0.07 - 0.12)/(1 + 0.12) = -4.46\%$ per annum against the US$.

The difference in interest rates simply reflects the market's best guess as to the change in the relative value of the respective currencies over the period of the loan.[3]

If the International Fisher Theory is valid and if the market's guess is always correct then, so far as cost is concerned, it would not matter in which currency the treasurer borrowed his funds since the present discounted cost of the repayment of interest and capital on the loan would be the same in all currencies "after conversion into the home currency"!

Unfortunately, life in the international capital markets is not as simple as this.

Exchange controls and other constraints are still applied to the export of many of the currencies of the world so the capital markets of the world are not very efficient, and even when exchange controls are not applied the market's "best guess" as to the future exchange rates between currencies is not very accurate. Research on the subject has found that private forecasters can, on average, over time, beat the market's guess concerning the likely future exchange rates between currencies.

Another interesting question is whether the currency market's "best guess" on future exchange rates is an "unbiased" estimate of the future rate. Does the interest rate differential between currencies consistently under- or overestimate the future exchange rate? Research on this less demanding requirement suggests a judgement following the Scottish verdict of "unproven".

In recent years much academic research has been focused on trying to find a convincing answer to these, and related, questions. The answers are less clear than one might have hoped.

SOME ACADEMIC RESEARCH ON THE RELATIVE COST OF BORROWING IN A FOREIGN CURRENCY

Does the International Fisher Theory actually work?

Most research on the question has concluded that either the theory does not work or that it does not work very well. Fisher's original paper (Fisher 1896)[4] found that interest rate differences did not predict future exchange rates very accurately and so he suggested that the international financial markets were not very efficient. Hansen and Hodrick (1980) also concluded that differential interest rates did not predict future exchange rates very accurately.

On the other hand Fama (1975) found that the Fisher effect relating interest differentials to inflation differentials in one country worked quite well on US data. Aliber and Stickney (1975), in a paper with a strong accounting bias, found that the International Fisher seemed to work quite well using long-term averaging over 10 years or so but it did not work in the short term when averaging out over three to four years. The prediction was closer for the currencies of developed than for developing countries.

Most of these studies looked at the macro picture. They used differences between national base interest rates to predict future exchange rates.

Research that tests the validity of the International Fisher when applied to loans taken out by individual companies are much harder to find. One of the few such studies was conducted by Morgan (1982). Morgan collected data on the interest cost of 130 fixed-interest loans raised by UK companies between 1965 and 1980. Data on the interest cost of loans of a similar value in alternative currencies for the same periods were also collected. Morgan could find no evidence to support the hypothesis that the cost of the loans in each currency was the same in terms of sterling over this period. He found no evidence to support the view that as time passed the cost of each loan in each currency, when translated into sterling, tended towards equality.

An example of Morgan's analysis of four loans in four currencies is provided in Exhibit 7.1 In each case the interest plus repayment cost of each loan, translated into sterling, is calculated up to each year end during the life of the loan. The annual cost in each foreign currency is converted into sterling at the year-end rate of exchange. As can be

Exhibit 7.1 The Real Cost of Loans Borrowed in a Foreign Currency

Borrower	Currency	Year Coupon rate%	70	71	72	73	74	75	76	77	78	79	80	81
			% Cost in the home currency up to the end of the year											
British Leyland	SF	5.75	5.50	5.57	6.73	12.18	13.22	14.84	16.89	16.94	18.34	17.22	15.72	14.98
	DM	6.60	6.51	11.87	12.17	15.10	16.64	16.26	17.13	18.01	17.89	16.76	15.69	14.91
	US$	7.60	7.07	7.11	4.67	6.60	7.41	7.34	10.25	11.17	10.16	9.14	8.80	8.63
	£	10.07	10.07	10.07	10.07	10.07	10.07	10.07	10.07	10.07	10.07	10.07	10.07	10.07
General Motors	US$	9.25		9.45	9.96	10.10	9.65	12.27	14.29	12.65	11.92	11.29	10.92	11.59
	DM	8.66		13.73	16.97	20.84	20.79	19.98	22.62	21.28	20.99	20.09	18.82	18.80
	SF	7.04		10.60	15.41	18.57	22.16	21.86	23.59	22.94	23.00	21.59	20.12	20.43
	£	11.96		11.96	11.96	11.96	11.96	11.96	11.96	11.96	11.96	11.96	11.96	11.96
Barclay's Bank	US$	8.25			14.74	11.80	10.98	13.89	16.88	14.15	12.75	11.46	10.86	11.61
	DM	7.59			18.10	24.53	21.40	20.38	24.13	21.38	20.82	19.64	17.82	17.66
	SF	5.58			17.13	20.91	22.34	22.57	25.80	23.08	23.15	21.05	19.06	19.31
	£	9.40			9.40	9.40	9.40	9.40	9.40	9.40	9.40	9.40	9.40	9.40
ICI	DM	8.00			14.88	27.91	19.23	20.05	23.78	21.73	20.82			
	US$	9.25			12.17	10.91	11.56	14.34	17.29	15.55	13.38			
	SF	4.02			10.99	20.48	17.16	19.51	23.34	20.35	22.64			
	£				10.00	10.00	10.00	10.00	10.00	10.00	10.00			

Source: Morgan, J. R. An empirical investigation into the interest rate theory of exchange rate expectations. Ph.D. Thesis: Bradford University, 1982, Table 6.

The table shows the cost of each loan in terms of pound sterling up to the end of each year. It is assumed that the loan was repaid in pound sterling at the year end. The interest and capital costs are translated at the year end rate and then discounted to the beginning of year one. The rates of exchange used for translating interest and capital are taken as the rates ruling at the end of each year. The alternative rates in each currency are taken from the loans book of a loans broker.

In the case of the loans taken out in £ sterling the coupon rate remains unchanged over the period of the loan. In the case of loans denominated in other currencies the overall cost to date is influenced by the change in the exchange rate between the £ sterling and the foreign currency over the period of the loan.

The table provides little evidence to support the hypothesis that the cost of each of these loans was converging towards equality in terms of the £ sterling as the loan period increased.

seen from Exhibit 7.1 the evidence does not support the view that the terminal cost of each loan in each currency when translated into sterling is equal or is even converging towards equality. The differences between the terminal cost of each loan in each of the four currencies in terms of sterling remains substantial in the case of all four loans.

The difference between the average annual cost of the sterling loan and the cost of the DM loan in each of the four cases is 4.84%, 6.84%, 8.26% and 10.82%!

We conclude that the jury is still out on the International Fisher Theory. Interest rate differences between long-term loans in different currencies seem to be a poor predictor of future exchange rates, even in the long term.

These studies suggest that the international financial markets are not very efficient, at least in the medium term, and so the currency in which a loan is denominated is a matter of some importance. By choosing the correct currency in which to denominate a loan a finance officer may be able to reduce the average cost of funding his company.

Note that all of these loans are fixed-rate loans, floating rate loans tied to an inter-bank rate present the finance officer with a quite different problem.

Practitioners in the bond market doubt that interest rates can be forecast. "We assume that no one can consistently call interest rates over an extended time period".[5]

Another question that is closely related to the previous one is whether the interest rate difference between two currencies is an "unbiased" predictor of the future exchange rate between the currencies.

Even if interest rate differences prove to be a poor predictor of the future exchange rate between the currencies the differences might provide an unbiased prediction of the future rate. On average, over many periods, the interest rate difference might neither overestimate nor underestimate the future exchange rate. The difference between the predicted future spot rate and the actual spot rate might tend towards zero in the long run.

On this question the research evidence provides rather stronger support. Aliber and Stickney (1975) and Morgan (1982) all found the predictions of future exchange rates to be very inaccurate but unbiased in the "very" long run.

If this is so then a finance officer can hedge the exposure risk on foreign loans by financing his company with several loans in several different currencies. The average interest cost on the portfolio of loans will be the same as the cost of a similar loan in the home currency but the variance on the cost of funds will be lower. The finance officer is simply applying the diversification principle, so well known in investment theory, to the funding of his company. The diversification of the loan portfolio reduces the variation in the cost of funding over time.

We conclude that the validity of the International Fisher Theory is unproven. It is possible that costs might be reduced by foreign rather than local funding. The variation in the cost of funding a company can be reduced by funding the company with a portfolio of loans denominated in several currencies.

DERIVATIVES AND FOREIGN BORROWING

Derivatives, such as forwards, futures and options can be used to hedge exposure to FX risk when funding a company with foreign currency loans. The derivatives will be placed in the same portfolio as the loans they are hedging. If the exchange rate moves against the local currency the value of the foreign loan will rise in terms of the home currency resulting in a translation loss. However, the market value of the hedging derivatives will also have risen, resulting in a roughly equivalent gain.

An interesting variant on this theme is the semi-fixed swap. In this case the swapper of the floating rate loan will substitute one of two fixed rates in place of the floating rate. The actual amount paid or received depends on the level of the periodic LIBOR rate. A semi-fixed swap can be into another currency.

Thus, if a finance officer believes that long-term borrowing will be cheaper in a foreign currency, he can raise a loan in that currency and hedge the currency risk via a derivative or he can raise the funds in the local currency and swap.

The calculation he must make is as follows: "Is the interest advantage of the foreign loan, adjusted for future expected FX changes and minus the cost of the derivatives, cheaper than a loan denominated in the local currency plus the cost of the swap?".

Currency swaps can be arranged to hedge the exposure risk inherent in a loans portfolio, but only in a few currencies. The mechanics of currency swaps were explained in Chapters 2 and 5. The finance officer swaps out of one currency into another which better suits the future needs of his company.

A swap is an "off-balance sheet" transaction. This accounting treatment can provide some benefits *re* disclosure but also raises some problems with regulatory bodies.

CONSTRAINTS ON BORROWING ABROAD

Despite the recent trend towards introducing more liberal economic policies into the world economy the international capital markets are still far from being free and efficient markets. Many restrictions are still imposed by many countries that limit the freedom of the finance officer when borrowing foreign currency. Let us now examine some of these restrictions.

First, there are the various exchange control restrictions imposed by many governments on the movement of capital out of, and even into, the given country. Even if borrowing by a foreign borrower is permitted by the monetary authority in a country the bureaucratic obstacles to be overcome in achieving this end may be so onerous as to dissuade a finance officer from following this route.

A further problem is taxation. The tax treatment of interest on loans denominated in a foreign currency and the tax treatment of profits or losses on instruments hedging the exposure on these loans can be complex. The interest paid on loans denominated in a foreign currency may not be allowed against company tax in the home country or may not be fully allowed. Any profit or loss arising on the currency exposure on the loan may be subject to eccentric tax treatment. The profits on derivatives such as futures and options that can be used to hedge exposure on foreign currency risk, may be taxed and losses may or may not be allowed against tax. The treatment of such matters by the tax authorities is often not symmetric, profits are taxed but losses are not allowed against tax. The problem is further discussed in Chapter 10.

In addition to these problems there is the question of the costs associated with the raising of foreign loans. A foreign loan may incur substantial up-front costs that can be avoided if the loan is taken out in the local currency where the borrower is more knowledgeable and is better known. The legal costs incurred in drafting foreign loans can be high and the charges made by the foreign financial advisers who are employed to sell the loan to local lenders can be significantly higher than the costs of selling a similar loan on the home market. This is why some companies prefer to raise the funds on the home market and swap the proceeds into a foreign currency via an international bank.

The size of the loan is another important determinant of cost. The legal and other loan costs are not much affected by the size of the amount borrowed. Thus small loans incur higher legal costs per monetary unit borrowed.[6]

Finally there is the cost of finding out about foreign borrowing. How does one go about borrowing in a foreign currency? From whom? From where? What are the overall costs involved? What hedging devices are available to cover the foreign exchange risk? How much do these devices cost? and so on. An expensive learning curve is attached to borrowing in a foreign currency.

For example, the current market value of existing bonds does not seem to be a good guide to the cost of making a new issue of similar bonds.[7]

SOME FURTHER CONSIDERATIONS

Much of the previous discussion was concerned with the cost of foreign funding. Will funds denominated in a foreign currency cost less than the same value of funds denominated in the home currency?

When finance officers in multinational companies are asked why they borrow funds in a foreign currency rather than in their home currency, the reduced cost of the funds comes low in their list of priorities (McRae 1992). Why then do finance officers borrow in a foreign currency?[8]

Matching Currency Flows

The primary reason why a company borrows funds in a foreign rather than in a home currency is to match currency flows.

Finance officers prefer to finance projects in the same currency as the currency generated by the project. An investment in Canada will be financed with Canadian dollars, a French project with French francs:

> "Within our portfolio we match against assets to ensure that the profits we make in our enterprise are not eroded by taking unplanned or irrelevant risks."[9]

Financing a project in the same currency as the currency generated by the profits from that project makes sense because it provides an automatic hedge of the currency exposure position. If a loan in Canadian dollars is used to buy Canadian assets that generate profits in Canadian dollars then, so long as the project is profitable, the Canadian dollar loan is self hedged. The cost of hedging is avoided.

The Maturity Date of the Debt

The maturity date of the debt is another important factor in raising long-term loans in whatever currency. McRae (1992) found that company treasurers favoured long-term maturities as against short-term even when the long-term interest rate was historically high. Long-term maturities in one currency were favoured above short-term maturities in another. The relative cost of the loans seemed to play a minor role in the currency of funding decision.

"The major factor influencing maturity preference was claimed to be the overall maturity pattern of the existing loan portfolio. Even with the new swap markets available treasurers do not like bond maturity dates 'bunching' around a given date". (McRae, 1992, pp. 8).

Tax Effects
Tax benefits may flow to a group of companies if they borrow in a foreign currency.

Under most tax regimes the interest paid on a loan by a company is allowed as a charge against profits. However, the rate of tax imposed on a company can vary between different regimes. These two facts, when taken together, can persuade a finance officer to raise a loan in one country, which imposes a high marginal tax rate, even if the money is needed in another country.

Another possibility is that the interest on a loan may be allowed against tax in one country but not allowed against tax in another.

The profits and losses that may arise out of exposure to exchange rate changes can also provide opportunities for tax reduction on loans. Some countries do not tax exchange rate gains on loans expressed in a foreign currency (but also do not allow such losses to be charged against profits).

Profit and loss on derivatives bought to hedge exposure on loans may offer similar opportunities. In some cases these profits are taxed, in other cases they are not.

We should note in passing that if profits on currency options are taxed then the hedge must be large enough to cover the exposure gross of the tax charge! McRae and Walker (1980) discuss the variety of approach adopted by tax authorities in major countries to the treatment of foreign exchange gains and losses.[10] This variety of approach has not changed much in the intervening years. This variety provides opportunities for tax reduction by shifting profits and losses between tax regimes.

Another factor that may persuade a finance officer to raise a loan in a foreign currency is the variation in the pattern of cash flow generated by loans denominated in different currencies. This is illustrated in Exhibit 7.4.

In the Apex case study, which we shall discuss later in the chapter, the company domiciled in Zatania has the choice of raising the loan in local Zatanian dollars (Z$), £ sterling, Swiss francs or Illyrian lyre.

Exhibit 7.3 shows the amount of foreign currency paid out in each of the five years and Exhibit 7.4 the equivalent value in the local currency, namely Z$.

Exhibit 7.4 shows that the cash flow pattern in Zatanian dollars over the five-year period is very different for each of the four currencies. The loan in lyre spreads the cash requirement in Z$ more evenly over the period than the Swiss franc or the £ sterling loan. These latter loans call for a large tranche of local funds to be built up for payment in the final year.

There are, of course, many other ways of spreading funding requirements over a period but Exhibit 7.4 shows that loans denominated in different foreign currencies generate different cash flow requirements in the home currency over the period of the loan.

Whatever the cash flow pattern may be the home company will have to set up a "sinking fund" to ensure that the funds are available to repay the foreign loan in the final year. This fund can be denominated in either the home or the foreign currency.

THE MECHANICS OF RAISING LOANS IN A FOREIGN CURRENCY

Most loans denominated in a foreign currency are arranged through banks, commercial banks or merchant banks.

If a finance officer wants to raise a loan in a specific foreign currency he simply has to ask his bank the current cost of such a loan or swap for the specified period in that particular currency. If the currency in which the loan is denominated is one of those used in international trade and if the company has a good prior credit record[11] there should be little difficulty in raising the loan in the foreign currency.

The risk ranking on the loan which will be calculated by a recognized credit rating agency such as the IBCA is also important. See Exhibit 7.7.

If the currency is not one of the "big five", that is US$, German DM, Swiss francs, £ sterling or Japanese yen there might be a time delay in arranging the loan. The permission of the monetary authority in the lending country may have to be sought.

If a direct loan in the foreign currency is not available the finance officer might consider swapping an existing loan in the local currency but the cost of the swap will be higher than the direct loan because of the risk of default by the counter party.

If the loan is to be raised in a country that imposes exchange control regulations on the movement of funds the foreign fund raising operation is not so simple. The foreign borrower will have to justify the need for the loan to the monetary authority in the foreign country and will probably have to accept a place in a queue for raising such loans. The funds may not become available for several months or even for some years.

If the finance officer is not sure as to the currency in which he wishes to raise the loan but would like to minimize the cost of funding in the home currency he might consult a specialist in forecasting exchange rates (if he believes that exchange rates can be forecast!).

Exhibit 3.2 illustrated the wide variation in interest rates that can exist at any one time in the currency markets. Based on these rates and forecasts he will select the currency that best suits the needs of the company. This may not be the currency that offers absolutely the cheapest loan in terms of the home currency over the specified period of the loan.

The next step is to work out a way of hedging the currency risk involved.

The type of hedge depends primarily on the size of the loan. If the loan is a large one, say for several million US$, then the finance officer can check whether a currency swap is available via the swap market or whether some other hedging technique is better suited to covering the exposure risk attached to the loan.

The next step will be to obtain the services of a legal firm experienced in drawing up loan contracts in foreign currencies. A loan contract will be drafted after consultation with a loans adviser and some hard bargaining between the borrower and the lender. Loan and bond contracts can be exceedingly complex legal documents. Exhibit 7.2 sets out some of the conditions that need to be specified precisely in a loan agreement regarding the issue of a bond denominated in a foreign currency.

Exhibit 7.2   Some Conditions that Might Be Attached to a Foreign Bond

International bonds and other international financial products are complex legal instruments. Before an international bond is issued the following conditions must be agreed between the borrower and the lender(s).

1. The value of the bond.
2. The currency in which the bond is to be denominated. Can the bond be repaid in a different currency?
3. The length and maturity date of the bond. Can the bond be repaid before maturity? Under what conditions? What is the cost of this option?
4. Is the bond to be repaid over its lifetime or repaid in one payment at the end of the bond period?
5. Is the bond renewable at the maturity date? Under what conditions?
6. Is the rate of interest on the bond to be fixed or will the rate float at x% above LIBOR? Can this rate be changed during the period of the bond? Under what conditions? Are "caps" applied to the floating rate?
7. What is the fixed interest rate to be? (Or excess over LIBOR.)
8. Is a permissible moratorium on the payment of interest available for a fixed period under specified conditions?
9. What is the security on the bond, if any? Do limit ratios apply such as market gearing ratios.
10. Is the bond registered or is it in "bearer" format?
11. Are any limitations placed on using the bond as security in a swap market deal?
12. Are any limitations placed on the bond by exchange control regulations? For example, must the proceeds of the bond be converted immediately into another currency?

Some other factors that may be important.

13. Legal, brokerage and syndication costs.
14. Under which legal framework is the bond set up? Where can remedies for non-payment be pursued?
15. Will a bond rating be available? From whom?
16. Is the bond negotiable? Is a secondary market available for trading the bond?
17. Will withholding taxes be applied to interest payments? At what rate? To be paid by whom? To whom?
18. Are limitations placed on the date when the bond can be floated? Will the bond be placed in a queue?

Many conditions can be imposed by either party to the deal. For example, clauses in the agreement may allow a moratorium on payment of interest for a period, early redemption of the bond and, possibly, a right to switch from fixed to floating interest rates or vice versa under certain conditions. The careful specification of conditions to cover rare or unusual circumstances can inject useful flexibility into a loan contract.

If the finance officer is wise he will maintain a library or set of files keeping himself up to date on such things as current rates and forecasts of future exchange rates, current international tax agreements, current exchange control regulations in those countries with which he trades, the benefits currently offered by tax havens, current developments in the fast changing swap market and so forth. It is not wise for a finance officer to rely solely on the advice of outside experts on such matters. The debt-raising strategy of Grand Metropolitan is illustrated in Exhibit 7.6.

A CASE STUDY: APEX PLC

A company called Apex PLC operates out of a country called Zatania in Eastern Europe. The company wish to raise a loan of Z$1 000 000 (Zatanian dollars) for a five-year period to assist in building a tourist hotel in Zatania. The company could raise the funds locally but a shortage of funds in the local economy means that Apex will have to wait in a queue for at least a year before the loan can be raised locally.

Table 26

			Year			
Currency	Beginning 1996	End 1996	1997	1998	1999	2000
Z$	100	100	100	100	100	100
£ sterling	60	55	50	46	42	39
Swiss francs	180	166	146	131	118	107
Lyre	2000	2110	2226	2348	2477	2614

Table 27

	Interest rate % per annum
Z$	25
£ sterling	17
Swiss franc	13
Lyre	30

The finance officer of Apex is considering the possibility of raising the funds abroad. He makes enquiries through the Zatanian National Bank (ZNB) and finds that funds are accessible in British pounds sterling, Swiss francs and Illyrian lyre. Illyria is a somewhat unstable state in the former Soviet bloc that enjoys the benefits of substantial oil reserves and so is currently lending money abroad.

A currency forecaster, which Apex has found to be quite reliable in the past, has put forward the forecasts shown in Table 26 of future spot rates for the £ sterling, Swiss francs and Illyrian lyre against the Z$.

The forecasts suggest that over the period considered the Z$ will depreciate in value against the £ and the Swiss franc but appreciate against the Illyrian lyre.

The current rates of interest on five-year, fixed interest loans in the four currencies are as shown in Table 27.

All of these loans are what are called "bullet" loans. A bullet loan being a type of loan requiring that only interest be paid during the period of the loan. The capital is repaid at the end of the final year of the loan.

The finance officer of Apex studies these costs and exchange rate forecasts. He must decide whether to wait and take up the loan in the local currency or raise the money in a foreign currency. The legal and other costs incurred in raising the loan will be approximately the same in all currencies. Tax treatment of the loans is also identical whatever the currency of the loan.

The cost of funds to Apex PLC is currently running at 25% per annum.

The finance officer decides to set out the cost of raising the funds in each currency. Exhibit 7.3 sets out the potential cash cost of the loan to Apex in each currency in each year of the loan.

Exhibit 7.4 sets out the cash that would have to be paid out by Apex in terms of Z$ in each year for each loan. Exhibit 7.4 shows that the amount and pattern of cash due

Exhibit 7.3 The Cost of the Loans to Apex Expressed in Each Currency

Cost in Zatanian $s:	1 000 000 Z$ at 25% per annum				
	1996	1997	1998	1999	2000
Interest	1 250 000	250 000	250 000	250 000	250 000	250 000
Capital	1 000 000					1 000 000
Total	2 250 000	250 000	250 000	250 000	250 000	1 250 000
Cost of loan discounted at 25% =		1 000 000 Z$			

Cost in £ sterling £	£600 000 sterling at 17% per annum				
	1996	1997	1998	1999	2000
Interest	510 000	102 000	102 000	102 000	102 000	102 000
Capital	600 000					600 000
Total	1 110 000	102 000	102 000	102 000	102 000	702 000

Cost in Swiss francs	1 800 000 Swiss Fr at 13% per annum				
	1996	1997	1998	1999	2000
Interest	1 170 000	234 000	234 000	234 000	234 000	234 000
Capital	1 800 000					1 800 000
Total	2 970 000	234 000	234 000	234 000	234 000	2 034 000

Cost in lyre	20 000 000 lyre at 30% per annum				
	Total	1996	1997	1998	1999	2000
Interest	30 000 000	6 000 000	6 000 000	6 000 000	6 000 000	6 000 000
Capital	20 000 000					20 000 000
Total	50 000 000	6 000 000	6 000 000	6 000 000	6 000 000	26 000 000

The table shows the amount of currency that Apex needs to buy in each year to pay the interest and the capital at the end of the five-year period.

to be paid out in Z$ in the case of each loan is very different. Initially the Swiss franc loan is cheapest in terms of Z$ but in the long run the lyre loan is the cheapest loan. In terms of Z$ the lyre loan turns out to be the cheapest option, the next cheapest is the Z$ loan, then the Swiss franc loan. The sterling loan turns out to be the most expensive in terms of Z$. These conclusions are only valid if the exchange rate forecasts are correct.

If we discount the amounts paid in Z$ in each year to the beginning of year one at 25%, the current cost of funds to Apex in the home currency, then the ordinal ranking remains the same but the absolute difference in the cost of each loan varies from the undiscounted figures. The pattern of the cash flow makes a significant difference to the relative discounted cost of each loan in terms of Z$.

We conclude that a loan denominated in Illyrian lyre appears to be the cheapest form of loan, but this conclusion is only valid if the currency forecasts are correct. A further problem arises from hedging the loan. The finance officer can hedge exposure risk in £ sterling and Swiss francs but can he hedge forward cover in lyre? This is unlikely since the lyre is an "exotic" currency.

Exhibit 7.4 The Potential Cost of Each Loan Expressed in Terms of Z$

Cost of £ sterling loan in Z$		$Z at end of 2000 1 538 462				
		1996	1997	1998	1999	2000
Interest	1 115 589	185 455	204 000	221 739	242 857	261 538
Capital	1 538 462					1 538 462
Total	2 654 051	185 455	204 000	221 739	242 857	1 800 000
Cost of loan discounted at 25% =		Z$ 1 081 752				

Cost of Swiss franc loan in Z$		$Z at end of 2000 1 682 243				
		1996	1997	1998	1999	2000
Interest	896 860	140 964	160 274	178 626	198 305	218 692
Capital	1 682 243					1 682 243
Total	2 579 103	140 964	160274	178 626	198 305	1 900 935
Cost of loan discounted at 25% =		Z$ 1 010 927				

Cost of lyre loan in terms of Z$		$Z at end of 2000 765 111				
		1996	1997	1998	1999	2000
Interest	1 281 200	284 360	269 542	255 537	242 229	229 533
Capital	765 111					765 111
Total	2 046 311	284 360	269 542	255 537	242 229	994 644
Cost of loan discounted at 25% =		Z$ 955 971				

	(A)	(B)	(B)/(A)
Z$ loan	1 000 000	2 250 000	2.25
Sterling loan	1 081 752	2 654 051	2.45
Swiss franc loan	1 010 927	2 579 103	2.55
Lyre loan	955 971	2 046 311	2.14

This table assumes that Apex will buy foreign currency to pay the interest charge at the end of each year. Currency will be bought at the forecast exchange rate at the end of the final year to pay the interest and repay the loan. Note that this is a "bullet" loan whereby the capital is repaid on the last day of the loan.

The financial officer of Apex may also consider the cost of the option of waiting one year until he is allowed to raise the loan in Z$, which is a relatively cheap currency. He may prefer this option because he knows more about local conditions than conditions abroad and the cash inflow is in Z$.

The Future Exchange Rates Implied in the Interest Rate Differentials

The future exchange rates used in the above calculations are based on the forecasts provided by the professional forecaster. Another exchange rate forecast is implied in the differences in the interest rates charged on loans in each currency. Exhibit 7.5 shows how to derive the future exchange rates that are implied by the differences in interest rates. It is assumed that no exchange controls apply to the movement of funds in these three currencies.

Exhibit 7.5   Future Spot Rates Implied by the Interest Rate Differences: Apex PLC

Calculation of the future exchange rates implied by the differing bond rates.
The relevant formula is:

$$(\text{Foreign rate} - \text{home rate})/(1 + \text{home rate})$$

In each case the implied future annual charge in the exchange rates are:

		%
Pound–Z$	$(0.17 - 0.25)/(1 + 0.25) \times 100 =$	−6.4
Swiss franc–Z$	$(0.13 - 0.25)/(1 + 0.25) \times 100 =$	−9.6
Lyre–Z$	$(0.30 - 0.25)/(1 + 0.25) \times 100 =$	4.0

For example, the Zatanian $ is expected to fall in value by approximately 6.4% against the £ sterling in each of the five years. In other words the interest rate differential implies that 6.4% fewer £s can be bought each year with each Z$.
Thus the exchange rates implied by the interest rate differentials are as follows:

	Year					
	0	1	2	3	4	5
£ per 100Z$	60	56	53	49	46	43
Swiss franc per 100Z$	180	163	147	133	120	109
Lyre per 100Z$	2000	2080	2163	2250	2340	2433

Note that there is a substantial difference between the future rates of exchange implied in the bond rates and the exchange rates forecast by the professional forecasting firm.
Interest rate differences have been found to be poor predictors of the future spot rate. However, the differences have also been found to be unbiased predictors of the future spot rate.

Exhibit 7.6   The Debt Raising Strategy of Grand Metropolitan in 1994

Grand Metropolitan won the "Corporate Finance" borrower of the year award for 1994. The UK-based company borrowed US$ 5.4 billion over the year. A difficult year for borrowers. Gearing, which had risen to 200% in 1989 when GM acquired Pilsbury, had fallen back to around 50% by the end of 1994. Interest cover is now around 10 times earnings and long-term debt has increased from 35% of total debt to almost 100% at the end of 1994.
Despite the fact that US government bond yields had increased by 200 basis points between February and November 1994 GM managed to reduce the average long-term cost of borrowing over the period.
On May 19 GM launched a US$400 million five-year Eurobond issue, its first such issue. The bond was priced at only 53 basis points over the US Treasury price, an aggressive price. The launch succeeded and allowed a further US$200 million Eurobond to be launched later in the year. This was priced at only 50 bp over the US Treasury issues.
On May 25 GM made another aggressive move by entering the "Yankee" market by arranging a 10-year US$1.224 billion zero coupon deal despite the fact that this particular market had been closed to Corporate borrowers for at least 10 years! Zero coupon bonds provide significant tax advantage since the difference between the issue and redemption price can be charged against tax even if no interest payments are made. Structuring the deal via inter-company loans provided further tax benefits.
In July GM arranged a US$3 billion five-year revolving credit with a small syndicate of banks. The fees of the banks were reduced by arranging the loan "in-house" through GM Finance, the group's financing subsidiary. The cost was only 5 bp above LIBOR plus commitment fees of 10 bp. A historically low cost. The reason for this was that during 1994 competition between banks and a lack of high quality borrowers in the market had forced syndicated loan costs to a low level. GM also managed to eliminate the "material adverse change" clause from the loan terms.
A series of structured loan swaps, all quite small, allowed GM to fill in gaps in its loan portfolio profile at low cost. All these small loans were fully hedged.

In November GM issued US$500 million of perpetual preferred securities via a subsidiary based in Delaware USA. A new fund raising device for UK based companies. These securities pay a fixed dividend but are treated as "minority interests" thus increasing the value of the conventional equity shares of GM. They have no voting rights but are deductible against tax. Perpetuals also increase the maturity profile of the debt of the company. After tax this form of debt only cost GM around 6%, that is only 40 basis points above the cost of fixed interest debt and 3% cheaper than preferred shares!

The debt raising strategy of GM in 1994 demonstrates a high degree of originality and aggressiveness on the part of the Treasury team at GM.

The relevant equation is:
$$r\% = (f\% - h\%)/(1 + h\%)$$
where $r\%$ is the expected average change in exchange rates in each year over the period of the loan. The interest cost of the foreign loan is represented by $f\%$, the interest cost of the home loan by $h\%$.

Exhibit 7.5 shows that if this formula is applied over the five-year period the Z$ is expected to fall by 6.4% a year against the £ and 9.6% a year against the Swiss franc but to rise by 4% a year against the Illyrian lyre. These changes in exchange rates contrast with the currency forecasts that expect the Z$ to depreciate by 9% a year against the £ and 11% a year against the Swiss franc but to appreciate by 5.5% a year against the Illyrian lyre over the five-year period.

Profits can be made from currency speculation if the predicted exchange rates are correct because they differ from the rates of exchange implied by the interest rate differentials.

The Strategy of Grand Metropolitan

Exhibit 7.6 describes the debt-raising strategy of Grand Metropolitan for the year 1994.

Debt Rating Agencies

Debt rating is a critical element in raising loans on the international bond market. Exhibit 7.7 lists a few of the more important debt rating agencies offering their services to potential lenders in 1995.

WHAT HAVE WE LEARNED IN THIS CHAPTER?

1. Exchange controls on the movement of funds between countries have been much reduced in recent years. This opening up of the world's financial markets has provided company treasurers with an opportunity to raise funds in currencies other than the home currency.
2. The cost of funding varies between the different capital markets of the world so it might be at least possible theoretically to reduce the average cost of funding a company by borrowing funds in a foreign currency.
3. If the International Fisher Theory works the differences between the cost of funds denominated in different currencies represents the market's best guess as to the exchange rates ruling between these currencies in the future. This guess by the market might not prove to be a very accurate estimate but it is the best estimate the market can make given all the facts available at that particular time.

Exhibit 7.7 Debt Rating Agencies

Most debts and financial institutions are rated as to creditworthiness by one credit rating agency or another. Some of the better known rating agencies are:

IBCA
A European rating agency. Initially specialized in rating banks but now rates most major corporate issuers. Based in Paris, France.

Thomson Bankwatch
Rates financial institutions and is particularly concerned with rating institutions in emerging markets. Based in London.

Duff and Phelps
Assigns credit ratings to around 85% of US corporate debt. Has special interest in Latin America.

Fitch Investors services
The Agency rates around 50 000 corporate bond issues. Based in the USA but rates many non-US corporates.

Before a company or an individual invests in a bond or enters into a swap with a counter-party the investor needs to check up on the creditworthiness of the issuer of the bond or swap.
   Many credit agencies specialize in this activity by grading bonds and other financial instruments as AAA, ABB, BBB, etc.
   The preferred short-term investment of most company treasurers is the commercial paper of other companies. Most treasurers are only allowed to invest in, at minimum, an investment graded double A. One-third are only allowed to invest in a triple A! This even applies to repo bonds although not to independently monitored repos.

4. If the International Fisher Theory works then, from a cost point of view, it would not matter in which currency funds are borrowed since the NPV of the future payments for these funds in terms of the local currency would be the same for all currencies.

5. Much doubt has been cast on the validity of the International Fisher Theory, not least by Fisher himself. The theory may work in the long term at the macro level but at the micro level of the individual firm empirical research and the questioning of international treasurers has not found much support for the theory. This suggests that international capital markets are relatively inefficient markets.

6. Within the time frame of 10 years or so, which is the relevant time frame for most international funding, there is little evidence to support the hypothesis that the cost of funding in different currencies moves towards a common cost in terms of the local currency.

7. The difference in interest rates on loans denominated in different currencies tends to be a poor estimator but an unbiased estimator of future changes in exchange rates. This finding may permit a treasurer to reduce the cost of funding a company by diversifying his funding over several currencies. The variance on the cost of funding over the period of the loan will be reduced.

8. The cost of the funding does not appear to be a primary consideration of finance officers when they are considering the currency in which a loan should be raised. The "matching" of currency outflows against currency inflows appears to be the primary consideration of a finance officer when selecting a foreign currency for funding his company's operations. In other words self-hedging is the primary consideration when selecting the currency for a foreign currency loan. The maturity date of the debt is another important consideration.

9. Tax allowances and up-front costs such as legal costs can be important considerations when selecting the currency in which to fund the future operations of a multinational company.

10. In recent years the remarkable growth of the currency swap market backed by the fast expanding Euromarkets has provided an alternative mechanism for altering the currency mix of a company's financial structure at relatively low cost. Currency swaps are, however, only available in the major trading currencies.

11. The application of exchange controls to the movement of funds across international frontiers reduces the efficiency of the world capital market and so reduces the applicability of the International Fisher and all the other theories based on free market assumptions. If exchange controlled currencies are accessible to a multi-national company the cost of these funds, after adjusting for inflation, may well be lower than the cost of funds raised in free market currencies.

12. The legal and financial mechanics of raising a loan in a foreign currency are quite formidable.

NOTES

1. Possibly because British companies found ways around the exchange control regulations. Devices such as "Back-to-back loans" were popular at that time.
2. Levich, R. M. On the efficiency of markets for foreign exchange, in R. Dornbusch et al. (eds) *International Economic Policy*, Johns Hopkins University Press, 1979.
3. There is, as we have noted, a second factor, namely, the political risk attached to the loan but this factor has been found in practice to have a relatively small effect on cost relative to the inflation factor.
4. Fisher, I. "Appreciation and interest", Publications of the AEA, vol. 11, 1896, 331–442.
5. Lay, Kenneth, Director of Financial Operations World Bank, *Euromoney*, 1 July 1994, 92.
6. "If we do a small transaction we require a much lower cost of borrowing, as much as 50 basis points lower, because legal costs are often as significant as those on a large deal", Peter Yngwe, Head of Finance, Swedish Export Credit. Quoted in *Euromoney*, July 1994, 93.
7. See, for example, Werner, Jeffrey, Corporate Treasury, General Electric Capital Corporation, *Euromoney*, July 1994, 95.
8. McRae, T. W. (1992) Topview of the cost of loans in a foreign currency. UPE Occasional paper 9202, April, 3.
9. Werner, Jeffrey, ibid., *Euromoney*, July 1994, 92.
10. McRae, T. W. and Walker, D. P. (1980) *Foreign Exchange Management*, Prentice Hall, chapter 11.
11. Standard and Poor's and Dun and Bradstreet provide credit ratings on bonds and companies issuing bonds.

FURTHER READING

Aliber, R. Z. and Stickney, C. P. (1975) Accounting measures of foreign exchange exposure. *Accounting Review*, January, pp. 44–57.

Bullock, G. (1987) Euro-notes and Euro-commercial Paper. Butterworth.

Chang, R., Koveos, P. and Rhee, S. G. (1990) Financial planning for long term debt financing, *Advances in Financial Planning and Forecasting*, vol. 4, 33–59.

Fama, E. F. (1976) Forward rate as a predictor of future spot rate. *Journal of Financial Economics*, October, pp. 361–377.

Fatemi, A. (1988) The effect of international diversification on corporate financing policy. *Journal of Business Research*, January, 17–30.

Fisher, F. G. (1987) *Euro-bonds*. Euromoney Publications.

Hansen, L. P. and Hodrick, R. K. (1980) Forward rates as optimal predictions of future spot rates. *Journal of Political Economy*, October, pp. 829–853.

PoLin, J. W. and Madura, J. (1993) Optimal debt financing for multinational projects. *Journal of Multinational Financial Management*, vol. 4, no. 1/2, 63–73.

Liu, A. and Hsueh, L. P. (1993) Tax effect on the debt denomination decision of multinational projects. *Journal of International Business Studies*, first quarter, 145–54.

Morgan, J. R. (1982) An empirical investigation into the interest rate theory of exchange rate expectations. *Phd Thesis*, Bradford University, UK.

Park, Y. S. (1984) Currency swaps as a long term international financing technique. *Journal of International Business Studies*, Winter, 47–54.

Rhee, S. G., Chang, R. P. and Koveos, P. E. (1985) The currency of denomination decision for debt financing. *Journal of International Business Studies*, Fall, 143–50.

Shapiro, A. C. (1984) The impact of taxation on the currency-of-denomination decision for long term borrowing and lending. *Journal of International Business Studies*, Spring, 15–25.

TUTORIAL QUESTIONS

1. Why was the relative cost of funds borrowed at home or abroad of limited importance to treasurers of UK companies prior to 1980?
2. The majority of the countries in the world still apply tight exchange controls to the flow of funds out of their country. How, therefore, can it be that a high proportion of international funds are today (1995) flowing between free capital markets?
3. A Canadian company wants to borrow US$50 million for four years to fund a venture in the USA. The money can be borrowed in US$ at 10% per annum or in C$ at 12% per annum. What does the treasurer of the Canadian company need to know before he can decide in which currency to borrow the required funds?
4. What does the International Fisher Theory claim about differences in interest rates on loans denominated in different currencies?
5. Under what specific conditions would you not expect the International Fisher Theory to work?
6. Is the International Fisher Theory supported by academic research? Explain how the theory could be tested.
7. Would the cost of a portfolio of loans in different currencies provide an unbiased estimate of the average future exchange rates in these currencies? Give an example of how a portfolio of loans in different currencies can provide an "unbiased estimate" of the future average exchange rates and so cancel out incorrect expectations of future spot rates.
8. What is a "parallel" currency? Does the data from Exhibit 7.1 suggest that any of these four currencies are "parallel" currencies?
9. Why is the International Fisher Theory not applicable to floating rate loans?
10. Even if the International Fisher Theory works why might the differences on the interest rates charged on long-term fixed interest rate loans denominated in different currencies not fully reflect future exchange rate changes?
11. Explain how the exposure risk incurred by a UK debtor taking on a one-year loan of US$50 000 might be hedged. How is it that the risk of wide swings in exchange rates can often be hedged relatively cheaply by using currency options?
12. Suggest four difficulties that might be faced by a finance officer raising a loan in a foreign currency that would not be faced when raising a similar loan in the home currency.
13. "The tax treatment of foreign loans is often not symmetric". Explain why this is so?
14. Why is "matching" usually the key consideration when borrowing in a foreign currency? What is being matched?
15. Why is it that "maturity date" rather than relative cost is often the key consideration in choosing between various loans on offer in different currencies?

16. What tax benefits might accrue to a company if the company raises a loan in a foreign rather than in the home currency?
17. In loan agreements what is meant by the terms "moratorium" on payment, "flexible" maturity, "convertibility"?
18. What is an "exotic" currency? Give an example. What problems might a finance officer meet when trading in an exotic currency?
19. The interest rate on a one-year loan in Australian dollars is 10% per annum. The interest rate on an identical loan in US$ is 6% per annum. The current exchange rate is A$1.6 to the US$. What does the market expect the rate of exchange between A$ and US$ to be in one year's time?

CASE STUDY: ELEK PLC

Let us assume that you are the international treasurer of a large UK multinational named Elek PLC. Your company has a market capitalization of £3 000 000 000. Elek has just been offered a major contract to instal a giant hydro-electric generator in Michigan, USA.

The contract is worth $440 000 000. Payments will be made to Elek in three slices of $50 million, $50 million and $340 million at the end of year one, two, and three respectively. Construction is expected to take three years. The quantity surveying on the contract has been carried out by the Bextel corporation.

The cost of construction is estimated by Bextel to lie between $270 million and $330 million. The cash flows will involve three currencies US$, £ sterling, and German DMs. The cash flow estimates are set out in Table 28 below.

Required: Write a memo to the Board of Elek advising on (a) the likely profitability of the project expressed in both £ sterling and US$; (b) the risks involved in the project and suggestions as to how to hedge against these risks; and (c) how much finance is needed for the project, when the finance is needed and how best the deal should be financed. What currencies should be used to finance this project?

Table 28   Estimated Contract Cash Flows

Year	0	1	2	3	
Inflow	0	50	50	340	US$
Outflow					
US$	5	20	20	30	US$
UK £	50	30	5	5	£
German DM	60	120	30	10	DM

Currency Forecasts

Private exchange rate forecasts made at the beginning of year 1 (year 0) predict that the US$ will rise by about 20% against the £ over the next three years and by 10% against the DM.

Current rates of exchange in year 0: £1 = 1.64 US$ = 3.0 DM.

The current costs of three year Eurobonds are:

£ sterling bond = 12%   US$ bond = 6%   DM bond = 4%

CASE STUDY: ELEK PLC:
NOTES TOWARDS A SOLUTION

Introduction

The basic approach is (1) to set out the cash flows under the various assumptions about the exchange rates; (2) calculate the implied IRR or yield; (3) identify the more important risks attached to the project; (4) work out ways of hedging these risks; and (5) examine the financing of the project.

Exchange Rates

Three possibilities suggest themselves:

1. No change in the exchange rates.
2. The private forecasts of future exchange rates are correct.
3. The future rates implied in the interest rate differentials are correct.

There is also the problem of deciding on the "timing" of the change in the rates. The change could come as a gradual change over the three years or a sudden change in years 1, 2 or 3. In practice the financial implications of each possibility would be examined. We have limited our examination by assuming a gradual change over the three years (Table 30).

Table 30

		Year		
The private forecasts:	0	1	2	3
1 × £ = US$	1.640	1.544	1.453	1.367
1 × £ = DM	3.000	2.912	2.832	2.751

The exchange rates implied in the interest rate differentials are as shown in Table 31.

Table 31

1 × £ = US$	1.640	1.552	1.469	1.390
1 × £ = DM	3.000	2.786	2.587	2.402

We see that there is a substantial difference between the private forecast prediction of the future DM spot rate and that implied by the interest rate differentials. The treasurer would be likely to query this difference with the forecaster. If the forecaster is right a speculative profit in DM is available.

Profitability of the Project

We use the private forecast rates to calculate the yield on the given cash flows expressed in both US$ and £ sterling.

The yield in terms of US$ is around 18% and in terms of the £ sterling is around 25%

These are good yields and they would seem to compensate for the limited risks involved. Especially if this project is being used as a "loss leader" to get into the US market.

Elek's estimate of its cost of capital is important here. It seems unlikely that the cost would exceed 20%, 15% is a more likely estimate. NOTE: The cost of capital must not be confused with the possibility of cheap DM financing. The possibility of "cheap" DM finance provides the opportunity for a gamble that can be taken whether or not the project is accepted. The likely profit and related risk on any speculative venture in DM should be calculated as a separate project.

It would also seem sensible to calculate the yield based on the "lower" Bechtel estimates. The project provides an acceptable cushion for risk at a cost of around US$280 million. Why are the cash flow estimates so pessimistic? Are the Elek project estimators building high estimates of cost into their projections to provide a cushion for risk?

The Risks Involved

The main risks attached to this project would seem to be:

1. The reliability of the Bextel forecasts of cost.
2. The creditworthiness of the US buyer who will sign the contract.
3. The future rates of exchange. These may change as may Euro-interest rates. We have assumed that the loan negotiated to finance the project will be a fixed interest rate loan of three years duration.

How to Hedge the Risks Involved

The cost risk can be hedged by arranging a guarantee from Bextel with regard to the reliability of their estimates. Also it is possible that the Elek cash flow estimates already include a large safety cushion re future cost increases.

The creditworthiness of the buyer can be tested by checking on the rating of the buyer with a credit rating agency, such as Standard and Poor, in the USA. The ECGD offers default insurance on large foreign contracts at a reasonable cost.

The exchange rate risks can be reduced but not eliminated by a series of rolling forward currency swaps. However, the simplest and probably cheapest solution to hedging the exchange rate risk attached to the project is to finance the project in US$. The cash inflows are denominated in this currency, so the US$ loan is self-hedged.

How Much Finance is Needed for the Project and When is it Needed?

We make the conservative assumption that all cash outflows occur at the beginning of a period and all cash inflows at the end. Elek must arrange a total US$ loan of about US$250 million, allowing for emergencies, and call down US$120 million during year 1 and the balance in year 2. We assume that the US$340 million cash inflow will not arrive until the end of year 3.

How Should the Deal be Financed?

This contract is very much "back-end-loaded" so a substantial amount of the funding must be raised by Elek in the early years to finance the project over the three years.

The treasurer must take a position on whether the currency of loan is important. If he believes in the international Fisher effect, which is unlikely, he might decide that the currency of the loan is of little importance because any interest rate differentials will be cancelled out by future exchange rate changes.

However, if he believes that the currency in which the loan is raised is important (and all the empirical evidence suggests that he will) then he is likely to look at borrowing in either US$, £ sterling, or German DM.

The currency inflow is all in US$s and the US$ is expected to rise in value over the next three years against both the £ and the DM, thus a "matching" strategy seems logical. A matching strategy would raise all the finance required in US$. This is a risk minimizing strategy since it makes the debt, in effect, self-hedging with regard to currency exposure.

However, the predicted fall in the value of the £ and DM against the US$ may present an opportunity to benefit from currency speculation by financing in £ sterling or DM. The differential between the current Euro-dollar rate of interest and the Eurosterling rate almost cancels out the benefit of raising the loan in £ sterling if the private currency projections are correct. However, the Euro-DM rate seems to present an opportunity for speculation in DM. The DM is expected to devalue by about 3% a year against the US$ over the next three years yet the DM loan is cheaper than the US$ loan! However, there is a definite risk that these currency forecasts are wrong. Is the risk involved worth the possible speculative gain? The treasurer must make up his mind on this before trying to "lock in" a speculative profit via the derivatives market.

Hedging Other Risks

The ECGD or NCM could be used to provide insurance guarantees re bankruptcy or non-payment by the US company. If the construction costs turn out to be well outside the range predicted then Elek may be able to sue the project surveyor. It all depends on the conditions that the surveyor attached to the cost estimates. Surveyors take out heavy insurance to cover this kind of risk.

Note that currency forecasters have been spectacularly wrong in the past about the future of the US$ to DM to £ sterling exchange rate. Particularly over a period as long as three years.

Other Information Required

In addition to the above Elek will need to collect further information on the following matters:

1. Details regarding exchange control the tax position re repatriating profits.
2. Study past performance as a guide to the reliability of the exchange rate forecasts provided by the private forecaster.
3. Whether Elek can raise euro-dollars at the prime rate given or if a risk premium will be added by lenders.
4. The extent and cost of insurance cover available in UK, Germany and USA.
5. The forward market rate of exchange between the US$, the £ sterling and the DM up to one year ahead. Do the forward market rates agree with the private rate forecasts? Are long term currency hedges available (through, for example, the swaps or options market)?
6. The credit rating of the US corporation offering the contract.

APPENDIX: ELEK PLC: NOTES TOWARDS A SOLUTION

Exhibit 7.8 Calculation of the Yield on the Elek Project Expressed in US$ and £s

.......Estimated yields in US$ and £ sterling

1. Translate all values into US$ at the forecast future spot rate.

	Year				
	0	1	2	3	Total
Estimated US$ inflow	0.00	50.00	50.00	340.00	440
Estimated cost outflow in US$:					
US$	5.00	20.00	20.00	30.00	75.00
UK£ in US$	82.00	46.31	7.26	6.84	142.41
DM in US$	32.80	63.60	15.39	4.97	116.76
Total outflow in US$	119.80	129.91	42.65	41.81	334.17
Net outflow in US$	−119.80	−79.91	7.35	298.19	105.83
Cumulative net outflow	−119.80	−199.71	−192.36	105.83	

The IRR expressed in US$ = 17.8%

The forecast exchange rates are as follows:

Predicted US$ per pound sterling	1.640	1.544	1.453	1.367
Predicted US$ per DM	0.547	0.530	0.513	0.497
Predicted DM per pound sterling	3.000	2.912	2.832	2.751

The US$ is predicted to rise by 20% against the £ sterling and 10% against the DM.

2. Translate all values into £ sterling at the forecast future spot rate.

	Year				
	0	1	2	3	Total
Estimated inflow in £s	0.00	32.39	34.42	248.67	315.48
Estimated cost outflow in £s:					
US$ in UK pound	3.05	12.96	13.77	21.94	51.71
UK pound	50.00	30.00	5.00	5.00	90.00
DM in UK pound	20.00	41.20	10.59	3.63	75.43
Total outflow in UK £	73.05	84.16	29.36	30.58	217.15
Net outflow in UK £	−73.05	−51.77	5.06	218.09	96.33
Cumulative net outflow in £s	−73.05	−124.82	−119.76	98.33	

The IRR expressed in UK £s = 25.2%

Elek: Yield on project expressed in UK pounds

The project offers a positive yield in both US$ and £s but the yield is higher in terms of £ sterling because of the forecast that the £ will fall in value by around 18% over the three-year period against the US$. Thus the US$s will become more valuable in terms of £s. The project evaluated in £s includes a speculative element in terms of US$s.

Exhibit 7.7 Future Spot Rates Implied by the Interest Rate Differences: Elek PLC

Calculation of the future exchange rates implied by the differing bond rates.
The relevant formula is:

$$(\text{Foreign rate} - \text{home rate})/(1 + \text{home rate})$$

In each case given the implied per annum future exchange rate is thus:

		%
US$–Pound	$(0.06 - 0.12)/(1 + 0.12) \times 100 =$	-5.36
DM–Pound	$(0.04 - 0.12)/(1 + 0.12) \times 100 =$	-7.14
DM–US$	$(0.04 - 0.06)/(1 + 0.06) \times 100 =$	-1.89

For example, the pound sterling is expected to fall in value by approximately 5.36% in each of the three years against the US$. In other words the interest rate differential implies that 5.36% fewer US$ can be bought each year with each £.
Thus the exchange rates implied by the interest rate differentials are as follows:

	Year			
	0	1	2	3
US$ per £	1.640	1.552	1.469	1.390
DM per £	3.000	2.786	2.587	2.402
US$ per DM	0.547	0.536	0.526	0.516

Note that there is a substantial difference between the future rates of exchange implied in the bond rates and the exchange rates forecast by the professional forecasting firm.

CASE STUDY: MOLSON'S DEBT STRATEGY

Molson's is a Canadian company that runs many subsidiary companies worldwide. Two of these companies are called Molson Breweries and the Diversey Corporation, which manufactures cleaning, sanitation and water cleaning products.

So far as global funding is concerned Molson's treasury aim to seek out the maximum tax shield they can find on their global debt.

"You always want to make sure that you have a tax deduction for your interest and your other corporate expenses." Molson aims at a stable cash flow: "Stability gives you a lower beta ... which means that you can invest in more projects because you have a lower cost of capital."

Molson hedges most of its debt since "several studies have shown that hedging decreases the beta of a firm ... and the lower beta lowers the cost of capital".

Diversey is a major company within the Molson group that operates in more than 50 countries around the world. Diversey manages its own currency risk and operates a Treasury Centre in Belgium that handles finance and tax for all 50 companies in the Diversey group.

The Molson Group treasurer states that: "At HQ we primarily concern ourselves, not with short-term currency transactions, but with the risks associated with the C$1 billion of assets we have around the globe."

Molson's key exposures fall into two groups: (1) the short-term currency, commodity and interest-rate exposures; and (2) the long-term asset, liability and cash flow exposures that arise out of operating businesses abroad.

The treasury at Molson's believes that shareholders want a similar amount of debt and equity in each country so gearing is not adapted to local conditions:

> "The debt financing of these businesses or their associated hedges often have to be put in place synthetically through derivatives for tax and accounting reasons".

For example, debt may be raised in Canada on cost or tax grounds and then swapped into foreign currencies to meet the foreign currency needs of the group.

The Molson Group does not subscribe to the popular view that the fixed to floating rate debt ratio should be correlated to the business cycle (via interest rate swaps) since the correlation of Molson's income to the business cycle is not high.

The duration of Molson's debt compared to the duration of its asset structure is the key factor in selecting suitable debt instruments.

> "The duration of fixed interest debt is far more important to us. The fixed/floating ratio does not capture the long-term nature of the debt, so we try to capture that [in the duration of the debt]".

The Molson group manages its interest rate exposures very actively. Its interest rate derivatives portfolio currently totals about C$600 million. The medium- and long-term debts are hedged primarily via floating for fixed swaps. "This allows Molson's to match the underlying debt obligations" while also allowing the treasury to "access spreads offered at the short end of the yield curve".

The swap portfolio is actively managed on a continuous basis. "We are monitoring our swaps constantly, considering whether we should buy out of our current . . . swaps". "You want to look continuously at refinancing of swaps through tax advantaged means." Tax planning of debt is particularly difficult in Canada because of the recent (post-1990) attack on tax avoiding measures on foreign financing mounted by the Canadian tax authorities.

For example, in 1994 if the value of foreign debt falls in value in terms of the C$ the "profit" is taxed but if the value of the foreign debt rises in value the loss is not allowable against tax. The only way to get around this lack of symmetry in the tax law is "through devising some fancy financing structures or some complex derivative transaction".

Molson, however, are very wary of using exotic derivative products. "We don't use them because we think the trader always knows better [than we do about their relative value]".

Molson revenue by region:

Canada: 58%. USA: 20% Europe: 16% Other 6%.

Answer the following questions about the case.

1. How does the hedging of corporate debt provide access to additional funds? Explain how the beta of the company is involved in this theory.
2. How can the treasury centre in Belgium increase the global cash flows of the Diversey group?
3. How can the gearing of foreign subsidiary be adapted to local conditions? How could this benefit the Group?
4. Explain how Molson uses synthetic derivatives to reduce funding costs and the global tax imposed on the Group.
5. "Molson's does not subscribe to the popular view that the fixed to floating debt ratio should be correlated to the business cycle." Why is this view popular? Why should the fixed to floating debt ratio be correlated to the business cycle? What benefits might accrue to a company that follows this philosophy? This philosophy is suited to what kinds of corporations?
6. Why do you think the matching of the duration of debt to the duration of asset structure is considered to be so important by the Molson treasury? (Rather than the fixed to floating debt ratio.)

7. What two advantages do the Molson treasury seek to gain by the active management of its interest rate exposures? What devices are used to hedge the medium- and longer-term interest exposures? How do these devices work? Explain why the treasury wishes to "access spreads offered at the short end of the yield curve".
8. Why do Molson's monitor their swap portfolio constantly? What might happen if they did not?
9. How can tax advantages be gained by refinancing of swaps (see Chapter 10 to assist in answering this question).
10. Why is the taxation of gains and losses on foreign denominated loans asymmetrical in Canada?
11. Can you think up any "fancy financing or derivative structure" that might overcome the tax asymmetry discussed in question 10?

CASE STUDY: HOSBILD PLC

Let us assume that you are the financial director of a large UK multinational named Hosbild PLC. Your company has a market capitalization of £1 750 000 000. During 1996 Hosbild PLC has won a major contract to build a hospital in Canada.

The contract is worth C$250 000 000 Canadian dollars. Payments will be made to Hosbild in four slices of C$50 million, C$50 million, C$50 million and C$100 million at the end of 1997, 1998, 1999 and 2000 respectively. Construction is expected to take four years, starting in January 1997. The quantity surveying on the contract has been carried out by the Aliber corporation, a well-established Canadian surveying company.

The total cost of construction is estimated by Aliber to be around C$165 million in C$ although other currencies will be used in the project. The cash flows will involve three currencies, the Canadian $, the £ sterling, and French francs. The cash flow estimates are set out in Table 29 below. The net of tax cost of funds to Hosbild PLC for international projects is estimated to be 14% per annum.

Required: Write a memo to the Board of Hosbild advising on (a) the likely profitability of the project in both Canadian $s and £ sterling; (b) the major risks involved in the project and suggestions as to how Hosbild might hedge these risks; and (c) suggestions as to how the deal should be financed. Only about £10 million is currently available from internal funds for financing the project so the balance, net of inflows, needs to be raised in the international capital markets. In what currency or currencies should the deal be financed? Hosbild is well known in the UK but little known outside the UK.

Table 29 Estimated Contract Cash Flows

Year	Begin 1997	End 1997	1998	1999	2000
Inflow	0	50	50	50	100 C$
Outflow					
C$ million	14	19	16	20	20 C$
UK £ million	20	9	4	6	4 £
French F million	25	30	25	10	20 FF

Currency Forecasts

Private exchange rate forecasts in late 1996 predict that the Canadian $ will fall to about C$2.10 to the £ over the next three-years and the FF will rise to about 8 francs to the £ over the same period assuming that the UK does not enter the ERM.

Current rates of exchange at the beginning of 1997 are:

$$£1 = 1.90 \text{ C\$} = 9.00 \text{ French francs}$$

The costs of three year international bonds at the beginning of 1997 are:

$$£ \text{ sterling bond} = 10\%, \text{ C\$ bond} = 11\%, \text{ FF bond} = 8\%$$

8
Multi-currency Accounting

INTRODUCTION: THE TRANSLATION PROBLEM

The growing internationalization of world trade has persuaded many companies to open up subsidiary companies abroad.

The accounts of these subsidiary companies are almost invariably denominated in the currency of the country in which they operate. The accounting regulations promulgated in many advanced industrial countries require that the parent company consolidate the accounts of the parent company together with the accounts of all of the subsidiaries into a single set of "consolidated" accounts denominated in the same currency. The currency used for the consolidation is usually the currency of the country in which the parent company resides.[1]

If a Canadian company owns three subsidiary companies operating in the UK, France and Taiwan then at the end of the company year the Canadian company must "add up" the accounts expressed in Canadian dollars, UK pounds sterling, French francs and Taiwanese dollars to make up the consolidated accounts of the group. Unfortunately Canadian dollars, francs, pounds and Taiwanese dollars cannot be added together in any meaningful way, so each set of accounts must be "translated" into a common currency. The common currency in this case will be Canadian dollars, the currency used to make up the accounts of the parent company.

The Canadian company must translate the accounts of the three subsidiaries into Canadian dollars, but at what rate of exchange?[2]

This key decision on what rate of exchange to use when translating the accounts into a common currency is a matter of some controversy. Over the last 50 years several different translation methods using differing rates of exchange have been used in different parts of the world. We shall discover later in the chapter that the calculation of the profit, debt and liquidity position of a group of companies can be much influenced by the method of translation chosen.

In recent years the various countries of the world would seem to be moving towards a common standard for translating accounts, but the differences are still substantial.

In this chapter we will describe the three most commonly used methods of translating company accounts from one currency to another. We will also illustrate the variation in financial results produced by each method.

It should be noted in passing that the process of consolidating company accounts that are denominated in several different currencies is one of the most complicated tasks faced by an accountant. Consolidation raises many tricky problems apart from translation. The treatment of goods and cash in transit, inter-company debts, the valuation of inventory and other matters raise difficult problems for the accountant. This chapter will examine only one small part of this large problem, namely the problem of translating accounts from one currency to another.

The Foreign Currency and the Home Currency

In this chapter we will refer to the currency in which the foreign subsidiary accounts are denominated as the "foreign currency" and the currency in which the parent company accounts are denominated as the "home currency".

For example, if a French company owns a subsidiary in Russia the "home currency" is French francs and the "foreign currency" is Russian roubles.

Accounting standards often refer to the currency used by the foreign subsidiary as the "functional currency" and the currency used for making up the consolidated accounts as the "reporting" currency.

The "functional" currency will nearly always be the same as the "foreign" currency unless the operations of the foreign subsidiary is very tightly tied into the operations of the parent company. In such a case the functional currency of the subsidiary is taken to be the reporting currency used by the parent.

For example if a US company with a Taiwanese subsidiary simply uses the Taiwanese subsidiary to put together parts made in the US and then sells the finished goods in the United States the Taiwanese company will be treated as if it were a department of the US company and the accounts of the subsidiary will be denominated in, or treated as if they were denominated in, US dollars.

This distinction is of some importance because of the US accounting standard FASB 52. In the situation described in the previous paragraph the US company would need to consolidate its accounts under the "temporal" and not the "current" method. In addition, and even more important, any translation gains or losses on the foreign accounts will need to be put through the income account of the US company and not simply transferred to a translation reserve account.

The significance of these requirements will become clearer later in the chapter.

Translation v Conversion

It is important to differentiate between the process of translation and the process of conversion. When a value in one currency is "translated" into a value in another currency the numerical value changes but no cash flows. If an amount in one currency is "converted" into another currency an amount of cash in one currency is converted into an amount of cash in another currency. A real flow of cash takes place.

Translating foreign currency values can result in a "paper" gain or loss on the values translated, but such a "paper" gain or loss can be reversed in a future period if the exchange rate reverses direction. A "paper" gain or loss is not a real gain or loss of cash. A gain or loss on conversion represents a real gain or loss of cash in terms of the home currency.

THE METHODS AVAILABLE FOR TRANSLATING ACCOUNTS FROM ONE CURRENCY TO ANOTHER

In practice, if not in theory, three methods of translation have been used to consolidate accounts denominated in different currencies into a single set of accounts denominated in a common currency.

These three methods are:

1. "The closing rate method" which is called the "current rate" method in the USA.
2. "The monetary–non-monetary method" and its associated method called the "temporal" method.
3. "The current–non-current method", not to be confused with the current method!

Let us now examine each of these translation methods in turn.

The Closing Rate (Current Rate) Method

This method is called the closing rate/net investment method in the UK and the current rate method in the USA.

Variations on this method of translation are currently recommended by the accounting standard boards in both the UK and the USA. The US standard is identified as FASB 52 and the UK standard as SSAP 20.

Under the closing/current rate method all of the items on the balance sheet of each foreign subsidiary, both assets and liabilities, are translated at the rate of exchange ruling on the last day of the company year.

The profit and loss account items can also be translated at this closing rate or at an average exchange rate for the year. A weighted exchange rate may also be used.

This method of translation, which is the most popular method in current use, enjoys many advantages over the other two methods in use.

Firstly, if only one rate is used for translation, it is simple to apply. There is only one exchange rate to apply to all of the many items in the accounts. Secondly, the current rate of exchange is easy to find, it is quoted at the end of each day in newspapers, etc., in each country. Thirdly, the financial ratios that measure the performance of the subsidiary remain the same whether these ratios are calculated in terms of the foreign or the home currency. Fourthly, the debt of the foreign subsidiary is correctly valued in terms of the home currency in the consolidated accounts.

In effect the method values the foreign subsidiary at "net worth" in terms of the currency of the parent company. In the UK the method is called the "closing rate–net investment method" to emphasize this fact.[3]

The closing rate method makes the net worth of the foreign subsidiary sensitive to any fall or rise in the value of the foreign currency relative to the home currency. A devaluation of the foreign currency results in a translation loss to the group, a revaluation awards a translation gain to the group. However, this gain or loss is a "paper" gain or loss, no cash actually flows, so the paper gain or loss could be reversed in a future period.

One major problem associated with using the closing rate method of translation is that the non-monetary assets of the foreign subsidiary might not be correctly valued in terms of the home currency unless the foreign non-monetary assets have been recently revalued.

The closing rate method, or some variant of it, is by far the most popular method currently in use. The method is recommended by the accounting institutes in North America and Europe and the method is followed by many countries in South America, Africa and South East Asia.

Although the methods of translation used in North America and Europe are similar, the methods are not identical in every respect. An accountant familiar with, say, the UK method of translation must be careful when applying the rather different US variant.

Also, under certain circumstances, an alternative method of translation might be recommended by the given accounting standard. If a subsidiary is bound so closely to its mother company that both are, for all practical purposes, one company then both the US and the UK authorities recommend the use of the temporal method of translation rather than the closing rate method for translating the foreign accounts.

If the foreign subsidiary is operating in a country suffering from hyperinflationary conditions[4] then all the foreign values must be translated directly into the "reporting" currency to arrive at any meaningful set of accounts for the purpose of consolidation. Under hyperinflationary conditions some accounting items may be difficult to value in any meaningful way.

The Monetary–Non-monetary Method

This method uses a very different approach to translating the accounts of each foreign subsidiary.

In this case all of the items in the balance sheet are identified as being either a monetary asset or a monetary liability or a non-monetary asset.

What is a Monetary Asset or a Monetary Liability?

A monetary asset or liability is an asset or liability whose value is defined as a fixed number of money units. For example, a debt that is owed to a creditor is a monetary liability and a company debenture is a monetary liability. Trade debtors (receivables), cash and most fixed interest government stocks are monetary assets.

A fixed-interest repayment mortgage on a house is a good example of a monetary liability. The lender lends the borrower a £100 000 repayment mortgage to buy a house. The repayment mortgage must be repaid over a 20-year period. The lender requires the borrower to pay back a portion of the £100 000 plus a fixed amount of interest each month for 20 years. The borrower is obligated to pay 100 000 money units plus interest to the lender over the repayment period.

If the rate of inflation rises above the rate of inflation expected by the lender the repayment value of the mortgage falls in real terms over the period of the loan. Monetary assets and liabilities are vulnerable to inflation. The reader will recall from Chapter 3 that the exchange rate between currencies is linked to the relative rates of inflation in the two currencies.

A non-monetary asset is defined in a negative sense as any balance sheet item that is not a monetary asset or liability. Land, buildings, equipment, equity shares, royalties and inventory are examples of non-monetary assets. Note particularly that an equity share is a non-monetary asset, its terminal value is not defined as a fixed number of money units.

The value of a non-monetary asset is determined by the market for the good, by the process of supply and demand. The price of a non-monetary asset is determined by that price that clears the market. The terminal sales value of a non-monetary asset, like a motor car, is not fixed in advance as it would be if it were a monetary asset like a government stock.

The Translation Process

Let us now return to the monetary–non-monetary method of translation.

The monetary–non-monetary method of translation applies a different rate of exchange to monetary items, both assets and liabilities, and non-monetary items.

Under the M–NM method monetary assets and liabilities are translated at the closing rate of exchange just as they were under the closing rate method. A non-monetary asset is translated at the "historic rate", that is the rate of exchange ruling on the date when the asset was acquired. If a non-monetary asset is later revalued the asset value is translated at the rate of exchange ruling on the date of the revaluation.

The profit or loss for the year is normally translated at the average rate of exchange, or weighted average rate, for the year, although under some translation standards there are exceptions to this rule.

If one of the costs charged in the profit and loss account is associated with a non-monetary asset, such as depreciation of equipment or cost of sales, then this cost will be translated at the same rate as the associated asset. Thus different rates of exchange could be applied to sales and cost of sales!

One advantage of the M–NM method is that if there has been substantial changes in the exchange rate in recent years, for example, if the home currency is rising in value against the foreign currency, the M–NM method is likely to translate the historic value of the subsidiary non-monetary assets into the home currency at a more realistic value than would be the case if the closing rate method is used.

The reader will recall from Chapter 3 that the PPP theory claims that changes in the exchange rate reflect the relative rates of inflation in the two countries over the time period. Thus if a foreign non-monetary asset, say equipment, is held in a country with a much higher inflation rate than the rate of inflation in the home country then the equipment held abroad will float up in value with the high foreign rate of inflation. The closing rate method of translation ignores this fact by translating the foreign non-monetary asset's historic cost at current exchange rates. Thus the closing rate method of translation ignores the PPP theory. If the PPP theory is correct the foreign equipment's value in terms of the foreign currency will have floated upwards in value but will not have risen in real terms in terms of the home currency.

If, however, the foreign held non-monetary assets are revalued on a regular basis then this limitation on the accuracy of the closing rate method is removed.

The perceptive reader, who recalls the theories set out in Chapter 3, will see that the M–NM method assumes that the PPP theory works but that the International Fisher Theory does not work! If the International Fisher worked, the rise in the value of a foreign loan, when translated into the home currency, would be exactly compensated by the advantage of a lower interest rate. This difference in the rates could be invested to repay the foreign loan on the maturity date.

We conclude that the M–NM method translates all money assets and liabilities at the closing rate and other assets at the historic rate. The method is favoured by most academic commentators.

The Temporal Method

A variation on the M–NM method is called the "temporal method". This method of translation was recommended by the US accounting standards board in 1976.[5] Later, in 1982, the US standards board switched to recommending a translation method called the "current method", that is very similar to the closing rate method advocated by the Accounting Standards Board in the UK under SSAP No. 20.

The temporal method is very similar to the M–NM method in practice but the theoretical foundations are rather different. When applying the temporal method to a set of foreign accounts the only practical difference from the M–NM method is that any inventory which is valued at year end market value in the accounts of the subsidiary is translated into the consolidated accounts of the parent company at the closing rate of exchange not at the historic rate; however, if the revaluation rule is applied under the M–NM method the result is the same.

In recent years the M–NM/temporal approach has fallen out of favour except in special circumstances. The reason for this may be because it is more complicated to understand and to apply compared to the closing rate method. For example, if an asset was acquired some time ago in an exotic currency then finding the rate of exchange ruling on the date the asset was acquired might present some difficulty.

However, the primary reason why the temporal method was discontinued in the United States seems to be a consequence of the fact that the US accounting standard enforced in 1976 insisted that any translation gains or losses thrown up by the method must be put through the group profit and loss account. These "paper" profits and losses destabilized the year by year trend in company profits. In other words the profits showed a higher year on year variance than they would have done if the translation losses or gains had not been put through the income account of the group. This higher variance on the profits figure could, in theory, push up the risk premium on the company share price and so push up the cost of funds to the company, which would, in turn, push down the share price.

However, research conducted on this hypothesis by Dukes (1978)[6] found that the method of translation employed did not seem to have much influence on the share price of the multinational companies included in his study.

Under the US standard FASB 52 if the functional currency of the foreign subsidiary is deemed to be the home (reporting) currency, then the temporal method of translation must be employed and profits or losses on translation must be carried to the group profit and loss account. The same rule may apply under the UK standard SSAP 20. The reader will recall that if the foreign subsidiary is tightly bound to the parent company then this rule applies.

The closing rate method does not throw out gains or losses on translation since all of the values in the balance sheet are translated at the same exchange rate.

If translation gains or losses are not put through the group profit and loss account they can be carried straight to a translation equalization reserve account. This approach means that any profit or loss on translation will not affect the profits reported in the year the translation gain or loss occurs.

The Current–Non-current Method

The third method of translation, called the current–non-current method, is only included as an historical footnote. It is generally agreed that this method suffers from one or two defects that eliminates it from serious consideration as a viable method of translating foreign accounts. However, the C–NC method was in almost universal use prior to 1970 and is still used by a few companies resident in countries that do not have accounting standards.

The current non-current (C–NC) method divides all of the assets and liabilities stated in the balance sheet into two groups.

The first group includes all of the assets and liabilities that are included under current assets and current liabilities in the company balance sheet. Examples of current assets and liabilities are inventory, debtors, cash, trade creditors and short-term bank loans.

The second group includes all of the other non-current items reported on the balance sheet. Assets such as land, buildings and equipment and long-term liabilities such as debentures.

Current assets and liabilities are translated at the closing rate of exchange, that is the rate of exchange ruling on the last day of the company year. The non-current assets and liabilities are translated at the historic rate ruling on the date when the asset or liability was acquired or revalued.

Most of the items in the profit and loss account are translated at the average exchange rate, or weighted average rate, for the accounting period. However, costs associated with non-current assets or liabilities will be translated at the same rate as the associated asset or liability.

The major difference between the C–NC method and the other methods is that long-term debts are translated at the historic rate when they were acquired and not at the closing rate. Inventory is translated at the end-of-year rate even if most of the inventory is valued at cost and was acquired some time previously.

Both of these differences introduce error into the C–NC method of translation. Particularly the translating of long-term debt at the historic rate. A company adopting such a translation procedure could bankrupt itself when the debt comes to be repaid!

The only thing that can be said in favour of the C–NC method is that it is intuitively appealing, particularly to accountants! Assets and liabilities acquired recently are translated at a recent exchange rate, assets and debt acquired some time ago are translated at a historic rate. However, the M–NM method provides all of the advantages of the C–NC method without suffering from any of the defects.

It has also been argued, incorrectly, that the C–NC method appears to offset gains or losses on translation of assets against the gain or loss on the financing of these assets.

The treatment of long-term debt is clearly wrong. If a five-year loan of FF10 million was incurred in 1990 when the rate of exchange was FF10 to the £ the UK company would, at that time, have needed to pay 1 million pound sterling to repay the loan. If by 1994 the rate of exchange has altered to FF8 to the £ the UK company needs FF10 million/8 = £1.25 million to repay the loan.

The cost of repaying the loan in the home currency depends on the closing rate of exchange not on the historic rate when the loan was acquired. If the group accounts show the debt as £1 million rather than £1.25 million the British parent company would be grossly understating the true value of the debt in terms of pounds sterling.

If the rate of exchange had moved in favour of the £ to, say, FF12 to the £ then the value of the French franc loan in terms of sterling would be FF10 million/12 = £833 333 not £1 million. The UK parent company would be overstating its debt by £166 667 if it used the C–NC method to translate the French accounts.

The mishandling of the translation of long-term debt eliminates the current–non-current method of translation from serious consideration as a translation method.

Another possible limitation of the C–NC method is that if the currency of the foreign subsidiary is rising in value against the home currency then the fixed assets of the foreign subsidiary might be seriously undervalued in terms of the home currency if the C–NC method is used and the foreign exchange market is not efficient.

Another less serious limitation of the C–NC method concerns the translated value of inventory. If the inventory was bought some time ago and is valued at cost in the subsidiary accounts, the end of year valuation in terms of the home currency might be quite inaccurate if the inventory is translated at the year end rate of exchange. The problem is similar to the problem that the closing rate method faces when translating non-monetary assets.

We conclude that the C–NC method of translation is today of no more than historical interest.

AN EXAMPLE OF TRANSLATION: THE PUMA CORPORATION

The problems inherent in translating accounts from one currency to another can best be explained by working through a simple example.

Exhibit 8.1(a) provides an example of a translation of accounts. A set of accounts of a foreign subsidiary denominated in a foreign currency, the P$, is to be translated into the currency of the home country, in this case into pound sterling. The British parent company is called the Puma Corporation. The parent company accounts are expressed in terms of £ sterling, so £ sterling is in this case the "reporting" currency.

The accounts of the subsidiary of the Puma Corporation are expressed in terms of a foreign currency called the $P. In the case of Exhibit 8.1(a) the closing rate of exchange at the company year end turns out to be $P8 to the £ sterling. When the fixed assets were bought and the debenture loans acquired the rate of exchange was P$4 to the £ sterling. The average rate of exchange over the last accounting year is calculated to be P$7 to the £ sterling. The inventory was bought, on average, three months before the company year end when the rate of exchange was P$7.5 to the £ sterling.

The closing rate method translates all values in the subsidiary company accounts, both the balance sheet and the profit and loss account values,[7] at the closing rate, namely P$8 to the £ sterling. Note that one result of using this method of translation is that the financial ratios of the subsidiary are the same whether they are expressed in terms of $P or £ sterling.

Exhibit 8.1(a)   Translating Foreign Accounts Using Different Translation Methods

Puma Corporation: Translating Accounts

Foreign subsidiary balances in P$	Item in balance sheet						
			Foreign currency falling in value £'000 Sterling				
		Exchange rate P$ per £	Closing rate method	Exchange rate P$ per £	Temporal method £	Exchange rate P$ per £	Current–non-current method £
10000	Fixed assets	8	1250	4	2500	4	2500
3000	Inventory (at cost)	8	375	7.5	400	8	375
2000	Inventory (NRV)	8	250	8	250	8	250
4000	Debtors	8	500	8	500	8	500
1000	Cash	8	125	8	125	8	125
20000	Total assets		2500		3775		3750
12000	Equity + reserves	8	1500	*	2775	*	2300
3600	Debenture loans	8	450	8	450	4	900
4400	Creditors	8	550	8	550	8	550
20000	Total finance		2500		3775		3750
2500 P$	Net profit	8 £	312.5	7 £	357	7 £	357
20.8%	Return on equity		20.8%		12.9%		15.5%
16.0%	Return on equity + loans		16.0%		11.1%		11.2%
23.1%	Gearing		23.1%		14.0%		28.1%

Rates of exchange

			P$
Historic rate for fixed assets and loans	1 pound sterling =		4
Average rate for year	1 pound sterling =		7
Historic rate for stocks	1 pound sterling =		7.5
Closing rate	1 pound sterling =		8

The financial results extracted from accounts expressed in a foreign currency can be affected by the method used to translate the foreign accounts. Much depends on whether the foreign currency is rising or falling in value compared to the home currency.

In the above example the return on equity varies from 20.83% to 12.9%. The gearing varies from 28.1% to 14.00%.

Where the foreign currency is falling in value against the home currency:

1. The Closing Rate method is likely to UNDERVALUE the Fixed Assets.
2. The Current–non-current method OVERVALUES the debt due.
3. The closing rate and C–NC method might well be UNDERVALUING inventory valued at cost.
4. The return on capital can be very different because of the inventory value and depreciation differences.
5. If the value of the $P is rising against the pound sterling the situation will be reversed.

The temporal version of the monetary–non-monetary method also translates all monetary assets and liabilities at the closing rate. The fixed assets, however, are translated at the historic rate ruling on the date the assets were acquired, namely P$4 to the £. Inventory valued at net realizable value at the year end is translated at the year end rate of P$8 to the £. The remaining inventory, which is valued at historic cost, is translated at the exchange rate ruling on the average acquisition date of the inventory.

Exhibit 8.1(b) Translating Foreign Accounts Using Different Translation Methods

Puma Corporation: Translating Accounts

				Foreign currency rising in value £'000 Sterling				
Foreign subsidiary balances in P$	Item in balance sheet	Exchange rate P$ per £	Closing rate method £	Exchange rate P$ per £	Temporal method £	Exchange rate P$ per £	Current non-current method £
10000	Fixed assets	2	5000	4	2500	4	2500
3000	Inventory (at cost)	2	1500	2.2	1364	2	1500
2000	Inventory (NRV)	2	1000	2	1000	2	1000
4000	Debtors	2	2000	2	2000	2	2000
1000	Cash	2	500	2	500	2	500
20000	Total assets		10000		7364		7500
12000	Equity + reserves	2	6000	*	3364	*	4400
3600	Debenture loans	2	1800	2	1800	4	900
4400	Creditors	2	2200	2	2200	2	2200
20000	Total finance		10000		7364		7500
2500 P$	Net profit	2 £	1250	4 £	1000	4 £	1000
20.8%	Return on equity		20.8%		29.7%		22.7%
16.0%	Return on equity + loans		16.0%		19.4%		18.9%
23.1%	Gearing		23.1%		34.9%		17.0%

Rates of exchange

		P$
Historic rate for fixed assets and loans	1 pound sterling =	4
Average rate for year	1 pound sterling =	2.5
Historic rate for stocks	1 pound sterling =	2.2
Closing rate	1 pound sterling =	2

The financial results extracted from accounts expressed in a foreign currency can be affected by the method used to translate the foreign accounts. Much depends on whether the foreign currency is rising or falling in value compared to the home currency.

In the above example the return on equity varies from 29.7% to 20.8%. The gearing varies from 34.9% to 17%.

Where the foreign currency is rising in value against the home currency:

1. The Closing Rate method is likely to OVERVALUE the Fixed Assets.
2. The Current–non-current method UNDERVALUES the debt due.
3. The closing rate and C–NC method might well be OVERVALUING inventory valued at cost.
4. The return on capital can be very different because of the inventory value and depreciation differences.
5. If the value of the $P is falling against the pound sterling the situation will be reversed.

The average acquisition date was three months before the accounting year end, the rate of exchange on this date was P$7.5 to the £ sterling

In the case of the temporal method the profit figure is translated at the average exchange rate for the year, namely P$7 to the £ sterling.

The current–non-current method translates all the working capital items at the closing rate of P$8 to the £ and the fixed assets and long-term debt (debentures) at the historic rate of P$4 to the £, the rate ruling when these assets and liabilities were acquired.

The profit figure is again translated at the average rate for the year, namely P$7 to the £.

Equity and Reserves

In all three cases the value we have allocated to equity and reserves is simply a balancing figure. This figure includes any foreign exchange gains or losses resulting from translating the foreign accounts into £ sterling at rates other than the closing rate. In real accounting practice these gains or losses arising out of translation would have to be individually identified within the reserve account or carried to the income account.[8]

The Impact of Each Method on the Financial Ratios

Exhibit 8.1(a) shows that the conventional financial ratios used to measure the performance of a foreign subsidiary can be affected by the method of translation chosen.

In Exhibit 8.1(a) we have calculated three financial ratios.

1. The ratio of net profit to equity. Equity being defined as (total assets − (creditors + long-term debt)).
2. The ratio of net profit to equity plus reserves plus loans (long-term financing).
3. The gearing ratio. Gearing being defined as the ratio of debenture loans to total long-term financing. (Debt + equity + reserves).

The lower half of Exhibits 8.1(a) and 8.1(b) illustrate these ratios as generated by the three different translation methods.

In the case of Exhibit 8.1(a) the exchange rate is moving in favour of the £ sterling. When the fixed assets were bought and the debenture loan raised the rate of exchange was P$4 to the £ sterling. The rate of exchange ruling on the date the accounts are prepared is P$8 to the £ sterling. The P$ has halved in value against the £ sterling over the intervening years.

The closing rate method translates all values, including the profit figure, at the closing rate of P$8 to the £. Under this system the financial ratios are identical whether the foreign accounts are denominated in P$ or £ sterling. This must be so since a common ratio has been applied to all the figures in the foreign accounts. Note that even if the P$ rises in value against the £, as shown in Exhibit 8.1(b), the ratios still remain the same.

The temporal method translates the fixed assets at the rate of exchange ruling when the assets were acquired, namely P$4 to the £. All monetary assets and liabilities are translated at the closing rate. That portion of the inventory valued at cost, rather than NRV, is translated at the rate of exchange ruling when the average item of inventory was bought, namely P$7.5 to the £. The profit for the year is translated at the average rate of exchange for the year, namely P$7 to the £.

Note that the temporal method doubles the value of the foreign fixed assets in terms of £ sterling compared to the closing rate method. Thus the return on both equity and equity plus loans is reduced relative to the closing rate method. For the same reason the temporal method reduces the gearing of the foreign subsidiary in terms of £ sterling, from 23.1% to 14%.

Under the temporal method the profit figure has increased slightly because the average rate and not the year end exchange rate was used to translate the annual profit figure.

The C–NC method translates the assets and also the debenture loans at the rate ruling when these items were acquired, namely P$4 to the £ sterling. All other items except equity are considered to be "working capital" items and are, therefore, translated at the closing rate of P$8 to the £ sterling.

Note that the value of the foreign debt is increased dramatically in terms of £ sterling under this translation method, the debt has doubled in value! Thus the gearing ratio is increased to 28.1%. The profit ratios are reduced, mainly but not exclusively, because of the substantial increase in the value of the fixed assets in terms of £ sterling.

If a full application of the temporal or C–NC method had been carried through, the profit figure under the C–NC method would have been substantially reduced, since the depreciation charge on the fixed assets in the translated accounts would have been recalculated and based on the higher value fixed asset figure used in the translated accounts.

Discussion

Exhibit 8.1(a) demonstrates that the method of translation can affect the perceived profitability and gearing of a foreign subsidiary as measured in terms of the home (reporting) currency, namely £ sterling.

In this example the closing rate method provides the highest profitability, the C–NC method the highest gearing.

Which method is the "best" method for translating the accounts of a foreign subsidiary company into the home currency?

First, let us eliminate the C–NC method from further consideration. The C–NC method values the debenture loan at £900 000. This is an incorrect valuation. If the Group wishes to repay the loan at the year end, the Group would only need to find £450 000 to repay the loan. The Group owes P$3 600 000. The rate of exchange ruling at the end of the year is P$8 to the £ sterling. Thus only £450 000 is need to repay the loan, not £900 000.

Another limitation of the C–NC method is that a portion of the inventory valued at cost is likely to be incorrectly valued. Translating inventory valued at cost at the closing rate will almost certainly undervalue the inventory if the foreign currency is falling in value relative to the home currency over the period.

These limitations must eliminate the C–NC approach from serious consideration as a translation method.

The closing rate method enjoys the not inconsiderable advantage that, if the profit is translated at the year end rate, the financial ratios remain unaffected whether denominated in terms of P$ or £ sterling. This means that the managers of the subsidiary and the management of the Group will use the same figures when assessing the performance of the foreign subsidiary. However, if some of these ratios are wrong this is not an advantage!

The closing rate method is also, technically, the simplest system. The method seems intuitively obvious to the non-financial manager and the relevant rate of exchange is easy to find.

The one major disadvantage of the closing rate method lies in the valuation of the non-monetary assets of the subsidiary in the Group accounts. If the assets were acquired some years ago when the rate of exchange was very different from what it is today the translated value of these assets may be very inaccurate in terms of the reporting currency.

For example, in the case of Exhibit 8.1(a) the fixed assets were acquired when the rate of exchange was P$4 to the £. Let us suppose that these assets were acquired ten years ago. Let us also suppose that the inflation rate in the foreign country has averaged 7.5% a year over the period and the inflation rate in the UK has averaged zero % a year over the same period.

Under these circumstances it is likely that if the fixed assets were valued at P$10 000 000 ten years ago, if they were properly maintained, they would be worth around P$20 million today. (P$10m $\times$ $(1.075)^\wedge 10$ = P$20 million approximately).

If these assets were sold and the proceeds sent back to the UK the value would be P$20 million/8 = £2.5 million. The closing rate method values these fixed assets at only £1.25 million. Both the M–NM and the C–NC method arrive at a valuation of £2.5 million.

The Temporal/M–NM method, at least in theory, avoids the major problems associated with the closing rate and the C–NC methods. The long-term debt is correctly valued in terms of current exchange rates. The non-monetary assets are raised in value to allow for the rise in the nominal value of the foreign held assets. This apparent rise in value is, of course, spurious. It simply represents a fall in value of the P$ in terms of £ sterling over the period.

The Temporal/M–NM method is thus, theoretically, the superior method but the closing rate method enjoys several practical advantages over the Temporal/M–NM method.

At present, in 1995, variations on the closing rate/net investment method, called the current rate method in the USA, is the approach most favoured by Accounting Institutes and Accounting Standard Boards throughout the world.

But What If the Foreign Currency Is Rising in Value?

Exhibit 8.1(a) illustrates a situation where the foreign currency is falling in value relative to the home currency. What happens if the reverse applies and the foreign currency rises in value relative to the home currency?

Such a situation is illustrated in Exhibit 8.1(b). In this case the foreign currency has risen in value from P$4 to the £ to P$2 to the £ since the fixed assets were bought. The average rate for the final year is taken to be P$2.5 to the £, and the historic rate for inventory is taken as P$2.2 to the £.

Under these very different circumstances the closing rate method provides identical ratios to those calculated when the P$ was falling in value against the pound sterling. But note that the absolute figures in terms of sterling are very different.

The temporal or M–NM method of translation now provides the highest profitability figures and also, at 34.9%, by far the highest gearing %.

These changes in the financial ratios result from two factors. The lower value of fixed assets as measured by the temporal and the C–NC method compared to the closing rate method and the equally dramatic fall in the value of the long-term debt as measured by the C–NC method.

A detailed discussion of the consequences flowing from the different sets of ratios generated by each translation method is beyond the scope of this book. This is a subject for accounting specialists.

The limited objective of this chapter is to demonstrate that the method of translation chosen can affect the performance of a foreign subsidiary as perceived by the management of a group of international companies. Therefore the management of any group of companies that includes a foreign subsidiary must be aware of these translation effects.

Special Problems in Translation

This chapter has attempted to introduce the reader to the problems encountered when an accountant translates the accounts of a foreign subsidiary into the currency of the parent company.

The consolidation of accounts from several currencies introduces many other tricky accounting problems which are not discussed above. For example, the opening balances of the subsidiary company must be translated into the reporting currency at a meaningful rate. Derivatives, such as forwards, futures and options need to be translated, inter-company debts need to be eliminated, the depreciation charge needs to be recalculated in relation to the translated value of the associated asset and so forth. Each of these problems calls for special consideration by the accountant but such problems are beyond the scope of this book. See Buckley (1993) and Demirag and Goddard (1994) for information on these topics in a UK context and Choi and Muller (1993) for a discussion in a wider international context. Appleyard and others (1990) describe current practice on multi-currency budgeting in British MNCs and Coates and others (1993) provide 15 case studies of performance measurement in MNCs in three countries.[9]

Some Other Translation Methods

The methods of translation described above are the three methods that have been used in practice to translate accounts expressed in a foreign currency into the home currency.

Other methods have been suggested, which, so far as we are aware, have never been used in practice.

For example, it has been suggested that accounts should be translated, not at the current spot rate of exchange at the company year end, but at the forward rate applicable to the date when the accounts will be published. Unless the company covers the net monetary asset position of the subsidiary forward the advantages to be derived from this approach are not clear.

Another suggestion is for the accounts to be translated using the purchasing power parity index, as calculated by the Central Bank or some other agency,[10] rather than using the spot exchange rate. This approach, it is claimed, would give the home shareholders a better idea of the real international purchasing power of the net worth of the foreign subsidiary.

So far as we are aware neither of these suggestions have been taken up by those who hold responsibility for preparing multi-currency accounts.

THE LIMITATIONS OF MULTI-CURRENCY ACCOUNTING

We noted above that the whole question of translating company accounts from one currency to another raises theoretical difficulties. For example the M–NM method of translation assumes that the international currency markets are efficient and that the PPP theory is working but it also assumes that the International Fisher Theory is not working. The closing/current rate method of translation might well apply the current rate of exchange to translating assets bought many years ago and valued in the accounts at historic cost, an obvious nonsense.

The problem stems from the fact that all of the translation methods described above are using accounts that look backward in time to arrive at values that are being used to look forward in time.

The primary use to which accounts are put is to forecast future cash flows from the investment represented by the foreign accounts. There can be no doubt that future changes in exchange rates will impact on the future cash flows of the Group. The problem is that accounts are designed in such a way that they do not include the present discounted value of future cash flows. Thus the impact of exchange rate changes on these future cash flows is ignored.

Accounting reports would ideally encapsulate not only the results of past events but also the present value of expected and predictable future events.

Some financial analysts are sceptical about the value of information derived from accounts consolidated from several currencies. They consider that because exchange rates vary through time this makes the results emerging from any consolidation process quite meaningless. These accounts are based on events that take place at different points in time.

We do not share this opinion. In our opinion the current methods of consolidating accounts expressed in different currencies may represent a compromise between different objectives but they are better than nothing. The consolidation of all of the many assets, liabilities, revenues and expenditures of a Group expressed in various currencies into a single set of accounts denominated in a single "numeraire" provides useful information to an analyst even if all the translation methods available suffer from one or other of the flaws noted above.

The crucial point is to ensure that the interpreters of consolidated accounts understand these limitations and allow for them when taking decisions based on the consolidated accounts. Exhibit 8.2 illustrates the kind of problems that can arise when they do not.

The primary objective of this chapter has been to point out these limitations.

WHAT HAVE WE LEARNED IN THIS CHAPTER?

1. Most of the governments in advanced industrialized countries require that companies resident on their territory produce consolidated accounts to bring together the financial results of the entire group even if the group is made up of several companies who denominate their accounts in various foreign currencies.

Exhibit 8.2   Translating the Polly Peck Accounts

Over the five years from 1984 to 1990 the company called Polly Peck was one of the fastest growing companies on the London Stock Exchange. The company grew from a market value of £193 million in 1984 to a market value of £1000 million over this five-year period. The company was, among other things, a producer and distributor of agricultural produce most of which was grown in Turkish Cyprus and the surrounding region.

In the latter half of 1990 some doubt was thrown on the accounting procedures used by Polly Peck in presenting its worldwide financial performance to its shareholders. The claim was made that the translation procedure used to translate the foreign income, costs and liabilities into pound sterling were flawed.

Accountancy Age (1991) reported that: "The study from the IBCA European rating agency suggests that accounting standards entirely inappropriate to Polly Peck's unusual multi-national financial structure were used." The report by the IBCA suggests that "much of the credit [for the profitability of the company] must go the group's accountant rather than to its business managers". The managers of Polly Peck have strenuously denied this allegation. They claim that they followed the accepted accounting principles in force at that time when preparing the accounts.

The argument revolves around the fact that Polly Peck took on hard currency debt without setting up adequate hedging arrangements to cover the exchange risk involved in holding this debt. The low interest charge on the debt concealed the fact that the value of the capital portion of the debt was growing substantially in terms of the local currency used by Polly Peck in Cyprus and Turkey.

The IBCA calculated that the foreign exchange losses suffered by Polly Peck exceeded the value of retained profits by 17% over the five-year period prior to 1990. The losses were transferred to reserves. This fact appears to have been ignored by the many financial analysts who recommended the purchase of Polly Peck shares over the period.

"In effect, says the IBCA, as a result of the ultra-high inflation [suffered by Cyprus and Turkey over the period] local profits would have benefited greatly from holding gains on stocks and purchases while taking no notice of the loss incurred on holding fast depreciating monetary working capital (debtors less creditors)."

The IBCA conclude that "consideration ought to be given to fully adjusting Turkish (and Turkish Cypriot) related profit figures for inflation before incorporating these figures into the consolidated statements".

The translation of the Polly Peck accounts over the period from 1984 to 1989 is a matter of some controversy. It has been claimed that the method of translation was inappropriate and resulted in profits being reported which were much higher than justified. The management of Polly Peck claim that they simply followed the accounting rules in force during the period. If erroneous conclusions were drawn from these accounts this was a consequence of the existing translation rules not the management of Polly Peck.

2. The financial markets prefer international groups to present their accounts as consolidated accounts denominated in a single reporting currency rather than as several sets of accounts denominated in several different functional currencies.

3. If accounts are to be consolidated from several different currencies into a single currency then a method of translating the foreign currency values into the "reporting" currency must be selected.

4. The method of translation in most common use today is the "closing" (UK) or "current rate" (USA) method. The "monetary–non-monetary" or "temporal" method is also recommended in certain special situations. The current–non-current method is seldom used today although it was the most popular method in times past.

5. The current–non-current method is a misleading method of consolidating accounts. The monetary–non-monetary method is permitted by many authorities but it is not widely used, however, the method is mandatory in certain circumstances.

6. The Accounting Institutes in most of the countries of the world have put forward mandatory standards for consolidating accounts from several currencies into a single

currency. In the USA this standard is called FASB 52. In the UK the standard is called SSAP 20. These standards are similar to one another but they are by no means identical. The US standard is more precise and technical than the UK standard.

7. Each translation method is likely to generate a different financial result in the reporting currency after consolidation. The profit, gearing and liquidity position of the consolidated accounts can look very different depending on the translation method used.

8. The relevance of these differential results is a bone of contention in the financial world. Some academic research has found that the method of consolidation may have little impact on the share price, and therefore the market value, of the company.

9. The technical side of international consolidation of accounts raises many tricky problems in addition to the basic "translation" problem discussed in this chapter. Most managers will have no need to peruse these technical matters further but if the need should arise the reader is referred to several specialist books on the subject written for accountants at the end of the chapter.

10. Multi-currency accounting is a controversial subject. Some analysts are sceptical about the usefulness of information derived from accounts built up from several different currencies. They consider that the analyst who is worried about the impact of exchange rate changes on a company should look forward by predicting future cash flows rather than backward by using accounts. We admit the importance of future cash flows in accounting analysis but consider that the consolidated accounts of a Group built up from accounts denominated in several different currencies does provide useful additional information to a financial analyst over and above what he or she could have obtained from a set of accounts denominated in each foreign currency.

NOTES

1. Occasionally the accounts are consolidated into the currency of some third currency, usually an international currency, such as the US$.

2. Assuming a common year end date. This is not always possible because the authorities in some countries insist that all companies operating in that country must arrange for their financial year to end on the same date.

3. The standard in the UK is issued under SSAP 20 *Foreign Currency Translation*, issued April 1983.

4. Hyperinflation is defined by FASB 52 as a mere 100% cumulative inflation over a three-year period!

5. The standard was called Financial Accounting Standard Board standard publication 8. (FASB 8) and was in force from January 1, 1976 to December 14, 1982.

6. Dukes, R. E. (1978) An empirical investigation of the effect of FASB 8 on security return behaviour. FASB (US).

7. The average rate for the year could have been used.

8. The US standard FASB 8 was thrown out because it insisted on carrying these translation gains or losses to the income account so destabilizing the income of the company from year to year with these "paper" profits and losses.

9. Appleyard, A. et al. *Multi-currency Budgeting*, CIMA UK, 1990. Coates et al. *Corporate Performance Evaluation in Multinationals*. CIMA UK, 1993.

10. Morgan Guaranty calculate the PPP adjusted value of many currencies on a regular basis.

FURTHER READING

Aliber, R. Z. and Stickney, C. P. (1975) Accounting measures of foreign exchange exposure. *Accounting Review*, January, 44–57.

Choi, F. D. and Mueller, G. G. (1992). *International Accounting*. Prentice-Hall.
    The standard work on the subject. The book includes a detailed discussion of the international consolidation problem.

Demirag, I. (1987) A review of the objectives of foreign currency translation. *International Journal of Accounting*, vol. 2, November, 69–85.

Houston, C. (1990). Translation exposure hedging post SFAS No. 52. *Journal of International Financial Management and Accounting*, vol. 2, nos 2 and 3, Summer and Autumn, 145–70.

Logue, D. and Oldfield, G. (1977) Managing foreign assets when foreign exchange markets are efficient. *Financial Management*, Summer, 16–22.

Nobes, C. and Parker, R. (1991) *Comparative International Accounting*. Prentice-Hall.
    A comprehensive review of current practice with regard to the reporting standards required in the various countries of the world. Discusses consolidation and translation rules in North America, the UK, USA, Japan, Australia, and Europe.

Rezaee, Z. et al. (1993) Capital markets response to SFAS Nos 8 and 52: professional adaptation. *Journal of Accounting, Auditing & Financing*, vol. 8, no. 3, Summer, 313–32.

Rosenfield, P. (1987) Accounting for foreign operations. *Journal of Accountancy*, August, 103–12.

Ross, D. (1992) Investors: for or against translation hedging? *Accountancy*, vol. 109, no. 1182, February 100–2.

Ruland, R. G. and Doupnik, T. (1988) Foreign currency translation and the behaviour of exchange rates. *Journal of International Business Studies*, Fall, 461–76.

TUTORIAL QUESTIONS

1. If the accounts of several foreign subsidiaries have to be consolidated why must they be translated?
2. A Swedish company owns a subsidiary in Norway. If the accounts are to be consolidated into Swedish krone what is the "functional" currency and what the "reporting" currency?
3. If a US company owns a subsidiary in Singapore that is used solely for assembling parts made in the USA and the assembled goods are all sold in the USA what effect does this have on any translation gains or losses made on the Singaporean accounts?
4. Explain the difference between translating an amount of money represented in a foreign currency and converting that amount.
5. Three methods have been used to consolidate the accounts of foreign subsidiaries into the home currency used by the parent company. Name these three methods.
6. Suggest four advantages that flow from using the closing rate/current rate method of translation. What is the one major problem that arises when this method is adopted?
7. Define a monetary asset.
8. Which of the following items are monetary assets?

   A Boeing 737 aircraft, 100 shares in IBM corporation, a royalty on a water cleaning process, a 7% bond from the Glaxo corporation, a debt owing from a customer, tax of US$500 000 owing to the US government, capital reserves on the balance sheet.

9. What advantage does the monetary–non-monetary method of translation enjoy over the closing/current rate method?
10. "The Monetary–Non-Monetary method of translation assumes that the PPP theory works but the international Fisher theory does not work." Explain.
11. "The temporal method requires that any exchange rate loss on translating net monetary liabilities should be charged against the profit and loss account of the group for that year. This results in an overseas subsidiary which is more valuable to the group actually appearing to be less valuable." Explain.

12. Since the temporal method of translation is favoured by most academics why do you think it has it fallen out of favour in recent years?
13. Explain the crucial difference between the M–NM and the C–NC methods of translating accounts.
14. Under the C–NC method of translation what rate of exchange would be used to translate the following items?
    Sales, inventory valued at cost, trade debts due to the company, production equipment, a debenture loan of £50 million acquired 1993 due to be repaid in the year 2000, government stock held as an asset, a bank loan, the profit for the year as per the P&L account.
15. A loan of DM50 million was incurred by a German subsidiary of a French parent company in 1993. The debt is due to be repaid in 1999. The rate of exchange when the debt was incurred was FF3.2 to the DM. In 1997, when the consolidated accounts of the French company are being prepared the rate of exchange is FF3.9 to the DM.
    What is the value of the loan in terms of French francs using the closing rate method, the M–NM method and the C–NC method? Which method do you believe gives the more accurate presentation of the facts?
16. Why do you think the C–NC method of translation was used by most accountants prior to 1970?
17. Using the data from Exhibit 8.1(b) calculate what the value of the foreign subsidiaries fixed assets might be if the fixed assets are shown at cost and rate of inflation in the foreign country is 2% and the rate in the UK 11%. Show the value in P$, after translation, using the closing rate of exchange.
18. What advantages might flow from using the PPP rate of exchange rather than the spot rate when translating foreign subsidiary accounts?
19. Suggest two serious limitations on using consolidated accounts made up from foreign accounts expressed in several currencies in making future decisions.

CASE STUDY: SIMEON INTERNATIONAL CORPORATION

The Simeon International Corporation is a UK multinational based in London. They own a large subsidiary company in Ruritania.

At the end of the year the company must consolidate the two sets of accounts, UK and Ruritanian, into £ sterling.

The Ruritanian accounts at the year end are set out below. The Ruritanian currency is the Ruritarian dollar ($R).

Required: Translate the Ruritanian accounts into £ sterling using (a) the closing rate method; (b) the temporal method; and (c) the current–non-current method.

Calculate the return on equity capital and the return on equity capital plus debt in each case and comment on the three different sets of results. Why is there a substantial difference between the results generated by the different translation methods? Also comment on the different degrees of gearing (leverage) resulting from the three methods.

Assume the following two rates of exchange apply for the year:

	(a)	(b)
Historic rate fixed assets and loans	£1 = $R7	£1 = $R7
Average rate for year	£1 = $R5.7	£1 = $R8.5
Historic rate for stocks	£1 = $R5.3	£1 = $R8.7
Closing rate	£1 = $R5	$1 = $R9

In the case of (a) the R$ is strengthening against the £. In the case of (b) the R$ is weakening against the £.

Table 32 The Ruritanian Accounts at the Year End

Finance	R$ 000s	Assets	
Equity + reserves	28000	Fixed assets	25000
Debenture loans 8%	20000	Inventory (cost)	12000
Creditors	6000	Inventory (NRV)	4000
		Debtors	9000
		Cash	4000
Totals	54000		54000
Profit for year: RS$10 000 000			

CASE STUDY: GARSTON ELECTRICS (SPAIN)

At the end of Chapter 5 we discussed a case study involving Garston Electrics PLC, a British company based in Leeds in the North of England.

Garston Electrics owns a subsidiary company based in Bilbao, Spain called Garston Electrics (Spain) S.A. This manufacturing subsidiary is exporting substantial amounts of electrical equipment to Germany.

Some 70% of the inputs to this subsidiary (labour, material etc.) are sourced in Spain. Most of the creditors and long-term debts of this subsidiary are denominated in pesetas. Mr Thomas calculates that on June 30, 1996 Garston Electrics (Spain) has net assets worth around Ps800 000 000 denominated in pesetas.

In common with almost all other UK companies Garston uses the closing rate method to consolidate the Garston (Spain) accounts with the UK company accounts at the end of the company year on September 30, 1996. The year end for both companies. This means that the net assets of Garston (Spain) will be consolidated on September 30, at a value, in terms of pound sterling, which is 10% less than the value on June 30, 1996 if a 10% fall in the peseta against the £ takes place over the intervening three months. Thus the exchange rate of 172 Ps to the £ is expected by Mr Thomas to fall to 191 Ps to the £ by September 30, 1996.

Assume that all the other facts noted in the Chapter 5 Garston case remain the same.

Mr Thomas decides to reduce the projected translation "loss" by ordering Mr Hermanes, the financial controller of the Spanish subsidiary to run down his working capital by reducing stock and limiting credit given.

On receiving this instruction by e-mail Mr Hermanes faxes back to Mr Thomas immediately to complain bitterly about this instruction. Mr Hermanes fax reads:

"I strongly disagree with your instructions to reduce stock and credit given. This will curtail the activities of the company over the next three months. I strongly advocate the opposite policy, namely to increase our production budget immediately. This will entail increasing our current stock levels and subsequently offering more credit to customers."

Required: Write a memo to Mr Thomas advising on this situation. Do you believe that the working capital of the subsidiary should be reduced until the expected devaluation of the peseta takes place or should production be increased? Explain your reasoning. What additional information would you need before you can make a final decision on this matter?

Table 33 Balance Sheet of Garston Electrics (Spain): June 30, 1996

		Ps m
Fixed assets		520
Inventory	120	
Debts	260	
Cash and bank	40	
	420	
Less:		
Trade creditors	140	280
Net assets		800
Financed by:		
Equity plus reserves		600
Debentures at 16% pa (1993–99)		200
Total financing		800

In particular:

1. Calculate the value of the expected translation loss in terms of £ sterling expected by Mr Thomas if the peseta is devalued to 191 Ps to the £ before September 30.
2. Calculate the actual translation loss in terms of £ sterling if the peseta only falls to 180 peseta to the £ by September 30.

Exhibit 8.3(a) Three Methods of Translating Simeon Corporation Accounts

Simeon International Corporation: Notes Towards a Solution   Part 1

Foreign Currency Rising in Value

Foreign subsidiary balances in R$ R$000	Item in balance sheet	Foreign currency falling in value £'000 Sterling						
		Exchange rate	Closing rate method	Exchange rate	Monetary non-mon. method	Exchange rate	Current– non-current method
25000	Fixed assets	5	5000	7	3571	7	3571
12000	Inventory (at cost)	5	2400	5.30	2264	5	2400
4000	Inventory (NRV)	5	800	5	800	5	800
9000	Debtors	5	1800	5	1800	5	1800
4000	Cash	5	800	5	800	5	800
54000	Total assets		10800		9235		9371
28000	Equity + reserves	5	5600	*	4035	*	5314
20000	Debenture loans	5	4000	5	4000	7	2857
6000	Creditors	5	1200	5	1200	5	1200
54000	Total finance		10800		9235		9371
10000 R$	Net profit	5	£2000	5.7	£1754	5.7	£1754
35.7%	Return on equity %		35.7%		43.5%		33%
20.8%	Return on equity + loans		20.8%		21.8%		21.5%
41.7%	Gearing		41.7%		49.8%		35.0%

Rates of exchange

		R$
Historic rate for fixed assets and loans	£ sterling =	7
Average rate for year	£ sterling =	5.7
Historic rate for stocks (average rate)	£ sterling =	5.3
Closing rate	£ sterling =	5

Note that the currency of the foreign country ($R) has been growing stronger against the £ over the period. It has, in fact, moved in value against the pound sterling from $R7 to the pound sterling to R$5 to the pound sterling over the period. Under these conditions:

1. The Closing Rate method is likely to OVERVALUE the Fixed Assets.
2. The Current–non-current method will UNDERVALUE the debt due.
3. The closing rate and C–NC method might well be OVERVALUING inventory valued at COST.
4. The return on capital can be very different (because of inventory and depreciation).
5. The gearing is affected by the change in the relative value of the assets and debt due.
6. If the $R was falling against the pound these factors would be reversed.
   * balancing figures.

Exhibit 8.3(b) Three Methods of Translating Simeon Corporation Accounts

Foreign Currency Falling in Value

Foreign subsidiary balances in R$ R$000	Item in balance sheet	Exchange rate	Closing rate method	Exchange rate	Monetary non-mon. method	Exchange rate	Current– non-current method
25000	Fixed assets	9	2778	7	3571	7	3571
12000	Inventory (at cost)	9	1333	8.70	1379	9	1333
4000	Inventory (NRV)	9	444	9	444	9	444
9000	Debtors	9	1000	9	1000	9	1000
4000	Cash	9	444	9	444	9	444
54000	Total assets		6000		9235		6794
28000	Equity + reserves	9	3111	*	6346	*	3270
20000	Debenture loans	9	2222	9	2222	7	2857
6000	Creditors	9	667	9	667	9	667
54000	Total finance		6000		9235		6794
10000 P$	Net profit	9	£1111	8.5	£1176	8.5	£1176
35.7%	Return on equity %		35.7%		18.5%		36.0%
20.8%	Return on equity + loans		20.8%		13.7%		19.2%
41.7%	Gearing		41.7%		25.9%		46.6%

Rates of exchange

		R$
Historic rate for fixed assets and loans	£ sterling =	7
Average rate for year	£ sterling =	8.5
Historic rate for stocks (average rate)	£ sterling =	8.7
Closing rate	£ sterling =	9

Note that the currency of the foreign country ($R) has been growing weaker against the £ over the period. It has, in fact, moved in value against the pound sterling from $R7 to the pound sterling to R$9 to the pound sterling over the period. Under these conditions:

1. The Closing Rate method is likely to UNDERVALUE the Fixed Assets.
2. The Current–non-current method will OVERVALUE the debt due.
3. The closing rate and C–NC method might well be UNDERVALUING inventory valued at COST.
4. The return on capital can be very different (because of inventory and depreciation).
5. The gearing is effected by the change in the relative value of the assets and debt due.
6. If the $R was rising against the pound these factors would be reversed.
   * balancing figures.

SIMEON INTERNATIONAL CORPORATION: CONSOLIDATION: NOTES TOWARDS A SOLUTION: PART 2

Closing Rate Method

This method of translation offers some substantial advantages over the other methods.

The financial ratios used by the managers of the subsidiary in Ruritania and the managers at Head Quarters (HQ) in the UK will be the same. This avoids disputes about policy and performance which can arise if the M–NM or C–NC methods are used in the consolidation. The exchange rate does not influence the evaluation of the performance of the subsidiary. Note that the ratios are the same whatever happens to the exchange rate. This does not mean to say that the CR method is either the most useful or the best method. It may suffer from other deficiencies which reduce its usefulness.

One possible weakness is the valuation of the fixed assets and inventory. If these are not recently revalued then the closing rate method might grossly over- or undervalue these assets. This can affect both the return on equity ratio and the gearing ratio. For example, if the R$ is rising against the £ are the foreign fixed assets in Ruritania actually worth £5 000 000? Probably not if the Ruritanian inflation rate is well below the inflation rate in the UK. Note how translating the annual profit figure at the closing rather than the average rate compensates to some extent for the higher equity plus reserve figure in calculating the return on equity capital ratio.

The Current–Non-current Method

The valuation of the debt in £ sterling is clearly wrong. No one can dispute this. If the HQ really believe that with R$ rising against the £ the debt due is only £2 857 000 then they will hit a liquidity crisis when the debt has to be repaid (unless they have set up a sinking fund in $R). The inventory at cost valuation may also be inaccurate but this is not a substantial error here although it could be if inventory at cost is a substantial fraction of net asset value. Of course if the R$ is falling in value relative to the pound sterling then the error is the other way around but not so serious. The HQ will overestimate the debt due and underestimate the value of inventory.

The Monetary–Non-monetary Method

This approach is likely to present the more accurate figures so far as economic theory is concerned. If the PPP holds then the debt and the fixed assets are more likely to be valued, in terms of £ sterling, at close to their realizable/repayment value.

Note that when using the M–NM method the return on equity is highest/lowest compared to the other two methods. This is the correct interpretation. For example with the R$ rising the returns per share are higher *but so is the risk* (i.e. the gearing)! The opposite conclusion applies to a falling R$ to the pound exchange rate.

Return on Equity

With the R$ rising in value the low value of fixed assets allied to the correctly valued debt provide the M–NM method with the highest return. This is probably the most accurate measure of the return on equity.

Return on Equity Plus Debt

Note the similarity between the figures in all three cases when the R$ is rising! This similarity arises because there are compensating mechanisms in operation. If the fixed assets are overvalued debt is increased. Using the average rate rather than the year end rate to translate the profit figure also compensates to some extent. This is not always so but it happens quite frequently.

Gearing

The differences in gearing are quite dramatic. This arises from the incorrect valuation of the year end debt in terms of the pound sterling when using the C–NC method. The degree of gearing is accentuated in the case of the M–NM method by the very low/very high value awarded to equity and reserves. This arises from the relatively low/high value awarded to the fixed assets by this translation method.

CASE STUDY: GARSTON ELECTRICS (SPAIN): NOTES TOWARDS A SOLUTION

The conflict between Mr Thomas and Mr Hermanes on policy regarding working capital arises because they are looking at different time horizons.

Mr Thomas is only considering the short term up to the next set of accounts on September 30. Mr Hermanes is looking to the long-term profits of the subsidiary.

Let us examine Mr Thomas's position.

The transition loss expected by Mr Thomas is based on an expected 10% fall in the sterling value of the net assets of Garston (Spain) caused by a change in the exchange rate. At a projected spot rate of 191 pesetas to the £ sterling if all the Ps800 000 000 were sent to the UK after the devaluation rather than before the devaluation the loss would be:

$$Ps\ (800\,000\,000/172) - (800\,000\,000/191) = ?$$

$$£4\,651\,162 - 4\,188\,482 = £462\,680$$

The actual translation loss on September 30, 1996 when the actual spot rate of exchange was 180 pesetas to the £ would have been:

$$Ps\ (800\,000\,000/172) - (800\,000\,000/180) =$$

$$£4\,651\,162 - 4\,444\,444 = £206\,718$$

However, these hypothetical losses are not real losses since Garston (UK) have no intention of liquidating the Garston (Spain) subsidiary and sending the proceeds to the UK before September 30. Note the apparent "loss" on translation might well be reversed in the following or a later period if the peseta grows stronger once again against the £ sterling. The more important question is whether or not a possible loss on the "net monetary asset" position should be hedged.

Such translation losses are "paper losses", they are not realized, no funds actually move, the cash flow of the group is not affected.

The net monetary asset position of Garston Electric (Spain) is as follows:

$$(Debors + cash and bank) - (Trade creditors + debentures)$$

$$Ps (260 + 40) - (140 + 200) = Ps - 40 million$$

Garston (Spain) owes money net and so a devaluation of the peseta against the £ sterling would result in a profit in terms of £ sterling! Mr Thomas is wrong in believing that a devaluation of the peseta will impose a loss on the Garston Group in terms of £ sterling.

However, a more interesting question relates to the future economic exposure of Garston Electric (Spain).

The Spanish manager, Mr Hermanes, is thinking in terms of economic exposure. Economic exposure is concerned with the effects of exchange rate changes on the future cash flows of a company.

Since the costs of Garston (Spain) are mainly denominated in local pesetas and the sales are mostly denominated in German DMs a devaluation of the peseta against the DM will either increase profits per unit sold or increase unit sales either option will widen the gap between costs and sales in terms of pesetas.

Much depends upon whether the German sales are denominated in DM or pesetas. If in DM then the profit per unit sold increases but not the volume of sales, if in pesetas the DM price will fall and the volume of sales will increase. Whichever strategy is chosen depends on whether the sales in Germany are price elastic or not. If the sales are price elastic a decrease in unit price will trigger a greater increase in unit sales.

However, there are several questions that still need answering. Namely:

1. Does the revaluation of the £ sterling apply only to the peseta or will it affect most other currencies including the DM? In other words is this exchange rate change really an appreciation of sterling against all other currencies?
2. Are exports to Germany denominated in DM or Ps? If in DM then, as we noted above, prices will be unchanged. If the sales are in Ps can Garston (Spain) increase its prices to keep the unit profit constant? How price elastic is demand for the products sold in Germany?
3. How will the input costs of the subsidiary be affected by the peseta devaluation? Even the domestically sourced costs may rise if the devaluation fuels local inflation and forces wages, etc., up. Will the Spanish government stand up against the higher inflation resulting from the devaluation? What is the immediate inflation forecast over the next few months?

Conclusion: Mr Hermanes is probably correct. A fall in the relative value of a currency will usually stimulate exports, at least in the short term. Production facilities should be increased and so inventory and debt increased. Mr Thomas is following a short-term profit maximization policy and his instruction to cut working capital is wrong. It would be more sensible for him to tell Mr Hermanes to take on more debt to increase productive capacity and increase advertising in Germany.

The value of this debt will fall in terms of £ sterling if a devaluation of the peseta takes place. However, higher interest charges on borrowing in pesetas could cancel this advantage.

CASE STUDY: PRETTY POLLY PLC

Pretty Polly PLC is a British multinational company that runs sales operations worldwide but limits production facilities to the UK and Turkey.

The accounts of Pretty Polly (Turkey) are presented below. These accounts must be consolidated into the UK accounts by translating the values expressed in Turkish lire into £ sterling.

Required: Translate the Turkish accounts into £ sterling using the closing rate method, the monetary–non-monetary method or temporal method and the current–non-current method.

Comment on the results. In particular comment on (a) the return on equity capital; (b) return on equity plus long-term debt; and (c) gearing under the three methods. Which figures do you consider to provide the most useful figures to the Board of Pretty Polly UK? Explain your reasoning.

The rates of exchange at various times in the past were as follows:

At the company year end	£1 = 80 000 Turkish lire
Average rate over the year	£1 = 70 000 Turkish lire
Rate when fixed assets required	£1 = 20 000 Turkish lire
Rate when debenture loans were raised	£1 = 20 000 Turkish lire

The company holds one year of inventory in stock.

The Pretty Polly accounts expressed in Turkish lire are set out in Table 34.

Table 34

		Lire '000 000
Fixed assets		50 000
Inventory (at cost)		15 000
Inventory (at NRV)		10 000
Debtors		24 000
Cash		5 000
	LR	104 000
Equity plus reserves		34 000
Debenture loans		50 000
Creditors		20 000
	LR	104 000
Net profit for year	LR	16 000

9

Financing and Insuring Exports

INTRODUCTION: PROBLEMS WITH EXPORTING

The first contact that most companies have with international finance is through exports.

The normal progression is for a company to start on its move into the international market by exporting goods abroad, then to take out a share in an agency before setting up a branch or subsidiary company abroad.

The activity of selling goods and services abroad will introduce the company to a novel set of risks and force the company to learn a range of new techniques involving transporting, financing and insuring the goods and services to be exported.

Transporting goods to a foreign country is a good deal more complicated than local shipment. Foreign sales impose a longer period of waiting between the shipment of the goods and the payment for the goods and foreign buyers may well present a greater credit risk to the seller than home buyers.

These additional problems have encouraged the growth of a range of intermediary companies who provide services to assist with exporting. Today most of these export service companies are located in the private sector but in the past many service companies were located in the public sector. "Export or die" was a motto proclaimed by many governments at the end of the Second World War. Some of these publicly funded export agencies still exist to help exporters and to subsidize the export industries of their country. The UK government set up the Export Credits Guarantee Department (ECGD) in 1948. In the past the ECGD played a major role in supporting and subsidizing British exports. Today its role is much emasculated.

Most export orders need to be financed. In order to raise the funds to finance an export contract the exporter will approach a lender, usually a bank, to raise a loan. The bank may be unwilling to provide the funds needed to finance the export contract without adequate security. This security can be provided by taking out an insurance contract on the export contract. Thus the two activities of financing and insuring export contracts are closely intertwined.

In this chapter we will first discuss the steps that need to be taken by an exporter prior to entering into an export contract. Then we will discuss insurance aspects of exporting. Finally we will examine the various techniques available to an exporter for financing and receiving payment for exports.

STEPS TO BE TAKEN PRIOR TO ENTERING INTO AN EXPORT CONTRACT

As we noted above selling goods and services abroad can prove to be a more complicated operation than selling goods and services at home.

Prior to entering into an export contract the exporter must:

1. *Identify the risks involved in the foreign sale.* Risks such as the loss of goods in transit, the non-payment or late payment for the goods, the risk of substantial changes in exchange rates taking place between writing the contract and receiving payment for the contract and so on. The exporter must work out ways of hedging these risks.

2. *Decide on the currency in which the export contract should be denominated.* The contract price must be denominated in a specific currency. Should the sale be denominated in the home currency of the exporter, the foreign currency of the buyer or some third international currency such as the US$?

3. *Decide on the method of payment.* Should the sale be paid "cash in advance" or payment on delivery of the goods to the foreign buyer? Should payment be made by way of a cheque drawn on a foreign bank account? Is a bill of exchange the most appropriate form of payment or possibly a letter of credit? Should the exporter insist on a banker's draft rather than a cheque? Perhaps some more exotic means of payment, such as a forfaiting agreement, is best suited to the conditions of the contract.

   The payment method chosen must be matched to the attributes of the contract.

4. *Decide on a method of financing the export order.* If the export contract will impose a substantial cost on the exporter between the date when the contract is signed and the date when the payment is received then the financing of the export contract might present the exporter with a problem.

   The method of financing the contract is likely to be closely related to the method of paying for the contract. For example, a bill of exchange or a forfaiting agreement can be used to both pay for and finance the contract. The more usual situation is for the exporter to ask a bank or other lending institution to finance the contract.

5. *Find out about the export documentation required.* The list of documents that must be completed before goods can be transferred from one country to another is quite formidable. In fact this activity can prove to be such a complicated process that it may be subcontracted to a specialist shipping agent. The documentation will include the bill of lading plus other shipping documents (at least six copies!), a certificate of origin to ensure that the goods are not exported from a country that is embargoed by the importing country, the invoice for the goods, a copy of the relevant insurance policy and an unsigned bill of exchange if it has been agreed that a bill is to be used to pay for the contract.

   The bill of lading is usually a negotiable instrument that gives title to the goods shipped. If the bill of lading is endorsed on the back this action can transfer the ownership of the goods to another party.

   One popular procedure is for the exporter to send the bill of lading to the exporter's bank who will later swap the bill of lading for a bill of exchange accepted by the importer.

6. *Agree with the importer whether the goods are to be shipped "Free on board" (FOB) or "Cost, insurance, freight" (CIF).* In the case of FOB the exporter must pay for getting the goods to the ship but then the responsibility for shipping, etc., lies with the buyer. In the case of CIF the exporter agrees to cover the costs of shipping the goods, insuring the goods and any other costs incurred in getting the goods to the buyer.

7. *Check out the exchange control regulations if such regulations apply to the contract.* If exchange controls are applied to the movement of funds out of or into the foreign country to which the goods are being shipped the exporter needs to study these controls carefully. The exporter would be wise to check on the following matters:

Does the importer have adequate authority and permission to buy these goods? Has the foreign monetary authority authorized the payment for the goods? Does a cash deposit need to be made to the foreign monetary authority before the contract can be signed?

THE RISKS INVOLVED IN A FOREIGN SALES CONTRACT

All business contracts entail a certain degree of risk. Even a local sale to a well established buyer can go wrong. However, sales to a foreign buyer moves the degree of risk thermometer up several notches on the risk scale.

Foreign sales can increase both the degree of conventional sales risk while introducing some entirely novel risks into the sales process.

Some of the changes introduced into the risk equation by moving into exporting are discussed below.

Geographical and Administrative Factors

Geography and bureaucracy can increase both the time needed to deliver the goods and the length of time before payment for the contract is received. Thus normal shipment and credit risks are increased simply because the period over which they extend is increased.

Personal Contact with, and Knowledge of, the Buyer

The exporter is less likely to know the buyer in a foreign sale contract. If the exporter does not know the buyer the exporter must approach a credit assessor, such as Dunn and Bradstreet, either in the UK or abroad to buy a credit assessment of the buyer.[1] Foreign sales are often arranged through a foreign agency, such agencies may have less to lose than the exporter if the sale contract goes wrong.

The Method of Payment

The additional risks involved in selling goods and services abroad means that the method of payment used for a foreign sale is likely to be a good deal more complicated than the method used for a local sale. Credit guarantees on payment may have to be obtained from a foreign bank and indirect payment systems such as factoring or forfaiting may have to be employed to ensure that the cash from the export contract will be received and received on time.

The Currency of the Contract

The foreign sale may be denominated in a foreign currency. This introduces foreign exchange exposure risk into the sales equation. Chapter 5 describes in some detail the many devices available for hedging this kind of risk. Several of these hedging devices are quite complicated to use and understand and will entail some investment in the learning process on the part of the exporter.

Exchange Controls

The exporter may well operate in a country with no exchange controls whatsoever and so he may be ignorant about the restrictions imposed by such regulations. Tight exchange controls may be applied by the government of the country in which the importer resides. Thus the exporter needs to check that the importer has implemented the proper exchange control procedures for importing the goods into his country. If these procedures have been improperly exercised difficulties can arise when the exporter tries to convert the proceeds of the sale denominated in a foreign currency into the home currency.

Law, Tax and Culture

Quite apart from the currency question a whole host of legal, tax and cultural differences can increase the risk attached to export sales compared to the risk attached to local sales. For example, the complexity of legal disputes can increase exponentially once an international frontier is crossed. Two legal systems may find themselves competing against one another.

The exporter needs to identify such risks and then select a suitable method for hedging each individual risk. We discussed the various methods that can be used to hedge exposure to exchange rate risk in Chapter 5. The most popular method of hedging most of the other, non-currency related, risks is to take out some form of insurance contract.

THE LINK BETWEEN INSURING AND FINANCING EXPORTS

There is a close link between financing exports and insuring exports. A lender, such as a commercial bank, may not be prepared to lend money to finance an export contract unless the more important risks attached to the export contract are already insured by an accredited insurance company or insurance agency.

There are three basic types of risk involved in an export contract.

1. *Credit or commercial risk.* Credit or commercial risk covers the risk that the importer may default on payment for the export contract. For example the importer may not pay for the goods bought and delivered to the importer or dispute that the terms of the contract have been implemented.

2. *Property risk.* This risk covers the possibility that the goods shipped to the importer may be damaged or lost in transit.
3. *Political risk.* This risk covers the possibility that the government of the importing country may expropriate the goods or block funds to prevent payment for the goods or commit a similar act so that the importer, "through no fault of his own", may default on the contract.

Once the exporter has obtained insurance to cover these risks then it is a relatively simple matter to raise the funds needed to finance the export contract.

A Typical Export Deal Might Proceed as Follows

A foreign buyer, previously unknown to the exporter, enquires about the goods sold by the exporter. The exporter sends details of the products he sells and the terms of sale to the foreign buyer. The foreign buyer indicates to the exporter that he would like to buy a quantity of the goods offered at the indicated price. The exporter now negotiates the terms of contract with the foreign buyer. The negotiations will cover the various points *re* delivery and payment terms outlined above.

The next step is for the exporter to obtain a credit assessment of the new customer, the foreign buyer, from a reputable credit agency, say NCM or Dunn and Bradstreet.

If the credit assessment is positive the exporter can proceed with the deal.

As the customer is a new one the exporter will be cautious about extending credit to the buyer. The exporter will either set up credit insurance cover on the deal or will insist on a secure payment method such as a letter of credit guaranteed by a bank.

The exporter now approaches a company such as NCM Credit Insurance Ltd to obtain insurance cover on the deal. The exporter will need to provide NCM with written evidence of the contract and the credit assessment on the buyer if this has not been obtained directly from NCM itself. Let us suppose that NCM agrees to insure the deal.

The exporter now goes to a lender, say a commercial bank, with the contract and the insurance guarantee from NCM and asks for a loan of a given amount to finance the export contract. For example, the exporter may need funds to buy in material to complete the contract.

The bank checks out the contract and the credit guarantee and if they are satisfied with these the bank makes a loan of the agreed amount to the exporter, possibly at a rate of interest subsidized by the government. In some cases the bank may make a loan directly to the foreign importer but only if the foreign importer can obtain a guarantee from his own local bank.

The exporter now has access to sufficient funds to manufacture the goods to be exported. The exporter can complete the goods ordered by the contract.

Let us assume that the exporter has agreed a payment system called "payment upon shipping the goods" with the importer. The exporter informs the foreign buyer that the goods have been shipped, sends him a copy of the relevant export documents outlined above except for the bill of lading, etc., that will give the holder legal possession of the goods. The bill of lading, etc., will be sent to the exporter's bank. The exporter will normally require the importer to pay for the goods before the importer can collect the goods at the port or elsewhere in his country.

The importer now pays for the goods or agrees to pay for them by the accepted payments method such as a bill of exchange.

Once the exporter's bank informs the exporter that payment has been received into the exporter's bank account or that the bill of exchange has been accepted by the importer the exporter or his bank gives the importer access to the bill of lading and various other documents that will allow the importer to take legal possession of the goods.

The export contract is now implemented. The importer has the goods and the exporter has the payment for the goods.

If payment is not forthcoming from the importer or his bank then the exporter re-directs the goods back home and informs the insurer, say NCM, and the bank who provided the loan of this fact. NCM will repay the loan amount to the exporter's bank and probably repay certain shipping costs, etc., to the exporter. NCM will then take proceedings against the foreign importer, or his bank, to recover the balance of the costs involved. Calculating the "balance of costs involved" can be a complicated operation in this kind of case.

The bank has received repayment of its loan to the exporter. The exporter will have lost around 5% to 10% of the value of the contract. The insurer will pursue its case against the offending party or parties.

EXPORT INSURANCE AGENCIES

Organizations that insure exports can operate in either the public or the private sector. Some years ago, when exporting to many countries of the world was a very risky business, a substantial proportion of export insurance was provided by government agencies. The USA set up the EXIM bank, the UK the ECGD, Germany HERMES, France COFACE, Italy the INA, Belgium the ONC, the Netherlands NCM and Japan JEXIM for insurance and EID for finance.

Today exporting is a far less risky business and the subsidizing of exports is frowned on by WTO and other international trading agencies. Countries adhering to the Berne Union have agreed some ground rules on calculating "fair" trade insurance rates for exporters. The EU have laid down certain "directives" that have outlawed direct government intervention in many sectors of trade.[2]

The insurance of exports by government agency still exists in many countries but the fraction of exports which are insured and financed by government agencies, as against private agencies, has been much scaled down in recent years.

In the UK the government privatized most of the short-term credit business of the ECGD in 1991. The business was bought by a Dutch company called NCM Credit Insurance Ltd. NCM's core product is insurance against the risk of non-payment for exported goods and services sold on credit terms of up to two years. NCM also acts as an agent for the UK government in providing credit insurance for some special risks and insurance of exports to some risky countries. Trade Indemnity, Sun Alliance and Commercial Union are other substantial export credit insurance agencies in the private sector

Lloyd's of London have offered UK companies cover on "political risk" on export contracts since the 1920s but recently they have expanded into insuring trade risks outside the mainstream. The Lloyd's ITCI facility provides cover to exporters from any country, not simply from the UK.

Insurance companies resident outside the UK also offer insurance cover for exports. For example, the American International Group, the Paris based Unistrat Assurances and the Bermuda based Exporter's Insurance Company (EIC).[3]

In the case of the EIC a multinational company can buy a tranche of shares in the company to allow it to set up a "captive insurance" facility.

In 1995 the ECGD still insured many medium- and long-term export contracts, most large-scale export contracts and certain specialized export contracts.

The facilities provided by the ECGD in insuring these medium- and long-term export contracts are basically unchanged since the sale to NCM. However, there have been one or two recent benefits added, for example, British companies can now insure against losses arising out of exchange rate changes between tendering and winning an export contract.

It is easy to find insurance cover for exports to advanced industrialized countries but insurance cover on exports to many "emerging" and "developing" countries can still be hard to come by although the EIC facility may be helpful.

Insurance cover may be offered but it may be too expensive to be worth taking up. In such cases an alternative form of hedge is likely to be sought out. For example a letter of credit from a bank in the foreign country who knows the importer as a customer or a forfeiting agreement or suchlike. These alternative forms of payment will be discussed later in this chapter.

WHAT SERVICES DOES AN EXPORT INSURER PROVIDE?

An export insurance contract can be designed to cover many different types of risk.

An export insurance contract can provide cover for the loss, damage or expropriation of the goods in transit from the exporter to the foreign buyer. This form of cover is provided by many insurance companies.

Credit insurance covers the risk of default by the importer on payment for the goods bought. In the UK most short-term credit insurance on exports is provided by NCM Credit Insurance Ltd and Trade Indemnity.

Credit insurance covers both commercial and non-commercial risk. Commercial risk means that the foreign buyer fails to pay for the goods. Non-commercial risk means that the default is not the fault of the buyer. Non-commercial risk covers failure to pay for the goods bought because of war, revolution, a freeze on foreign currency payments by the foreign government and so forth.

We explained above that an important service provided by an export insurer is that the insurer guarantees to repay an export loan made to the exporter by his bank if the importer fails to pay for the goods.

In addition to providing a guarantee to a local bank an insurance agency may provide a guarantee to a foreign bank thus allowing the foreign bank to provide a loan to the foreign buyer to finance the import of the goods. The loan will be used by the importer to pay for the goods imported.

Most export guarantees to foreign entities are made between banks rather than between the exporter's bank and the importer, but straight loans to the foreign buyer can be arranged.

An example of the principal risks covered by one agency, along with the proportion of the loss covered in each case, is set out in Exhibit 9.1. Normally 90% to 95% of the potential loss is covered by the insurance contract so long as the exporter is not negligent in pursuing his claim.

SERVICES OFFERED BY THE ECGD

Although the services provided by the ECGD to British exporters has been much scaled down in recent years substantial assistance is still provided by the ECGD Projects Group. Cover is now provided for longer-term contracts, some medium-sized contracts and large contracts. As noted above the insurance of smaller short-term export contracts has been taken over by NCM Credit Insurance and other private agencies.

The services provided to UK exporters by the ECGD vary year by year as circumstances change in the export markets of the world. The current principal objective of the Projects Group is to assist in the insurance and financing of large-scale capital projects in foreign countries.

Some of the services currently provided by the ECGD include:

Insurance guarantees on loans provided to exporters by British banks and other lenders who finance foreign sales contracts of a capital nature. Supplier credit guaranteed for up to 85% of the value of the foreign contract. A favourable rate of interest on loans financing exports to certain "third world" countries. The rate is subsidized by the ECGD

Exhibit 9.1 Principal Types of Risk Covered by an Export Insurance Contract

Type of Risk	% Cover
1. Insolvency of client	90
2. Buyer's failure to pay within six months	90
3. Loss or damage to goods transported	95–100
4. Government action that blocks payment	95
5. War preventing payment or loss of goods	95
6. Additional handling resulting from diversion	95
7. Repudiation of contract without just cause	95
8. Any other cause for non-payment:	95
(a) outside the UK	
(b) outwith control of client	

Normally the policy assumes that the insured has taken advantage of any legal remedy open to him in the home or importer's country. The policy does not cover loss due to events preventing completion of the contract in circumstances that could free the client from his obligation to make payment under the contract.

Losses incurred on export contracts can be insured in the private sector in the UK through companies such as NCM Ltd and Trade Indemnity and in the public sector through the ECGD.

Most types of potential losses can be covered by one or other of these agencies. The ECGD covers larger and long-term contracts and contracts where special risks are involved.

The above lists the principal risks covered. Many other less common risks can be covered at a price.

but the rate of subsidy must be acceptable to the Berne Union. If the buyer defaults on payment insurance cover is provided for up to 100% of the loan value, that is 85% of the contract value.

Various forms of cover are provided for "political risk". Political risk covers losses arising from such things as blocked profits, confiscation of goods, expropriation of the foreign company and other losses arising from government interference in the trading process. This type of insurance covers up to 90% of the contract value.

Financial guarantees are offered to allow foreign buyers to finance the purchase of British goods via loans from British banks. Loans are available for up to 85% of the value of the contract. The loan may be provided at a subsidized rate but the foreign buyer must be prepared to put down a deposit equal to 20% of the contract value to receive this particular form of subsidized loan.

Special facilities are offered by the ECGD to cover potential losses arising from such matters as unpredictable cost escalation, consortium projects that go wrong, bond support, pre-shipment finance, tender to contract finance, the costs involved in the unwinding of collapsed foreign contracts and many other specialized risks.

If a British exporter can prove that some foreign government is providing a special subsidy to its exporters the ECGD may provide an equivalent subsidy and then complain to the relevant committee of WTO or the Berne Union.

PAYING FOR EXPORTS

An exporter can offer an importer a wide variety of options when it comes to paying for the goods or services imported.

If the exporter is dubious about the credit-worthiness of the foreign importer the exporter can insist that payment for the exported goods is made and cleared before the goods are shipped. An exporter needs to be in a strong bargaining position vis-à-vis the importer to insist on this particular payment method. The offer of credit on the goods bought is an important accessory to encouraging foreign sales.

At the other extreme on the payments spectrum an exporter who knows the customer well can ship the goods "on open account". The goods are shipped with the invoice attached. The exporter sends on the bill of lading and other documents to the importer and waits for payment by foreign cheque, etc., to be forwarded after the goods have been delivered and inspected. The exporter must know his customer very well indeed to employ this form of payment system because all of the risks associated with non-payment are shifted onto the exporter.

Most export payment systems lie at an intermediary point between these two extremes on the payment spectrum.

The key point is this. The risk of non-payment by the buyer needs to be balanced against the risk of non-delivery by the seller. All payment systems will vary the distribution of these two risks between the seller and buyer. Pre-payment by the buyer is strongly biased towards the interests of the seller, post payment by the buyer is strongly biased towards the interests of the buyer.

A payment system must be viewed as a marketing tool. Who is in the stronger position on the deal? Who really needs the deal to go through, the buyer or the seller? The buyer is usually in the stronger position but it could be the seller. If the buyer is in the stronger position the seller must balance the risk of losing the profit on the sale against the risk of default by the buyer.

Therefore, when choosing a payment system the exporter must balance the cost of operating the system against the security of payment provided by that system. If excellent security is provided to the seller, as in the case of a letter of credit from an established bank, then the payment method will tend to be relatively expensive to the exporter. It is expensive because the amount the bank will charge for a letter of credit includes, in effect, an insurance premium covering non-payment by the importer.

The payment methods used in exporting include:

Cash and credit
Bills of exchange
Documentary letters of credit
International factoring
Forfaiting

Cash and Credit

If the sale to the importer is on "open account" or "payment on shipping the goods" the importer will send a foreign cheque, banker's draft or payment order to the exporter at a time to be agreed between the two parties to the deal.

A cheque is the simplest method of payment. If the cheque is denominated in a foreign currency then the exporter must ask his bank to clear the cheque with the foreign bank. The foreign currency must then be converted into the home currency at a cost to the exporter.

As an alternative to the cheque the importer can ask his bank to provide him with a banker's draft for the given amount. This device is safer than a cheque since the bank and not the importer is liable for the value stated on the cheque. The foreign bank draws the banker's draft, which is an inter-bank cheque, on a bank in the country of the exporter. The draft is now given to the importer who sends it to the exporter who in his turn cashes it with his own bank.

A payment order is a written instruction from one bank to another to pay a given amount of money to a specific person or company.

Money transfers can be by mail, telegraph or telex but today most money transfers are sent electronically by one or other of the inter-bank electronic money transfer systems which are currently in operation.

The Bill of Exchange

A bill of exchange is a credit document sent by a seller to a buyer setting out the amount of money owed by the buyer to the seller and stipulating a date by which the payment must be made.

The buyer receives the bill, checks that the terms agree with the export contract, signs the bill and sends it back to the seller, the exporter.

At this point the bill, if it is associated with a letter of credit (see ahead), can become what is known as a "negotiable instrument". This means that the bill can be sold in the discount market.

If a bill of exchange is in the form which is known as a "documentary bill" the goods to which the bill relates will only be released to the importer once the bill is paid.

Once the seller, the exporter, receives the "accepted" bill he can discount the bill with an organization that specializes in discounting bills of exchange. This organization might be a commercial bank or a specialist "discount house". The discounter pays the exporter a fraction of the face value of the bill, say 98% of its face value. The amount the exporter receives on the discounted bill depends on the rate of interest ruling in the money market of the country where the bill is discounted at that particular time. Once the bank accepts the bill it signs the bill and turns it into a "fine" or "bank" bill, which is negotiable like money.

However, if the acceptor of the bill, the importer, defaults on paying the bill on the due date the bank that discounted the bill has recourse to the exporter to recover the money.

A bill of exchange can pass through many hands before the time comes for the bill to be paid by the original acceptor. Eventually the bill matures and the payment date arrives. The owner of the bill at that point in time presents the bill to the original acceptor for settlement.

If the original acceptor of the bill pays over an amount equal to the face value of the bill then everyone is happy.

The above procedure applies to a home bill. In the case of a foreign bill the procedure is slightly more complicated. The bill is drawn up by the exporter and then sent by the exporter's bank to the importer's bank in the foreign country. The importer's bank presents the "term" bill to the importer for acceptance. If the importer accepts the bill the document of title to the goods stated in the contract will probably be given to the importer. The importer can now claim the goods when they arrive in the foreign country.

The accepted bill is now sent back to the exporter via his bank. The exporter can now discount the bill as explained above.

An exporter may be able to discount a bill of exchange with a bank even before the bill is accepted by the foreign importer! The bank discounts the bill and then sends it to the foreign importer for payment. If the foreign importer refuses to accept the bill the bank, of course, has recourse against the exporter.

Note that a bill of exchange injects some additional purchasing power into the economy during the period of its existence.

The negotiability of a bill depends to a great extent on the reputation of the bank that initially discounts the bill, since, if the buyer and seller both renege on the bill the final owner of the bill can present the bill to this bank for payment.

A "term" bill of exchange provides the seller with immediate liquidity while allowing the buyer a credit period of, possibly, two to three months during which time the goods can be shipped to him.

There is also a form of bill called a "sight" bill. In this case the importer must pay the bill immediately it is presented to him by his (foreign) bank.

Bills of exchange have been the backbone of international credit trading for hundreds of years. The procedures are well tested and understood by all the parties involved.

The Documentary Letter of Credit

If the exporter is worried about the credit-worthiness of the importer or if the transaction is a large one the exporter and the foreign importer may agree that the contract will be financed by means of a "letter of credit".

A letter of credit provides good security to the exporter because it places the responsibility for financing the deal and to some extent the insuring of the deal onto the shoulders of the foreign importer and his bank.

The foreign importer must find a bank that is prepared to provide a letter of credit guaranteeing the deal. This may not be a simple task if the importer resides in a country that has been allocated a poor credit rating by an international credit rating agency such as Standard and Poor's.[4]

The importer's bank then contacts the exporter's bank and tells this bank that the letter of credit has been arranged and the terms of the letter of credit. The exporter's bank may also guarantee the letter of credit to the exporter making it a "confirmed" credit.

Note that the importer's bank gives an irrevocable undertaking to the exporter that the money will be paid once the correct shipping documents are received by the bank.

Once the exporter receives confirmation that a letter of credit has been set up between the two banks it is very unlikely that the exporter can lose money on the deal. The letter of credit is guaranteed by both banks. It is what is called a "confirmed" letter of credit. Note that the letter of credit is a contract that is legally separate from the export/import contract between the exporter and his customer.

Once the goods have been shipped the relevant documentation is sent to the importer's bank and copies are sent to the importer. The importer's bank checks that the documents are in good order[5] and then forwards the cash to the exporter's bank as per the letter of credit. The importer's bank then debits its client's account with this amount.

These shipping documents must be filled in accurately. If even one document does not comply with the export contract the foreign bank can refuse payment!

The exporter's bank now informs the exporter that the money for the export contract has been received from the foreign bank and has been credited to his account.

Instructions can now be given for the bill of lading, etc., to be handed over to the importer so that the goods, held abroad, can be released to the importer. The exporter has ensured that he has been paid for his goods via the letter of credit before the goods are in the possession of the importer.

A letter of credit guarantees either that payment for the goods is secured or that the goods are returned to the exporter. A letter of credit from a bank is only valid for a fixed period of time. The surety is provided by the knowledge which banks possess about the credit-worthiness of their own customers.

On the negative side some exporters claim that a letter of credit is a relatively expensive form of payment, that it is complicated to set up and that it is open to fraud.

Several cases of fraud based on fraudulent documentary credits have come to light in recent years so exporters need to ensure that the foreign bank is a genuine guarantor and that forged bills of lading, etc., are not presented to the foreign warehouse when releasing the goods.

The banks receive a good fee for providing a letter of credit but the charge is not unreasonable relative to the value of the service provided.

International Factoring of Foreign Debts

Factoring is a process whereby an institution called a factor "buys" a debt from a creditor by paying him a fraction of the face value of the debt. A factor takes over the debt from the creditor once the amount of the debt has been agreed between the debtor and the creditor. The factor then collects the payment from the debtor when the payment falls due. International factoring is only available to companies who export a substantial volume of goods or services.

The factor pays the creditor a fraction of the face value of the debt, say 70% to 80%, immediately and the balance, less his charges, once the debt has been settled.

The factor might be prepared to accept, for a fee, most of the risks attached to the debt. For example, he might be prepared to accept the risk of non-payment by the debtor on the due date, this is called "factoring without recourse". As was noted in Chapter 5 an international factor might even be willing to accept the risk of any exchange rate exposure on the debt since the factor may be able to match-off debts in the same currency from several different clients if the factor is operating in several countries or currencies.

Thus if an exporter hands all of his foreign debts to an international factor he gains immediate liquidity and, possibly, insurance against both the non-payment of the debt and exchange rate risk. A useful service.

The one snag with international factoring of debts is the cost of the service. Since the international factor is providing a range of very useful services to his client he will tend to charge an appropriately high fee, which is likely to amount to 2% to 3% of the value of the debt.

However, on the credit side, factoring debts may save the exporter the cost of financing the deal, insuring the deal, collecting or pursuing the debt in the courts and hedging foreign exchange exposure.

In order to weigh up the relative advantage of factoring foreign debts the exporter needs to compare the cost of factoring against the cost of providing these individual services for himself or buying them piecemeal from other external agencies.

Forfaiting

A method of payment called "forfaiting" has been introduced into international trade in recent years.

Under this system of paying for exports the foreign importer provides a series of promissory notes or bills to the exporter. The notes pay a fixed rate of interest. These notes will be converted into cash on a regular basis by the exporter over a period of time varying from one to five years. The notes will provide the exporter with a regular cash inflow sufficient to finance the manufacture of the goods being exported.

The method is normally used by importers operating in countries that are short of foreign currency to finance the import of capital goods. Contracts financed in this way are always relatively long-term contracts.

The key point about forfaiting is that the notes are guaranteed by the importer's bank in the foreign country.[6] Normally the guarantee is given to the bank that will discount the notes in the exporter's country. Thus the process is not unlike a series of guaranteed letter of credit.

The promissory notes are, as we noted in the previous paragraph, discounted by the exporter with a bank in his own country. This local bank, unusually for a transaction of this sort, has no recourse to the exporter if the promissory notes are not paid on time. So these promissory notes are as good as money to the exporter.

For a forfaiting system to be viable the exporter's bank must have complete confidence in the surety of the foreign bank that guarantees the notes. In addition the foreign bank must have complete confidence in the credit-worthiness of its customer, the importer.

Forfaiting is used for paying for imports when foreign currency is in short supply in the importer's country and the exporter has difficulty in financing the export contract by more conventional means.

The London Forfaiting Company states that "if companies have a buyer in a country which is not palatable to the seller or his bank as a risk, the risk might be acceptable to the forfait market".

If forfaiting is the method of payment used in an export contract there is no need for the exporter to take out credit insurance. The banks are, in effect, insuring that the future payments to the exporter will take place on time. Another benefit provided by the forfaiting system is that the fixed rate of interest on the credit contract is guaranteed over the period of the contract.

Another advantage of forfaiting is the speed at which the contract can be set up. If the foreign country into which the exporter is exporting is assessed as suffering from a high degree of political risk then the more traditional forms of insurance and finance might take three months or more to organize. A forfaiting contract can be set up very quickly.

The above description of forfaiting represents what might be called the "mainstream" approach, a wide range of variations are currently being played on this particular theme.

Counter-trading and Barter Trading

The technique of forfaiting is designed to assist companies who wish to buy foreign goods but who reside in countries with limited foreign exchange reserves

An alternative method of accessing scarce foreign currency, which can be used in larger contracts, is to use a system of payment called "counter-trading" or in its original form, "barter trading".

Counter-trading allows a company to swap the goods or services it produces for other goods or services of approximately equivalent value produced in the exporting country.

The problem with counter-trading lies in defining the term "of approximately equivalent value". If both sets of goods are not valued by a common "numeraire" called money, how does either party to the transaction know that the other goods are of approximately equivalent value? Of value to whom?

Counter-trading can take many forms. The straight swapping of goods is rare. A more common form of counter-trading is called counter-purchase. Under this system a part of the export price paid to the exporter is paid for in terms of the goods of the importing company. The balance is covered by allowing the foreign exporter to purchase other goods from the given foreign country.

A variant of counter-purchase occurs when an exporter sells equipment to a foreign importer and agrees to take a fraction of the goods produced by this equipment as part payment for the equipment. For example, a British company sells jam-making equipment to Poland and takes some of the jam produced as payment for the equipment.

A further variant on this theme occurs when the exporter manufacturing equipment for export accepts parts for this equipment from the foreign importer of the equipment and gives a credit for these parts. For example, a German company selling motor machine tools to a company in the Czech Republic accepts machine parts in exchange.

In all of the above cases the exporter accepts goods or services in place of cash for the goods exported.

Counter-trading exists because the potential importer of the goods or service operates in a country which is short of foreign currency and so the government applies stringent exchange control regulations on access to such foreign currency.

Obviously barter trading is less efficient, in an economic sense, than cash trading. It is very difficult for free competitive markets to operate if free market pricing is abolished. However, if an exporter cannot sell to a willing importer simply because the importer cannot pay for the goods in the exporter's currency then counter-trading expands world trade and makes sense. The exporter can break into markets otherwise closed to him.

Counter-trading also removes the problem of exposure to exchange rate risk since money has been removed from the trading equation.

Where developing countries counter-trade their raw materials, such as sugar or oil, for industrial equipment bought from developed countries the process of counter-trading can help to stabilize the price of the exports and imports of the developing country.

For all of these reasons companies operating in developing and emerging economies have adopted counter-trading as an important means of paying for imports when foreign currency is scarce. Thus exporters in developed economies must study the practice of counter-trading if they wish to operate in foreign markets which are lacking in foreign currency reserves.

One consequence of counter-trading is that exporters may find themselves saddled with stocks of goods which they do not need and do not know how to sell. The growth of counter-trading has thus encouraged the emergence of a breed of intermediaries called "counter-traders" and "counter-trade brokers". The broker finds a buyer for the unwanted goods. The counter-trader will offer to buy the unwanted goods from the exporter. The counter-trader will offer to take the unwanted goods off the hands of the exporter at a discounted price. Counter-trade broking has expanded since 1990 and the profession has developed a remarkable degree of sophistication.

Counter-trading supports the aphorism that if a need is there markets will adapt to satisfy it.

Cross-border Leasing

Rather than selling goods outright exporters have the option of leasing assets to foreign buyers. This technique is particularly suited to exporting capital equipment of high value.

Unfortunately, at present, the UK tax code works against UK companies using this technique[7] although it is popular in other European countries.

If the UK tax code changes with regard to leasing then leasing will provide UK exporters with an alternative payment option. Leasing works in the following way. The exporter makes the foreign contact, he then sells the goods to a leasing company who sets up the foreign lease on behalf of the exporter. The exporter gets his money immediately from the leasing company and need not worry about insuring credit sales.

CONCLUSIONS ON SELECTING THE MOST SUITABLE PAYMENTS SYSTEM

All payment systems are not available to all exporters. The exporter must set down all of the payment systems that could be employed in a given contract and select from among these systems the system best suited to the particular deal.

As we noted above that the risks attached to the payment system must be balanced against the cost of the system. If the customer is known to the exporter an inexpensive but risky payment system, like "open account", will be chosen. If the exporter is dubious about the credentials of the importer the exporter will insist on employing an expensive but very safe payments system like a 30-day sight draft or a confirmed letter of credit or a forfaiting agreement. The exporter will try to pass on the cost of the payment system to the foreign importer in the price of the goods supplied.

Thus the level of cost does not, by itself, determine the payment system best suited to the deal. The cost of a payment system must be compared to the risk of default by the importer under the given system to arrive at a decision on the payment system best suited to the particular deal.

WHAT HAVE WE LEARNED IN THIS CHAPTER?

1. The insuring and financing of export contracts is an important aspect of international financial management. Since these activities lack the glamour of hedging exchange risk, investing abroad or raising funds abroad they tend to be marginalized when the major problems of international finance are being discussed but they are important in practice.

2. An exporter must decide on a number of important factors before a foreign sale contract is finalized. The currency of contract, the method of payment, the method of financing and insuring the contract must be decided. In addition the relevant export documentation must be assembled and any exchange control restrictions on payment explored.

3. Many of the risks associated with a home sale, risks such as buyer default on payment or the loss of goods in transit, are augmented when the sale is made to a foreign buyer. Some novel risks are added to the sales contract. Risks such as those attached to foreign exchange exposure, the risks arising from novel forms of insuring and financing the foreign sales contract, the risks attached to novel types of payment systems and the risk of expropriation or other form of intervention by a foreign government.

4. The financing of export contracts is closely linked to the insurance of export contracts. It often happens that financing cannot be obtained for an export contract until the contract is adequately insured.

5. Insurance cover for exports is available from both the private and the public sector. In the past a good proportion of export insurance in the UK and elsewhere was provided by government agency. Today these government schemes have been scaled down and private insurance companies have taken over most of the responsibility for insuring exports. Almost all short-term cover in the developed world is now provided by private agencies. Long-term contracts, very large contracts and unusual export contracts may still be covered by government agency. The agency that covers such contracts in the UK is called the ECGD. Public agencies play a greater role in emerging markets.

6. Cheap export loan finance, subsidized by government, is available in the UK and elsewhere to encourage foreign sales of a substantial size to certain countries. The rate of subsidy is controlled by international monitoring agencies.

7. The insurance agencies provide cover for payment and other default by the buyer and for any loss or damage to the goods in transit. Insurance cover is also available to cover many other risks such as the costs arising from interference by foreign government in normal trade practice.

8. An export insurer will provide a loan guarantee to a lender who provides funds to an exporter to finance an export contract. A guarantee may even be offered by a UK insurer to a foreign lender who finances the purchase of British goods by a foreign importer.

9. A wide range of payment systems are used for paying for foreign sales. Examples of these are "payment on open account", "payment on shipping the goods", the use of bills of exchange and documentary letters of credit, pre-payment by an international factor and the more exotic forms of forfaiting and counter-trading.

10. The method of payment chosen by the parties to the deal must try to balance the costs associated with the payment method against the risk of default by the buyer. Cheap payment systems for the exporter tend to be risky and safe payment systems expensive. It might be possible to pass the incremental cost of the safer payment system on to the foreign buyer via an increase in price.

11. "Counter-trading" is a comparatively recent development in international trade. This method of swapping goods and services rather than paying for goods and services in cash has grown rapidly in recent years. It is claimed that around one quarter by value of world trade might involve some form of counter-trading in 1995.

12. Counter-trading allows exporters to sell into foreign markets where they would otherwise be excluded because of a lack of foreign currency. The recent growth in the profession of counter-trade dealers and brokers is encouraging the growth of the method.

NOTES

1. A credit assessment can cost as little as £1!
2. The Callut committee studied short-term credit insurance and the Tufrau committee medium-term insurance.
3. EIC provides immediate access to US$2 million of credit if US$100 000 of shares are bought in EIC. Maximum cover on one deal in 1994 was US$6.6 million (*Financial Times*, October 5, 1994).
4. For example, in 1994 S&P gave a poor credit rating to Turkey and many banks pulled out of providing letters of credit or forfaiting for Turkish companies. When S&P upgraded the Turkish credit rating the banks moved back in to providing credit for Turkish importers.

5. SITPRO claim that almost half the sets of export documentation sent to UK banks in these circumstances are rejected as being incomplete! See Gee "International Trade Finance" (updated), p. 12/26. It was estimated in 1991 that these errors and omissions had cost UK exporters £100 million in that one year alone.
6. Occasionally the bank guaranteeing the forfait notes resides outside the country of the importer. For example, the bank providing the guarantee may be a bank operating in a country in Western Europe that has good contacts in Eastern Europe.
7. Equipment leased abroad can only be written off against tax at a rate of 10% a year as against 25% a year for equipment leased in the UK. Thus, most UK leasing companies have currently pulled out of leasing abroad.

FURTHER READING

Dunford, C. (ed.) (1991) *A Handbook of International Trade Finance*. Woodhead-Faulkner.
A collection of articles on the problems encountered when financing international trade.
Gee & Co. (updated) *International Trade Finance*.
A compendium of information on financing and insuring international trade. Comprehensive and well indexed.
Guild, I. and Harris, R. (1985) *Forfeiting*. Euromoney Publications.
Hennart, J. (1990) Some empirical dimensions of countertrade. *Journal of International Business Studies*, second quarter, 243–70.
Korth, C. M. (1987) *International Countertrade*. Quorum Books.
Schmitthoff, C. M. (1992) *Export Trade: Law and Practice of International Trade*. Stevens.
The bible on the subject of international trading law. Extremely comprehensive but only recommended to an avid student of the subject.
Venedikian, H. and Warfield, G. (1986) *Export–Import Financing*. New York, John Wiley.
A very clear introduction to the various methods of financing exports and imports. The book takes an international perspective. Factoring, forfaiting and counter-trading are well covered.
Watson, I. (1994) *Finance of International Trade*. CIB.
The recommended book for the banker's exams on the subject of financing international trade. Clearly presented and very comprehensive. Lots of self testing.
Whiting, D. P. (latest edition) *Finance of International Trade*. Macdonald and Evans.
Another useful presentation of the basic facts *re* insuring and financing international trade.

TUTORIAL QUESTIONS

1. Why are the insurance and financing of exports so closely intertwined?
2. Suggest four major risks that may face an exporter with regard to a foreign contract.
3. Why should an export contract be denominated in a third currency? A contract denominated in a third currency is a contract which is denominated in a currency that is neither the currency used by the buyer or the seller. Can you think of an alternative strategy for solving this problem?
4. Suggest three methods of financing an export contract.
5. Provide the names and uses of four of the shipping documents which are needed to allow goods to be shipped to a specific destination abroad.
6. What is meant by the terms FOB and CIF in export contracts? What is the difference between them?
7. Describe the three major types of risk that need to be covered by insurance contracts on an export contract.
8. A British exporter signs a contract to export £15 million worth of brake linings to an Italian company in Italy. The British company needs to raise a £10 million loan for six months to finance the contract. Outline the procedures that the British firm must follow to finance the deal.
9. What types of risk are still insured by the ECGD in 1995?

10. Provide two examples of commercial and non-commercial risk attached to an export contract.
11. Suggest three services provided to an exporter by an export insurance company.
12. The Projects Department of the ECGD provides insurance cover on long-term and large export contracts. What type of risks are covered?
13. Exports can be paid for using various payment methods. What two factors need to be balanced against one another when selecting a suitable payment method?
14. Describe the five most commonly used methods of paying for exports.
15. What is the difference between a banker's draft and a payment order?
16. Explain the procedures that must be followed before a "term" bill of exchange becomes a negotiable instrument.
17. What is the difference between a "term" bill and a "sight" bill?
18. A British company secures an export order for selling desalinization equipment to a company in Argentina. The British company insists that payment be made via a letter of credit. Explain the procedures involved in setting up this letter of credit to pay for the export order.
19. What services might an international factor who operates in several countries provide to an exporter?
20. What advantages accrue to the exporter and the importer of goods which are paid for through a "forfaiting" system rather than through the more conventional "letter of credit"?
21. A French company is approached by a company resident in Poland. The Polish company wishes to purchase machine tools worth FF500 000 from the French company.

    Unfortunately the Polish company cannot gain access to sufficient French currency to complete the deal. The Polish company manufactures agricultural equipment.

    Describe how the French company might use counter-trading to allow the export sale to take place.
22. Why is counter-trading likely to produce a less efficient trading system than trading paid for in a generally accepted currency?
23. What are the key factors to consider when selecting a payment system on an export contract?

EXERCISES

Zenink PLC

A case study on Zenink PLC is attached to Chapter 5. In this case study Zenink is exporting high-purity dyes to Canada and South Africa. The contracts have a value of C$10 million and rand 50 million respectively. Zenink denominates both contracts in the foreign currency.

Zenink needs a loan from a bank or some other source of credit to finance these export contracts.

Zenink uses the services of the Natsouth Bank in the UK. The Canadian importer uses the services of the Toronto Bank, Ontario and the South African importer the services of the Standard Bank in Port Elizabeth.

Zenink decides to insure the Canadian contract in the UK through NCM Credit insurance and to insist on a documentary letter of credit from the South African importer.

Required: Explain the procedures that Zenink will need to follow to finance both deals and to ensure that payment will be received in due time from the importer.

Applecraft PLC

Applecraft PLC is a British company that exports fruit processing machines throughout the world. An order for six machines worth over £2 million is received from a newly privatized jam-making company in Poland called Letza industries.

Applecraft have never heard of this company but the marketing director, Mr Tom Bayliss, flies out to Poland to find out more about Letza Industries.

Mr Bayliss finds that the Polish company seems to be well run but he is told by the finance director of Letza Industries that Poland lacks sufficient UK currency to allow Letza Industries to pay for the contract immediately in pound sterling. Mr Bayliss is keen to win the contract because he believes that the Polish market has great potential in the future.

The marketing director has heard of several exotic techniques of paying for imports called "forfaiting" and "counter-trading". Applecraft have never used these techniques in the past so the marketing director asks the Financial Director of Applecraft, Mr Alec Watson, to explain how they work.

Required: Write a memo to the Marketing Director of Applecraft explaining how "forfaiting" and "counter-trading" work. Suggest how these techniques might be used to gain this Polish order for Applecraft. Which of the many forms of counter-trading would be best suited to this particular situation? What additional information would Applecraft need to find out before it could go ahead with setting up a contract based on either of the two payment methods?

Diggerskill PLC

A British company called Diggerskill PLC receives an order from an Argentinian company called Pecos Mining for tunnelling equipment worth around £1.5 million in pound sterling.

The companies agree that the contract will be financed with an international Bill of Exchange.

Required. Explain (a) how the bill is drawn up; (b) what key information is stated on the bill; (c) how the bill is processed; (d) what happens if the bill is discounted by Diggerskill; (e) how much cash does Diggerskill receive if the bill is discounted; and (f) how the bill is finally paid, by whom and to whom?

Suppose Pecos Mining fail to honour the bill on its due date, what happens then?

Ozsoft PLC

A UK software house with Australian connections called Ozsoft PLC receives an enquiry from a company in Malaysia called Rahman Finance about the possibility of Rahman becoming an agent in Malaysia for Ozsoft. Ozsoft sell some highly specialized software that is used for controlling customer credit.

Ozsoft have never heard of this Malaysian company and, in fact, have never even traded with Malaysia in the past.

Required. Outline the steps that need to be followed by Ozsoft before it can set up a trading link with Rahman Finance. What are the key factors that need to be agreed between Ozsoft and Rahman Finance before the Agency can be run on a regular basis?

Wincott PLC

Wincott PLC have moved into exporting to markets in Eastern Europe. They are having problems with slow payment (one month average) and bad debts (1%) on these sales. The average period of credit given is 90 days. The expected volume of credit sales is £1 500 000 per annum. All sales are in pound sterling.

Wincott consider two options for financing these export sales and covering the increased credit risk involved:

1. To insure the credit sales with a private credit insurer called "Forncredit" who cover credit risk up to 95% of value. Once the export contract is insured Wincott can finance the deal by

raising a loan of £1 200 000 from a commercial bank at a rate 2% below the usual charge of 14% charged by banks for financing such deals if uninsured.
2. To hand the debts over to a factor called "Exfacto Ltd" who will (a) pay Wincott 80% of the value of the sale immediately, the finance being provided at a charge of 17% p.a.; and (b) take over the credit management operation from Wincott (this would cost Wincott £23 000 for all £1 500 000 of East European sales). The factoring is without recourse if the debt is late or unpaid.

Other costs associated with each option are as follows:

Forncredit charges an insurance premium of 50 pence per £100 of exports insured. The charge for debt collection, etc., by the factor is 3% of the value of sales.

Which do you consider to be the better option?

10

International Tax Planning

INTRODUCTION: THE BURDEN OF FOREIGN TAXATION

"Taxation represents a business cost like any other. Accordingly, most companies will endeavour to use whatever legitimate means are available to keep such costs to a minimum in order to enhance shareholder value. This is not easy to achieve. Many UK based multinationals have reported tax charges far in excess of the UK corporate tax rate because of overseas taxation, the cost of repatriating funds to the UK and the burden of unrelieved advance corporation tax. Unusable losses in an overseas jurisdiction are particularly damaging to a multinational's reported tax rate".

Ernst and Young *International tax.*

If a parent company sets up a subsidiary company in a foreign country the profits earned by that subsidiary will be subject to tax in the foreign country. Two forms of direct tax are likely to be imposed on the foreign subsidiary, first, the subsidiary company will be required to pay direct income tax on the profits earned in the foreign country, secondly, the subsidiary will be required to pay a form of tax called a "withholding" tax, which will be deducted from any dividends which the subsidiary company might decide to repatriate abroad to its parent.

There are many variations on this basic theme, especially in countries which are called "tax havens", but the tax set up described in the previous paragraph illustrates the normal situation with regard to taxing foreign subsidiaries.

In addition to these direct taxes the foreign subsidiary will normally be required to pay additional indirect taxes such as VAT, an excise duty on imports and various social and payroll taxes.

We now turn to the tax demands of the home country where the parent company resides.

In addition to paying tax on the profits of the foreign subsidiary to the tax authority in the foreign country the group that owns the subsidiary may have to pay additional income tax on these profits in its home country! Also the shareholders of the multinational group may well have to pay further personal income tax on the dividends paid out to them by the parent company. These dividends will be paid out of profits including the net profits from the foreign subsidiary which have already been double taxed abroad!

It would seem that the profits made by the foreign subsidiary are being taxed four times over!

Clearly if the profits made by foreign subsidiaries were actually subject to the quadruple tax regime described above there would be very little investment in foreign subsidiaries! Many years ago the governments of the world realized that something had to be done about this excessive tax burden on foreign subsidiaries and so a series of treaties called "double taxation agreements" have been signed between the tax authorities of many of the countries of the world. These treaties allow the tax paid on the profits of subsidiaries in one country to be offset against the tax bill paid in the other country.

Despite the existence of these treaties foreign tax remains a serious burden on multinational companies and if mishandled foreign taxation can impose a formidable cost on a multinational company.

The OECD published a report entitled "Taxing profits in a global economy" in 1992. The report concluded that "double taxation by home and host countries of company profits earned abroad emerge as a real barrier [to foreign investment]". The report calculated that the average return needed on a home investment to match a 5% near risk free post tax bond yield of 5% per annum was 5.9% before tax. An identical investment overseas would have needed to produce a yield of 7.5% before tax to provide the same post tax yield. The higher return required from the foreign investment is a consequence of the taxes imposed on the income from the foreign investment by foreign governments.

Exhibit 10.1 illustrates the pre-tax returns needed to produce a 5% after tax return on domestic, outward and inward investment in seven major OECD countries in 1991.

If a company is trading in only one country tax planning is complex enough but once a company begins to trade overseas, and particularly to manufacture overseas, the complexity of the tax planning process increases exponentially with the number of foreign subsidiaries.

The process of international tax planning is complex yet the objectives of tax planning are quite straightforward. The principal objective of international tax planning is to minimize the global tax bill of the MNC. This can be best effected by ensuring that full advantage is taken of "tax arbitrage". Profits should be made within tax regimes that charge a low rate of tax while, at the same time, ensuring that costs are incurred in those tax regimes which charge a high rate of tax!

The real challenge in constructing an international tax plan does not lie in the conceptual difficulty of the subject but in collecting the myriad of relevant facts about the tax regimes of the world. It is not easy to keep up to date with the changes in tax rates, tax allowances, tax legislation and novel tax efficient techniques that are changing continuously within every tax regime. A review of the annual publication called the *International Bureau of Fiscal Documentation* (IBFC, 1994), which lists and discusses the major tax changes that have taken place worldwide during the previous year, will underline this point.

We will describe how to keep up to date on worldwide tax changes later in the chapter.

The continual state of flux in the international tax field may explain the dearth of books of an analytical nature on international tax planning.[1]

Exhibit 10.1 The Impact of Foreign Taxation on the Return on Foreign Investment

	Investment		
Country	Domestic %	Outward %	Inward %
France	5.4	6.6	7.9
Germany	5.6	7.9	6.3
UK	5.9	6.8	7.0
USA	5.8	7.1	7.5
Italy	5.9	8.6	7.2
Canada	6.3	7.5	8.5
Japan	6.3	8.0	8.1
Average	5.9	7.5	7.5

Notes:
Inflation rate of 4.5% pa assumed in all cases.
No tax liability for investor assumed.
Investment financed by a range of normal sources.

The table shows the gross of tax return needed to achieve a return of 5% after tax in seven major countries in the OECD in 1991.

Note that in most cases inward investment needs to achieve a higher return than outward investment. However, Germany and Italy are exceptions to this rule.

The table shows that because of foreign taxes external investment needs to achieve a higher return than that generated by a similar investment in the home country.

Source: *Taxing Profits in a Global Economy*. OECD Report.

In order to reduce the global tax bill of her company the tax officer needs to identify those tax devices and tax stratagems that best match the global cash flow and asset structure of her company. This is easier said than done when tax legislation and anti-avoidance legislation are in a constant state of flux.

The opportunity cost of adapting the global tax policy of a company to the constantly changing kaleidoscope of tax rates, tax allowances and tax law in all of the countries of the world is high.

The problem is so complex that some multinational companies have evolved a simulation computer model to provide a "satisficing" solution to the international tax conundrum.

It may be that one day, far in the future, electronic data bases developed from LEXIS, NEXIS or HYPERTAX, data bases that store and continuously update current information on tax matters, can be linked into a financial model of a company to generate an optimal tax plan. Such a linkage may alleviate the cost of international tax planning somewhat, but that time has not yet arrived.

DIFFERENCES IN THE TAX SYSTEMS OF THE WORLD

In 1995 there were some 180 different tax regimes operating in the various countries of the world. No two of these tax regimes were exactly alike.

Exhibit 10.2 Corporate Tax Rates and Withholding Taxes Applied by Various Countries in 1994

Country	Rate of company tax %	Rate of capital gains tax %	Rate of tax on branches %	Withholding tax				Net operating losses	
				Dividends %	Interest %	Royalties patents knowhow %	Branch remittances %	Carry-back	Carry-forward
Argentina	30	30	30	0	12	24	0	0	5
Australia	33	33	33	0/30	10	30	0	0	No limit
Barbados	40	0	40	15	15	15	10	0	9
Belgium	40.17	40.17	44.29	25.75	13.39	13.39	0	0	No limit
Bermuda	0	0	0	0	0	0	0	0	No limit
Brazil	25	25	25	15	25	25	15	0	4
Canada	28.84	21.63	25	25	25	25	0	3	7
Cayman Islands	0	0	0	0	0	0	0	0	No limit
China	30	33	33	20	20	20	0	0	5
Denmark	34	34	34	30	0	30	0	0	5
Germany	45	45	42	25	0	25	0	2	No limit
Greece	35	35	35	0	15	20	0	0	5
Guernsey	20	0	20	0	20	20	0	1	No limit
Hong Kong	17.5	0	17.5	0	0	1.75/17.5	0	0	No limit
India	45	40	65	25	25	30	0	0	8
Ireland	40	40	40	0	27	27	0	1	No limit
Italy	36	36	36	32.4	15	21	0	0	5
Japan	37.5	37.5	37.5	20	20	20	0	1	5
Korea	32	25	32	0	20	0	0	0	5
Liechtenstein	20(a)	35.64	20	4	4	0	0	0	2
Malaysia	32	0	32	0	20	15	0	0	No limit
Netherlands	35	35	35	25/0	0	0	0	3	8
Neth. Antilles	36.8/44.85	36.8/44.85	36.8/44.85	0	0	0	0	0	5
Singapore	27	0	27	0	27	27	0	0	No limit
South Africa	40(b)	0	40	15	0	12	0	0	No limit
Spain	35	35	35	25	25	25	25	0	5
Sweden	28	28	28	30	0	0	0	0	No limit
Switzerland	10/27(c)	0	10/27(c)	35	35	0	0	1	6
Taiwan	25	25	25	35/20	20	20	0	0	5
Turkey	25	25	25	20	0	25	20	0	5
UK	33	33	33	0	25	25	0	3	No limit
USA	35(d)	35	35	30	30	30	30	3	15
Zimbabwe	42.5/20	10/30	50.9	20	10	20	0	0	6

Notes:
(a) Holding companies are exempt from income tax.
(b) Plus STC tax on dividends declared at 15%.
(c) Total tax is made up of cantonal plus state tax.
(d) Plus local state tax.

Source: *Worldwide Corporate Tax Guide and Directory*, Ernst & Young, 1994.

Many variations are played on the rates shown above. The rates and allowances are varied in relation to specific circumstances. The rules applying in each country must be carefully studied before designing a tax strategy.

The most obvious differences between the tax regimes of the world relate to tax rates and tax allowances. The basic rate of company tax, capital gains tax, branch tax and withholding tax in various countries of the world in 1993 are shown in Exhibit 10.2. Note that the basic corporate tax rate varied from 0% in Bermuda to 45% in India. The capital gains tax varied from 0% in South Africa to 45% in Germany. "Withholding" taxes on dividends, interest, etc., varied from 0% in Greece to 35% in

Switzerland. Tax "havens" such as Bermuda and the Cayman islands impose no taxes whatsoever on so-called "non-resident" companies that operate out of these countries.

Some countries apply the "classical" system of taxing foreign income whereby the foreign income is taxed once in the foreign and once in the home country while others apply the "imputation" system whereby tax is based on the worldwide income of the group but a tax credit is allowed against the foreign tax paid.

Differences in the tax rates charged and tax allowances offered represent only a small fraction of the differences that exist between the tax regimes of the world. For example, as shown in Exhibit 10.2, most countries of the world, but not all, insist on applying a "withholding" tax on dividends.

Exhibit 10.3 sets out some of the key questions that need to be asked by a finance officer to identify these differences.

As we noted above the aim of international tax planning is to take advantage of these differences to reduce global tax. The tax officer can take advantage of what has been called "tax arbitrage" and use these differences between tax regimes to reduce the global tax bill of her company. The tax officer will attempt to organize the financial affairs of her company in order to take advantage of any tax reduction or tax avoidance devices that are available within the several tax regimes within which her company operates, often setting one regime off against another.

However, the basic strategic thrust of a company must not be tax driven. Tax minimization must be treated as a constraint on strategy not as an objective in itself. Corporate policy must not be reduced to a subplot of tax planning, as sometimes happens.

GOVERNMENT ATTITUDES TO THE TAXING OF FOREIGN COMPANIES

Governments often take up a somewhat schizoid attitude to the taxing of foreign companies, particularly multinational companies (MNCs), operating on their territory.

The conflict arises because most countries wish to extract the maximum possible revenue from the foreign company resident in their territory while at the same time soliciting the maximum amount of investment, in the form of capital and know-how, from these same companies. These objectives conflict with one another. A high tax regime will discourage foreign investment.

A great deal of bargaining goes on between the multinational company and the relevant department within the government of the country in which an investment might be made. The final results of this bargaining process concerning such things as the tax to be paid by the MNC and the grants, etc., to be awarded for inward investment may never be published in any tax manual.

These negotiations about tax rates, tax allowances, repatriation of dividends, payment for services rendered by other subsidiaries, repayment of value added tax on exports, transfer pricing and associated matters are the bread and butter of the bargaining process that takes place between the MNC and the government of the foreign country before a foreign investment is made.

Exhibit 10.3 Key Questions on International Tax

1. What is the corporate tax rate?
2. What is the capital gains tax rate?
3. What is the rate of tax applied to the profits of a branch?
4. What are the withholding taxes charged?
   On dividends?
   On interest?
   On royalties, patents and "know-how"?
   On Director's fees?
   On remittances from branches?
5. Can net operating losses be carried forward or back?
   How many years forward?
   How many years back?
6. What capital allowances are available? On what assets?
7. Are resident companies treated differently from non-resident companies for tax purposes? What are the differences?
8. What tax relief is allowed against foreign tax?
9. What double tax treaties have been signed? With which countries?
10. Can a group of companies be taxed as a single entity?
11. What other significant taxes are paid by a company?
    Value added tax? At what rate?
    Average customs duties on imports?
    Employee insurance tax?
    Social security and pension tax?
12. What anti-tax avoidance legislation is in force?
13. Are debt to equity rules (thin capitalization) in place? What is the maximum debt % allowable?
14. How is the tax assessment and charge administered? What are the timings of tax payment?

The above table lists some of the key questions to ask about a foreign tax regime.
Source: The table is adapted from the *World-wide Corporate Tax Guide* published annually by Ernst and Young.

As with all bargaining processes the balance of benefit in the final agreement depends on how much each party to the negotiations really wants the investment to take place.

We conclude that just because a tax treaty or a tax schedule states that the tax to be paid is such-and-such it does not mean that these rules are set in granite. Negotiation on the official tax rules may well be possible if the government of the country where the investment might take place really needs the foreign investment or the trade or the know-how.

FORMS OF INTERNATIONAL TAX

Companies operating abroad can find themselves taxed both at home and abroad in several different ways. The more common forms of foreign taxation imposed on international companies are direct tax on company profits earned abroad, withholding taxes on dividends, interest, consulting fees, etc., repatriated to a parent by a foreign subsidiary, taxes on translation gains on assets and liabilities denominated in a foreign currency and taxes on capital gains.

Direct Taxation of Profit

The most common form of tax paid by an MNC to a foreign government is the direct tax charged on the profits of a subsidiary company operating abroad.

Currently the basic rate of company tax imposed on the profits of foreign subsidiaries varies from zero to around 50%. If a company is operating in several countries that charge varying rates of tax on company profit then obvious opportunities exist for applying "tax arbitrage" between these various tax regimes. The multinational company can charge costs that benefit the global company against the profits of subsidiary companies operating in countries that apply the highest corporate tax rates or offer the most favourable tax allowances. Conversely very profitable activities undertaken within a multinational group can be allocated to subsidiaries operating in countries that charge relatively low corporate tax rates.

Exhibit 10.4 illustrates some of the items that are subject to differing tax treatment by the tax regimes in various countries of the world.

Transfer Pricing

Transfer pricing has an obvious part to play in minimizing global tax. Relatively high charges can be imposed on subsidiaries operating in high tax regimes and relatively low charges imposed on subsidiaries operating in low tax regimes. Subsidiaries operating in high tax regimes can be advised to raise funds for the Group locally and so offset the interest charge against the high local tax rate.

Many tax authorities set down strict rules on methods of transfer pricing. The OECD has put forward a "convention" for transfer pricing that is followed by many multinational companies. Under this convention all transfer prices within a group should be priced at an "arm's length price". This price can be negotiated with the relevant tax authority in advance of an investment being made in the given country via a bilateral advanced pricing agreement.

The overall objective in such matters is to minimize the global tax bill of the company. The distribution of the total costs of the Group for accounting purposes may be no more than a paper entry in the consolidated accounts of a holding company. This is why the United States tried, but failed, to introduce a "unitary" tax system in 1986 that would have taxed multinational companies operating in the USA on a fraction of their global profits rather than simply on the "accounting" profits earned in the USA.[2]

If a "weighted" transfer pricing scheme is used to reduce the global tax bill of an MNC we must assume that the foreign subsidiaries of the Group are mere satellites of the parent company who will do what they are told by the head office. We must also assume that the governments in the high tax countries are somewhat naive about the use of transfer values in varying the distribution of profits within a multinational group of companies. Tough anti-tax-avoidance legislation in the foreign country or the ethical stance adopted by the parent company may well negate the use of transfer pricing stratagems for reducing the global tax bill of a group of companies.

The United States tax authorities impose very strict regulations on international transfer pricing. The US authorities insist that all transfer prices are fixed at "arm's length" between the parent and the subsidiary and, in addition, they impose a "super-royalty" rule on the amount that can be charged to foreign subsidiaries for the transfer of intangible assets such as consulting advice.

The careful planning of the time when a cost is debited or a profit taken is another stratagem that can reduce the global tax bill of a company. For example tax may not need to be paid on the profits from a transaction until the transaction is "closed". This closure process can be delayed in order to shift the profit into a later period when the marginal tax rate of the company is lower than it was in the previous period.

We should note in passing that if the repatriation of profits to a parent is blocked by a foreign government then the invariable rule is that no taxes are imposed on these foreign profits by the tax regime in the country where the parent resides until the profits are unblocked.

Double Tax Agreements

If a parent company is taxed on its worldwide profits the profits of any foreign subsidiary might be taxed twice. Once in the foreign country and once in the country where the parent company resides.

Double tax agreements are signed between the tax regimes of two countries in order to split the tax revenue to be received by each regime from a common source of profit. The treaty regulates the taxing rights of the two tax regimes.

Double tax treaties may also clarify some other matters. For example, they might determine the residency of a company under various circumstances, they will prevent a foreign company from one country being charged at a higher tax rate than a local company and they may arrange for the two tax authorities to exchange information about the financial dealings of local companies controlled by companies in the other's country.

Most of the advanced industrial countries of the world have worked out double tax agreements with one another. These agreements ensure that the profits and the dividends paid out of these profits are not taxed twice by two different tax regimes.

The OECD put forward a model double tax convention in 1977 that has been very influential in harmonizing such agreements worldwide.

Tax Credits

A government might exclude foreign profits from tax using the so-called "classical" or "partial exemption method" as in South Africa or France. However, most countries tax their resident companies on their worldwide profits, the so-called "credit" method of imposing tax.

Although the worldwide profits of an MNC are subject to tax in the home country of the parent the profits made by any non-resident subsidiary are usually only taxed on the dividends remitted by the subsidiary to the parent since "tax credits" are allowed.

If the profits of a foreign subsidiary and/or the dividends repatriated from these profits to the parent company are already taxed by a foreign tax regime then under the credit method some kind of "tax credit" is likely to be allowed on the dividend income repatriated to the parent. This tax credit can be offset against the tax bill of the parent company. This tax credit is in addition to any tax relief available on "withholding" taxes deducted by the foreign government.

If the rate of company tax in the foreign country is lower than the rate charged in the home country then an additional tax charge may be imposed by the tax authorities in the home country to bring the tax rate up to the home country rate. If such a scheme is applied the parent company with a foreign subsidiary in a low tax regime may decide not to repatriate profits to the home country, at least not in the form of dividends, but in some other form such as consultancy fees.

If the rate of company tax in the foreign country is higher than the rate charged in the home country the tax authorities in the home country may allow the parent company an additional tax credit to compensate for the higher tax paid abroad, although this is unusual. The tax authority in the United States has run a compensation scheme on these lines in the past. Normally this excess tax credit is lost by the parent unless some scheme is set up to "mix" the tax credits from several foreign subsidiaries via a "stepping stones" company so that they can be set off against one another to absorb all the credits available. We will return to "stepping stone" companies later in this chapter.

In the UK the tax credits allowed cannot exceed the UK company tax attributed to the grossed up foreign income of the subsidiary.[3] If the UK parent makes a loss the foreign tax credit on foreign profits is lost for that year.[4]

Unless countervailing measures are taken the net result of a double tax agreement will usually be that profits earned by a foreign subsidiary are taxed at the higher of the two rates, the foreign rate or the home rate. Obviously a tax officer will try to avoid this result by careful tax planning.

Double tax agreements designed on the lines described above will tend, in the long run, to equalize the rate of company tax charged in all the countries involved in the double tax network since, if the corporate tax rate is not equal, one country, the country with the higher tax rate, can take advantage of a low rate of company tax in another country to raise additional tax on foreign profits earned in that country.

As noted above the OECD in 1977 put forward a "model" double tax convention for consideration by its members. Most agreements take this model scheme as a starting point for discussions but all double tax agreements do not use the same formula to calculate the taxing of foreign income.

Double tax agreements tend to be favoured by high taxing regimes. Countries which impose low or zero tax, such as tax havens, have difficulty in setting up double tax agreements with other countries. If, however, two high tax regimes, A and C, do not have a double tax agreement between them for some reason then a third country, B, may be allowed to set up a double tax agreement with both A and C to allow a multinational company trading in both A and C to minimize its tax bill.

Carry-forwards and Carry-backs

If a subsidiary company operating in a foreign country makes a loss it pays no income tax. Most countries allow such losses to be carried forward for several years to be set off against future profits. Carry-forwards of three years' to five years' duration are common. In the case of the UK or South Africa there is currently no limit to the number of years a loss can be carried forward. These losses can be set off against future profits to reduce future income tax. Some tax authorities even allow losses to be set off against tax paid on past profits running back to five years or more, however, as shown in

Exhibit 10.1 such concessions are rare. Currently (1995) Canada, the USA and the UK allow a three year carry-back.

These carry-backs and carry-forwards of losses against the tax on past, current or future profits are valuable assets. They can substantially increase the value of a target company in a merger or take-over bid.

Tax credits can be carried forward and even backwards by some tax regimes. The UK does not allow this but the US does.

Dividends

Dividends are normally awarded a different tax treatment to the profits out of which the dividends are paid.

Dividends create tax problems both as payments and receipts. Let us first examine the tax problems associated with the payment of dividends by a foreign-based subsidiary to its parent company in another country under a "credit" system. For example, if the subsidiary of a German company resident in Indonesia pays out dividends from profits to its European parent it will have to deduct a 15% withholding tax from these payments and pay this to the government in Indonesia. The Indonesian subsidiary has already paid corporate tax on its local profits at 35%.

Few countries object to a foreign-based company making good profits, what they object to is that company repatriating substantial cash sums, usually in the form of dividends, out of the country.

Taxes on dividends and other distributions are called "withholding" taxes. "Withholding" taxes are usually imposed on dividends repatriated abroad to foreign shareholders. The mechanism of a "withholding" tax consists of the tax authority in the foreign country retaining a part of the dividend before it is sent abroad. If withholding taxes are imposed the fraction of the dividend withheld may vary from a figure as low as 4% in the case of Liechtenstein to above 50% in the case of Zimbabwe. Most tax havens impose no or very low withholding taxes on dividends sent abroad by resident companies.

The rate of the withholding tax may vary depending on the nature of the payment to the foreign entity. The payment may be in the form of dividends but it may also be in the form of interest or rent or royalty or licence fee or a payment for "know-how". For example, in the case of Malaysia in 1993, corporate tax on foreign subsidiaries was paid at a rate of 32% on profits, the withholding % on dividends repatriated abroad was zero, on royalties and patents and payments for "know-how" it was 15% and on interest repatriated abroad it was 20%.

As explained above the parent company receiving the dividend will normally be entitled to some form of tax relief on its home country tax bill for this foreign "withholding" tax.

Whatever the situation relatively high withholding taxes on foreign payments have proved to be a strong disincentive to foreign investment in the country imposing them.

The withholding taxes described above should be differentiated from advanced payment of corporation tax. The tax authorities in several countries operate an advanced corporation tax (ACT) payment scheme that speeds up tax payments to the local Inland Revenue. An ACT scheme causes problems for foreign owners of shares in the countries operating such a scheme. The UK tax authorities offer foreign companies operating in the UK several solutions to this problem. Tax concessions by the UK authorities allow a foreign subsidiary resident in the UK to pay dividends plus a fraction of the ACT directly to their foreign shareholders.

The rules on taxing dividends received from abroad vary from country to country. The UK situation regarding the taxation of foreign dividends received by UK companies is fairly typical.

If the foreign operation is not a subsidiary but a branch or agency of the UK company then the UK company must pay tax on all profits made by the foreign-based branch or agency. If the foreign operation is a subsidiary company then tax at the standard rate is assessed on any dividends or interest received from the foreign subsidiary. Even though tax is based on worldwide profits, double tax relief in the form of tax credits will be available to compensate for any foreign taxes paid by the subsidiary as long as a double tax treaty is in place with the foreign government.

Some countries refuse to enter into double tax agreements with other countries. These countries are mainly tax havens or countries run by socialist governments.

A tax officer must give careful consideration to the amount and timing of any dividend paid to the parent company by a subsidiary resident in a country that refuses, or is unable, to enter into double tax agreements with other countries. He must also pay attention to the routing of this dividend to the parent. As will be explained later if the dividend is routed via a "stepping stones" company the global tax bill of the group might be reduced quite substantially.

The Treatment of "Translation" Profits or Losses on Items Exposed to FX Risk

If a company operates abroad it is likely to own assets and owe debts abroad. These assets and liabilities will be expressed in terms of a foreign currency.

Between the beginning and end of an accounting period the value of such assets and liabilities are likely to change in value in terms of the home currency because of changes in exchange rates.

If the foreign currency rises in value against the home currency the foreign assets and liabilities will also rise in value in terms of the home currency, if the foreign currency falls in value during the period, foreign currency denominated assets and liabilities will, at least temporarily, fall in value in terms of the home currency.

These "paper" profits or losses on assets and liabilities denominated in a foreign currency may have tax effects in the home country. Such translation gains and losses are only "paper" gains and losses, no actual cash flows. The "paper" gain or loss may well be reversed in a future period.

We will recall from Chapter 4 that real assets denominated in a foreign currency are self-hedged but that monetary assets and liabilities are not. A rise in the value of a debt denominated in a foreign currency in terms of the home currency represents a real loss if the exchange rate does not reverse itself before the debt matures.

The tax treatment of translation gains and losses varies a great deal between the tax regimes of the world. Under most tax regimes translation gains and losses on assets and liabilities are ignored unless converted into cash.

As a general rule translation gains and losses are only taxed or allowed against tax once the asset, which has risen in value, is sold or the debt repaid. However, a translation loss on a rise in debt in terms of the home currency may be allowed against tax even if the debt has not yet matured. Exchange losses incurred on short-term revolving loans are often allowed as an immediate charge against company profits while similar losses against longer term loans of a similar amount, beyond a year, are not allowed until the loan is repaid. In a few rare cases translation gains are taxed but translation losses are not allowed against tax!

In some tax regimes the "accrual method" is used. The accrual method allows any translation gain or loss on assets denominated in a foreign currency to be netted off against gains or losses on liabilities at the end of the accounting year. This net gain or loss is taxed at the current corporate tax rate or at some special rate. The UK is due to introduce such a system in 1995.

Profits or Losses on Derivatives

Many companies guard against potential losses on FX exposure by taking out cover via a forward, future, option or swap contract. The tax treatment of any profit or loss arising out of these derivative or swap contracts can be complex.

Ernst and Young write that: "The cross border taxation aspects of new financial products is one of the most complex and uncertain areas of international tax".[5]

If the associated business transaction is a normal business transaction, for example if the derivative is to be used to cover the risk of loss on a future payment for exports denominated in a foreign currency, then the gain or loss on the forward cover is usually taxed, or allowed against tax, just like normal trading profits or losses. The gain on the derivative transaction is taxed or the loss allowed against tax once the contract is closed.

If the gain or loss is made on a hedge set up to cover a "translation" loss then either the transaction will have no tax effect or it may be treated as a capital transaction and a capital gains tax rate applied to any profit. If this rule is applied to the contract then losses on the derivative contract will only be allowed against capital gains not against normal profits. Capital gains may not, of course, be available to offset such losses.

Gains or losses on very long-term hedges, for example, on swap transactions, may have no tax effect or may be treated as if they are capital transactions as above.

These matters may seem to be somewhat esoteric but they have one very important practical effect. This arises from the fact that it is difficult to calculate the precise amount of a hedge needed to cover an exposure position if the tax to be charged on any profit from the hedge is not certain. The amount hedged will need to be "grossed up" to cover the tax charge on any profit that may be made from the hedge ... but if the value of the profit on the hedge is not known with certainty when the hedge is taken out the finance officer has a problem! Note that losses on derivatives may not be allowed against normal trading profits.

The precise tax treatment of the profit or loss on derivative contracts needs to be clarified in many tax regimes, not least in the British regime. However, "financial products frequently offer an opportunity to exploit mismatches in taxation between two [tax] jurisdictions".[4] For example, between Portugal and Germany and Italy and Holland.

Recent anti-tax-avoidance legislation has closed up many of the tax-avoidance schemes based on debt and so in recent years structured tax-avoidance schemes have concentrated on using derivatives to reduce the tax burden of MNCs. Around 60% of tax-avoidance schemes sold in the USA in 1994 were based on derivatives.

Capital Gains and Losses

Capital gains on transactions in foreign assets and liabilities may be taxed at the normal rate applied to company profits or at a different "capital gains" rate or may not be subject to tax.

Capital losses may not be allowed against normal trading profits but only allowed as a set off against capital gains. Under some tax regimes capital losses have no tax effect, particularly if capital gains are not taxed.

The Use of Sensitivity Analysis in Tax Planning

The relative importance of each of the above taxes in the global tax plan can be tested by applying "sensitivity analysis" to a financial model of the group. The tax officer can apply sensitivity analysis to the model to identify those tax-saving devices which are significant relative to global profits and concentrate his efforts on using these particular devices to reduce global tax.

Tax allowances and the tax treatment of various costs and revenues vary between countries. An MNC may be able to use these differences to reduce the global tax bill. Variations in tax treatment, such as those listed in Exhibit 10.4, can be inserted into a tax planning model and the impact on the global tax bill deduced.

THE LEGAL FORM OF THE FOREIGN ENTITY

Trading abroad is normally initiated through exporting goods or services. Later in the day trading is expanded by selling through a foreign agent who may act for several customers. In such cases the company is said to be "trading with" but not "trading in" the foreign country. All profits on these deals will probably be taxed in the country of the parent as normal company profits but not taxed in the foreign country where the sales are made.

As the foreign operations of the company expand the company may decide to set up an independent entity in the foreign country. At this point the company must decide whether to set up a branch or a subsidiary company in the foreign country. The choice between operating abroad through a branch or a subsidiary company is determined by many factors among which tax advantage is only one but tax planning can play an important role in the decision.

Both the branch and the subsidiary company will be considered to be "trading in" rather than "trading with" the foreign country. Therefore both these entities will normally be subject to tax in the foreign country. If the branch and the subsidiary company are considered to be "permanent establishments" by the foreign tax authority then the income tax paid to the foreign government on any profits earned in the foreign country will normally be the same,[6] but the branch will not usually have to pay a "withholding" tax on remittances to the home country.[7]

The situation is different if the foreign entity is a subsidiary company. If the profits of the foreign subsidiary are repatriated to the home country in the form of dividends or some other form then these dividends will normally be subject to a withholding tax as discussed above.

Exhibit 10.4 Tax Deductions, Exemptions and Incentives

The tax regimes in the various countries of the world offer a wide range of tax deductions, tax exemptions and tax incentives. These vary widely between countries and offer the able tax officer an opportunity to minimize the global tax bill of her company.

Some of these deductions and incentives are listed below:

Depreciation of assets

The rates of depreciation and the speed with that an asset can be written off the company books varies widely between tax regimes. In some cases 100% of the value of the asset can be written off against profits immediately. In other cases no offset is allowed until the asset is sold. Most regimes allow the asset to be written off against profits over n years using various write-down methods.

The rules regarding the assets that can be depreciated also vary a great deal between countries. Equipment can invariably be written off but what about land and buildings, franchises, patents, goodwill and suchlike? Must the write-down for tax purposes be the same as write-down in the annual accounts?

Research and development costs

The tax treatment of R&D costs varies a great deal between tax regimes. Many allow immediate write-off against profits. A few do not allow R&D as an allowable expense except against the product produced. Some regimes allow special tax credits in excess of the R&D actually expended to encourage research.

Investment reserve and pension reserve

Some tax regimes, such as in Scandinavia, allow a percentage of company tax to be placed in a special investment reserve that can be used for future investment. The money must be deposited in a government account. The same procedure may apply to money set aside for an employee pension fund.

Tax on distributed and retained profits

There is a wide variation in the tax treatment of dividends. In some cases profits distributed are taxed at a lower rate than profits retained in the business. In other cases the reverse procedure applies. Some tax regimes allow dividends to be deducted from taxable profit. The rate of withholding tax on dividends varies a great deal from country to country as illustrated in Exhibit 10.2. The rate of advanced corporation tax may affect the value of the dividend received by a foreign shareholder.

The tax treatment of inflation

Under inflationary conditions some of the "profits" of a company are not real profits but simply represent a decline in the value of money. It would not be fair to tax such inflationary profits so many tax authorities provide tax allowances to compensate for inflation. The value of inventory can be adjusted for inflation and capital gains on the sale of assets are reduced to allow for the inflationary effect. Many allowances are adjusted annually to allow for inflation.

These rules vary widely betweeen countries. Some tax regimes are more sympathetic to inflationary effects than others.

Since the rules regarding tax deductions, tax exemptions and tax incentives vary widely between the tax regimes of different countries this allows an able tax officer to seek out those regimes that provide the highest allowances, the fastest write-offs and the highest incentives for transactions taking place within a multinational group of companies.

The rate of corporate tax in the foreign and the home country is an important factor in deciding between setting up a branch or a subsidiary company abroad.

If the rate of tax in the foreign country is lower than the rate in the home country then it may pay the parent company to set up a subsidiary abroad and advise the subsidiary to pay low dividends out of these foreign profits to the parent company and so retain cash within the Group. If the rate of corporate tax in the foreign country is higher than the home rate a branch may prove to be the better option since, although the foreign income tax on profits is likely to be the same, there is no additional high rate of withholding tax to pay on remittances.

If the new foreign operation is likely to run at a loss for several years then the parent company may decide to operate through a branch rather than a subsidiary. The branch will give the parent company immediate access to the foreign losses to reduce tax at home.

Subsidiaries but not branches can be charged for the cost of head office services.

There are so many variable factors influencing the branch versus subsidiary decision that a general rule cannot be formulated. For example, the carry forward of losses, if permitted, may bias the decision back towards a subsidiary even if early losses are anticipated on the foreign venture.

ORGANIZATIONAL DEVICES FOR REDUCING THE GLOBAL TAX BILL

Once a company, which is operating abroad, reaches a given size it may find that the complexity of its foreign operations allows it to re-organize its worldwide structure in such a way as to minimize its global tax bill.

Some organizational devices which have proved useful in reducing the global tax bill of MNCs are (a) the setting up of a holding company at home or abroad; (b) the setting up of a management and finance centre within the group; and (c) using the facilities offered by a tax haven.

Setting Up a Holding Company

Holding companies within a group of companies can be set up usually in a foreign country but possibly in the home country. The holding company may be able to better exploit potential benefits inherent in tax treaties.

Once the parent company of the group has set up several subsidiary companies abroad it may consider setting up a "holding" company. The main asset of a holding company is the shares it owns in other companies. The holding company may own shares in both the parent company and the subsidiaries or only in the subsidiaries. In the latter case the parent company holds the shares in the holding company.

Many variations can be played on the holding company theme. The holding company can be set up in the country of the parent or in a foreign country where one of the subsidiary companies is resident or in some third country that caters for holding companies.

The holding company may be set up in a tax haven, although this approach has its disadvantages. Within the EU the Netherlands is far and away the favourite country but Luxembourg and Austria provide helpful legislation. Outside the EU Switzerland is favoured and Bermuda. Much depends upon the terms of the tax treaties that have been signed between the country in which the parent resides and the foreign country in which the holding company resides.

Situations Where Holding Companies Are Not Tax Efficient Vehicles

Holding companies may not be tax efficient in all cases. For example, under some double tax agreements no domestic tax is charged on foreign dividends received from a subsidiary registered in the other country. Under a specific EU directive a subsidiary registered in the EU which pays dividends to a parent in another country of the EU will benefit from a zero withholding tax. A subsidiary, for the purposes of this directive, is defined as a company where 25% of the shares are owned by the recipient of the dividend.

If dividends are paid by a US company to a UK company that owns more than 10% of the stock of the US company the withholding tax is charged at a low 5% rate. The normal rate of withholding tax on dividends repatriated from the USA is 30%. In addition the UK company will receive a tax credit for corporate tax paid on the profits earned by the US company which may well eliminate all UK tax on these US profits. This is a very efficient tax arrangement and interposing a holding company between the USA and the UK companies could not hope to improve on this degree of tax efficiency. For example if the shares in the US subsidiary were held by a holding company in a tax haven the withholding tax would be charged at 30%!

Under such circumstances a holding company is of limited value in avoiding foreign or local tax.

What then are the advantages to be derived from setting up a holding company within a group for the purpose of tax planning?

The Advantages To Be Derived from a Holding Company

The advantages may have nothing to do with tax. The group may wish to consolidate its assets or income for financial reasons or it may wish to set up a head office in a stable political regime if the parent or subsidiaries reside in unstable regimes. Many South African companies followed this course in the run up to the April 1994 elections. But the usual reason for setting up a holding company within a group is to take full advantage of foreign tax credits, to reduce the rate of withholding tax or to defer tax payment on overseas income or the tax on profits from disposing of overseas assets.

Setting Up a "Stepping Stones" Company

If two countries, A and C, with high corporate tax rates, say at 30%, have failed to set up a tax treaty between themselves a significant reduction in global tax may be effected by setting up a holding company in a third country, B, which has tax treaties with both A and C. Such a company is often called a "stepping stones" company.

Dividends repatriated from A to B will be subject to a low withholding tax at, say, 5% as per the tax treaty between A and B. These dividends can now be repatriated from country B to country C at a withholding tax rate of, say, 5%. The 30% withholding tax has been reduced to less than 10%.

Another "stepping stones" company device is the "tax credit mixer company". By setting up a "stepping stones" holding company to mix dividends received from several different subsidiaries operating under different tax regimes a loss of tax credits can be avoided. The "mixed" dividend stream can now be repatriated as dividend to the parent from the holding company taking full advantage of the tax credits that might otherwise be lost to the parent.

In both of the above cases we are assuming that country B in which the "stepping stone" company resides does not impose significant income taxes on the holding company. If it does impose such taxes the advantages of the exercise may be negated. The tax regimes of the Netherlands and the Netherlands Antilles are particularly suited to this type of tax planning.

The tax authorities in high tax countries are very wary of multinationals who interpose holding companies between subsidiaries and parents and such arrangements are only permitted if they are seen to be "fair" and not simply tax-avoidance vehicles. If the holding company is a trading company or is providing other services to the group this helps to make the "fairness" case to the relevant tax authority.

Where Should a Holding Company Be Set Up?

The objective is to find a tax regime that reduces the total "throughput tax" of a Group to a minimum. We have already noted the favourable tax treatment accorded to withholding taxes between a subsidiary and a parent residing in different countries in the EU. A company residing in the EU would be wise to set up its holding company in the EU to avoid investigation of its tax affairs by the tax authority in the EU country where it resides.

The finance officer is seeking a tax regime that imposes no tax on foreign dividends received, exemption from withholding tax on dividends repatriated abroad and exemption from capital gains tax on the sale of assets, particularly shares. The second of these aims is the most difficult to achieve. Within the EU the Netherlands, Denmark and Portugal offer tax provisions that are useful to holding companies.

The Netherlands have negotiated a wide range of double tax treaties with other countries. Thus dividend income flowing into the Netherlands will be subject to low withholding taxes. Also it can be arranged that these dividends (and capital gains) are not taxed in the Netherlands (via the participation exemption scheme). The dividend income can now be repatriated abroad to the parent company at a low or zero withholding tax rate.

A parent or subsidiary resident in the Netherlands is able to pass dividends to a company in the Netherlands Antilles at a very low rate of "throughput" tax. Holding companies based in the Netherlands Antilles can repatriate funds at a zero withholding tax rate but this device is currently the subject of anti-tax-avoidance legislation in many countries.

Gibraltar, Malta, Cyprus, Hungary and Madeira also offer certain tax benefits to holding companies.

If the objective is simply to avoid local tax, rather than to minimize throughput tax, any tax haven will do. We discuss tax havens later in this chapter but Bermuda and the Bahamas offer excellent facilities for holding companies. These countries have not signed any tax treaties with other countries so dividends sent to them will be likely to have been subject to a high rate of withholding tax. Note that several holding companies resident in Bermuda are listed on the New York stock exchange.

The Highly Geared Holding Company

One well-known stratagem for reducing global tax is to substitute interest for dividends as the vehicle for transmitting value across an international frontier. This can be effected by creating a highly geared holding company.

Denmark and Luxembourg currently impose no withholding tax on interest repatriated abroad so if the Danish or Luxembourg holding company is highly geared this may suggest a solution to a high withholding tax problem. Although Luxembourg places limits on such an arrangement since only 50% of the interest repatriated abroad can be used to reduce the tax payable by a group.

We conclude that a holding company offers finance officers and tax planners a great deal of flexibility in reorganizing the company's tax affairs. It is at least theoretically possible that dividends paid out by a subsidiary company to a holding company situated in a third country with suitable tax treaties will not be taxed by the foreign tax regime and suffer a relatively low tax when repatriated to the parent.

Other Tax Advantages of Holding Companies

A holding company may allow the total profits of a group and the costs of a group, such as the cost of financing group loans, to be distributed between countries in a tax efficient way. Profits can be allocated to a low tax regime and costs to a high tax regime. The timing of the crediting of profits and the debiting of costs can also be shifted by using holding companies.

Insurance payments, patent and trade mark royalty receipts and franchise payments can be channelled through a holding company resident in a low tax regime to reduce the global tax due on these profits or payments.

A holding company also allows profits on the sale of shares in a subsidiary to take place in a preferred tax regime to minimize the global capital gains tax to be paid by the Group if the shares are sold. The rate of capital gains tax varies widely between tax regimes, in some tax regimes it is zero.

In summary, a holding company allows the finance officer a choice of tax regime within which to conduct a financial transaction, to mix tax credits and to provide a mechanism for shifting the timing of various financial transactions so as to minimize the global tax paid by the group.

Characteristics of Tax Regimes Suited to Setting Up a Holding Company

An ideal regime for setting up a holding company would offer the following facilities.

1. A wide range of tax treaties with important trading countries:
2. A low or zero rate of income tax on the foreign owned holding company.
3. A low or zero rate of withholding tax on dividends repatriated from the country.
4. A low or zero rate of capital gains tax.

A tax regime offering all of these facilities would be hard to find but there are a few that come close. Apart from the Netherlands the tax regimes in Luxembourg, Switzerland, Cyprus and Hungary offer useful facilities.[8]

Setting Up a Management and Finance Centre (MFC)

Once an international company becomes very large it may decide to centralize its international financing, international tax planning and international management service activities into one centre (see Exhibit 10.5). This centre may be located in a tax haven or in a country that provides special concessions to MFCs.[9]

Belgium provides special tax concessions to MFCs incorporated on its territory. For example income tax is calculated as a % of its costs and dividends, etc., which are repatriated abroad are exempt from any withholding tax. Interest received by an MFC in Belgium is deemed to have a withholding tax attached to it which can be charged against local tax.

Management and finance centres (MFCs) can be used to reduce global taxes and costs in a variety of ways. For example if the rate of tax on the income of the MFC is low the MFC can charge other subsidiaries in the group for management services rendered to them. These charges become the income of the MFC and this income is taxed at a low or zero rate in the tax haven but the charges are allowed against tax in the foreign country where the subsidiary resides. We assume that the corporate tax rate is higher in these countries. On the debit side MFCs are expensive to set up and maintain so only companies of a sufficient size can achieve a net financial benefit from setting up an MFC.

The types of operation that can be profitably channelled through an MFC are:

- The raising of finance for the group.
- Foreign exchange exposure management.
- Withholding tax management.
- Tax credit management.
- The provision of a re-invoicing vehicle.
- Financial and consultancy services.
- The residency of a holding company.
- The insurance needs of a group.
- Exchange control management.
- Certain shipping and transport facilities for a group.

Choosing the country in which to set up an MFC is a tricky problem. Even if the local corporate tax rate is low or zero this might be of little benefit if the MFC wishes to offset group costs against local profits. Tax authorities are suspicious of MFCs and so MFCs must be organized in such a way as to ameliorate these suspicions.[10]

Thus the MFC might be set up in the country of the parent company or in a foreign country in which the company runs a major operation. Both of these options will defuse the suspicions of the tax authorities that the MFC is no more than a tax-avoidance vehicle.

A further problem with MFCs concerns the impact of the MFC on the morale of the managers running the other foreign subsidiaries. If the MFC demands and obtains tight control over such things as the financing, exposure management, tax planning and even transfer pricing policy of the other companies in the group this degree of control can emasculate local management. This loss of sovereignty, in turn, can impact on the morale of the management in the subsidiary company. The quality of local management may suffer, it may become difficult to recruit and retain good managers in these subsidiaries.

Using the Facilities of a Tax Haven

Some countries, particularly some very small countries, have designed their legal, financial and tax regimes with the specific objective of encouraging multinational companies and rich individuals to set up subsidiary companies in their country. Countries that have followed this course of action have been given the name "tax havens".

The foreign entity that sets up a subsidiary or a holding company in a tax haven must usually pay an initial registration fee plus a fixed sum each year, say a few thousand US dollars, to the government of the tax haven for the privilege of operating a subsidiary company in that country.

Tax havens are of two types. The first and most common type impose no or very low taxes on resident companies. The second type charge conventional rates of tax but provide special tax concessions to certain companies. The Cayman Islands and the Bahamas are good examples of the first. The Netherlands and Ireland good examples of the second.

Tax havens may provide several useful facilities to a foreign company operating in the tax haven. First, the rates of tax imposed on income and capital gains are likely to be either low or zero. No withholding tax will be deducted from any dividends, interest, etc., repatriated abroad to a parent company.

The tax haven may allow a foreign controlled resident company to conceal much of the detail about the operating activities of the subsidiary in the tax haven. In some cases, such as Luxembourg, the degree of secrecy is so complete that it is not even possible to find out who owns the company! Some tax havens require no accounts to be published, require no audit of the accounts, apply no form of local tax whatsoever, not even VAT, to any of the transactions of the company and apply no exchange controls whatever on the movement of currency out of or into the country!

If a multinational company can find a way of channelling its profits or dividends tax free into a subsidiary or trust registered in a tax haven then various tax-saving stratagems become possible. For example, these untaxed funds can be used to buy assets, etc., for the group, these assets can than be leased back to other companies in the group and the profits from the leasing operation saved in the tax haven at a minimal tax charge.

The costs of running a subsidiary in a tax haven will normally be recovered by charging an annual fee to the various subsidiaries which it services. This fee will, hopefully, be allowed as a charge against the profits of the foreign subsidiaries operating in countries with a much higher tax rate than the tax haven.

Choosing a Tax Haven

All tax havens do not offer identical facilities. Some tax havens have been set up to satisfy the needs of a specific type of company or individual.

So far as the multinational company is concerned most of the following facilities will need to be available in a tax haven to make that tax haven viable:

- Political stability
- Low or zero rate taxes on profits, capital gains, etc.

- Low set up and annual running costs.
- No or very low withholding taxes on dividends, interest, etc., sent abroad.
- No exchange controls on capital movements.
- Suitable tax treaties *re* double taxation or no such treaties if that is what the MNC wishes.
- Tight legislation *re* secrecy and long-term guarantees *re* exemption from future legislation. But beware against . . .

  A tax information exchange agreement (TIEA). If such an agreement exists the tax haven has agreed to pass on information about individuals or companies registered in the tax haven to the tax authorities in certain major countries such as the USA "if asked" to do so.

- Good communication facilities.
- Good transportation facilities to and from the tax haven.
- Good banking facilities and connections to foreign banks.
- Good legal and accounting facilities for local advice on technical matters.

Much depends on what the MNC wishes to do in the tax haven. Access, etc., may not be important if the tax haven is no more than a convenient "intermediate" legal entity for channelling funds between subsidiaries.

Anti Tax-avoidance Legislation

As tax havens can reduce the tax collected by government tax authorities these same authorities pay a great deal of attention to the activities of subsidiary companies registered in tax havens. Much international tax legislation in recent years, particularly in the UK's 1994 Finance Act, has been targeted at preventing multinational companies from using tax havens to avoid tax.

In the case of profits channelled through a tax haven subsidiary some countries treat such profits as though the tax haven subsidiary does not exist. Profits are taxed in the country of the parent as if they had been sent directly to the parent. Profits retained by a subsidiary company resident in a tax haven may be taxed as if they had actually been remitted directly to the home country.

The war against tax avoidance devices has been fought so intensely by the tax authorities in recent years that most of the traditional devices have been closed down and the emphasis has shifted to derivative based schemes such as those outlined in Exhibit 10.6.

In the UK if a foreign subsidiary, controlled by persons resident in the UK, is deemed to be a controlled foreign company (CFC) then special tax rules apply. If the rate of tax applied to the CFC by the foreign tax regime is low or zero then the UK tax authorities can impose tax on the profits of the CFC as if it were a resident UK company. A low rate of foreign corporate tax is deemed to be a rate below 75% of the current UK corporate tax rate.

If the UK parent company instructs its foreign subsidiary to follow certain procedures it may be able to avoid the CFC legislation. For example, if the subsidiary operates as a normal trading company in the foreign country or if it distributes at least half of its profits to the UK it may avoid the legislation. Subsidiary companies set up in certain foreign countries are specifically excluded from the CFC regulations.

Exhibit 10.5   Perkin-Elmer Centralizes its Treasury Management

Perkin-Elmer is a US Corporation manufacturing monitoring instruments that are used in many industries. P-E had a turnover of over a billion US$ in 1994. Two-thirds of turnover and a higher fraction of profits are made outside the USA. The company runs 30 subsidiary companies worldwide.

In 1992 P-E decided to restructure its international treasury management operations. Initially each subsidiary operated autonomously, each subsidiary ran its own financing, cash management and foreign exchange.

In 1992 P-E decided to centralize its FX operations to "neutralize the impact of FX on the company". The stages in this operation were as follows:

1. A "netting centre" was set up in London, UK. Inter-company debts were netted once a month.
2. A captive finance house was set up in Dublin, Ireland. Dublin was chosen because "you have to look at where you get the best tax benefits". The FMC in Dublin provides a vehicle to manage cash and debt for European operations.
3. The FMC set up a centralized billing system so that each subsidiary is billed in its own currency so that local FX exposure is eliminated. The FX exposure is shifted from the subsidiary to the billing centre where it is managed centrally. This arrangement allows P-E to "offset exposures internally and reduce the total number of currency transactions".
4. The hedging instruments used are forwards of one-year or shorter duration and options. The company would like to hedge anticipated transactions but the SEC and the FASB disapprove of this practice.
5. By 1994 the company had paid off its long-term debt and only held short-term floating rate debt. However, in 1994 it was considering locking into longer-term Japanese debt since interest rates are low in Japan and corporate taxes high. The idea is to swap out of short-term US$ debt into long-term fixed interest yen debt. The FX risk on such debt would be formidable except for the fact that P-E had merged with Applied Biosystems and A-B have a sizeable manufacturing capacity in Japan which generates yen receivables.

Source: Lawrence Quinn, Perkin-Elmer centralizes as it grows. *Corporate Finance*, May 1994.

Appendix 10.1 provides information about the facilities provided, the needs catered for and the benefits arising in three tax havens that are used by multinational companies. Some other popular tax reduction schemes are set out in Exhibit 10.6.

TAX ARBITRAGE

A raft of tax planning devices have been designed by tax consultants to use the varying treatment of tax allowances and rates in various tax regimes to reduce the global tax bill of the multinational company via "tax arbitrage". Some vehicles for implementing tax arbitrage are outlined in Exhibit 10.6.

Exhibit 10.5 describes how one large multinational, Perkin-Elmer, restructured its international treasury operations in 1992 to, among other things, reduce its overall tax bill.

A CASE STUDY IN INTERNATIONAL TAX PLANNING

A UK company called the Madrax corporation manufacture and sell specialized machine parts for heavy industrial vehicles. The first contact the company had with international trading occurred when it began to export its products to Germany and

Exhibit 10.6 Some Tax Planning Devices

The tax regimes of the various countries of the world differ from one another. This allows a tax planner to reduce the global tax of an international company by redistributing income and costs in such a way as to take advantage of the tax concessions and allowances offered by each country. This process is often called "tax arbitrage". Some examples of tax arbitrage are illustrated below.

Leasing

If a company cannot absorb all available tax deductions in a given year it can allow a profit-rich company to buy the equipment and lease it from that company. The profit-rich company is usually an international bank. The bank can absorb the high initial tax allowances on the equipment and reduce the leasing cost to return some of this benefit to the less profitable company.

The French have a law of "credit bail" whereby the lessor of equipment has legal ownership of the item leased during the lease. In the UK the legal ownership rests with the lessee. Thus if a French company leases equipment to an English company both companies can claim capital depreciation allowances on the equipment to reduce their tax bills.

Converting equity to Debt

The interest on debt is allowable against tax but high gearing can put up the cost of funding a company. Thus a financial instrument that can be treated as both debt and equity at the same time is tax efficient.

Convertible preference shares can be issued by a subsidiary resident in, say, the Cayman Islands. The subsidiary now lends the proceeds of this issue to its parent company resident in a high tax regime in the form of an inter-company loan. The interest costs of the loan can now be charged against tax by the parent company while the preference shares are treated as equity in the consolidated accounts of the group. Companies such as Tarmac and British Airways have used variants of this theme in the past.

Asymmetrical tax systems: "double-dip devices"

Where the tax systems of two countries are not identical opportunities arise for tax arbitrage. For example, a German company can make a loan to a subsidiary in Portugal. The Portuguese subsidiary pays interest on this loan to the German company. The German company qualifies for a tax credit against its tax bill on this interest received from Portugal. However Portugal does not impose a withholding tax on interest paid to Germany. Thus the German parent has gained a fictional tax credit!

The same type of scheme can be applied between an Italian parent and a Dutch subsidiary or a Dutch parent with a French subsidiary.

Stepping stone companies

A group can insert a stepping stone company between a foreign subsidiary and the parent company. This structure can provide a whole host of tax advantages.

For example, an Australian company owns all the shares in an Italian company. The Australian company sets up a stepping stone "exempt" company in Jersey. The Australian company borrows A\$50 million at 12% pa in Australia and invests this in the company in Jersey. The Jersey company lends this amount on to the Italian subsidiary at 17% pa. The interest charge at 17% pa can now be charged against the profits of the Italian company reducing its tax bill. The Jersey company passes the interest payments back to the Australian parent as dividend payments with no withholding tax deducted. The Australian company can charge the 10% interest charge against its Australian tax bill. If the Italian company had simply paid dividends to its Australian parent the Group would have had to pay the withholding tax at 15% as per the current Italy/Australia double tax agreement.

Using derivatives in tax planning schemes

The attack on conventional tax planning devices has persuaded tax advisers to seek out new pastures. Most of the new tax planning devices are based on derivatives.

Option matching

A British company buys an interest rate option for £10 million. This is allowable against the UK company's tax bill. An offshore subsidiary of the parent company in the Cayman Islands sells an identical option for £10 million. The net exposure of the Group is zero. The Cayman Island option is a "contingent premium" option. No premium is payable unless the option is exercised. Neither option is exercised so no premium is paid by the Cayman Islands company but the UK parent has created a synthetic tax credit worth £10 million.

International tax is a constant battle between the tax authorities and the tax advisers. The above exhibit describes some tax planning devices used in the past but many of these devices have already been outlawed by the UK and US tax authorities. However, the ingenuity of the tax experts is endless, new structural devices for reducing tax will be forthcoming.

Sweden. The only tax problem the company encountered at this stage of its development was in ensuring that any gains or losses resulting from exposure to foreign currency fluctuations were taxed as ordinary business profits and losses on the foreign transactions.

A few years later the company began to export to the USA and Canada. Madrax decided that it would be wise to set up a manufacturing unit in the USA. As this unit would be unlikely to make substantial profits for some years to come it was decided to set up a branch of the company in Detroit. The expected early losses on the venture could be almost immediately offset against company profits in the UK.

A few years later the US branch began to make a substantial profit so Madrax converted the branch into a full-blown subsidiary company. The Detroit subsidiary was taxed as a US company but the double tax treaty between the USA and the UK ensured that the withholding taxes at 5% on dividends repatriated to the UK parent would receive a tax credit which could be offset against the UK tax charged on the parent company.

The following year Madrax decided to set up a manufacturing subsidiary company in the Far East. After a long search process which involved re-location consultants, the Board of Madrax decided on Australia. The company entered into tough negotiations with the Australian Development Corporation and acquired substantial capital grants and tax concessions by setting the subsidiary up in a designated "Development Area" in Australia. The company also set up a sales subsidiary in Singapore to service its products in the growing South East Asian market. Double tax agreements with both countries ensured that tax credits were available in the UK to set against the foreign income and withholding taxes on dividends repatriated by the subsidiaries to the UK parent.

Later still further sales subsidiaries are set up in Brazil and South Africa. Both countries have negotiated double tax agreements with the UK.

At this point the company decided to set up a holding company to hold the shares of the various subsidiary companies in the Group. It was originally intended to set this company up in Switzerland but the UK tax authorities warned that this arrangement might affect the tax credits allowed against UK company taxes via the various double tax treaties in force. It was decided to set up the holding company in the Netherlands with a branch in Switzerland.

Madrax now considers itself to be a fully developed multinational company owing specific allegiance to no particular country. The Board of Madrax are not happy about the aforementioned interference by the UK tax authorities in the desired world wide organizational structure of Madrax, the board therefore decides to set up a Management and Finance subsidiary in Belgium to give the company more freedom in organizing its international affairs.

Belgium provides generous tax allowances to multinational groups setting up their management and finance centres in the country. For example, tax is based on a percentage of the administration costs and there are no withholding taxes charged on dividends, interest payments or royalties.

The treasury function, international tax, internal audit and public relations are switched into this subsidiary.

A working party is set up to consider the cost and other implications of shifting the residency of the Madrax parent company from the UK to another country within the

EU, possibly to the Netherlands. The tax implications of such a move are subjected to particular scrutiny and international tax experts are consulted. The working party is also asked to study the implications of the conclusions of the Ruding committee report re the possible creation of a unified EU corporate tax system out of the present highly fragmented system.

The international treasury department of Madrax now believes that it has put everything in place to be able to minimize its global tax bill in the future.

FINDING OUT ABOUT FOREIGN TAX

We noted earlier in this chapter that a major difficulty encountered by international tax planners is how to keep up to date with the myriad of tax systems that operate throughout the world and how to monitor the regular changes in these systems.

Many international companies subcontract the job of tax planning by buying in the services of international tax experts, such as J.F. Chown & Company, to handle their global tax affairs. The accounting firms of Ernst and Young, Price Waterhouse and Coopers and Lybrand, who all have international tax divisions, publish annual booklets setting out the basic facts about the various tax systems of the world.

An alternative policy is to buy in the services of a local accounting firm in each country where a subsidiary resides to handle the local tax problems of that subsidiary. The inter-company tax problems being handled in-house or via an outside expert.

M. Ray Saunders (see readings) publishes a regular update describing ten of the major tax systems of the world. The book also provides useful advice on minimizing the global tax burden of companies with extensive activities abroad.

Tolley's publish an annual guide to the international taxation of both companies and individuals. Giovannini (1993) provides a useful set of essays on various aspects of international tax. CCH publications also publish a regular and well-indexed update on international tax.

With regard to tax havens Diamond and Diamond (annual update) provide a most extensive guide to the tax havens of the world. This multi-volume publication covers most of the things a tax officer needs to know about each individual tax haven covered. Grundy (1994) provides a useful summary of the facilities provided by tax havens and the uses of tax havens but in rather less detail than Diamond.

The annual changes that take place within the major tax systems of the world are covered in an annual publication of the International Bureaux of Fiscal Documentation. This publication (IBFD (1994)) covers both corporate tax and personal tax.

Several journals such as *Tax Planning International Review* and *Journal of Strategy in International Tax* provide useful discussions on important changes in international tax.

It is often more important to anticipate tax changes before they are implemented rather than immediately after they are enacted. Some international tax firms provide such a service to clients. The organizations monitoring country and political risk, which are listed in the Appendix to Chapter 6, also provide this kind of information on a regular basis.

Several data bases stored on computers and accessed via modems hold valuable information on international tax. Two of these are called LEXIS, a legal data base, and NEXIS a business information data base. HYPERTAX is a tax law database stored on a CD-ROM and regularly updated. Several thousand data bases can now be accessed by computer terminal but, in the author's experience, finding out what exactly is stored in each data base and how to access it is exceedingly difficult even with the use of NETSCAPE, MOSAIC and the other search tools currently available. Several international accounting firms have designed data bases on tax which can be accessed by their own staff from any location in the world.

WHAT HAVE WE LEARNED IN THIS CHAPTER?

1. Every company trading internationally will attempt to minimize its global tax bill as long as this objective does not conflict with other more important business objectives.

2. Companies with branches and subsidiaries based in foreign countries pay tax on the profits earned in the foreign country to the foreign government. In addition subsidiaries will normally pay a withholding tax on any dividends, etc., repatriated to the home country.

3. International tax planning is not difficult in any fundamental sense since the prime objectives of reducing the global tax bill are easy to understand. The problems arise from the difficulty inherent in retrieving the relevant tax information and in selecting an optimal permutation from among the many tax saving devices available. There are a myriad of tax rules applied within any single tax system and every country in the world runs a different tax system. Attempts are being made by the EU, the OECD and the WTO and other international organizations to standardize company tax rates and rules but the world is still a very long way from achieving a standardized corporate tax system.

4. Tax systems differ with respect to tax rates, tax allowances and tax rules. These differences allow the officer responsible for minimizing the company's global tax bill to shift revenues and costs around the globe to minimize the global tax burden of the company. This process is called "tax arbitrage".

5. International tax planning consists of four basic activities. First, find the most suitable organizational structure to minimize tax, second choose from among the many tax planning devices available those best suited to the needs of the company, third, work out the most tax efficient way of distributing income and costs within the organization and fourth, work out how to channel the profits of foreign subsidiaries back to the parent company so as to minimize the "throughput" tax.

6. Global tax planning will often entail tough bargaining between a finance officer and the tax authority of a foreign government. There is a direct conflict between the desire of foreign governments to maximize their tax revenues while at the same time maximizing foreign investment in their country. These conflicting objectives give the finance officer of an MNC an opportunity to display her negotiating skills.

7. International tax can take many forms. For example, royalties paid to governments based on mineral extraction may be considered to be a form of international tax. The major forms of international tax imposed on MNCs are income tax on profits earned in the foreign country, withholding tax on dividends, interest, etc., repatriated

to the home country, taxes imposed on "translation" profits resulting from changes in exchange rates and taxes on profits arising out of capital transactions.

8. The double charging of tax on the same profit stream by two tax regimes can normally be avoided by using the provisions of a double tax treaty agreed between the two countries involved. Tax credits on foreign taxes are made available to MNCs to offset home taxes. Various tax concessions such as "carry-forwards" and "carry-backs" of losses are made available to MNCs to shift losses around in time to offset the tax charged on current profits.

9. Dividends repatriated from a foreign subsidiary to a parent company will almost certainly be subject to a "withholding tax" in the foreign country. However, as noted in the previous paragraph this tax can often be offset against some form of tax credit.

10. The tax treatment of translation gains and losses varies a great deal between the tax regimes of the world. Under most tax regimes translation gains and losses are ignored unless converted into cash.

11. Special tax rules may be applied by a home government to capital gains and losses which arise in a foreign country.

12. If a trading or manufacturing entity is to be set up abroad the form of this entity will be influenced by tax considerations. Expected early losses on the venture may favour setting up a branch network abroad rather than a subsidiary, but a foreign subsidiary provides more opportunity for tax reduction in the long run.

13. Several organizational devices provide opportunities for reducing the global tax burden of a multinational company. Devices such as a holding company, a management and finance subsidiary or the facilities provided by a tax haven.

14. The tax authorities in all of the countries of the world know that tax planning devices can be used to reduce company tax and so tough anti tax-avoidance legislation has been passed by most governments in recent years to reduce the scope for MNCs to avoid tax by switching profits around the globe via these structures.

15. A game is constantly being played between the tax authorities and the tax experts. The prize is the share-out of the profits made by the multinational companies. Debt based tax planning devices are falling out of favour to be replaced by derivative based products.

16. An extensive literature now exists on international tax but most of it is descriptive rather than analytical. If, in the future, international tax legislation is stored and "efficiently indexed" within an electronic data base the cost and speed of access to relevant information on the various tax systems of the world could be much reduced.

NOTES

1. Hughes and Payne (1994) provide a short analytical introduction to the subject. Ogley (1993) discusses the problem in more depth. Saunders (see suggested readings) is also a partial exception to this rule since he provides a discussion of alternative tax strategies. Several collections of essays such as Tolley's annual book on international tax are available but they lack a proper analytical structure. Tomsett (1989) provides an analytical approach.
2. However, some States in the USA have introduced unitary tax systems.
3. Tax Act, 1988, section 797.
4. *George Wimpey* v *Rolfe* (1989) STC 609.
5. *International Tax*, Ernst and Young, 1994.

6. There are exceptions to every rule in international tax. For example, Papua New Guinea in 1993 charged a corporate tax rate of 25% and a branch tax rate of 40%.
7. The USA has introduced a branch profits tax to eliminate this benefit using a "deemed" dividend. Thus, branches may be worse off than subsidiaries if they make a loss or need capital.
8. Unfortunately (1) is incompatible with (2), (3) and (4).
9. Many tax havens are not suited to setting up a management and finance centre because they have not signed double tax treaties with many, or even any, of the larger countries of the world. These larger countries are suspicious of the intentions of tax havens. Many tax havens are deemed by foreign tax authorities to be no more than vehicles for tax avoidance.
10. To assuage suspicion the MFC can provide full consulting services on an "arm's length" fee basis to the subsidiaries in the group, provide similar services to other companies outside the Group or simply not to be set up in a tax haven!

FURTHER READING

CCH International (updated regularly) *International Tax Planning Manual.* Horwath International.
  A detailed and well-indexed manual on international tax planning for companies that trade internationally. Easy to use unlike some other competitive manuals.
Diamond, W. H. and D. B. (Updated regularly) *Tax Havens of the World.* Matthew Bender.
  An exceptionally detailed review of current developments in all of the best-known tax havens of the world. Details are provided on the legal code, the tax regulations, secrecy laws, communications, local infrastructure and living conditions.
Dolan, D. K. (1990) Intercompany transfer pricing for the layman. *Tax Notes,* October 8, 211–28.
Ernst and Young (annual) *World-wide Corporate Tax Guide and Directory.* E & Y.
  A useful listing of the main corporate tax rates and concessions in most of the countries of the world. An annual update is provided. Useful information is provided on the exchange controls applied in each country, if such controls exist.
Grundy, M. (1994 or latest) *Grundy's Tax Havens.* Sweet and Maxwell.
  A resumé of the key facts about many of the tax havens in the world plus information on the advantageous tax benefits offered by each country. Much shorter but also much cheaper than the Diamond's compendious book on the same subject.
Hemelt, J. and Spencer, C. (1990) United States: tax effective management of foreign exchange risks. *European Taxation,* vol. 30, no. 3, 67–71.
Hughes, T. and Payne, D. (1994) *International Tax Planning for UK Companies. Tax Digest No. 129,* 43 pp.
  A brief but cogent discussion of the problems of planning and minimizing global company tax. A useful book for beginners to get a complete picture of the problems faced by UK tax officers when planning international tax.
Hypertax. HMSO Electronic Publishing.
  This is a data base stored on a CD-ROM. Hypertax is a UK tax law database but it contains some information that is relevant to an international tax planner. A companion volume targeted at international tax would be useful.
International Bureaux of Fiscal Documentation (1994) *Worldwide Survey of Trends and Developments in Taxation.* Published annually by IBFC.
  This booklet summarizes all of the major changes in taxation, corporate and personal, in the major countries of the world over the previous year. A commentary and discussion of the changes and the reasons for the changes is also provided.
Ogley, A. (1993) *The Principles of International Tax.* Interfisc Publishing.
  A masterly summary of the current state of play in the international tax arena. Written with commendable concision and clarity.
Saunders, M. Ray (annual) *International Tax Systems and Planning Techniques.* Longman.
  A detailed country by country analysis of current tax legislation in 10 major countries of the world. The book also provides a list of the tax concessions provided by certain countries, like Ireland, plus a list of countries set up as tax havens and how these tax havens can be used to minimize tax internationally. This book does not simply list the facts but provides a tutorial on how to set up tax minimizing techniques internationally. A case study is provided explaining how a small company can expand into a major multinational company and the various tax planning techniques that can be developed along the way.

Shapiro, A. (1984) The impact of taxation on the currency of denomination decision for long term borrowing and lending. *Journal of International Business Studies*, Spring/Summer, 15–25.

Sherman, H. A. (1987) Managing taxes in the multi-national corporation. *The Tax Executive*, Winter, 171–81.

Tolley, *International Tax Planning*.
   A set of articles on various aspects of tax planning. Volume 1 of the series is concerned with planning company tax internationally.

Tomsett, E. (1989) Tax planning for multinational companies. Woodhead Faulkner.
   An admirable introduction to the principles and techniques of international tax planning for MNC's. Commendably practical in its approach.

Specialized tax journals

Tax Planning International Review

Journal of Strategy in International Tax.

The Tax Journal, *The Tax Executive* and *European Taxation* offer many articles on international tax.

TUTORIAL QUESTIONS

1. What are the two forms of direct tax that are usually imposed by a foreign tax authority on a subsidiary company operating in the foreign country?

2. If the profits of a foreign subsidiary are taxed in the foreign country what prevents these same profits from being taxed as profits of the parent company in the home country when the world-wide accounts are consolidated into the home country currency?

3. What is meant by the term "tax arbitrage"? Give an example illustrating how tax arbitrage can reduce the global tax bill of a company.

4. Suggest four factors that could be negotiated between an MNC and the tax authority in a country where the MNC is considering an investment.

5. How can transfer pricing be used to reduce a multinational company's tax bill? What rules do the US tax authorities impose on transfer pricing within a multinational group of companies?

6. How do double taxation agreements work? Suppose the corporate tax rate in country A is 40% and in country B it is 20%. Country A imposes a 25% withholding tax on dividends expatriated by foreign subsidiaries, country B imposes no withholding tax. If an MNC whose parent is resident in country H owns one subsidiary in country A and another subsidiary in country B what tax would the tax authorities in country A impose on the A subsidiary? What advice would you give to the parent company in country H *re* their global tax position in this situation?

7. In the context of international taxation what is a "carry-back" and a "carry-forward"? How can such tax concessions be treated as an asset in a take-over bid situation?

8. What is a "withholding" tax and how does it operate? What is the difference between a "withholding" tax and "advanced corporation tax"?

9. A parent company resident in the UK controls three wholly owned subsidiary companies in Canada, Spain and South Africa. Is the UK parent company assessed for tax in the UK on (a) only the profits made in the UK; (b) the UK profits plus dividends sent from the subsidiary companies to the UK; or (c) the worldwide profits of the company from whatever source?

10. The translation gains or losses incurred by a parent company when translating assets and liabilities denominated in a foreign currency into the home currency are treated differently by different tax regimes. Suggest three approaches used by the tax authorities for taxing (or not taxing) such profits or allowing the losses.

11. Why is it that the tax treatment of derivatives, like currency options, sometimes makes it difficult to calculate the precise amount of the hedge needed to cover a potential foreign exchange profit or loss?

12. "Sensitivity analysis can be used in tax planning". Describe the technique called "sensitivity

analysis". How can this technique be used by a tax officer in an MNC to optimize her global tax plan?

13. A company can sell its goods abroad through several different types of entities. What are the criteria that decide whether or not income tax will have to be paid on profits earned in the foreign country?

14. What tax advantages might a foreign branch enjoy over a foreign subsidiary?

15. Suggest three organizational devices that can be used to reduce the global tax bill of a multinational company.

16. How can a holding company assist with optimizing international tax planning?

17. A parent company with subsidiaries in five foreign countries decides to set up a Management and Finance Centre to control certain aspects of a group's activities. What activities can an MNC channel through an MFC that will bring tax benefits to the MNC? How can an MFC be set up so as not to excite the suspicions of the local tax authorities?

18. Explain in detail how a tax haven can be of use to a tax planner in a multinational company if (a) goods are invoiced through the tax haven; and (b) all insurance in a group is insured via a captive insurance company sited in a tax haven.

19. A tax haven needs to provide what key facilities to off-shore companies to persuade these companies to set up subsidiaries in the tax haven?

20. How does the CFC legislation currently operating in the UK affect the taxation of profits earned by the foreign subsidiary companies of UK multinationals? How can an MNC avoid the CFC legislation being applied to one of its subsidiaries?

EXERCISE: AUCKLAND ENGINEERING

Auckland Engineering (UK), the subsidiary of a New Zealand company Auckland Engineering, has built up a large debt of £50 million denominated in £ sterling. A current gearing ratio of 70%. The debt is due to be repaid over a ten-year period. The interest charged is floating at 3% above LIBOR. Auckland Engineering (NZ) would like to eliminate the foreign exchange risk attached to this debt since the treasurer believes that the pound sterling is likely to rise in the future against the New Zealand dollar and AE (UK) output is mainly sold to countries with weak currencies relative to the UK pound sterling.

Five methods of eliminating the FX risk on the debt have been suggested:

1. Repay the debt early. This strategy is allowed by the debt agreement. This course would, however, entail providing additional capital for the UK subsidiary.

2. The debt could be swapped into some other currency but NZ$ swaps are not available.

3. A one year rolling forward contract can be set up to cover FX risk for one year ahead at any point in time.

4. UK government stock could be purchased with the same value and maturity as the debt.

5. Auckland could try to convert the debt into ordinary shares in AE (UK) or the parent company.

Required: Study these options. Which of these options would most effectively eliminate the FX risk on the debt of the UK subsidiary? Which would be the cheapest and which the most expensive options?

What additional information would you need to know about the corporate tax rules in the UK and New Zealand before you can answer this question? What do think would be the tax implications of each of these options? What additional tax might have to be paid or what additional charges might be allowed against the Group's global tax bill? Can you suggest an alternative strategy for eliminating the FX risk that might also provide superior tax benefits?

INTERNATIONAL TAX CASE STUDY: PUREFON PLC

Purefon PLC is a British company quoted on the London Stock Exchange. The company designs and manufactures water purifying equipment. Although the equipment is assembled from a set of basic parts manufactured by Purefon in Bradford, West Yorkshire, each installation requires to be independently designed to meet the local needs.

In 1990 the company was exporting 10% of its production to the Far East and South America. In that year the company decided that it would make sense to set up two foreign Agencies in Singapore and Buenos Aires, Argentina. This will allow the company to store parts in these two foreign locations which will, in turn, allow the company to answer queries and satisfy orders coming from these parts of the world more quickly. Sales can still only be contracted from the UK.

In 1992 the demand for the products of Purefon in South America has risen to such an extent that the company can no longer handle the work through an agency. The company opens a warehouse in the industrial sector of Buenos Aires and within months the tax authorities in Buenos Aires are writing to the local manager claiming that Purefon has set up a "taxable presence" in Argentina and the local warehouse is presumably a branch of Purefon (UK). The sales in South America are hardly sufficient to carry the full costs of a branch, however, the South East Asian business is very profitable.

The tax authorities in both Argentina and Singapore are now adamant that Purefon has established a "taxable presence" in those countries. Thus Purefon decides to set up a sales branch in Buenos Aires and a manufacturing subsidiary in Singapore. Purefon claim exemption for five years from Singapore corporate tax on the basis that this new company is a "pioneer industry". This claim is disallowed so Purefon claim exemption from half their exports under the "ware-housing and services" tax incentives scheme. This is allowed.

The branch in Buenos Aires only sells to Argentinian companies; other South American sales are still handled from the UK. In 1994 the Argentinian branch expands its activities and begins to make substantial profits. Purefon therefore decides to convert the branch into a subsidiary company handling all trade with South America.

Double tax treaties have been signed between the UK and Argentina and Singapore.

Purefon now sets up a third subsidiary company in Istanbul, Turkey to service its growing trade in the Middle East. This company will assemble parts shipped from the UK. The company is funded by 60% equity and 40% from a loan from Purefon (UK).

Purefon now decides to set up a holding company in the Netherlands. This holding company will own all the shares in the three subsidiaries. Purefon Holdings (Netherlands) is, in its turn owned by Purefon UK. Dividends from all the three subsidiaries are sent to the Netherlands company who, in turn, pay a single annual dividend to the UK parent company. A substantial part of the management services of the Purefon group are provided by the holding company who charge a management fee to each subsidiary for these services.

In 1996 Purefon decides to set up a Finance subsidiary in the Netherlands Antilles. Parts sent to the various subsidiaries are invoiced through this Purefon (Antilles) subsidiary and dividends are channelled from Purefon (Antilles) to the holding company in the Netherlands.

The financing of the group is re-arranged through the Netherlands Antilles finance subsidiary although funds borrowed in "hard" currencies are still borrowed by Purefon (UK). In time Purefon (Antilles) builds up surplus funds and uses those funds to buy assets that it leases to other companies in the group.

A further subsidiary Purefon (Patents Netherlands) is set up in Holland to hold the patent rights of the group. The Purefon group are considering licensing some of their water purification techniques to other companies worldwide.

Purefon (UK) begins to have arguments about tax avoidance with the UK tax authorities. The UK tax authorities threaten to treat certain interest payments within the Group as ordinary dividend payments. Because of these arguments with the tax authorities the Board of Purefon (UK) consider moving their UK operations to some other country such as the Netherlands.

Answer the Following Questions With Regard to the International Tax Position of Purefon

1. Is it likely that Purefon PLC will be taxed in Singapore and Argentina when it sets up an Agency in these countries? What factors will decide this issue?
2. How will the foreign tax authority decide whether or not Purefon has a "taxable presence" in Argentina or Singapore?
3. How much tax is likely to be levied by the foreign tax authority on the income derived by Purefon from using the warehouse for storage of imported parts and promotional activities?
4. How will the agency and the service warehouse handle indirect taxes, for example value added tax on goods bought?
5. Now that Purefon is considered to have a taxable presence in Argentina and Singapore why did Purefon decide to set up a branch in Argentina but a subsidiary in Singapore?
6. Why might all South American sales not be handled by the branch in Argentina?
7. Purefon try to gain two special tax benefits from the Singaporean authorities. Suggest three other types of tax benefits that some countries provide to try to induce foreign companies to their shores.
8. Why does Purefon convert the branch in Argentina into a subsidiary once the branch becomes profitable?
9. What tax advantages might accrue to Purefon (UK) by setting up a holding company in the Netherlands? Why the Netherlands?
10. Why are most of the management services provided to the subsidiaries provided from the Holding Company rather than from the parent company?
11. What tax advantages might the Purefon Group hope to gain by setting up a Finance subsidiary in the Netherlands Antilles?
12. Purefon (Antilles) controls the financing of the group but loans in "hard" currencies are still borrowed by the parent company in the UK. Why does the Group follow this procedure?
13. Why does Purefon (Antilles) use its surplus funds to buy assets that it leases to other companies in the group? What tax advantages can accrue from such a procedure?
14. What tax advantages might accrue to the Purefon Group if funds are raised by Purefon (Antilles) and then loaned on to other subsidiaries in the Group? What are the problems inherent in such a policy?
15. Why should the Purefon Group place all their patent rights within a separate subsidiary company registered in the Netherlands? What tax advantages might accrue to the Group from this move?
16. What "anti-avoidance" tax legislation might the Purefon Group have breached with the above arrangements that have caused the UK tax authorities to question these arrangements?
17. Why is the parent company in the UK considering moving its whole operation to another country? Why might the tax consequences of such a move prove to be very expensive for the group?

APPENDIX 10.1: TAX HAVENS

The Cayman Islands

Background

The Cayman Islands consist of three small islands lying in the Caribbean Sea between Jamaica and Cuba. The capital is called Georgetown. The Cayman Islands are a British colony. The legal system in force is based on the UK legal system. The currency, the Cayman dollar, is tied in value to the US$. The language in popular use is English.

The islands are relatively rich and so the political risk attached to the islands is low. The level of unemployment is negligible.

The Cayman Islands are currently the second largest of the world's Offshore financial centres. Some 600 banks have set up in the islands of whom around 90 have fully staffed offices and advice centres. Deposits amounted to around US$500 billion dollars in 1993.

The regulatory apparatus is exemplary, a model for other financial centres. Company law is based on the 1948 UK companies act.

A wide range of high quality if expensive professional advice is available to companies and individuals in the Cayman Islands.

Tax

There are no taxes imposed on income or capital gains or on dividends repatriated or received in the islands. The Cayman Islands has concluded no tax treaties with other countries. A guarantee can be obtained from the relevant government authority that exempts what is defined as an "exempt" company from any future taxes for 30 years from the date of registration.

Exchange Controls

The monetary authority in the Cayman Islands imposes no exchange controls whatsoever on the movement of cash into or out of the islands.

Setting Up a Company in the Cayman Islands

For a small fee a foreign company can set up a subsidiary company in the islands that is defined as being either "resident", "non-resident" or "exempt". Most foreign companies (95%) opt for the "exempt" category. The registration fees are low, ranging from US$1000 to US$3000 for incorporation plus an annual fee of US$700 to US$1700.

An "exempt" company is not permitted to conduct business within the Cayman Islands but can conduct any business it wishes relative to its foreign operations including negotiating contracts and opening bank accounts.

An "exempt" company need not file annual returns, be audited, keep a register of members or hold annual general meetings. An exempt company can be re-domiciled into or out of the Cayman Islands to any other country, such as the Isle of Man, offering a similar facility.

Shares can be issued in the form of bearer shares or no-par-value shares if the company wishes.

Banks and insurance companies pay a licence fee ranging from US$6000 to around US$50 000 depending on the size of the company.

Specialisms

The Cayman Islands specialize in offering facilities to international banks (600), trusts, captive insurance companies (400)[1] and management and finance subsidiaries of multinational companies. The Cayman Islands has been granted a "class one" category as a shipping registry by the government of the UK.

The Cayman Islands is as close as a country can get to being a perfect tax haven.[2]

Ireland: the IFSC Project

Background

The Irish government has set up the International Financial Services Centre (IFSC) on the North bank of the Liffey river in Dublin, the capital of Ireland. The Centre is designed to provide a financial link between the European Union and the rest of the world.

Ireland is an enthusiastic member of the European Union and so goes out of its way to provide foreign companies with easy access to this huge financial market.

Political risk on economic matters in Ireland is low and excellent professional services are on tap. The Centre itself will provide advice to enquirers on matters such as captive insurance, asset financing, investment management, corporate finance and re-insurance.

Dublin provides easy access to the major financial centres of Europe. London can be accessed in a one hour flight from Dublin. Paris in two hours.

Tax

Income tax is limited to a 10% rate on profits earned on all non-Irish transactions plus a further allowance against trading income related to rents paid. The 10% rate has been accepted by the EU Commission up to the year 2005. Generous capital allowances are granted to IFSC companies plus cheap rents plus full remission from municipal taxes for 10 years. Generous income tax allowances are available to employees of the IFSC registered company.

Since IFSC companies are considered to be resident in Ireland they can benefit from the 25 tax treaties which Ireland has signed with foreign countries. This is an important concession.[3]

Companies that are controlled and managed abroad are allowed to set up a branch of the company rather than a subsidiary company in the IFSC. Profits from such a branch are also taxed at the low 10% rate but branches cannot benefit from utilizing the aforesaid tax treaties.

No withholding taxes are imposed on dividends or interest repatriated abroad from companies registered in the IFSC. IFSC companies are also exempt from paying value added tax.

Setting Up a Company in the IFSC

Foreign companies working in the financial services sector in their own country are actively encouraged to set up subsidiaries in the IFSC. Companies which are managed and controlled within the IFSC are treated as being resident in Ireland. IFSC companies can then benefit from the aforementioned low concessionary tax rate at 10% on corporate profits earned in currencies other than the punt (until the year 2005).

In order to obtain an operating certificate to set up a company in the IFSC the company must be involved with one or other of the following financial activities:

- Banking and foreign exchange business
- money management
- factoring

- dealing in derivatives
- share and bond dealing
- insurance
- franchising
- accounting and legal work
- storing or processing or selling financial information
- developing and selling financial software

Every application for a certificate to set up a subsidiary or branch in the IFSC is vetted by the Irish Development Agency. The Agency requires the following information from an applicant:

- The recent accounts and history of the company.
- An analysis of the accounts, finances and budgets for three years ahead.
- Details of the goods or services to be produced.
- Details as to how the goods are to be marketed.
- Accommodation and equipment required in the Centre.
- Management structures and evidence of competence.
- A note as to how the new company will help the Irish economy.

Applications for new projects within the IFSC may be terminated on December 31, 1995. This is currently under discussion.

Conclusion

The IFSC has attracted many financial companies from the United States and Canada who find the IFSC a socially and economically attractive entry point into the European Union.

The IFSC project has achieved a great success during its short life. By 1994 150 companies had set up in the IFSC plus 100 captive insurance and finance companies.

It should be noted that many incentives are offered to foreign companies who set up in Ireland outside the IFSC. For example non-resident companies pay no corporate tax on profits earned outside of Ireland as they would if they were registered in the UK. However, most financial companies will choose to operate inside the IFSC.

Bahamas

Background

The Bahamas are situated in the Caribbean and are a string of islands in the archipelago running from the coast of Florida to Haiti. The capital city, Nassau, sited on the island of New Providence, is the main centre of financial activity. A duty free zone has been set up on the island of Grand Bahama.

The population of the Bahamas are not as rich as those resident in Bermuda or the Cayman Islands but there is very little social unrest so political risk is low.

The Bahamas are a member of the British Commonwealth of Nations. There is an elected parliament and a free press. The law is based on the English legal system.

The local currency is the Bahamian dollar, which is tied in value to the US$. There are strong links between the government of the Bahamas and the United States. The US government is happy with the current tax status of US companies registered in the Bahamas because an information sharing agreement exists on criminal or drug related activities.

A wide range of high quality professional advice is available in Nassau.

Nassau is only 30 minutes flying time from Miami.

Tax

Companies registered in the Bahamas which are conducting off-shore business are subject to no taxes on income or capital gains. Withholding taxes are not imposed on dividends or interest repatriated abroad from the Bahamas.

Custom duties average 35% and various stamp duties are payable on financial transactions. The rate on remittances of cash is around 1.5% of the value remitted.

The Bahamas have signed no tax agreements with other countries.

Exchange control

There are no exchange control regulations applied to the movement of funds by non-resident companies or IBCs (see ahead) into or out of the Bahamas. However there are restrictions placed on the transfer of shares of such companies. The Central Bank must be informed of any share transfers.

Setting Up a Company in the Bahamas

Any company or person can set up a business in the Bahamas for offshore operations as long as the operations are legal under the Bahamanian legal code. An International Business Company (IBC) can be set up which is subject to less stringent regulation than a conventional company which can trade in the Bahamas. An IBC is exempt from all taxes for a period of twenty years from date of incorporation.

Before a bank, insurance company or trust business can be set up in the Bahamas a licence must be bought from the government. The cost of the licence is not high being in the region of US$2500 to US$10 000 per year. A cheaper and simpler form of licensing can form an International Business Company which requires minimal disclosure requirements.

The Bahamas have been described by experts on such matters as the "Universal tax haven". It caters for all tax haven requirements. It offers facilities for international banking, captive insurance companies, trusts, management and finance centres, holding companies, a shipping registry and the formation and management of unit and investment trusts.

The government is careful not to upset the off-shore financial services sector because this accounts for a significant fraction of government revenue.

NOTES

1. The legal infrastructure is based on the 1979 insurance law. There are two status levels for insurance companies, a class A licence or a class B licence. Underwriting is also undertaken in the islands.
2. The Gallagher Report, which reviewed the efficiency and legal underpinning of tax havens in 1989, considered the Cayman Islands to be an "exemplary" tax haven. An example to be followed by other tax havens.
3. Germany has reduced these benefits to some extent by passing certain internal tax legislation relating to special purpose investment companies within the IFSC.

Leading Textbooks on International Finance

Balling, M. (1993) *Financial Management in the New Europe*. Blackwell, 245 pp.
  A description of how financial management is operating in the European Union.
Belkaoui, A. R. (1994) *International and Multinational Accounting*. Dryden.
  A standard textbook on international accounting.
Buckley, A. (1992) *Multinational Finance*. Prentice-Hall, 708 pp.
  A leading British textbook with the emphasis on the operation of multinationals based in the UK.
Clark, E., Levasseur, M. and Rousseau, P. (1993) *International Finance*. Chapman and Hall.
  A leading European textbook. The book is written by two French and one British author. Very good on the technical side of international financial management. A bias towards Europe rather than the UK.
Demireg, I. and Goddard, S. (1994) *Financial Management for International Business*. McGraw-Hill.
  Another popular textbook with the emphasis on UK based multinationals.
Eiteman, D. E., Stonehill, A. I. and Moffett, M. H. (1995) *Multinational Business Finance*. Addison-Wesley, 697 pp.
  A masterly exposition of IFM, based mainly but not exclusively on US material. Exceedingly comprehensive but also clearly and simply written. A leading world text on the subject.
Holland, J. (1993) *International Financial Management*. Blackwell, 470 pp.
  Another popular British textbook. Provides many practical illustrations taken from the accounts of British companies and British markets.
Madura, J. (1995) *International Financial Management*. West Publishing Co.
  A leading US textbook. Explains complicated matters with admirable simplicity. Useful associated tutor's guide.
Shapiro, A. C. (1992) *Multinational Financial Management*. Allyn and Bacon, 729 pp.
  The other leading US textbook. Strong bias towards the United States but possibly the best book on the theoretical side of multinational finance.
Shapiro, A. C. (1994) *Financial Management for Multinationals*. Allyn and Bacon, 652 pp.
  A more popular version of the previous book, but not much shorter. Intended for post-experience courses.

Table 35

Discounting Tables

Present value of a series of future payments of £1 discounted back n periods of time at r% interest.
(Present value of an annuity of £1 per period).

Period	Percentage % 1	2	3	4	5	6	7	8	9	10	12	14	16	20	25	30	40	50
1	0.9901	0.9804	0.9709	0.9615	0.9524	0.9434	0.9346	0.9259	0.9174	0.9091	0.8929	0.8772	0.8621	0.8333	0.8000	0.7692	0.7143	0.6667
2	1.9704	1.9416	1.9135	1.8861	1.8594	1.8334	1.8080	1.7833	1.7591	1.7355	1.6901	1.6467	1.6052	1.5278	1.4400	1.3609	1.2245	1.1111
3	2.9410	2.8839	2.8286	2.7751	2.7232	2.6730	2.6243	2.5771	2.5313	2.4869	2.4018	2.3216	2.2459	2.1065	1.9520	1.8161	1.5889	1.4074
4	3.9020	3.8077	3.7171	3.6299	3.5460	3.4651	3.3872	3.3121	3.2397	3.1699	3.0373	2.9137	2.7982	2.5887	2.3616	2.1662	1.8492	1.6049
5	4.8534	4.7135	4.5797	4.4518	4.3295	4.2124	4.1002	3.9927	3.8897	3.7908	3.6048	3.4331	3.2743	2.9906	2.6893	2.4356	2.0352	1.7366
6	5.7955	5.6014	5.4172	5.2421	5.0757	4.9173	4.7665	4.6229	4.4859	4.3553	4.1114	3.8887	3.6847	3.3255	2.9514	2.6427	2.1680	1.8244
7	6.7282	6.4720	6.2303	6.0021	5.7864	5.5824	5.3893	5.2064	5.0330	4.8684	4.5638	4.2883	4.0386	3.6046	3.1611	2.8021	2.2628	1.8829
8	7.6517	7.3255	7.0197	6.7327	6.4632	6.2098	5.9713	5.7466	5.5348	5.3349	4.9676	4.6389	4.3436	3.8372	3.3289	2.9247	2.3306	1.9220
9	8.5660	8.1622	7.7861	7.4353	7.1078	6.8017	6.5152	6.2469	5.9952	5.7590	5.3282	4.9464	4.6065	4.0310	3.4631	3.0190	2.3790	1.9480
10	9.4713	8.9826	8.5302	8.1109	7.7217	7.3601	7.0236	6.7101	6.4177	6.1446	5.6502	5.2161	4.8332	4.1925	3.5705	3.0915	2.4136	1.9653
11	10.3676	9.7868	9.2526	8.7605	8.3064	7.8869	7.4987	7.1390	6.8052	6.4951	5.9377	5.4527	5.0286	4.3271	3.6564	3.1473	2.4383	1.9769
12	11.2551	10.5753	9.9540	9.3851	8.8633	8.3838	7.9427	7.5361	7.1607	6.8137	6.1944	5.6603	5.1971	4.4392	3.7251	3.1903	2.4559	1.9846
13	12.1337	11.3484	10.6350	9.9856	9.3936	8.8527	8.3577	7.9038	7.4869	7.1034	6.4235	5.8424	5.3423	4.5327	3.7801	3.2233	2.4685	1.9897
14	13.0037	12.1062	11.2961	10.5631	9.8986	9.2950	8.7455	8.2442	7.7862	7.3667	6.6282	6.0021	5.4675	4.6106	3.8241	3.2487	2.4775	1.9931
15	13.8651	12.8493	11.9379	11.1184	10.3797	9.7122	9.1079	8.5595	8.0607	7.6061	6.8109	6.1422	5.5755	4.6755	3.8593	3.2682	2.4839	1.9954
20	18.0456	16.3514	14.8775	13.5903	12.4622	11.4699	10.5940	9.8181	9.1285	8.5136	7.4694	6.6231	5.9288	4.8696	3.9539	3.3158	2.4970	1.9994
25	22.0232	19.5235	17.4131	15.6221	14.0939	12.7834	11.6536	10.6748	9.8226	9.0770	7.8431	6.8729	6.0971	4.9476	3.9849	3.3286	2.4994	1.9999
30	25.8077	22.3965	19.6004	17.2920	15.3725	13.7648	12.4090	11.2578	10.2737	9.4269	8.0552	7.0027	6.1772	4.9789	3.9950	3.3321	2.4999	1.9999
40	32.8347	27.3555	23.1148	19.7928	17.1591	15.0463	13.3317	11.9246	10.7574	9.7791	8.2438	7.1050	6.2335	4.9966	3.9995	3.3332	2.5000	2.0000
50	39.1961	31.4236	25.7298	21.4822	18.2559	15.7619	13.8007	12.2335	10.9617	9.9148	8.3045	7.1327	6.2463	4.9995	3.9999	3.3333	2.5000	2.0000
100	63.0289	43.0984	31.5989	24.5050	19.8479	16.6175	14.2693	12.4943	11.1091	9.9993	8.3332	7.1428	6.2500	5.0000	4.0000	3.3333	2.5000	2.0000

Table 36

Future value of a series of payments of £1 for n periods of time at r% interest.

Period	1	2	3	4	5	6	7	8	9	10	12	14	16	20	25	30	40	50
	Percentage %																	
1	1.0000	1.0000	1.0000	1.0000	1.0000	1.0000	1.0000	1.0000	1.0000	1.0000	1.0000	1.0000	1.0000	1.0000	1.0000	1.0000	1.0000	1.0000
2	2.0100	2.0200	2.0300	2.0400	2.0500	2.0600	2.0700	2.0800	2.0900	2.1000	2.1200	2.1400	2.1600	2.2000	2.2500	2.3000	2.4000	2.5000
3	3.0301	3.0604	3.0909	3.1216	3.1525	3.1836	3.2149	3.2464	3.2781	3.3100	3.3744	3.4396	3.5056	3.6400	3.8125	3.9900	4.3600	4.7500
4	4.0604	4.1216	4.1836	4.2465	4.3101	4.3746	4.4399	4.5061	4.5731	4.6410	4.7793	4.9211	5.0665	5.3680	5.7656	6.1870	7.1040	8.1250
5	5.1010	5.2040	5.3091	5.4163	5.5256	5.6371	5.7507	5.8666	5.9847	6.1051	6.3528	6.6101	6.8771	7.4416	8.2070	9.0431	10.9456	13.1875
6	6.1520	6.3081	6.4684	6.6330	6.8019	6.9753	7.1533	7.3359	7.5233	7.7156	8.1152	8.5355	8.9775	9.9299	11.2588	12.7560	16.3238	20.7813
7	7.2135	7.4343	7.6625	7.8983	8.1420	8.3938	8.6540	8.9228	9.2004	9.4872	10.0890	10.7305	11.4139	12.9159	15.0735	17.5828	23.8534	32.1719
8	8.2857	8.5830	8.8923	9.2142	9.5491	9.8975	10.2598	10.6366	11.0285	11.4359	12.2997	13.2328	14.2401	16.4991	19.8419	23.8577	34.3947	49.2578
9	9.3685	9.7546	10.1591	10.5828	11.0266	11.4913	11.9780	12.4876	13.0210	13.5795	14.7757	16.0853	17.5185	20.7989	25.8023	32.0150	49.1526	74.8867
10	10.4622	10.9497	11.4639	12.0061	12.5779	13.1808	13.8165	14.4866	15.1929	15.9374	17.5487	19.3373	21.3215	25.9587	33.2529	42.6195	69.8137	
11	11.5668	12.1687	12.8078	13.4864	14.2068	14.9716	15.7836	16.6455	17.5603	18.5312	20.6546	23.0445	25.7329	32.1504	42.5661	56.4053	98.7391	
12	12.6825	13.4121	14.1920	15.0258	15.9171	16.8699	17.8885	18.9771	20.1407	21.3843	24.1331	27.2707	30.8502	39.5805	54.2077	74.3270		
13	13.8093	14.6803	15.6178	16.6268	17.7130	18.8821	20.1406	21.4953	22.9534	24.5227	28.0291	32.0887	36.7862	48.4966	68.7596	97.6250		
14	14.9474	15.9739	17.0863	18.2919	19.5986	21.0151	22.5505	24.2149	26.0192	27.9750	32.3926	37.5811	43.6720	59.1959	86.9495			
15	16.0969	17.2934	18.5989	20.0236	21.5786	23.2760	25.1290	27.1521	29.3609	31.7725	37.2797	43.8424	51.6595	72.0351				
20	22.0190	24.2974	26.8704	29.7781	33.0660	36.7856	40.9955	45.7620	51.1601	57.2750	72.0524	91.0249						
25	28.2432	32.0303	36.4593	41.6459	47.7271	54.8645	63.2490	73.1059	84.7009	98.3471								
30	34.7849	40.5681	47.5754	56.0849	66.4388	79.0582	94.4608											
40	48.8864	60.4020	75.4013	95.0255	120.7998	154.7620												
50	64.4632	84.5794	112.797	152.6671	209.3480	290.3359												
100	170.4814	312.2323	607.288	1237.6237	2610.0252													

Table 37

Present value of £1 discounted back n periods of time at r% interest.

Period	Percentage % 1	2	3	4	5	6	7	8	9	10	12	14	16	20	25	30	40	50
1	0.9901	0.9804	0.9709	0.9615	0.9524	0.9434	0.9346	0.9259	0.9174	0.9091	0.8929	0.8772	0.8621	0.8333	0.8000	0.7692	0.7143	0.6667
2	0.9803	0.9612	0.9426	0.9246	0.9070	0.8900	0.8734	0.8573	0.8417	0.8264	0.7972	0.7695	0.7432	0.6944	0.6400	0.5917	0.5102	0.4444
3	0.9706	0.9423	0.9151	0.8890	0.8638	0.8396	0.8163	0.7938	0.7722	0.7513	0.7118	0.6750	0.6407	0.5787	0.5120	0.4552	0.3644	0.2963
4	0.9610	0.9238	0.8885	0.8548	0.8227	0.7921	0.7629	0.7350	0.7084	0.6830	0.6355	0.5921	0.5523	0.4823	0.4096	0.3501	0.2603	0.1975
5	0.9515	0.9057	0.8626	0.8219	0.7835	0.7473	0.7130	0.6806	0.6499	0.6209	0.5674	0.5194	0.4761	0.4019	0.3277	0.2693	0.1859	0.1317
6	0.9420	0.8880	0.8375	0.7903	0.7462	0.7050	0.6663	0.6302	0.5963	0.5645	0.5066	0.4556	0.4104	0.3349	0.2621	0.2072	0.1328	0.0878
7	0.9327	0.8706	0.8131	0.7599	0.7107	0.6651	0.6227	0.5835	0.5470	0.5132	0.4523	0.3996	0.3538	0.2791	0.2097	0.1594	0.0949	0.0585
8	0.9235	0.8535	0.7894	0.7307	0.6768	0.6274	0.5820	0.5403	0.5019	0.4665	0.4039	0.3506	0.3050	0.2326	0.1678	0.1226	0.0678	0.0390
9	0.9143	0.8368	0.7664	0.7026	0.6446	0.5919	0.5439	0.5002	0.4604	0.4241	0.3606	0.3075	0.2630	0.1938	0.1342	0.0943	0.0484	0.0260
10	0.9053	0.8203	0.7441	0.6756	0.6139	0.5584	0.5083	0.4632	0.4224	0.3855	0.3220	0.2697	0.2267	0.1615	0.1074	0.0725	0.0346	0.0173
11	0.8963	0.8043	0.7224	0.6496	0.5847	0.5268	0.4751	0.4289	0.3875	0.3505	0.2875	0.2366	0.1954	0.1346	0.0859	0.0558	0.0247	0.0116
12	0.8874	0.7885	0.7014	0.6246	0.5568	0.4970	0.4440	0.3971	0.3555	0.3186	0.2567	0.2076	0.1685	0.1122	0.0687	0.0429	0.0176	0.0077
13	0.8787	0.7730	0.6810	0.6006	0.5303	0.4688	0.4150	0.3677	0.3262	0.2897	0.2292	0.1821	0.1452	0.0935	0.0550	0.0330	0.0126	0.0051
14	0.8700	0.7579	0.6611	0.5775	0.5051	0.4423	0.3878	0.3405	0.2992	0.2633	0.2046	0.1597	0.1252	0.0779	0.0440	0.0254	0.0090	0.0034
15	0.8613	0.7430	0.6419	0.5553	0.4810	0.4173	0.3624	0.3152	0.2745	0.2394	0.1827	0.1401	0.1079	0.0649	0.0352	0.0195	0.0064	0.0023
20	0.8195	0.6730	0.5537	0.4564	0.3769	0.3118	0.2584	0.2145	0.1784	0.1486	0.1037	0.0728	0.0514	0.0261	0.0115	0.0053	0.0012	0.0003
25	0.7798	0.6095	0.4776	0.3751	0.2953	0.2330	0.1842	0.1460	0.1160	0.0923	0.0588	0.0378	0.0245	0.0105	0.0038	0.0014	0.0002	0.0000
30	0.7419	0.5521	0.4120	0.3083	0.2314	0.1741	0.1314	0.0994	0.0754	0.0573	0.0334	0.0196	0.0116	0.0042	0.0012	0.0004	0.0000	0.0000
40	0.6717	0.4529	0.3066	0.2083	0.1420	0.0972	0.0668	0.0460	0.0318	0.0221	0.0107	0.0053	0.0026	0.0007	0.0001	0.0000	0.0000	0.0000
50	0.6080	0.3715	0.2281	0.1407	0.0872	0.0543	0.0339	0.0213	0.0134	0.0085	0.0035	0.0014	0.0006	0.0000	0.0000	0.0000	0.0000	0.0000
100	0.3697	0.1380	0.0520	0.0198	0.0076	0.0029	0.0012	0.0005	0.0002	0.0001	0.0000	0.0000	0.0000	0.0000	0.0000	0.0000	0.0000	0.0000

Table 38

Future value of £1 at the end of n periods of time at r% interest.

Period	|						Percentage %											
	1	2	3	4	5	6	7	8	9	10	12	14	16	20	25	30	40	50
1	1.0100	1.0200	1.0300	1.0400	1.0500	1.0600	1.0700	1.0800	1.0900	1.1000	1.1200	1.1400	1.1600	1.2000	1.2500	1.3000	1.4000	1.5000
2	1.0201	1.0404	1.0609	1.0816	1.1025	1.1236	1.1449	1.1664	1.1881	1.2100	1.2544	1.2996	1.3456	1.4400	1.5625	1.6900	1.9600	2.2500
3	1.0303	1.0612	1.0927	1.1249	1.1576	1.1910	1.2250	1.2597	1.2950	1.3310	1.4049	1.4815	1.5609	1.7280	1.9531	2.1970	2.7440	3.3750
4	1.0406	1.0824	1.1255	1.1699	1.2155	1.2625	1.3108	1.3605	1.4116	1.4641	1.5735	1.6890	1.8106	2.0736	2.4414	2.8561	3.8416	5.0625
5	1.0510	1.1041	1.1593	1.2167	1.2763	1.3382	1.4026	1.4693	1.5386	1.6105	1.7623	1.9254	2.1003	2.4883	3.0518	3.7129	5.3782	7.5938
6	1.0615	1.1262	1.1941	1.2653	1.3401	1.4185	1.5007	1.5869	1.6771	1.7716	1.9738	2.1950	2.4364	2.9860	3.8147	4.8268	7.5295	11.3906
7	1.0721	1.1487	1.2299	1.3159	1.4071	1.5036	1.6058	1.7138	1.8280	1.9487	2.2107	2.5023	2.8262	3.5832	4.7684	6.2749	10.5414	17.0859
8	1.0829	1.1717	1.2668	1.3686	1.4775	1.5938	1.7182	1.8509	1.9926	2.1436	2.4760	2.8526	3.2784	4.2998	5.9605	8.1573	14.7579	25.6289
9	1.0937	1.1951	1.3048	1.4233	1.5513	1.6895	1.8385	1.9990	2.1719	2.3579	2.7731	3.2519	3.8030	4.1598	7.4506	10.6045	20.6610	38.4434
10	1.1046	1.2190	1.3439	1.4802	1.6289	1.7908	1.9672	2.1589	2.3674	2.5937	3.1058	3.7072	4.4114	6.1917	9.3132	13.7858	28.9255	57.6650
11	1.1157	1.2434	1.3842	1.5395	1.7103	1.8983	2.1049	2.3316	2.5804	2.8531	3.4785	4.2262	5.1173	7.4301	11.6415	17.9216	40.4957	86.4976
12	1.1268	1.2682	1.4258	1.6010	1.7959	2.0122	2.2522	2.5182	2.8127	3.1384	3.8960	4.8179	5.9360	8.9161	14.5519	23.2981	56.6939	
13	1.1381	1.2936	1.4685	1.6651	1.8856	2.1329	2.4098	2.7196	3.0658	3.4523	4.3635	5.4924	6.8858	10.6993	18.1899	30.2875	79.3715	
14	1.1495	1.3195	1.5126	1.7317	1.9799	2.2609	2.5785	2.9372	3.3417	3.7975	4.8871	6.2613	7.9875	12.8392	22.7374	39.3738		
15	1.1610	1.3459	1.5580	1.8009	2.0789	2.3966	2.7590	3.1722	3.6425	4.1772	5.4736	7.1379	9.2655	15.4070	28.4217	51.1859		
20	1.2202	1.4859	1.8061	2.1911	2.6533	3.2071	3.8697	4.6610	5.6044	6.7275	9.6463	13.7435	19.4608	38.3376	86.7362			
25	1.2824	1.6406	2.0938	2.6658	3.3864	4.2919	5.4274	6.8485	8.6231	10.8347	17.0001	26.4619	40.8742	95.3962				
30	1.3478	1.8114	2.4273	3.2434	4.3219	5.7435	7.6123	10.0627	13.2677	17.4494	29.9599	50.9502	85.8499					
40	1.4889	2.2080	3.2620	4.8010	7.0400	10.2857	14.9745	21.7245	31.4094	45.2593	93.0510							
50	1.6466	2.6916	4.3839	7.1067	11.4674	18.4202	29.4570	46.9016	74.3575									
100	2.7048	7.2446	19.2186	50.5049														

Glossary

Agio The charge for converting an asset from one form to another.

Arbitrageur If the value of assets differs between different markets an arbitrageur brings them into line by buying in the cheaper market and selling into the dearer.

Arm's Length If companies in a group sell to one another then the sale is at "arm's length" if the price is the same as if they were selling to companies outside the group.

Authorized Depository If exchange controls are imposed on a country an authorized depository is allowed to hold assets denominated in a foreign currency on behalf of clients.

Autodealing Buying or selling financial assets via a computer/telecommunication system.

Back-to-back Loan A company in one country swaps its loan obligation with a company in another country. Seldom used today.

Banker's Draft A banker's cheque drawn on another bank. A very safe payment mechanism.

Barter Trading Swapping goods rather than paying by cash.

Basis Points A method of pricing currency. Uses the most junior digits in an exchange rate rather than the full quote. US$1.5633 could be quoted as "33".

Beta Measure of the market risk attached to a company share quoted on an efficient stock exchange. Relation between the return on a share and return on all shares in the market.

Bill of Exchange A promise to pay a fixed amount of money to a third party on some date in the future. The bill might be a "sight" bill payable immediately or a "term" bill.

Bill of Lading A document that accompanies goods shipped to a foreign port. Gives details about the shipment.

Blocked Currency Money held in a foreign bank account that cannot be repatriated to the home country. Usually because of exchange restrictions by a foreign government.

Bond A financial instrument issued by a company or government that promises to pay an agreed amount of interest for a given period and then to repay the money paid for the bond.

Call   A term used with options. The right to buy a fixed amount of currency at a fixed price on a given date in the future.

Captive Insurance Company   A group of companies set up such a company in a tax haven for tax reasons. Most insurance of the group is insured via the captive.

Carry Forward/Back   Losses can be carried forward and/or backwards in time to be set off against future or past profits to reduce tax. Some countries, not the UK, allow tax credits to be carried backwards and forwards in time.

Closing Rate (Current Rate) Method   Method of translating accounts from one currency to another. The rate used in this case being the rate on the closing day of the accounting year. Method called the current rate method in the USA.

Cocktail, Currency   A loan denominated in a mixture of currencies.

Consolidated Accounts   The accounts of several companies in a group added together. These accounts may be denominated in several different currencies so they must be "translated".

Country Risk   The risk of investing in a foreign country varies a great deal between countries. "Country risk" tries to measure the risk differential between countries.

Conversion   Selling one currency for another. Not to be confused with "translation".

Credit Grading   Allotting a grade to the credit-worthiness of a company. The grade is usually expressed as AAA to CCC. Several agencies supply such gradings for a fee.

Cross Rates   An exchange rate expresses the rate of exchange between two currencies A and B. When a third currency C is introduced the cross rate is the rate of B in terms of A derived from the rate between A and C and B and C.

Current–Non-current Method   A method of translating foreign accounts into the home currency of the parent. Current items are translated at the closing rate, other items at the historical or revalued rate of exchange.

Direct Investment   Foreign investment made with the objective of controlling the foreign venture. (C.f. portfolio investment.)

Derivative   A financial product the value of which is derived from the value of some other financial product. For example, the value of an option to buy an amount of currency at a fixed price in the future depends on the current value of the currency.

Double Tax Agreement   If the income of a company can be taxed by two different tax authorities in two different countries both countries sign a tax agreement that decides how much tax goes to either tax authority.

Economic Exposure   The exchange risk attached to the long-term cash flows of a company.

ECU   A monetary unit used by the European Union.

Exchange Control   The control by a government of the flow of funds out of and, possibly, into a country.

Exotic Currency   A currency that is seldom used for international trading.

Exposure   The amount of currency that may suffer or gain from a change in exchange rates.

Factoring   A financial procedure whereby an institution called a factor takes over the debts owed by a debter.

Fisher Theory (International)   A theory that relates the current difference between interest rates on loans in different currencies to future changes in exchange rates.

Forfaiting   A payment and financing procedure in international trade whereby the importer arranges for a local bank to guarantee a series of payments to the exporter in another country.

Forward Market   A market that allows currency to be bought and sold at a fixed price on a future date.

Forward Premium/Discount   The difference between the spot rate and the forward rate on a currency.

Futures Market   A market which allows a standardized packet of currency to be bought and sold at a fixed price for a future date.

Functional Currency   If a parent company runs a subsidiary company in a foreign country the currency used to denominate the foreign accounts is said to be the "functional currency" (C.f. reporting currency.)

Gearing (Leverage)   A measure of the volume of debt incorporated into the total funding of a company.

Guarantee   A surety given by one party to another about the future behaviour of a third party. For example, the future payment of a debt might be guaranteed or the future exchange rate on a foreign deal.

Hedge   Any device that reduces the loss on a future risk. Forwards, futures and options are hedging devices.

Holding Company   A company whose major asset is the shares held in other companies in a group of companies.

Hyper-inflation   When the value of money falls relative to other goods the result is called "inflation". If the value of money falls very fast the result is called "hyper-inflation". A rate above 25% a year is officially described by the WTO as hyper-inflation.

Invisible Exports   The export of services rather than goods.

In-the-money   An option that will make a profit if exercised.

Interest Rate Parity Theory   A theory that relates the differences between short-term interest rates to the premium or discount on the forward exchange rate.

Leading and Lagging   Speeding up or delaying payment to a foreign creditor.

Leasing   Transferring the use but not the ownership of an asset to a user (in the UK). The user pays an agreed periodic sum to use the asset. The user may have a right to buy the asset after n periods.

Letter of Credit   A method of paying for goods, usually goods sent abroad. A bank guarantees the payment.

Levered Derivative   A derivative that allows the owner to invest in a financial instrument at a cost well below that of the cost of the underlying product on the open market.

LIBOR   The London interbank rate. The rate at which banks lend money to one another.

Matching   Equating the inflow of funds in a given currency to the outflow in the same currency.

Monetary Asset   An asset the terminal value of which is fixed in money terms at the outset.

Monetary–Non-monetary Method   A method of translating accounts from one currency to another.

Net Monetary Position   The monetary assets of a company less the monetary liabilities.

Netting   Offsetting the debts of two subsidiaries against one another.

Numeraire   A good selected to measure the value of all other goods.

Off-balance Sheet   An asset of a company that is not listed or valued on the balance sheet in the annual accounts. At one time in the UK lease commitments were not stated on the balance sheet of UK companies.

Option   The right but not the obligation to buy or sell an asset at a fixed price on some future date. The option can be a traded option or an over-the-counter-option.

Out-of-the-money   An option that will not make a profit if exercised.

Over-the-counter   Not traded on an official market.

Parallel Currency   A currency whose exchange value is highly correlated to the movement of another currency.

Portfolio Investment   Securities held for income rather than control. (C.f. direct investment.)

Purchasing Power Parity Theory   A theory that relates changes in exchange rates between two currencies to changes in inflation rates in the two currencies.

Put   A term used with options. The right to sell a fixed amount of currency at a fixed price on a given date in the future.

Ratchet Clause   A clause in a price contract that limits the future change in price to some fixed periodic amount, say 5% per annum.

Real Asset   An asset the terminal value of which is not fixed in money terms at the outset.

Recourse   If a factor or a bank discounts a debt for a creditor then if the debt is not paid by the debtor the factor or bank may have recourse to the original creditor to recover the money.

Reporting Currency   If consolidated accounts are produced from accounts denominated in several currencies the currency in which the accounts are denominated is called the "reporting currency". It is usually the currency of the parent company.

Sensitivity Analysis   A technique for finding the factors that have a major impact on the return from an investment project.

Sinking Fund   A fund set up to repay a loan.

Snake, Currency   A device for limiting the movement in the exchange rates between currencies.

Spot Rate   The current rate of exchange between currencies.

Spread The difference between the buying and selling price of any financial product. Also the excess above some "base" rate.

Stepping Stones Company A company set up in country C that has a beneficial double tax agreement with two other countries A and B. Dividends, etc., can be repatriated from A to B via C to reduce the through-put tax for a group.

Strike Price The price at which an option can be exercised.

Swap Market A market for swapping streams of currencies. Mostly run by the international banks.

Synthetic Derivative A hedging product manufactured by a merchant bank to solve some hedging problem for an MNC if a "natural" derivative is not available.

Tax Arbitrage A tax officer can shift revenues and costs between subsidiaries in different countries in a group to minimize global tax. To take advantage of different tax rules in different countries.

Tax Credit A credit to compensate for tax paid abroad.

Tax Haven A country that provides facilities for reducing the tax bill in other countries.

Temporal Method A method of translating accounts denominated in a foreign currency. Similar in practice to the monetary–non-monetary method.

Thin Capitalization A technique that allows a company, which is very highly geared, to pay high interest charges to an associated company abroad. A tax-avoidance device.

Transfer Price The price at which one subsidiary or department charges goods or services to another subsidiary in the same group.

Transaction Exposure The exchange risk attached to short-term payments or receipts in a foreign currency.

Translation The calculation of a value in one currency from a value in another currency, no cash is involved. (C.f. conversion.)

Translation Exposure The net exposure to exchange risk of items in a balance sheet and P and L account.

Unitary Tax A method of taxing a group of companies that bases the tax due on a proportion of the worldwide profits of the company rather than on the local profits.

Withholding Tax When a subsidiary in one country sends dividends to its parent or other shareholder in another country a "withholding" tax is usually deducted from the dividend by the host government.

Writing an Option Underwriting the liability on an option.

Zone, Currency Several countries agree to fix the value of their currencies to one major currency.

Solutions to Odd-numbered Tutorial Questions

CHAPTER 1

1. Around 180 currencies are used in world trade but many of these currencies are fixed in value relative to some other currency like the US$. The five most important currencies are the US$, the DM, the Japanese yen, the UK£ sterling and the Swiss franc.

    Saudi Arabia: riyal, Guatamala: quetzal, South Korea: wan, Thailand: baht.

3. Contracts can be paid in any currency agreed by the two parties to the contract. Once the currency in which a contract is to be paid is settled it is said that the contract is "denominated" in that currency. The exchange rate between currencies varies minute by minute, very large variations can occur over short periods of time. Thus a contractor who allows a contract to be denominated in a foreign currency is taking a risk. The exchange rate may move against him before the contract is settled. The pound sterling fell in value by 25% against many currencies on September 16, 1992.

5. The value of a contract denominated in a foreign currency is "hedged" if another countervailing contract is set up at the same time as the initial contract that cancels any loss caused by changes in exchange rates between the time the contract is set up and the foreign currency is received.

    If "you" are not a Japanese company and the contract is denominated in Japanese yen then there is an exchange rate risk that the value of the contract in your own currency may rise if the yen increases in value against your own currency. The risk can be eliminated by taking out a forward contract to buy yen at the current rate six months forward or to buy a Japanese yen futures contract of equal value. See Chapters 2 and 5.

7. The financial officer can become an "arbitrageur". For example, if she believes that the Italian lire is being undervalued by the interest rate difference she can buy lire forward with a short-term loan at the current forward rate of exchange and make a profit when she sells these lire in six months' time.

9. A tax haven charges low or zero rates of tax on company profits and low or zero withholding taxes on dividends sent abroad from the tax haven. A finance officer can reduce the global tax bill of her company by arranging for group profits to be made in a tax haven subsidiary by, for example, setting up a captive insurance company in the tax haven. The subsequent profits can be used to buy equipment that can now be leased to other companies in the group who will charge the leasing costs against their local profits that are taxed at a higher rate in that country.

11. Your company is not allowed to repatriate cash but there is unlikely to be any objections to you repatriating other goods or services you buy in the country where the funds are blocked. You may be able to work through a barter dealer who will buy the goods from you and sell them himself. Your company may be allowed to invest in local funds, say government stock, and repatriate the proceeds after a number of years. Counter-trading is by far the best option in most cases. See Chapter 9 for a further discussion of the problem.

13. Interest cannot be charged on funds loaned in many Muslim countries. Bribery is common in many developing countries and is not unknown at home. Family relations play an important part in awarding contracts in many countries. Some governments prefer to deal with counter parties operating in a similar political or religious system.

15. The religious authorities in Muslim countries object to interest being paid on funds loaned but not to profit being made from these funds. Thus banks in some Muslim countries take an equity interest in a deal, fund the deal, and take a slice of the profits in place of interest. Examples of such contracts are called "Musharakah", "Modarabah" and "Murabahah".

17. The legal systems of the UK and the USA are based on common law, legal precedent. The legal systems of continental Europe are mainly based on an interpretation of constitutional laws, such as the "Code Napoleon", passed by parliament or some other constitutional body .

19. In some African countries it is difficult to win a contract without giving some small, or perhaps not so small, gift to the counter party in the contract. Some Muslim countries may not sign a contract with a company which deals with Israel.

CHAPTER 2

1. (a) The US dollar is standing at a premium of 7 cents to the UK £ sterling one year forward.

   (b) If you buy a one year US$100 000 bond at 10% per annum on November 1, 1995 and also take out a forward contract to sell US$100 000 on October 31, 1996 at US$1.85 to the £ the figures come out as follows:

   Buy bond   US$100 000/1.92 = £52 083

   US$ received 31.10.96

   Interest   US$10 000

   Capital   US$100 000

   Received in £ sterling   110 000/1.85 = £59 459

If £52,083 had been invested in the UK market at 15% then ... £52 083 × 1.15 = £59 895 would have been received on October 31, 1996.

Conclusion: It is not worth while buying the US$ bond. It is better to invest in the UK £ sterling market. The 3.8% expected devaluation of sterling against the US$ over the year does not fully compensate for the 5% differential on the interest rates available.

3. A wide spread between the buy and sell rate on a currency tells us that the market is either a "shallow" market with few transactions taking place each period or that there is great uncertainty about the movement in the future spot rate of exchange, possibly both.

If an exchange rate is quoted "34–71" these figures refer to the last two digits in the quote rate, for example, 8.2034–8.2071. This method of quotation can only be used between experienced dealers who know from experience that the other figures will be unchanged.

5. A future currency contract is a contract to sell a fixed amount of currency at a fixed price at some future date to a buyer of the contract. The factors that are standardized in a futures currency contract are (1) the value of one contract, i.e., 12 500 000 yen, and (2) the terminal dates for completion of the contract March, June, September, December. A futures contract is more liquid than a forward contract. The cost is the same.

If the spot rate changes the writer (seller) of the futures contract must pay the futures clearing house the difference between the spot rate and the futures rate each trading day. If a British investor writes a £25 000 US$ contract when the futures price is US$1.67 to the US$ and the spot price falls to US$1.65 to the £ sterling (the US$ costs more in terms of sterling). The writer of the futures contract must pay the clearing house US$(1.67 − 1.65) = 2 cents × £25 000 = US$500. Thus on the next day the "write price" of the futures contract now stands at US$1.65 to the £. This will be done on each day while the contract is in force so that the "write" price of the futures contract changes day by day. This reduces the risk of default by the writer of the contract and so protects the clearing house who guarantee implementation of the contract.

7. A currency call option gives the buyer of the option the right, but not the obligation, to buy a fixed amount of currency at a fixed price at some date, or between two dates, in the future. A currency option market such as the Philadelphia market quotes "strike" prices for fixed amounts of currency for various dates in the future. A price, or premium, is quoted for each price/date option. For example, a single "call" option contract for £32 000 at a strike price of US$1.67 to the £ sterling for the end of December might be quoted at a price of 10 cents a £. The risk in the currency option market is taken by the "writer" (seller) of the option. The writer must implement the contract if asked to do so by the buyer of the option. The maximum loss possible to a buyer of an option is option price plus the interest lost on the option price invested over the period of the option. The loss to the writer of a "call" option is theoretically infinite unless he places a "cap" on his liability by buying an equivalent option at a different price.

9. (a) 0.72 cent × 31 250 × 10 = US$2250.

(b) 0.24 cent × 31 250 × 2 = US$150.

11. The finance officer will contact the foreign exchange department of the bank that handles the company business and ask for a six-month forward quote on the lire/sterling exchange rate. Alternatively he may first study the prices quoted by a screen based system such as Telerate. The finance officer will not say whether he wishes to buy or sell lire. He may contact other dealers or even a broker if the company is a large one to find the most competitive rate. Eventually he accepts the best quote offered for buying lire six months' forward.

A written acceptance is delivered to the company. In six months' time when the lire arrives from the Italian company the Finance officer sells it to the dealer at the fixed rate as per the contract.

If the importer fails to pay the amount due in six months' time the finance officer must buy the lire on the open market on behalf of his company at the exchange rate ruling on that date to implement his side of the contract with the currency dealer. He can, of course, sue the Italian company for any loss incurred and the contract may be insured.

13. Several committees of the US government have studied the likely fall-out if a major bank collapses because of the failure to meet its obligations in the swap market. There is no regulator of the swap market and no one knows the actual figures on how many swaps are held by the various participants at any one time. The real danger lies with swapping in the secondary market and swapping between different swap markets The entry of lesser known participants into the swap market is the main risk faced at present.

15. (a) $1.5623 - 0.00125 = US\$1.56105$

$1.5711 + 0.00375 = US\$1.57485$

(b) $£1/1.56105 = 64.06$ pence.

(c) Cartel PLC sends the US\$ cheque for US\$2 million to its bank along with the forward contract and the £1 269 962 is credited to its account. The transfer of funds is likely to be effected by electronic transfer via SWIFT.

(d) $US\$2m/1.57485 = £1 269 962$

(e) The cost or profit of the forward cover is the difference between the amount received on the forward cover rate contract and what would have been received if no forward cover had been taken out. If no forward cover had been taken out Cartel would have received $US\$2 million/1.5344 = £1 303 441$. So by taking out a forward contract Cartel lost $£1 303 441 - £1 269 962 = £33 479$. The currency moved the "wrong" way over the six-month period.

CHAPTER 3

1. The IRPT claims that the difference on the interest rates charged on loans offered in different currencies is directly related to the premium or discount on the forward exchange rate between the currencies.

The IRPT works because individuals called "arbitrageurs" note any discrepancy that exists between the difference in interest rates between currencies and the forward premium or discount on the exchange rate between the currencies. If these two values are out of line the arbitrageur takes out a short-term loan in the advantageous currency and covers the currency risk forward with a forward contract. This will eventually drive the interest rate difference into line with the discount or premium on the forward rate.

The IRPT can only operate if a forward currency market exists to set up forward exchange contracts between the two currencies. Many currencies have no forward market. Few forward markets quote for a period ahead of more than one year (except against the US$). In the case of some currencies the government of the country forbids the setting up of a forward market or even using foreign markets in the currency. The swap market can be used to set up long-term forward contracts between currencies.

3. The PPP theory states that changes in exchange rates reflect parallel changes in inflation rates in the local currencies of the two countries. If this assumption is true future rates of exchange can be predicted if inflation rates in both countries can be predicted.

The net monetary balance in pesetas is as shown in Table 39:

Table 39

	SP million
Debtors	70
Cash	40
	110
Creditors	50
Net balance	60

The Spanish subsidiary is holding a net positive balance of 60 million pesetas, if, therefore, the peseta is devalued by 5% against the £ sterling the subsidiary will suffer a real loss in terms of £ sterling.

Advice: The inventory value is not at risk, the value will float up with inflation. If net working capital of SP60 million is essential to the running of the business it may be difficult to run down debtors and cash at short notice. Transferring the liquid pesetas into £s may be considered or the taking out of an additional 60 million of loans in pesetas for further expansion of the business to take advantage of the cheaper peseta. Much depends on the forward rate. If this already discounts the expected 5% fall in the value of the peseta little can be done with derivatives to hedge the fall in value.

5. The word "efficient" refers to the efficiency with which information is processed by the currency markets. "Information efficient" means that all facts influencing the value of currencies traded on the international financial markets are available to all traders very quickly after the event which triggers the new information. Future changes in the value of a currency are determined by future events which are themselves unpredictable. If this theory is true then past price trends can give no guide to future price trends. The movement of currency prices form a "random walk". Note that many currency markets are controlled and therefore not efficient. "Chartism", which extrapolates currency trends forward, cannot work if this theory is true. There is a good deal of published research work supporting the theory that currency movements are a random walk.

7. All the relevant data to test the IRPT is available every day in the *Financial Times* and other newspapers abroad. In order to test the Open Fisher theory a researcher needs to wait for many years until the foreign fixed interest loans under study have matured and been repaid. You cannot test the Open Fisher on a 25-year loan until the 25 years are up! This fact has discouraged research on the subject until recently. The tight exchange controls applied by many countries prior to 1980 also discouraged testing the theory.

9.
$$(1 + s\%)/(1 + f\%) = f/e$$
$$(1 + 0.10)/(1 + 0.04) = f/1.32$$
$$f = 1.0576 \times 1.32 = C\$1.396$$

11. The international Fisher may not work because the international funds market is not efficient. Exchange controls may be imposed by the monetary authority in a country prohibiting the free flow of funds into or out of the country. Even if the free flow of funds is allowed governments may influence the cost of funds by interfering in the markets by buying or selling funds in an attempt to control the rate of exchange. Country risk may also impose a premium on the rate of exchange between currencies.

13. Research suggests that a risk premium on currencies does exist, in addition to the inflation differential factor, but the effect of differential risk is small. The reason appears to be that international investors can diversify the risk away by investing in a wide range of currencies.

15. A "currency snake" is an agreement between the monetary authorities of several countries to keep the value of their exchange rates between given bounds relative to one another. The best-known example in recent years is the "snake" operated by most of the countries in the European Union. Stable predictable exchange rates can remove FX risk, a major risk in international trading. If currencies are placed into a currency snake a currency speculator faces an asymmetric bet. A floor on the value of the exchange rate limits a speculator's potential loss if he guesses the wrong way. The rate he is speculating on can rise or fall only within the given limits. Without limits on exchange rates there is no limit to possible losses. Cover, via derivatives is available but is much more expensive than a government guaranteed limit on loss.

CHAPTER 4

1. An amount is exposed to exchange rate risk if a change in the exchange rate might impose a loss on a company in terms of the home currency. This "exposure" will include any asset or liability denominated in a foreign currency plus the amount of any cash that will cross a currency frontier in the near future plus the long-term cash flows of the company. The value of any of these items may change in terms of the home currency because of future changes in exchange rates.

3. (a) A monetary asset or liability is any asset or liability whose terminal value is determined as a fixed number of money units. A debt is a monetary asset, a machine tool is not a monetary asset, its terminal value is not fixed in value.

(b) The value of any non-monetary asset, such as inventory held abroad, will tend to float up with the foreign inflation rate. In theory the real value of non-monetary assets which can be traded internationally will remain constant in terms of the home currency. The value of ordinary (equity shares) is determined by the expected future profits of the company issuing the shares. These profits are likely to float up with the local rate of inflation.

5. The price elasticity of demand for a product allows an exporter to estimate the likely impact on the volume of sales of a given percentage increase in the price of the product. We assume that the product is priced in terms of the foreign currency in the foreign market. If an increase or decrease in the exchange rate with the foreign market occurs the price elasticity of demand for the product in the foreign market determines whether the change in the exchange rate will be reflected in increased (decreased) sales or increased (decreased) profits in the foreign market. Inelastic demand would suggest that the price as denominated in the foreign currency should remain constant and increased profit be taken in the form of increased profit per unit sold.

7. "Risk minimizing" means that the finance officer aims to reduce the foreign exchange exposure of his company to a minimum. "Profit maximizing" means that the finance officer is prepared to speculate in the future value of a foreign currency if the opportunity should arise to make this activity profitable.

The two essential conditions that must be satisfied if a finance officer decides to speculate in currency are:
(a) that the market is not an efficient market;
(b) that future exchange rates can be predicted with a fair degree of accuracy; and
(c) that the Board of his company gives the international treasurer permission to speculate.

9. The government must interfere with the free flow of currency between the two countries involved or some other form of inefficiency must exist in the currency markets. The exchange rate must be fixed in some way or operate within a "currency snake". The probability of the rate moving up or down at a particular point in time is not symmetric. Reason: the government who are controlling the rate via intervention in the market do not mind losing money to control the exchange rate. The speculator is gambling with an opponent who does not mind losing his money!

11. If a forward market exists in the currency then the IRPT ensures that any expected differences in inflation rates in the two countries involved are reflected in the differences in the interest rates on short-term loans or bonds in the two currencies. Thus expected changes in exchange rates are already discounted into the interest rate differential, such changes are already hedged. The situation is different with unexpected changes in inflation or any other unexpected event. These events are not discounted into the interest rate differential thus if the risk or the amount involved is substantial these risks should be hedged via the derivatives market.

13. Information needs to be collected on
(a) assets and liabilities currently denominated in foreign currencies
(b) budget on future transactions in each foreign currency by all companies in the group over the next few months
(c) predictions on future exchange rates
(d) changes in long-term economic exposure.

15. An internal exchange rate hedging technique is devised and controlled by the treasury department of the company using the technique. An external technique uses the facilities provided by external currency markets.

"Matching" and "leading and lagging" are examples of internal techniques. "Futures contracts" and "currency options" are examples of external techniques.

17. If the forward rate is an unbiased predictor of the future spot rate then a finance officer who covers all FX transactions forward will not make a profit or a loss on forward cover in the long run. However, this a long-run strategy for covering many small transactions, large individual contracts should be covered on the forward market if the exchange rate loss on the contract might jeopardize the future of the company.

CHAPTER 5

1. Parallel currencies are two currencies whose values relative to other currencies move in parallel to one another. For many years the German DM and the Dutch florin have been parallel currencies. If the value of two currencies run parallel to one another they can be used a substitutes for one another. If an MNC is exposed in one currency it can hedge the risk with an opposite exposed position in the other currency.

3. (a) The cost of using the FX markets is reduced since less currency is bought and sold in the currency markets.
   (b) The total exposure position of the group which needs to be hedged is reduced.
   (c) The liquidity position of the individual companies at both ends of the netting process is improved.

5. If the matching of individual payments in each currency used by a group is to be employed, a very tight discipline needs to be imposed on the individual treasurers who are responsible for managing the cash flows. The precise form of payment, the amount and the timing of each payment must be specified in advance and strictly adhered to if the system is to work. Finance officers in foreign subsidiaries that operate in countries with underdeveloped financial systems may find such tight financial discipline difficult to manage.

7. If the price of an export contract is based on the forward rather than the spot rate of exchange the exporter passes the cost of or benefit from forward cover onto the importer. This method of pricing bases the price on market expectations as to the future spot price when the contract is paid.

9. In 1944 at Bretton Woods in the USA the major countries of the world agreed on a system of fixed exchange rates. Exchange rates could be changed but only with prior agreement between the major monetary authorities of the world. The US$ was tied to the price of gold at $35 an ounce and the other currencies tied to the US$. In 1970 the United States government broke the link between the US$ and gold. In consequence the Bretton Woods agreement itself broke down and the breakdown in agreed exchange rates followed. The currency markets of the world have suffered from extreme turbulence ever since.

11. A foreign currency dealer makes a profit on a forward contract out of the "spread" between the buying and the selling price of the currency. This "spread" is his profit.

The seller of a "futures" contract makes a profit out of the commission charged on the contract.

13. The Italian exporter must first ask his own bank in Italy or a corresponding bank in Australia for a six-month loan in A$ with a value equivalent to 200 million lire. The proceeds of the A$ loan will be immediately converted into lire at the current exchange rate and invested in Italy. In six months' time when the Australian company pays the amount due on the contract the proceeds are used to repay the loan in Australian dollars. The profit or otherwise on the loan depends on the rates of interest in Italy and Australia and any movements in exchange rates over the period.

    Such a hedging scheme might not be possible if the Italian company cannot raise a loan in A$ because it has been allocated a low credit rating by the market. Such a hedging scheme might not be wise if the real interest rates in Australia are a good deal higher than in Italy.

15. An international factor can offer the following services to an exporter; (1) Immediate cash up to 80% to 90% of the value of the contract; (2) to absorb the risk of credit default by the importer; (3) to absorb the foreign exchange risk on the contract; and (4) to run the credit control operations on behalf of the exporter.

    An international factor may well be dealing in many currencies in many countries. The factor may be able to "internally" hedge debts in various currencies rather than having to cover the FX risk by using the facilities provided by the more expensive external markets.

17. The contract traded on a currency option market is a "standardized" contract. The attributes of the contract which are standardized are (1) the value of the contract (2) the length of the contract (3) the maturity dates of the contract (4) the strike (exercise) price spread.

    As the product is a standard product the buyer and seller know exactly what it is they are buying and selling. If the attributes of the contract were not standardized each individual product sold would have to be individually examined before bidding to check out the particular attributes of this product. Trading between buyer and seller would be greatly slowed by such a process.

19. A traded currency option covers the buyer of the option against losses that might be incurred by unexpected shifts in exchange rates; it is thus a kind of insurance policy. In addition a traded currency option gives the buyer of the option the opportunity of making a speculative profit on unexpected changes in exchange rates. If the currency rises in value above the strike price the option will rise in value resulting in a speculative profit to the buyer.

    Suppose a US finance officer buys $10 \times £31\,250$ "put" (sell) options on £ sterling for December 1994 at a strike price of US$1.60 for 3.61 cents per £. The deal costs $10 \times 31\,250 \times 3.61¢ = $ US$11\,281.25. If on the due date in December 1994 the US$/£ exchange rate stands at US$1.55 to the £ the finance officer can sell his £312\,500 for $312\,500/1.6 = $ US$500\,000 rather than $312\,500 \times 1.55 = $ US$484\,375. However, the profit of US$15\,675 must be reduced by the cost of the option US$11\,282 plus the interest lost on this investment of US$11\,282 over the six months so the net profit is small on this contract but the FX risk was covered.

21. The British company can arrange through an international bank to swap £10 million for DM 25 million with a German company, the swap to be reversed in three years

time at an agreed exchange rate. The bank would charge a commission of around 0.25% of the value of the deal for arranging the swap.

23. There are a number of reasons why a company trading internationally might choose an exchange rate guarantee to a forward or other derivative contract for the purpose of hedging exchange rate risk. The most likely reason is that a forward market is not available in this particular currency or that a forward contract of the required maturity is not available. A second reason might be that even if a derivative contract is available the rate guarantee might provide cheaper cover than the derivative contract if the currency is unstable.

CHAPTER 6

1. Buying control is the key idea here. Direct investment buys control of a company or a foreign venture, which, hopefully, will make a profit for the investing company. Control is a key objective. Portfolio investment does not normally give the investing company control of the company issuing the shares. The investment is made to earn income but not to gain control.

3. (a) What exchange control regulations are applied by the foreign government to inward investment?
   (b) How has the exchange rate and inflation rate moved in recent years between the home and the foreign currency? Are hedging devices available to cover foreign exchange risk in this currency?
   (c) Are there significant cultural differences between the culture of the foreign and the home country? Religious prohibitions, language barriers, ethical differences, type of government?
   (d) Is the growth rate in the economy of the foreign country cyclical or counter-cyclical to the growth rate in the home country?
   (e) What kinds of taxes are imposed on foreign investment in this country? What income taxes, withholding taxes, indirect taxes and social security taxes, personal income taxes?

5. The traditional view of the risk attached to foreign investment was that the degree of risk attached to foreign investment is much greater than the risk attached to home investment. The investor knows so much more about the conditions attached to investment at home. The only type of risk considered in this case is the "specific" risk attached to the foreign investment.

7. The beta of a share quoted on an information efficient stock exchange measures the change in the return on the share during a given period compared to the change in the return on an index of all of the shares quoted on that stock exchange. The beta measures the market risk attached to the share as against the company's specific risk. A share of average risk is awarded a beta of 1. A lower beta, of say 0.8, indicates that the share is less risky than average while a higher beta, say 1.8, indicates that the share is more risky than average.

9. According to the table of inter-country correlation of share indices given in the text of Chapter 6 the correlation between the share indices in the UK and Japan between 1972 and 1992 was 0.45 and between the UK and Canada was 0.51 over this period. The correlation between the UK and Canada was 0.55 so the

UK/USA share index correlation was higher than that of the UK/Canada over this period.

11. If the government of the foreign country where the investment is to take place is involved in the project in some way there is much less chance of new laws and rules, altered rates of tax or new rules regarding the remittance of profits abroad being imposed on the project. Government involvement can be achieved by offering free shares in the project to the government in return for tax free remittance of profits, taking on local staff, appointing government ministers to the Board of the company or maximizing the value of goods and services that are bought locally. The introduction of substantial foreign capital and importing free "know-how" from abroad into the country will also help to persuade foreign governments of the good intentions of the foreign investing company.

13. The UK: ECGD, France: COFACE, Germany: HERMES, Japan MITI, JEXIM.

   The private sector is often unwilling to cover unusual risks, such as expropriation, because the total cost might be huge if all the foreign projects in a foreign country are affected at the same time. Examples are Iran in 1980 and Argentina in 1986. The total pool of risks is not large enough for the law of large numbers to apply to the risk or for the actual odds against this event to be calculated.

15. An investing company can take expert advice from a consulting company in measuring the degree of risk attached to some aspect of a project. For example, the volume of oil underground or the cost of extracting wood from a difficult site. If the advice proves to be invalid the investing company can sue the consultant. International surveying and consulting firms carry heavy insurance to cover this possibility and pass this cost on to their clients in the form of higher fees. It is an oblique type of insurance policy. It is difficult and expensive but not impossible to use the International Court of Justice at the Hague to mediate on international business disputes.

17. The exporter can try the export credits guarantee branch of government in his own country such as the ECGD in the UK or HERMES in Germany or he might try finding credit cover in the importer's country via "forfaiting" or a "letter of credit" from the importer's bank. See Chapter 9 for a fuller discussion of this question.

CHAPTER 7

1. Prior to 1979 most of the countries of the world, even major industrialized countries such the USA, France and the UK, imposed exchange control regulations of varying degrees of tightness on the movement of funds out of their countries. A few countries, such as Switzerland, enjoyed free markets but foreign finance, for the most part, could only be accessed via "back-to-back" loans and suchlike stratagems. In 1979 the UK abolished almost all exchange control regulations and so access to foreign currency became feasible. Following 1980 many other countries followed this lead.

3. The treasurer of the Canadian company needs to know: (a) the likely pattern of the currency inflows to his company over the next four years, particularly the inflow in US$; (b) the likely movements in the exchange rate between the Canadian dollar and the US$ over the next four years; (c) whether he will be able to swap out of C$

into US$ for four years if funds are more easily accessible in Canada; and (d) the tax implications in Canada of loans in C$ and US$.

5. The international Fisher theory will not work if exchange controls are imposed on the movement of funds into or out of a country. For the international Fisher to work funds must be allowed to flow freely between the financial markets of the two countries issuing the currencies. The difference in interest rates may also be influenced by "country risk". Some currencies may be perceived as being riskier to hold than others. Thus a "risk premium" may be added to the fixed interest rate on a loan in addition to the "expected inflation differential".

7. Let us assume that the treasurer of a UK company finances his company by taking out five-year loans in US$, C$, Swiss francs and Spanish pesetas of approximately equal value in terms of £ sterling.

The fixed rates of interest are as shown in Table 40.

Table 40

Currency	Cost (% p.a.)	Expected inflation (% p.a.)	Cost diff. (%)	Actual inflation (%)
US$	8	6	−2	4
C$	9	7	−1	6
Swiss francs	5	3	+2	5
Spanish pesetas	11	9	+1	10
UK£	8	6	0	6

Assuming that the differential inflation rate determines the future exchange rate the "average" cost of the financing in terms of £ sterling will be much as expected despite the fact that not one exchange rate actually matches the exchange rate expected over the five-year period. The cost differences cancel out. The interest differential is an inaccurate predictor of the future spot rates but, on average, they are unbiased predictors.

9. The cost of a floating interest rate loan is determined by adding a given percentage, say 1.5%, to some base rate such as the London Interbank rate (LIBOR). Since the rate is adjusted on a regular basis, say every three months, the international Fisher could only apply to the short periods between the adjustment of the floating rate. This period is well within the IRPT horizon so the forward rate can supply cover.

11. The debtor can use a forward contract, a futures contract, a set of options, or a swap. A currency option allows the UK debtor to hedge the foreign exchange risk and open the possibility of a speculative profit. For example, let us suppose that the rate of exchange when the loan is raised is US$1.60 to the £ sterling. The UK borrower can take out a series of call (buy) options one year forward at a strike price of, say, US$1.55 that may cost, say, 10 cents per £, which means that the maximum repayment cost of the loan in sterling is limited to US$50 000/1.55 = £32 258. At US$1.60 to the £ the repayment cost would have been US$50 000/1.60 = £31 450. The cost of the option would be about US$3000. If a strike price is chosen that is well "out of the money" the cost of the option cover can be low.

13. If a loan is raised in a foreign currency the repayment cost of the loan in terms of the home currency may differ from the initial cost of the loan in terms of the home currency. It can thus be said that a "profit" or a "loss" is made on the foreign loan in terms of the home currency. The tax authorities in various countries treat this profit or loss in different ways. In some countries such "conversion" profits or losses are ignored for the purpose of tax assessment. In others the profit is taxed at either the normal rate charged on trading profits or charged at a capital profit rate. The same applies to the allowing of losses against tax, these may only be allowed against capital taxes or even only on currency conversion profits. However, in some countries "conversion" profits are taxed but "conversion" losses are not allowed against tax. The treatment can thus be said to be "asymmetric".

15. A finance officer will normally try to avoid a batch of foreign loans reaching maturity at around the same time. Re-financing a batch of loans at one point in time raises funding problems. A more sensible policy is to distribute the maturity dates over time. Thus the maturity date of the loan is a key consideration when raising a loan. The cost is not so important since the currency cost is probably matched by budgeted inflows in the same currency or the international Fisher may apply.

17. (a) A "moratorium" on interest payments on a loan means that the borrower can miss an agreed number of interest payments on the loan at his discretion without breaking the loan agreement.

(b) "Flexible" maturity means that the borrower can, within agreed limits, alter the period over which the loan will be repaid.

(c) "Convertibility" means that the currency in which the loan will be repaid can be chosen by the borrower. A list of possible currencies for repayment is agreed between the borrower and the lender at the inception of the loan.

19. The relevant equation is:

$$h\% - f\% = (s_{t+1} - s_t)/s_t$$

where $h\%$ is the interest rate in the home currency

$f\%$ is the interest rate in the foreign currency

s_{t+1} is the rate of exchange at the end of the period

s_t is the rate of exchange at the beginning of the period

Thus

$$0.10 - 0.06 = (s_{t+1} - 1.6)/1.6$$

$$s_{t+1} = 1.664$$

The exchange rate between A\$ and US\$ is expected to be A\$1.664 to the US\$ at the end of the year.

CHAPTER 8

1. The return on an investment is measured by comparing the profit on the investment with a measure of the capital tied up in the investment. If an overall return is needed on a group of companies operating in several different countries then both the profits and the value of the investment in each country must be translated into a single currency. Adding together pound sterling, French francs

and South African rand is economically meaningless unless these currencies are all translated into a common "numeraire".

3. According to the US accounting code the Singapore company is really no more than a branch of the US company. The balance sheet and profit and loss account of the Singaporean company must be translated using the "temporal" not the "current" method of translation. The Singapore accounts must be translated using the reporting currency (US dollars) not the functional currency (S$). This rule is promulgated in FASB 52 of the US Accounting Standards Board.

5. The three methods of translation commonly used in the present or the past are: (a) The closing rate/current rate method; (b) The monetary–non-monetary or temporal method; and (c) the current–non-current method.

7. A monetary asset can be defined as an asset the terminal value of which is represented as a fixed number of money units. The terminal value of the asset is not determined by the supply and demand for the asset on the date it is sold. If the asset is an interest bearing bond the market value is determined by the market rate of interest on the date the asset is sold. If the value of the money unit that defines the value of the asset falls in value relative to other assets then a real loss occurs. The value of the asset, say a bond, will not float up with inflation to compensate.

9. The monetary–non-monetary method of translation enjoys one major advantage over the closing/current rate method. This advantage is that non-monetary assets bought at some time in the past are likely to be translated into a value in the home (reporting) currency at a value closer to their actual current value in the home currency. However, if the foreign non-monetary assets have been re-valued recently in the foreign currency then this advantage will no longer apply.

11. If the foreign currency is rising in value relative to the home currency the foreign debts will be rising in value in terms of the home currency. This "loss" will be charged against the group Profit and Loss account reducing the profits of the Group for the given year. However, the same revaluation of the foreign currency will increase the future value of the dividends flowing from the foreign subsidiary. This fact is not reflected in the group accounts for that year. Thus an increase in the value of the foreign subsidiary will be shown in the accounts translated by the temporal method as a fall in the return from the subsidiary! The closing rate method of translation does not commit this error.

13. The C–NC method of translation divides the assets and liabilities in the balance sheet between those items that are in working capital and those that are not.

The M–NM method of translation divides the assets and liabilities on the balance sheet between those that are monetary items and those that are not. The C–NC method translates any debt due at the rate of exchange ruling when the debt was acquired and inventory at the rate of exchange ruling on the date the accounts were closed. Both these operations will almost certainly provide wrong values in the reporting currency.

15. The value using:

The closing rate method:	FF195 million
The M–NM method	FF195 million
The C–NC method	FF160 million

If the Group wish to repay this debt on the last day of the company year they will have to pay FF195 million not FF160 million. Therefore the closing rate method and the M–NM method give the more accurate representation of the facts at the year end.

17. If the rate of inflation in the foreign country averaged 2% per annum over the ten-year period and the fixed assets of the foreign subsidiary float up with inflation then the value of these fixed assets in terms of P$ would be P$ $(10\,000 \times (1.02)^{10}) =$ P$12\,190$. If the P$12\,190 is translated at P$2 to the £ sterling then the value in the reporting currency will be £6095.

19. (a) The impact of future changes in exchange rates on the future cash flows from the foreign subsidiary are ignored under current accounting conventions. The present value of the subsidiary to the Group is the discounted present value of these cash flows.

(b) Exchange rates are in a continuous state of flux. The rates of exchange chosen to translate the accounts, using whichever method, are chosen at random points in time which might not provide rates that truly represent the underlying economic phenomena. The translation process thus includes a large random element.

CHAPTER 9

1. The financing and insuring of exports are closely intertwined because it is difficult to raise the finance for an export contract unless the contract is insured against non-payment by the importer and any other consequent risks such as the loss of the goods in transit or expropriation. Once the contract is insured it is easy to raise export finance from a bank or other credit institution.

3. Many currencies are very unstable in value through time. If a contract is denominated in such a currency the exporter cannot evaluate the value of the contract if it is denominated in the importer's currency and the importer cannot evaluate the value of the contract if it is denominated in the exporter's currency. One solution to this problem is to denominate the contract in a third currency, usually the currency of a major country such as the United States dollar or the German Deutschmark. An alternative solution is to take out a forward contract at the time the contract is signed and base the price of the contract on this forward rate.

5. Four shipping documents:
   (a) The bill of lading. (Describing goods and shipping instructions to importer.)
   (b) The certificate proving ownership of the goods.
   (c) The certificate proving origination of the goods in a specific country. (Some countries forbid imports from certain countries.)
   (d) The invoice setting out a description of the goods and the price of the goods plus name of exporter and importer.

7. The three major risks which need to be covered by an insurance export contract are:
   (a) The risk of non-payment by the importer.
   (b) The risk of loss or damage to the goods in transit.
   (c) The risk of expropriation of the goods or the blocking of funds by a foreign government.

9. In 1995 the ECGD projects group, a UK government agency, still insures long-term contracts, very large contracts even if short-term and unusual export contracts which are substantial in money terms and cannot gain insurance in the private sector.

   Loans on large contracts of a capital nature are guaranteed for up to 85% of the contract value. Losses caused by "political risk", for example, blocked funds, are guaranteed for up to 90% of the contract value. These guarantees can also provide the exporter with access to subsidized rates of interest on the finance under specific conditions. Special cover is offered to insure against such things as the collapse of a consortium and tender to contract finance.

11. An export insurance company can provide the following services to an exporter.
    (a) A guarantee allowing the exporter to raise finance for the export contract.
    (b) Compensation of up to 90% if the importer fails to pay for the goods or services exported.
    (c) Compensation of up to 95% if the goods are lost or damaged in transit.

13. The two factors that need to be balanced against one another with regard to selecting a suitable payment system for an export contract are:
    (a) The risk that the importer will not pay for the contract.
    (b) The risk that the exporter will not deliver the goods.

    In addition a balance needs to be struck between the risk of non-payment and the cost of the payment system. As the former is reduced the latter is increased.

15. A banker's draft is an inter-bank cheque drawn by one bank on another bank for the favour of a specific person or institution. It is a very safe form of payment since it is guaranteed by a bank.

    A payment order is a written instruction sent by one bank to another bank instructing the other bank to make payment of a specific amount to a specific person or institution.

17. A "term bill" will be paid by the "drawee", the acceptor of the bill, at some time in the future depending on the conditions in the bill. A "sight" bill is paid "on sight" by the drawee of the bill.

19. An international factor can pay the exporter around 80% to 90% of the value of the debt immediately in his own currency. The factor may accept the risk of non-payment by the importer, "payment without recourse". The factor may take over the entire credit control operation of the exporter including billing the foreign importer. The factor may even take over the risk of a change in exchange rates between the contract being signed and the payment for the goods being made. In return for all this the factor will charge a substantial fee to the exporter.

21. As the Polish company cannot gain access to sufficient French francs to finance the deal the French company may try to set up a barter type deal to solve the problem. All or part of the cost of the machine tools may be paid for in terms of the agricultural equipment being manufactured by the Polish company. This equipment can either be imported directly from Poland by the French machine tool company and sold by them or, more likely, the French company will find a counter-trade broker or dealer who will find a buyer for the agricultural equipment possibly in some third country.

23. The key factors to consider when setting up a payments system for an export contract are:

(a) Adopt a system that balances the risk of non-payment against the cost of the payment system. Risky payment systems are cheap to operate, safe systems expensive.

(b) Choose the safest currency available in which to denominate the export deal.

(c) Choose a system that allows the exporter to receive payment in the shortest possible time. The longer the delay between signing the contract and receiving payment the greater the risk involved.

CHAPTER 10

1. The two forms of direct tax imposed on a foreign subsidiary are (a) income tax and (b) a withholding tax on dividends, etc., repatriated abroad. Additional taxes may be imposed in the form of VAT, excise duties on imports, social security taxes and salary taxes.

3. The term "tax arbitrage" has been used to describe a process whereby a tax officer shifts global costs to those countries that impose high relative tax on companies and shifts profits to those countries that impose low relative taxes on resident companies. An example might be to set up a captive insurance company in a tax haven. The other subsidiaries in the group pay their insurance premiums to the "captive" subsidiary in the tax haven that pays no tax on any profits made on insuring the group risks while the premium costs are charged against the subsidiary profits in their resident country. Franchise payments, licences and leasing payments on equipment provide other examples of potential tax arbitrage.

5. As transfer pricing is an internal matter that does not affect the profit of the group opportunities exist within a multinational group to charge out costs to subsidiary companies at a cost at some distance from "arm's length cost" which would be charged if the product or process were being sold to a company external to the group. For example, if the corporate tax rate on a specific subsidiary H is very high and on subsidiary L very low, then the MNC might charge out costs from L to H at a cost well above the true cost of production. This would increase costs and so reduce tax in regime H and increase profits in regime L. An example of "tax arbitrage".

The US government insists that all inter-group pricing must be proved to be at "arm's length" just as if the sale were to an external company. Also a "super-royalty" rule is imposed on payments for intangibles such as consulting advice and the licensing of techniques of production.

7. Most tax regimes allow losses made by a company to be carried forward to be set against future profits. Three- to five year carry-forwards are common and some tax authorities allow such losses to be carried forward indefinitely. A few countries allow losses to be carried back and set against tax previously paid on past profits. Up to three-year carry-backs are allowed by the tax authorities in certain countries.

If a company has incurred losses in the past that can be used to reduce either future profits of the company itself or the profits of the company buying the loss making company, this reduction in future tax is an asset which enhances the value of the target company in a takeover bid situation.

9. The UK parent is assessed on global profits from whatever source by the UK tax authorities. However, if a double tax treaty is in operation then tax credits will be available to offset any income and withholding taxes on dividends paid abroad.

11. If profits made from a derivatives contract are subject to tax the hedge itself must be large enough to cover this tax which will be due to the tax authority. However, the profit on the derivatives contract, and so the tax due to be paid on this profit, will not be known until the contract has matured. The finance officer must guess the likely profit or loss on the contract and hedge accordingly.

13. Tax will have to be paid on income earned from foreign trading if the company concerned is considered by the tax authorities in the foreign country to be "trading-in" rather than simply "trading with" the foreign country. The precise definition of trading-in varies between countries but if the MNC simply owns a storehouse in a country it may get away with the "trading-with" definition. If it starts to sell from the warehouse it will almost certainly be considered to be "trading-in" the country . . . and have to pay income tax.

15. (a) a holding company (b) a management and finance centre (c) a subsidiary that can use the benefits provided by a tax haven.

17. Tax benefits can be forthcoming if the MNC channels the following activities through an MFC.

FX exposure management, withholding tax management (utilizing tax credits), handling the insurance of the group, exchange control management, raising finance internationally, providing financial and consultancy services to the group, leasing assets to the group subsidiaries, handling royalties and patents, re-invoicing the billing procedures of the group and many more!

The tax authorities in most of the countries of the world are very suspicious of management and finance centres set up by MNCs. One way of allaying these suspicions is to allow the MFC to conduct similar activities for companies outside the group, to conduct activities with other group subsidiaries at an "arm's length" basis *re* charges and not to set the MFC up in a tax haven. Set the MFC up in the same country as the parent or in a country with a relatively high tax rate.

19. If a tax haven wishes to attract MNCs to its shores it must provide most, but not necessarily all, of the following facilities:

   (a) Very low or zero tax rates on income or dividends for resident companies. Tax treaties with other countries may be desirable in certain instances.
   (b) No exchange controls on the flow of funds out of or into the country.
   (c) Tight legislation *re* secrecy as to the activities pursued by resident companies and, in certain cases, ownership of the companies.
   (d) Long-term guarantees to offshore companies with regard to changes in current legislation
   (e) Good facilities for telecommunication 24 hours a day
   (f) Good banking, accounting, foreign tax and legal services
   (g) Low set up and running costs for offshore companies
   (h) Adequate transportation facilities to a major country.

Index